Springer Texts in Business and Economics

Springer Texts in Business and Economics (STBE) delivers high-quality instructional content for undergraduates and graduates in all areas of Business/Management Science and Economics. The series is comprised of self-contained books with a broad and comprehensive coverage that are suitable for class as well as for individual self-study. All texts are authored by established experts in their fields and offer a solid methodological background, often accompanied by problems and exercises.

More information about this series at http://www.springer.com/series/10099

Peter Schuster • Mareike Heinemann • Peter Cleary

Management Accounting

Springer

Peter Schuster
Faculty of Business and Economics
Schmalkalden University of Applied Sciences
Schmalkalden, Germany

Mareike Heinemann
VALNES Corporate Finance GmbH
Frankfurt am Main, Germany

Peter Cleary
Cork University Business School
University College Cork
Cork, Ireland

ISSN 2192-4333 ISSN 2192-4341 (electronic)
Springer Texts in Business and Economics
ISBN 978-3-030-62021-9 ISBN 978-3-030-62022-6 (eBook)
https://doi.org/10.1007/978-3-030-62022-6

This Springer imprint is published by the registered company Springer Nature Switzerland AG
The registered company address is: Gewerbestrasse 11, 6330 Cham, Switzerland

About This Book

This book is partially the result of a book originally planned by the first author together with Ralf Ewert and Alfred Wagenhofer, building on their highly successful German textbook (2014) which took a wide approach to management accounting, predominantly from a German perspective. Their permission to use material derived from this German textbook is greatly appreciated. Part of the book's last chapter received some attention as a publication in the Springer Briefs in Accounting series (2015).

Contents

List of Symbols

a	action parameter, productivity
a	actual
A	action space
ABC	activity-based costing
AVF	annuity value factor
b	budgeted
b	budgeted, planned
B	bonus
bc	basic unit cost
BV	basis variable
BEA	break-even amount
BATNA	best alternative to a negotiated agreement
c	variable cost per unit
$\overline{c}$	preliminary variable cost (before particular cost)
c	cumulated (index)
C	cost, total cost
cm	contribution margin per unit
cm	specific contribution margin per unit
$\overline{cm}$	sum of the weighted contribution margins of all products
cm^{m}	modified contribution margin per unit
CF	cash flow
CM	total contribution margin
CT	capital tied up
COF	cash outflow
Cov	covariance operator
CRF	capital recovery factor
CFaR	cash flow at risk
D	depreciation
E[ ]	expected value function
f	density function (continuous)
F	probability function (continuous)
F	fixed (index)
GPK	'Grenzplankostenrechnung'
H	high (index)
i	uniform discount rate
I	initial investment outlay
i, j, l, m, n	running index, from 0 or 1, ..., *I, J, L, M, N*
k	cost, cash outflows per unit of the period capacity
k(x)	change factor of the costs per unit
l	low (index)
LG	LAGRANGE function
LQ	residual value, liquidation value
lmi	induced by volume, 'leistungsmengeninduziert'
lmn	not induced by volume, 'leistungsmengenneutral'
min	minute
NPV	net present value
NPV_{o}	net present value of the cash outflows
OC	opportunity cost
OL	operating leverage
p	price per unit
Pr	probability

PKR	'Prozesskostenrechnung'
q	factor unit, factor quantity
r	factor price
R	revenue, turnover, sales, cash inflow
RS	right side
ROI	return on investment
ROS	return on sales
$RORAC$	return on risk-adjusted capital
s	remuneration function
SC	safety coefficient
t	time index, from 0 or 1, ..., T
T	end of the planning period
TC	total cost
TP	transfer price
u	capacity utilisation
U	utility function
U^A	utility function of the manager (agent)
$\underline{U}^A$	reservation utility of the manager (agent)
v	direct consumption coefficient, consumption factor
v	variable (index)
V	capacity
$V(a)$	disutility or private cost at the productivity level a
VC	variation coefficient
VaR	value at risk
w	slack variable
x	output in units or in monetary terms
X	cumulated production amount
$\hat{\mathbf{X}}$	quantity combinations of sales volumes
y	influencing factor
$ZOPA$	zone of potential agreement
α, β, γ	coefficients
δ	smaller figure
Δ	difference, change
ε	random number
η	elasticity
θ	environmental condition, information, type
κ	output-related alternative costs, cost elasticity
λ, μ	multipliers (in LAGRANGE approaches)
ρ	discount factor
σ	standard deviation
σ^2	variance
τ	time (index)
ϕ	probability (discrete distribution)
Φ	cumulated probability (discrete distribution)
Π	profit
$*$	optimal value

Introduction to Management Accounting

Contents

P. Schuster et al., *Management Accounting*,
Springer Texts in Business and Economics,
https://doi.org/10.1007/978-3-030-62022-6_1

1

Learning Objectives

After studying this chapter, you should be able to:

- Illustrate the contents and main focus of management accounting
- Discuss the decision support and the behavioural control functions of management accounting
- Understand why and what types of simplifications are necessary in designing management accounting systems
- Analyse management accounting and its use for short-term decision-making

1.1 Management Accounting

1.1.1 The Accounting System

The accounting system can be **conceptualised as one element** of a company's information systems. Internal or **management accounting** covers all information systems designed for the internal user, predominantly the manager as the decision-maker in the company. In contrast, external or **financial accounting** is directed towards external users, such as investors, creditors, customers, suppliers, competitors and the general public.

The reason for distinguishing between internal and external accounting – or management and financial accounting – is influenced by the different relationships between the **information producer** and the **information user** in both forms of accounting. For **financial accounting**, the producer and the user are different people; the producer essentially has a better knowledge about the data that enter the system, than the user. Consequently, a higher degree of regulation is required to guarantee a certain quality attaching to this information, which forms an integral part of the accounting system. Legislation enables this, for example, in the area of auditing or in the context of specific agreements between producers and users (e.g. loan contracts). The split between management and financial accounting is particularly rigid in German-speaking countries as will be demonstrated in this text.

Management accounting fulfils its tasks free of legal and other restrictive rules. Conflicting targets with external parties do not seem to appear, at least at first glance. Yet, this does not imply that management accounting is free from conflicting targets, as, for example, they may occur in the form of conflicts between decision-makers of different hierarchical levels within the company. The company's structure and the resulting allocation of decision competences and responsibilities therefore assume an essential importance within the management accounting system.

Three typical accounting **information systems** and their corresponding measures are as follows:

- **Accounting for investment and finance**: cash inflows and cash outflows
- **The financial (external) accounting system**: expenditures and yields
- **The management (internal) accounting system**: costs and revenues

For certain purposes **non-monetary measures** (e.g. production volumes and times) are applied. Their advantage lies in the fact that measures connected with the respective decisions are directly reported. The disadvantage is that they cannot be aggregated and do not permit an economic comparison of effects.

▪ **Accounting for Investment and Finance**

Accounting for investment and finance is mainly used for the determination of **investment and finance projects' profitability** (for an exhaustive coverage, see Götze, Northcott and Schuster, 2015). Cash flow statements determine a company's liquidity and are used both within internal and external accounting systems. **Cash outflows** and **cash inflows** are the components of such statements.

▪ **The Financial Accounting System**

The most essential tasks of the financial accounting system are to provide information about the **company's assets and its financial and profit situation**. It uses **expenditures** and **yields**, which are derived from a periodisation of cash inflows and cash outflows according to certain rules and criteria and are reported to the public.

▪ **The Management Accounting System**

The management accounting system supports the **planning** and **coordination** of company decisions, particularly in the short run. The reporting of costs and **revenues facilitates a determination of** resource consumption, that is, the production of goods (and/or services) according to the company's objectives within a particular time period. Usually they are derived from expenditures and yields. Their content and relationship to cash outflows and inflows is shown in more detail below.

Management accounting in the German-speaking countries is highly independent from financial accounting. This becomes obvious when considering **cost classification (into cost types), although a trend of convergence** or **harmonisation of the management and the financial accounting systems** is observable internationally. There are a number of practical reasons for this convergence, such as: to maintain two parallel accounting information systems requires a lot of time, effort and resources and it can be difficult to interpret the results from both; also, the internationalisation of (external) accounting standards and the focus on the information requirements of shareholders (investors) support this development and allow it to become relevant to management accounting and **management control**, as top management carries out the shareholder's function of the company or its daughter companies to a certain extent.

1.1.2 The Decision-Making Function of Management Accounting

Management accounting has **two main functions, as follows**:
- Decision-making (decision support): 'influencing one's own decisions'
- Behavioural guidance (or behavioural control) (decision influencing): 'influencing other people's decisions'

According to the **decision-making function**, management accounting is an instrument of information that provides a basis for decisions made by management. **Conflicting objectives** are not considered further. Either there are no conflicting objectives if an individual acts of his or her own accord (**one-person context**) or the company implicitly considers congruency of targets between the user (upper management) and the producer of the information. This function can then be referred to as '**influencing one's own decisions**'.

Traditional management accounting literature mainly deals with this function, that is, specific accounting systems that deliver the best information support for **certain types of decisions. Although more precise information** never impairs an improvement in decision-making, only when the additional costs of such information are fully considered in comparison to the gains obtainable will it become obvious whether the trade-off is favourable or not.

Typical decisions that the management accounting system supports are related to the production programme (for manufacturing companies), sales price determination, procurement policy, as well as cost management. To be able to make appropriate decisions, information about costs, cost dynamics and possible effects are important to consider.

1.1.3 The Behavioural Control Function of Management Accounting

Decision support is also at the centre of the behavioural control function but in a different way, as its objective is to influence decisions made by others, that is, '**influencing other people's decisions**'. This function explicitly considers the company and takes place in a **multiple-persons context**. Decision-makers can have different targets/objectives on which they base their subsequent decisions.

Presuppositions for the behavioural control function are as follows:

- There are, or at least potentially are, **conflicting objectives/targets** between decision-makers in the company. *Example*: a divisional manager strives for an increase in his[1] staff because the number of assistants assigned to him is an indication of his importance in the company.
- There is **asymmetrically distributed information** between the company's upper management and decentralised decision-makers. This is frequently the case: a divisional manager will have better knowledge about the details of his division than head office will. After all, this is one of the main reasons for the delegation of decisions to him.

This latter point can potentially result in the head office losing **control**. *Example*: head office may not be able to assess the efficiency of the research department's

1 The male gender used throughout this book is applied for matters of simplicity and without intention of any form of discrimination, nor to emphasise aspects of male versus female managers, etc.

activities because it possesses no specialised competence in this area; or a lack of time may prevent them to adequately evaluate all (subordinate) company divisions' activities.

▪ Information and Behavioural Control

There are a number of instruments to reduce conflicts amongst targets and asymmetric information, such as delegation, monitoring or the appointment of suitable personnel. Management accounting can contribute here via the use of:

- **Management control information**
- **Coordination information**

Management accounting enables decision-makers to control **costs** and **revenues**. Variance analysis determines differences between budgeted and actual values and provides potential reasons for their existence. This is meaningful not only for receiving knowledge about new environmental conditions but also for motivating the decision-maker to complete his tasks well since he is ultimately responsible for the variance. This form of control generally triggers a positive behavioural control effect in advance.

Management accounting also supplies decentralised decision-makers with information to be used for the **coordination** of their decisions, and decentralised decisions can be subliminally influenced by it. *Examples*: if the inherent risk of particular decisions is not reflected by the management accounting information, a divisional manager may put inappropriate emphasis on it. If the costs of a central service (e.g. electronic data processing [EDP]) are allocated on the basis of the number of PCs in the departments, incentives arise to invest more in PC equipment but not in the service activities of the service department. The coordination of the management system is an essential feature of the **management control** system, with approaches including budgeting, performance measures, transfer prices and cost allocations, discussed in this book.

The behavioural control function can have peculiar effects on the organisation of the management accounting system: suddenly 'correctness' and precision may not be a critical feature anymore. *More information is not always better*, even without explicit consideration of the additional information costs. As regards the **decision-making function**, this is not generally the case: certainly, management will not deliberately procure incorrect data for their own decisions. The same logic does not always apply for influencing other people's decisions. A management accounting system that supplies more or less precise information that reduces information or delays reports can be advantageous. *Examples*: a divisional manager can use more information to better pursue his own objectives and to make decisions, which in turn may not be optimal for the company as a whole. Too much information reduces the control options of head office or senior management. Aggregate information can induce head office *not* to use individual performance measures; this can provide positive work incentives in the long term. On the sales side, senior management frequently demand full costs as a 'lowest price limit', despite knowing that the 'correct' product costs for sales and price decisions are marginal costs. Many companies providing marginal cost information to their sales representatives find that they are then too obliging in price negotiations.

> If there is a central thesis in this discussion it is this: that cost accounting has a number of functions, calling for different, if not inconsistent, information. As a result, if cost accounting sets out, determined to discover what the cost of everything is and convinced in advance that there is one figure which can be found and which will furnish exactly the information which is desired for every possible purpose, it will necessarily fail, because there is no such figure. If it finds a figure which is right for some purposes it must necessarily be wrong for others. (Clark, 1923, p. 234)

1.1.4 Focus of This Text

This text emphasises the **two main functions** of management accounting, namely *decision-making* and *behavioural control*. Hence, **cost accounting** techniques are not explicitly considered in this text. Rather, the approach adopted here represents the definition of **management accounting**, that is, to consider the *managerial use of accounting information* retrieved from the accounting system.

We believe that this approach is meaningful for at least two reasons:

1. Management accounting has become an important instrument to support companies' **management**.
2. This textbook addresses the **advanced reader**. Prior knowledge of basic cost accounting techniques is assumed, ensuring that the focus here is on the *application* of accounting information.

The fact that 'the costs' to manufacture a product are extremely difficult to determine may not be immediately obvious from a practitioner's perspective, despite being generally understood amongst academics. In theory, accurately allocating fixed costs or synergies to products is impossible, as every allocation is ultimately arbitrary. Interestingly, in multi-product companies even average costs are not definable. The fact that variances of higher order cannot be related to individual causes is also known. Nevertheless, in practice this is frequently implied when applying the 'right' method of variance analysis. However, even 'incorrect' cost allocations can actually serve 'correctly' for the purposes of the behavioural control function; this however requires a conceptual understanding of the management accounting system within the organisation. Such **conceptual considerations** are at the centre of this text.

We have tried to consider many **newer developments** in this textbook, particularly the following:

- **The consideration of uncertainty**. For example, the question of decision relevance of fixed costs is increasingly under discussion.
- **The emphasis on information-economic approaches**. Features and ideas from agency theory and, more generally, from game theory are applied to management accounting problems.

The latter point is closely connected with the behavioural control function. Information-economic models are practically inevitable for the treatment of coordination instruments and partly for management control instruments. Frequently, such models are implicitly or explicitly accused of single results usage in specific situations. However, with the discussion of simple information-economic models in this textbook, we want to show that the **way of thinking** and the **solution of ideas**, which are behind these models, are relevant to company practice. The models sharpen the look of fundamental *mechanisms* and *incentives* that can, but not necessarily have to, be released by certain institutions (e.g. the way to determine variances, budgeting procedures, management assessment). These attempts supply a **theoretical foundation** for management accounting and management control as a practice-oriented discipline.

Literature sometimes distinguishes between the approaches of **information economics** and **behavioural science**. Behavioural-scientific approaches are based on psychological and sociological knowledge. They do not assume the same definition of rationality that information-economic approaches do. Instead behavioural approaches empirically observe actual decision behaviour often deviating from the optimum objective. Another difference lies in the methods applied: the information-economic approach uses deductive methods, whilst the behavioural-scientific approach uses inductive or other methods. Both attempts have their advantages and disadvantages. However, despite being frequently demanded, combining both is quite difficult due to their conceptual differences and primary focuses. This text concentrates on the information-economic approach, although some examples are based on behavioural-scientific knowledge. This approach conforms to the decision-making function as treated in 'traditional' management accounting systems. **Organisational aspects** of the application of management accounting systems are also not at the centre of attention here.

1.2 Introduction to Management Accounting and Decision-Making

A company's success significantly depends on the quality of its decision-making, and solving decision problems requires information about the decisions' consequences. Accounting systems provide such information using performance measures such as **costs, revenues** and **profits**. Costs and revenues generally comprise the (company's) monetary resource consumption and production in one time period; a period's profit (or loss) is the difference between revenues and costs. However, how 'good' are business decisions that are predominantly orientated towards the maximisation of such periodic measures? Are decision-makers really focusing on these figures rather than the consumption opportunities that arise from business activities (and their own income)? Upon closer reflection and despite the initial impressions, it seems that this apparent understanding cannot and should not be assumed.

A **management accounting system** can be characterised by specific assumptions and restrictive conditions. Thus, before starting to discuss 'optimal' decisions derived from a management accounting system, we need to clarify the relationship between accounting procedures and their results. We show what **differentiates** management accounting systems and whether the necessary inherent assumptions are ambiguous or in some way problematic.

The **starting point** is a normative question: *How should we proceed to find the solution to decision problems?* To approach the concepts of costs and revenues, we gradually introduce **simplifications**; for example, focusing solely on financial measures. Further simplifications are also necessary, for example, neglecting certain interdependences that result in focusing on **short-term decisions**. Having done so, useable definitions of costs and revenues emerge.

1.2.1 The Concepts of Costs and Revenues

Definition

Costs: Resource (goods) consumption by a company according to its objectives and within a period.
Revenues: Resource (goods) production by a company according to its objectives and within a period.

The defined concepts serve as a basis for solving multiple decision problems aimed at the maximisation of the **period's success**, or **profit** – the difference between a company's revenues and costs.

What is the relationship between the measures and their foundation for decision-making? In other words, how 'good' are decisions based on such measures? Costs and revenues are **derived from cash flows**, are explicitly limited to one single period and capture the resource consumption or production in that period. Therefore, the split between short-term and long-term decisions is of great importance.

1.2.2 Short-Term and Long-Term Decision-Making

If there are no temporal interdependences and all cash flow effects of procurement, production and sales occur in the respective time period, the decision problem can be separated into several, isolated partial problems in each period. In that case, decisions in these periods have only '**short-term effects**', which implies the ability to make the decision exclusively based on a short-term period consideration without facing the risk of choosing a suboptimal action from a long-term perspective. Ignoring temporal interdependences – if they in fact exist – is a significant restriction because long-term and short-term decisions are inevitably related. Every short-term decision can immediately have '**long-term effects**' because the conditions in future periods depend on decisions made in the current period. Thus, a decision problem with short-term effects cannot be fully characterised by the given factors or capacities only, because cost or cash outflow interdependences (e.g. learning effects) may occur. In addition, revenue or cash inflow interdependences usually exist. Hence, short-term effects in a strict sense are not likely to exist in reality and decisions based on these considerations alone may be inaccurate.

The above-mentioned categorisation of decision problems divides them by their time dimensions. Moreover, decision problems with long-term effects include decisions about capacity dimensions, whilst short-term effects do not.

Decision Problems with Short-Term Effects

Costs and revenues, as defined above, are suitable for solving decision problems with short-term effects and are typical in determining the **'optimal' degree of complexity** of decision models (other concepts of costs and revenues exist but are not discussed further at this point). Therefore, the quality of 'optimal' decisions determined based on such models should be evaluated in the context of their assumptions and simplifications and are primarily **situation-specific**. This applies to all models presented in this book; more extensive considerations of all circumstances usually do not solve practical decision problems. Nevertheless, decision models developed in the management accounting literature often show a considerable theoretical level, and their principles for various decision problems are also applied in other areas of business and economics (e.g. methods to determine optimal production programmes with limited capacities). Additionally, procedures and methods of management accounting systems can be supplemented with specific aspects where needed for a particular decision problem at hand.

The following illustration shows the **decision problems** that are often regarded by the literature as having short-term effects (► Box 1.1). They can be solved by considering the revenues and costs as defined. The following chapters of this book address selected problems in more detail and show how the management accounting system helps find optimal solutions.

Box 1.1 Decisions with Short-Term Effects

- **Procurement decisions**
  - Order quantities
  - Procurement sources and channels
  - Upper (purchase) price limits
- **Production decisions**
  - Production procedures
  - Production programmes
  - Lot sizes and production sequences
  - Acceptance and rejections of one-time special orders
- **Sales decisions**
  - Lowest price limits and sales prices
  - Sales inventory
  - Distribution channels, sales regions and customer groups
- **Integrative decisions**
  - Make-or-buy
  - Transfer prices between subunits and subsidiary companies
  - In-plant transportation and stock-keeping

- **Strategic Decisions**

Management accounting systems were originally not designed for supporting decisions with long-term, i.e. strategic effects. The principal aim of strategic decisions does not lie in short-term cost reductions (keeping performance at the same level) or performance increases (keeping costs at the same level) within given capacities, but rather in achieving and defending a successful position attained by the company in the market. By definition, strategic management accounting might be considered a contradiction in itself because **investment appraisal methods** – as opposed to management accounting systems – seem to be preferred for such long-term decision-making.

Investment appraisal requires more explicit information about the effects of strategic decisions than the management accounting system. For instance, a forecast of the temporal distribution of current cash flows, the consideration of risk and the planning of alternate options are important. Due to the nature of strategic decisions, the effects of a decision or a competitive situation in, say, ten years (provided the demand for the company's products still exists) are hard to forecast and budget.

Such effects are implicitly taken care of in the management accounting system by certain assumptions, whereas, in practice, they are rarely questioned since they are not explicitly stated. Therefore, the management accounting system appears to be more **robust** than investment appraisal methods; however, those latent assumptions mostly go unquestioned.

Example: In practice, not all **future cash flows** are considered because certain cash outflows and cash inflows may be underestimated. For instance, an investment in new manufacturing technologies may not appropriately consider software costs for production process control. The cash inflows may not include advantages accruing from the increased manufacturing flexibility expressed by lower stocks and faster adaptation to the customers' wishes. Potential advantages of subsequent investments, such as a first investment that increases the chance to enter the market more broadly, may be insufficiently analysed. Moreover, strategic decisions sometimes require organisational changes and their costs are usually underestimated.

Another difficulty – and similar to the management accounting system – in the practical application of investment appraisal methods is that often the **implications of the methods** and parameters are insufficiently considered and understood and, thus, the advantage of the management accounting system appears to be that they have not been dealt with explicitly.

Example: The **risk** connected to future cash inflows is often not appropriately taken into account, for example, the **length of the time period being** considered. Strategic decisions often show effects rather late in time; however, the later this is, the more uncertain and the more difficult is it to accurately forecast the cash flows. Therefore, many companies plan only a relatively short period of time ahead. The payback period then becomes the (main) relevant measure. Alternatively, higher **discount rates may be** applied to capture that risk. However, the risk of success or failure is often higher in the first years and lower in the long run, such that lower discount rates should in theory be applied in later years.

Example: Investment appraisal often deals with **single investment** projects rather than with extensive projects or programmes. Organisational rules in practice often connect decision-making power to budgets for the initial investment outlay and partially lead to situations where it is easier to invest in many smaller projects than in one large project. In this case, the company's response to changes in technologies or markets may take longer than optimal. Another problem with single projects is the fact that the risk diversification with other projects is not – or only inadequately – considered.

The complexity of including such considerations in the investment appraisal process has led to developing specific approaches within the management accounting system to support strategic decisions. We will discuss strategic management accounting systems in more detail in ▶ Chap. 5.

1.2.3 Orientation Towards Goods Consumption and Production

With the cost and revenue concepts applied, it cannot be assumed that all cash flows occur within the considered time period. Therefore, the orientation towards the production and the consumption of goods takes care of the timing differences between cash flows. Companies take credit from suppliers and grant credit to customers, and thus, even without the existence of temporal interdependences, cash flows related to regularly buying or selling of products will *not* occur in the same period. The consumption of production factors does not necessarily lead to cash outflows in the current period if the consumption is purely from existing stocks. Similarly, sales of the current period do not necessarily lead to an increase in the same period's cash inflows due to delayed payments that result from customers' credit terms. To account for such temporal overlaps, costs and revenues as defined do not directly use and represent current period cash flows; in fact, they refer to the **consumption** and **production of goods**. Decisions based on the current period's cash flows would neglect the effects of the decisions on other periods' cash flows. Instead, costs and revenues are based on all cash flows that result from the activities of the current period.

▪ Harmonisation of the Management and Financial Accounting Systems

The orientation towards the consumption and production of goods does not imply a **specific matching (or accounting) principle**. Such principles can be developed within a company or by referring to financial accounting principles, such as the *International Financial Reporting Standards* (IFRS). The harmonisation, that is, convergence of management and financial accounting systems, requires a cost-benefit analysis. **Advantages** include the following:

- **Lower costs**, when using the mandatory financial accounting system.
- **Internal consistency of control and reporting systems**, since management is publicly evaluated based on the financial accounting system.
- **More objective and less manipulatable costs** of the financial accounting system because it uses well-known rules and is audited.

Disadvantages of harmonisation include the following:

- **Objectives of the management accounting system may deviate** from those of the financial accounting system. For example, we noted above that one of the fundamental guiding principles of management accounting systems is: *Different costs for different purposes.*
- **Matching rules of the financial accounting system may be inappropriate** in some cases (e.g. certain research and development expenses are not capitalised in the balance sheet but are treated as expenses and, hence, costs rather than an investment).
- **Decisions require budgeted** (planned) **measures** and not actual measures, but the financial accounting system is largely oriented towards actual measures. Therefore, meaningful budgets may only be derived in times of stable environmental conditions.
- The cash flow-based **determination of costs and revenues is not in accordance with opportunity costs** that may be needed for specific decisions.

These advantages and disadvantages suggest that with regard to their usefulness, it could be argued that the accounting systems should be kept separate, whereas with regard to the **behavioural control function** a convergence between them could be more appropriate. But even if harmonisation were beneficial, certain characteristics of the management accounting system still differ from the financial accounting system (for instance, if the management accounting system is used for management control and coordination in specific situations).

1.3 Guided Tour of This Text

1.3.1 Contents of the Text

The text is divided into two parts, which are dedicated to the two primary applications of the management accounting system, that is, decision support and behavioural control.

▪ Part I: Decision Support

Part I deals with instruments and ideas to support *one's own* decisions. ▶ Chapter 2 provides a foundation about management accounting systems based on decision theory. Particularly, the (mostly implicit) simplifying assumptions that underlie the 'traditional' determination of costs and revenues are illustrated. Due to the variety of decisions which the management accounting system can be applied to, only the most essential decision problems are selected (e.g. decisions of procurement and stock-keeping are excluded). Questions with a short-term focus, such as which products should be produced, what quantities sold and with what (existing) procedures in the relevant time period, are selected in this part. The most essential instruments for the solution of linear and non-linear problems are explained based upon different restrictive situations. The application of opportunity costs to the decision under consideration is also discussed.

► Chapter 3 deals with one of the 'classical' problems of management accounting systems, even though it does not completely treat *price decisions* in the traditional way. Here, the determination of lowest price limits is discussed for many different situations in which some are not 'standard'; for example, capacity decisions for the acceptance of additional orders under uncertainty. This similarly applies to optimal prices.

► Chapter 4 is dedicated to an often-neglected question: what is the influence of uncertainty on the usability of management accounting instruments? In traditional textbooks, uncertainty is often not discussed at all, or, if so, only superficially. This chapter treats cost-volume-profit relationships and their relevance to uncertainty as an extension of ► Chap. 2: production programme decisions under uncertainty. It is shown under which circumstances fixed costs can be relevant for decision-making.

► Chapter 5 deals with cost management and so-called 'strategic management accounting'. The chapter encompasses a compact presentation of the activity-based costing system. Other important instruments of cost management are also presented: target costing and life-cycle costing.

- **Part II: Management Control and Coordination**

► Chapter 6 is dedicated to the second principal purpose and function of the management accounting system: behavioural control. Variance analyses are an essential instrument for it. In a world of certainty, it would be unnecessary to compare actual and budgeted results as variances would not exist. This chapter discusses many different forms of (costs and revenue) variances and their analyses, as there is no single procedure or method applicable in all circumstances. This appears to be important particularly because the assignment of responsibility for variances can often be arbitrary. The final part of this chapter questions to what extent the different causes of variances can be differentiated, and discusses several methods to do so.

► Chapter 7 deals with coordination and further addresses the behavioural control function. It examines an important instrument of management control of decentralised companies: Budgeting. Activities of divisional managers should be mutually coordinated and adjusted in accordance with company targets. The considered personnel coordination problems are based on the divisional managers' better state of information about the situation in their respective division (asymmetric distribution of information) *and* in potential conflicts of interest, especially when the divisional managers are assessed by their *divisional profits*. The existence of uncertainty is an essential reason for coordination problems. The chapter therefore describes the necessity for coordination through budgeting and for the assessment of managers. Different forms of budgeting participation and their effects on management performance are illustrated in more detail in this chapter.

The concluding chapter, ► Chap. 8, considers one of the most important issues in Management: transfer prices and cost allocations. Cost allocations can be understood as a special form of transfer prices. Both relate to influencing decentralised decision-making. Transfer prices based on costs, market prices and negotiations are examined for their coordination efficiency. With regard to cost allocations, several possible reasons for the allocation of fixed costs to divisions (cost centres) are shown.

1.3.2 Formal Structure of This Text

The chapters of this text are structured in the following manner. **Learning Objectives** describe the main points of attention, whilst **Chapter Summaries** conclude the text of each chapter. **Review Questions** that can be directly answered from the chapter text are included at the end of each chapter, but they also partially build upon an examination of the relationships amongst the main issues discussed, which may foster further reflection. **Exercises** conclude each chapter. The text itself does not contain solutions, as we believe that the questions should cause no difficulties to answer.

As far as possible, **symbols** are generally and uniformly applied throughout the text. Occasionally, it is necessary to apply identical symbols for *similar* measures to avoid 'eccentric' symbols. *Example*: the symbol x sometimes denotes the output in quantity units and sometimes in monetary units. The **list of symbols used in the text** precedes this first chapter.

1.3.3 Use of the Text

As already mentioned, this book is aimed at the **advanced reader**. Therefore, a **basic knowledge of management and cost accounting** is a prerequisite to the extent of average business administration courses in the initial undergraduate years. Required basic knowledge particularly includes **cost accounting techniques** and a knowledge of **investment appraisal methods** (e.g. net present value method). Some parts of this text are mathematically demanding, so a fundamental knowledge of mathematics is certainly an advantage. However, we have tried to emphasise the way of thinking and the conceptual understanding rather than presenting purely mathematical problems.

The individual chapters are organised in such a way that treats the respective topic under consideration **in a closed form**. Therefore, within certain limits the reader can deviate from the given sequence and omit a chapter. The parts of the text are only loosely connected.

1.4 Summary

The management accounting system is used to support decision-making in companies. In considering how this is achieved, **various simplifications** are explicitly made. For example, **decisions** are differentiated between those with **long-term effects** and those with **short-term effects**, with the latter relating to areas such as procurement, production and sales programmes within a given capacity. Furthermore, assuming a given capacity, it is assumed that the conditions are independent for all time periods and that all cash flow consequences of all periods' activities occur in the respective period under consideration. These simplifications are a typical solution to the issue of complexity within decision models. They eventually lead to costs and revenues used to support decisions with short-term effects.

Management accounting provides **information relevant to decision-making**. The main functions are the decision support function and the behavioural control function. The **decision support function** of management accounting supports company management decisions of one's own. In doing so, it assumes the congruence of targets of other decision-makers in the company with those of head office.

The **behavioural control function** explicitly considers the company's organisation; and management accounting serves to influence decisions of subordinated decision-makers to whom company head office has delegated certain decisions. The supplied information is used to **control** and **coordinate** the decision-makers in the company.

This text analyses these two main functions in detail. **Conceptual considerations** are given special emphasis, and **newer theoretical developments**, particularly the information-economic approach, are also considered.

1.5 Assessment Material

Review Questions

1. How do cash outflows, expenditures and costs differ from each other?
2. What is the relationship between financial (external) and management (internal) accounting?
3. Why does the behavioural control function depend on the company's organisation/structure?
4. What conditions are required for management accounting to fulfil the behavioural control function?
5. How would you judge the following behaviour? Marc Harding is notoriously always late. He feels guilty about it and, therefore, puts his wristwatch forward by 5 minutes.
6. Why, and under what conditions, can 'incorrect' information be productive for management accounting?

Exercise

Purposes-dependent costs. Joanna Varley is puzzled. She keeps looking at the costing calculated by her EDP system for a product in her area (figures rounded off, per unit):

Direct materials	54
Material overhead (12% of manufacturing materials)	6
Direct labour costs	45
Manufacturing overhead (121% of direct labour costs)	55
Cost of production	**160**
Administrative costs (14% of production costs)	22
Distribution costs (8% of production costs)	13
Total costs	**195**

(a) A competitor is offering a practically identical product for 189 in the market. Joanna Varley is quite certain that the competitor does not enjoy any cost advantages in comparison to her department. Therefore, she concludes there must be a mistake in the costing. Let us assume that instead of a relatively high-value material part costing 11, she uses another part with the same function costing only 7. By how much do total costs fall?
(b) Joanna Varley knows that the overhead contains high portions of fixed costs. In the material overhead, 50% are fixed, in the manufacturing overhead 70%, in the administration costs 95%, and in the distribution costs 80%. Recently she accepted a special order at 140, which, according to her calculations, had been a good deal. A later analysis, however, showed that she had incurred a loss of 140 – 195 = 55. The results for the month were accordingly frustrating. What is correct?
(c) Joanna Varley complains to the management accountant that she has absolutely no influence on administration costs. She does not understand why so much is allocated to her department. The management accountant explains to her that she must calculate it in this way in order to improve cost consciousness in the departments. Is that a convincing reason?

Accounting Information and Production Decisions

Contents

P. Schuster et al., *Management Accounting*,
Springer Texts in Business and Economics,
https://doi.org/10.1007/978-3-030-62022-6_2

Learning Objectives

After studying this chapter, you should be able to:

- Determine the optimal short-term production programme with and without capacity restrictions using appropriate procedures
- Analyse the influence of fixed costs on the optimal decision
- Understand the contents and the use of different opportunity cost concepts

2.1 Basics

2.1.1 Preliminary Remarks and Assumptions

This chapter deals with production programme problems. The optimal solution is usually based upon costs and revenues in the traditional sense. The principles and procedures needed to maximise the company's profit are at the centre of attention; thus, concepts of **cost and revenue management** (see also ► Chap. 5: 'Cost Management') and of the **managerial use of accounting information** (*management accounting*) for decision-making are also stressed.

Implicitly, certain data (e.g. costs of intermediate and final products, orders and production methods) are assumed for the decision problems described in this chapter. The determination of such data is part of cost accounting and therefore not discussed in this book.

Naturally, issues of *cost and revenue management* and of *cost (and revenue) accounting* cannot be considered completely independently of each other. The use of cost and revenue information determines the quality of a management accounting system, and, conversely, the **quality** of the information from a management accounting system determines the **quality of the decisions subsequently made**. This interdependence will be discussed in this chapter for the following two reasons:

1. **Opportunity costs** are a central component of costs. The relevance of such costs for the solution of decision problems can only be discussed in direct relation to the solution structure of these decision problems. They also concern aspects of *cost management* as well as aspects of *cost accounting* and are further discussed in ► Chap. 3: Accounting Information and Pricing Decisions.
2. The question of **absorbed costs** versus **marginal costs** is addressed in the following chapters. For production programme decisions, this question is addressed in a meaningful way when discussing some of the assumptions made.

Basic Scenario

Production programme decision problems are based on the following **scenario**:

- A **given capacity** and a **short-term perspective exists**. The type and number of production procedures (i.e. machines) are determined by long-term decisions and are unchangeable for the period under consideration. Furthermore, the procurement and sales potentials are predetermined by the long-term procurement and sales policies (e.g. in the form of maximum order sizes of raw materials, maximum sales volumes of finished products or a price-demand curve). Minimum requirements for procurement and sales in the current period may result from long-term market strategies, long-term contracts with suppliers, the existence of minimum order sizes, minimum sales volumes for single products based upon particular market strategies, etc.

- Production programme decisions are made by deciding **what products should be produced and sold in what quantities using existing production procedures** during the period under consideration. It is assumed that the quantities produced equal those sold, that is, inventory is not considered. Procedural decisions are included when a number of different production procedures exist.
- **Certain expectations** (i.e. certainty) are assumed for the period under consideration in order to illustrate the fundamental principles. That is, the company knows all relations in the procurement markets and sales markets as well as the internal production conditions and cost relationships. Uncertain expectations are introduced in ▶ Chap. 4.
- Only financial **measures** are considered. The amount preferred is strictly monotonously increasing (i.e. maximised) with regard to the period profit Π and calculated on the basis of **costs and revenues**. Linkages between multiple periods' assessments do not exist.

2.1.2 Absorption Costing

The following basic scenario can be applied to choose between the use of absorbed and marginal costs. As the decision problem has short-term effects, it is implicitly assumed that current activities show no, or only negligibly low effects on the decision fields of the following periods. Since intertemporal interdependencies are not considered, the current period's results can be exclusively analysed. Thus, due to the assumption of certain expectations, **neither time preferences nor certainty preferences** need to be considered for decision-making in this context. As the quantity preference with regard to the period's profit Π is strictly monotonously rising, the **period's maximum profit** characterises the optimal company policy.

With regard to the (periodic) decision's scope, the following should be noted: due to the dismantling of the problem according to the time perspectives, not all action parameters are viable options. Variable action parameters of the specific period are limited by long-term effective decisions, particularly in relation to capacity. An action a^V results from a combination of variable action parameters (e.g. final and intermediate product amounts), and $\mathbf{A}^V\bar{a}$ is the action space relevant to it depending on 'fixed' action parameters $\bar{a}$

The remaining **decision problem** then can be described as follows:

$$\max_{a^V} \Pi\left(a^V, \bar{a}^F\right) \text{ with } a^V \in \mathbf{A}^V\left(\bar{a}^F\right) \tag{2.1}$$

The period's profit Π depends on the action parameters and can be split into two parts. On the one hand, a **fixed part of the profit** $\Pi^F\bar{a}$ which is determined exclusively by the action parameters decided in the beginning; in fact, as fixed revenues hardly exist, $\Pi^F \bar{a}$ mainly consists of fixed costs, like (fixed) deprecation. On the other hand, there is a **variable part of the profit** $\Pi^V(a^V|\bar{a})$, which depends on the action parameters still under consideration and possibly affected by the parameters $\bar{a}$ (e.g. the slope of the price-demand curve and/or the prohibitive price can depend on long-term effective marketing activities or the cost functions can be affected by the degree of automation of the available production technologies). Thus, the problem presented in (2.1) can be written as follows:

$$\max_{a^V} \Pi^V\left(a^V|\bar{a}^F\right)+\Pi^F\left(\bar{a}^F\right) \text{ with } a^V \in \mathbf{A}^V\left(\bar{a}^F\right) \tag{2.2}$$

Because the fixed part of the profit $\Pi^F \bar{a}$ remains *constant* for the presented problem, the optimal solution a^{V*} is the one with the maximised variable part of the profit $\Pi^V(a^V|\bar{a})$.

To determine the **maximum profit** of company policies with **short-term effects**, it is, therefore, sufficient under the above conditions to only consider the **variable part of the profit** and with it a management accounting system based on **marginal costs**. However, if an **absorption costing system** is used, this is not a *necessary* condition. In periodic accounting, fixed costs are *not* allocated to cost objects (e.g. products) but are simply registered as a block by cost type. Then, fixed costs are constant and without influence on the determination of the optimum quantity. The question of 'absorbed costs versus marginal costs' is therefore simply irrelevant here.

However, in most cases, **absorbed costing** is used for a (unit) cost accounting system that allocates variable and proportionate fixed costs to cost objects. This may not automatically lead to mistakes for the solution of decision problems, provided that the total costs of an action formed from the cost objects are always equal to the total costs of cost accounting. However, in general, this is only achieved when the alternative considered for decision-making purposes is also the basis for the added fixed costs related to the cost objects. This, of course, is very complicated because the determination of the period's profit **neutralises** the original **fixed cost allocation**, so it would have been dispensable in the first place.

▪ ***Example***

Two final products are considered as cost objects. The constant variable costs of Product 1 (2) amount to 20 (40), and fixed costs are forecasted to be 21,000. The (variable) action space consists of only two alternatives: Alternative 1 with the production of 100 (200) units of Product 1 (2) and Alternative 2 with the production of 150 (100) units of Product 1 (2). The allocation of the fixed costs is done by a simple job costing procedure with the total variable costs applied on an allocation basis.

Alternative 1: variable costs amount to 20·100 + 40·200 = 10,000. An allocation percentage for the fixed costs amounts to 21,000/10,000 = 2.1 (or 210%). The periodic costs are 10,000 + 21,000 = 31,000. Then, unit costs based on absorbed costs are:

For Product 1: 20 + 20·2.1 = 62
For Product 2: 40 + 40·2.1 = 124
The total costs of Alternative 1 on the basis of the unit cost will be:
100·62 + 200·124 = 31,000

Alternative 2: variable costs are 20·150 + 40·100 = 7,000. Now the allocation is 21,000/7,000 = 3 (or 300%). The periodic costs amount to 7,000 + 21,000 = 28,000. Absorbed costs per unit are as follows:

For Product 1: 20 + 20·3 = 80
For Product 2: 40 + 40·3 = 160
The total costs of Alternative 2 on the basis of the unit cost will be:
150·80 + 100·160 = 28,000

Alternative 1 leads to higher costs. The same cost difference is obtained by comparing the variable costs: 10,000 – 7,000 = 3,000. The total costs of both alternatives are always determined correctly, despite the use of absorption unit cost accounting. Consequently, a decision on the basis of the period's profit is also always correct.

- ***Sources of Error***

The previous example illustrated the sources of error of a unit cost accounting system based on absorbed costs. Incorrect decisions result if the **unit** cost of one level (of outputs) is calculated and then **used** for the determination of the **total cost of other alternatives**. In the example, the total costs of Alternative 2 would have been incorrectly calculated based on the unit cost of Alternative 1. In this case, cost allocations are no longer neutralised. An incorrect assumption of the relations between the action parameters and the total costs can be seen and with it, incorrect decisions may subsequently arise.

The second source of incorrect decisions lies in the immediate **use of unit costs** for decision-making **without the determination of the period's profits**. This is clear in the above example if it is assumed that Product 2 could also be purchased from the market at a price of 50 each. Both accounting results based on absorbed costs suggest purchasing *only* if unit costs are used. However, the absorbed costs contain arbitrarily allocated fixed costs, which will occur independently from the make-or-buy decision for Product 2. However, this effect would only be shown in periodic accounting. On the contrary, the use of variable unit costs in the above example leads to the correct decision: that is, purchasing is more expensive than manufacturing Product 2.

Since the variable part of the profit was shown to be *sufficient* for the determination of optima, these variable measures will be predominantly used in the following considerations of this book. Yet it should be stressed again that the above results occur only **under the assumptions made**, particularly the absence of uncertainty. ▶ Chapter 4 shows that with consideration of uncertainty, situations may appear when the measure $\Pi^F \overline{a}$ – even though it might be certain – may not be ignored; moreover, there may be situations when *only* **periodic cost accounting based on absorbed costs** will guarantee a correct decision while the exclusive consideration of variable cost profit components can lead to incorrect decisions.

2.1.3 Contribution Margins, Profit Functions and Restriction Types

Some additional terminology has to be introduced to further illustrate the production programme problem described in the preceding section.

- *Contribution Margins and Profit Functions*

Thus far, profit's **functional dependence** on the variable action parameters a^V has not been described. Linear as well as non-linear relations are possible; linear relations imply constant sales prices and variable unit costs of the final products. Consequently, **contribution margin** plays a major role in the production programme decision. It is calculated as the difference between the sales price p and the variable cost c of a product:

$$cm = p - c \tag{2.3}$$

The **units** of the final products remain the single action parameter within given production procedures. If the company can produce J types of final product with its existing machines, the period's profit can be written in the following form of linear relations:

$$\Pi = \sum_{j=1}^{J} \left(p_j - c_j\right) \cdot x_j - C^F = \sum_{j=1}^{J} cm_j \cdot x_j - C^F = CM\left(x_1, \ldots, x_J\right) - C^F \tag{2.4}$$

Where:

p_j is constant sales price of the product j
c_j is constant variable unit cost of the product j
cm_j is contribution margin per unit of the product j
x_j is production/sales volume of the product j
C^F is the fixed costs ($= -\Pi^F(\bar{a})$)
$CM(x_1, \ldots, x_J)$ is total contribution margin ($= \Pi^V(a^V|\bar{a})$)

The origin of the term **contribution margin** is reflected by the amount shown in (2.3) respectively (2.4): A unit sold of the final product contributes to the coverage of fixed costs. In the case of linear functions, the contribution margin also equals the **marginal profit** of the final product:

$$\frac{\partial \Pi}{\partial x_j} = \frac{\partial CM\left(x_1, \ldots, x_J\right)}{\partial x_j} = cm_j \text{ for } j = 1, \ldots, J \tag{2.5}$$

Only in the case of purely linear relations does it make sense to designate *the* contribution margin and *the* marginal profit of a product; otherwise the marginal profit of a product is affected by the previous production and sales volume.

- *Restriction Types*

Restrictions arise from the given capacity and the given market conditions for production planning in the current period. They are represented by the (variable) action space $\mathbf{A}^V\bar{a}$ whereas limitations can refer to procurement, production and/or sales areas.

The dependencies expressed by the restrictions can be **linear**, partially linear or **non-linear**. As an example, the raw material consumption per unit of the final product may depend on the amounts produced, as higher amounts are only achievable with an increased production intensity (quantity produced per unit of time) connected with additional consumption.

The limitations can be in form of **upper limits** (restrictions of the type 'smaller or equal than'), **lower limits** (restrictions of the type 'larger or equal than') or **equations**. Not all restrictions apply to all products. For example, there is a sales-side restriction for the production of 2,000 units, which directly concerns the specific product type and is a **restriction applicable to one product**. They can be found in all functional areas, such as in the form of a limited supply of raw material. In contrast, if a limitation refers to at least two product types, it is a **restriction applicable to multiple products**, which may also be found in all functional areas. Such restrictions are due to the fact that products compete for limited resources, and resources used for one product cannot be used for other products, therefore reducing their production quantities.

» For a production programme decision, it is important whether these competing relations affect **multiple products** or not. A machine needed for the production of several product types may be limited, but if the sales limits are more restrictive, the multiple-product restriction, while existing, will be irrelevant and so will the competing relationship. The decision criteria and methods applied for the production decision largely depend on whether, and if, how many effective multiple-product restrictions exist. This aspect will be discussed later in this chapter.

2.1.4 Basic Model of the 'Pure' Production Programme Decision

Based on the assumptions described, production decisions are firstly shown in this section without the explicit inclusion of procedural decisions. This so-called basic model is used to explain the fundamental decision criteria and methods and serves as a basis for the analysis of opportunity costs. In these 'pure' production programme decision problems, the production methods and procedures are decided a priori.

In the basic model, the period's profit Π (or more precisely: the total contribution margin *CM* or the variable part of the profits Π_V) is maximised and is solely based on the amount x_j of the J product types. An upper sales limit $\overline{x}_j > 0$ (as a restriction applicable to one product) is assumed for each product type and additionally, other limitations may exist in different functional areas as restrictions applicable to one and/or multiple products. In the case of restrictions applicable to one product, only the most restrictive limitations are applicable and it is assumed that they are the respective upper sales limits of the products. In this sense, other restrictions are exclusively applicable to multiple products and I such restrictions ('resources') exist; v_{ij} shows the consumption of the resource i for the production of one unit of the product j, and $\overline{V}_i$ indicates the available capacity of this resource. Non-negativity conditions for all products apply to prevent solutions with negative amounts of production. Restrictions in the form of linear inequations of the type 'smaller than' characterise the action space $\mathbf{A}^V(\overline{a})$.

- ***The Planning Problem***

The planning problem can generally be written as follows:

$$\max_{x_j} \Pi(x_1,\ldots,x_J) = CM(x_1,\ldots,x_J) - C^F \tag{2.6a}$$

With the restrictions:

$$\sum_{j=1}^{J} v_{ij} \cdot x_j \leq \overline{V}_i \qquad i = 1,\ldots,I \tag{2.6b}$$

$$0 \leq x_j \leq \overline{x}_j \qquad j = 1,\ldots,J \tag{2.6c}$$

All v_{ij} are non-negative and all capacity $\overline{V}_i$ are positive, when no lower limits exist among the I restrictions applicable to multiple products; this is the '**standard case**'. More complex problems and the inclusion of **opportunity costs**, and their significance for decision-making, will be discussed later in this chapter.

2.2 Production Programme Decisions in Different Scenarios

Different **solution structures** and **solution procedures** arise depending on the form of the profit function and the restriction types (◘ Table 2.1).

◘ **Table 2.1** Solution procedures in different types of production scenarios

	Linear profit function	**Non-linear profit function**
No effective multiple-product restriction	Production of all products with positive contribution margins up to their sales limits (marginal solution)	Production of the products with positive contribution margin up to their sales limits or as long as marginal profit > 0
One effective multiple-product restriction	Sorting the products according to their specific contribution margins (marginal solution)	Production of the products according to the same marginal contribution margins
Several effective multiple-product restrictions	Standard case of linear programming; for instance, the Simplex method ('corner-point solution')	Solution with the LAGRANGE function and the KUHN-TUCKER conditions

2.2.1 Initial Example

The relations relevant to the decision situations are analysed with the use of an example, which is modified in the course of the discussion to consider additional situations.

A company is considering producing $J = 3$ product types on $I = 2$ machines. The fixed costs amount $C^F = 4{,}000$, and all other data are shown in ◘ Table 2.2. Constant sales prices, unit costs and, therefore, linear functions exist. Non-linearities are introduced in the course of the further discussion. The demands v_{ij} of both machines are measured in terms of machine hours and the capacities of the machines are shown in the second part of ◘ Table 2.2.

2.2.2 No Effective Multiple-Product Restriction

According to the previous analysis, fixed costs are irrelevant for the solution of the decision problem and, thus, the contribution margin *CM* of the production programme is to be maximised.

Equation (2.5) implies that only products with **positive contribution margins**, cm_j, should be produced, as only these products contribute to covering the fixed costs and to increasing the company's profit. The inclusion of products with **negative contribution margins**, therefore, cannot be optimal. According to these considerations, Product 3 is excluded from production.

Sales limits for Products 1 and 2 both demonstrate that **production restrictions** are not applicable, as the total consumption v_i of the resource i by fully exhausting the sales potential amounts to:

$$2 \cdot \bar{x}_1 + 8 \cdot \bar{x}_2 = 2 \cdot 300 + 8 \cdot 200 = 2{,}000 = V_1 < \bar{V}_1 = 2{,}500$$

◘ **Table 2.2** Data of the initial example

Product	$j = 1$	$j = 2$	$j = 3$
Price p_j	200	480	1,100
Variable costs c_j	160	400	1,170
Contribution margin cm_j	40	80	−70
Sales limit $\bar{x}_j$	300	200	600
Consumption v_{1j}	2	8	5
Consumption v_{2j}	9	4	1

Machine	$i = 1$	$i = 2$
Capacity $\bar{V}_i$	2,500	3,700

$$9{\cdot}\overline{x}_1+4{\cdot}\overline{x}_2=9{\cdot}300+4{\cdot}200=3{,}500=V_2<\overline{V}_2=3{,}700$$

Therefore, the **optimal policy** is to produce Products 1 and 2 up to their respective sales limits and not to produce Product 3 at all:

$$x_1^* = 300;\quad x_2^* = 200;\quad x_3^* = 0.$$

The resulting contribution margin amounts to CM = 28,000 and the profit $\Pi = CM - C^F = 24{,}000$.

- ***Solution Structure***

In summary, the procedure can be described as follows: a linear situation without a multiple-product restriction exists when the consumptive demands of all product types with **positive contribution margins** to be produced in the amount of their respective sales limits do not exceed the available capacities. Then, the optimal production programme is: $x_j^* = \overline{x}_j$ for all products j with $cm_j > 0$ and $x_j^* = 0$ otherwise.

In the optimum at least, some **sales limits**, and therefore some restrictions, are entirely exhausted. In this linear case, without effective multiple-product restrictions, the optimal production policy lies at the **corner point of the 'area of feasible solutions'**. The area of feasible solutions is the set of possible solutions where all restrictions are satisfied; it is graphically delineated by the restrictions, that is, their (linear) equations (see ▶ Sect. 2.2.4). The **corner points** are combinations of the products within the area of feasible solutions, with which at least one restriction is fulfilled. The following sections will show that this is a general result for linear relations.

The above rule is modified if minimum amounts are to be produced for some or all products. In this case, the programme is only feasible if it also fulfils all lower limits. In the example, a minimum quantity of Product 3 in the amount of 100 may exist.

Such a **lower limit** could result, for example, from **long-term considerations**. To have the chance to sell Product 3 in a future year, it may not be possible to fully withdraw it from sales in the current year and, thus, become invisible to customers. Additionally, products at the beginning of their life cycle often show a negative contribution margin.

In the circumstance described, the amount of Product 3 would have to be set at 100. However, due to the negative contribution margin, *not more* than 100 units would be produced. Product 3 would require capacities of both machines, namely 500 machine hours of the first machine and 100 machine hours of the second machine. Then, however, only 2000 machine hours are available for the first machine for the two remaining products; and with it, this multiple-product restriction becomes effective because full production to the level of the sales limits of the remaining two products would require 2200 machine hours.

- ***Evaluation of the Solution***

Based on the optimal solution, other questions can also be answered. First, to improve the profit situation, a short-term **increase in capacity** can be considered, possibly by the introduction of an additional shift or the delay of maintenance. However, in the initial example described above, such activities cannot lead to improved profits because the capacities are not exhausted.

2

Non-linear Profit Functions

With non-linear relations, contribution margins depend on production levels. In the following, it is assumed that they depend only on the amount produced of the respective product *j* but not on the amount of the other products. The non-linearity is caused by price-demand curves of every product with the usual features, so it is:

$$cm_j = cm_j(x_j) = p_j(x_j) - c_j \text{ with } p_j'(x_j) < 0 \text{ and } p_j''(x_j) \leq 0 \text{ for } j = 1, \ldots, J$$

The *marginal contribution margins* of the products are relevant for testing the effectiveness of the multiple-product restrictions and can be derived from the contribution margin $CM_j = cm_j(x_j) \cdot x_j$ of the product type *j*:

1. First, the **unrestricted optimum** for every product is determined. It describes the point at which the respective marginal contribution margin is *zero*.
2. Provided that this unrestricted optimum is below the respective sales limit, it can be accepted **temporarily as a feasible solution**. Otherwise, only the appropriate sales limit is allowed where the respective marginal contribution margin is still positive.
3. With these production amounts arising from it, the demand of the multiple-product restrictions is examined. Their effectiveness results from it.

The essential difference in the linear case is in Step 2. If all unrestricted optima are feasible in respect to the sales limits, optimal production policy is regularly **not found at any corner point** of the area of feasible solutions anymore (see illustration of linear situation shown in **Fig. 2.1**).

Example

Based on the initial example (**Table 2.2**) and with the previous sales prices (except for Product 3) being prohibitive, the respective price-demand curves are as follows:

$$p_1(x_1) = 200 - x_1;\ p_2(x_2) = 480 - 2 \cdot x_2;\ p_3(x_3) = 1{,}260 - 1.5 \cdot x_3$$

The following contribution margins per unit arise for the different product types:

$$cm_1(x_1) = 40 - x_1;\ cm_1(x_1) \cdot x_1 = 40 \cdot x_1 - x_1^2$$
$$cm_2(x_2) = 80 - 2 \cdot x_2;\ cm_2(x_2) \cdot x_2 = 80 \cdot x_2 - 2 \cdot x_2^2$$
$$cm_3(x_3) = 90 - 1.5 \cdot x_3;\ cm_3(x_3) \cdot x_3 = 90 \cdot x_3 - 1.5 \cdot x_3^2$$

The unlimited optimum calculated by setting the marginal profit or the marginal contribution margin to zero is as follows:

$$x_1^{*u} = 20 = x_2^{*u}; \qquad x_3^{*u} = 30$$

All three are feasible, and their use in both production restrictions shows the ineffectiveness of both restrictions and with it the ineffectiveness of *all restrictions*. The optimum is a real inner point of the area of feasible solutions. This changes, for instance, if the price-demand curve of Product 1 is assumed as:

$$p_1(x_1) = 200 - 0.05 \cdot x_1$$

From it arises $x_1^{*u} = 400$, which evidently is not feasible. In this case, the amount would have to be lowered for Product 1 to the sales limit of 300. Both multiple-product restrictions then remain ineffective.

Certainly, a **delay in inspections** or other maintenance activities can lead to a reduction in the **fixed costs** C^F, but its long-term effects also need to be considered. A decrease in the current maintenance activity level may induce increased future repairs or machine failures. In this respect, the **dependencies of fixed costs** and the embedding of the current period's decisions in long-term decision-making become obvious and visible.

To achieve profit improvements at short notice, the company should instead consider an **expansion of their sales limits**. If both sales limits can be increased by 10 each, there would still not be any bottlenecks within production. With the given contribution margins, profit improvements are $10{\cdot}40 + 10{\cdot}80 = 1200$. This should be compared to the **additional costs** of the sales activities to determine the net effect.

Long-term aspects could also be considered here. With the additional costs of 1500 it may be favourable from a long-term perspective, provided that the sales levels rise in subsequent periods. Conversely, additional sales costs of 900, for instance, do not necessarily imply favourable activities if the current sales increase comes with a decrease in future sales volumes.

These explanations clarify the statement made earlier in this chapter that the demarcation **at 'short notice effects'** cannot always be perfectly drawn, and whether it can be assumed valid or not, depends on the specific situation and the individual case. The solution of the production decision problem, nevertheless, gives important indications for improvements. The optimal solution is the only meaningful **starting point** so as to at least estimate the short-term profit effects. This especially applies with appropriate restrictions to multiple products because changes in the optimal strategy cannot be easily achieved as shown above.

2.2.3 One Effective Multiple-Product Restriction

Now the initial example is slightly modified with the available machine hours of the first machine lowered to 1000 (as shown in ◘ Table 2.3). Since the chosen production level requires 2200 machine hours on Machine 1, the restriction of Machine 1

◘ Table 2.3 Changed capacity

Machine	$i = 1$	$i = 2$
Capacity $\bar{V}_i$	1,000	3,700

represents an effective limitation. Product 3 can continuously be neglected and the optimal production amounts of Products 1 and 2 are to be decided upon anew.

At first glance, it may look meaningful to highlight Product 2. Its contribution margin is twice as high as that of Product 1. If initially prioritising the production of Product 2, it seems that 200 units could potentially be sold, that is, the upper sales limit. However, due to the strict production capacity restriction of the first machine, only 125 units can actually be produced, and this would fully exhaust the capacity of the first machine, meaning that Product 1 cannot be produced at all. This policy would lead to a total contribution margin of 10,000.

This, however, cannot be the optimum. A comparison of the *exclusive* production of 300 units of Product 1 (whereby 600 machine hours on the first machine are needed and 400 machine hours remain unused) shows that this policy produces a contribution margin of 12,000, which is superior to the first alternative considered. Due to unused capacities on the first machine, the contribution margin can be further increased above 12,000.

In the case of a single multiple-product restriction, the **competitive relations between the products** restrict and waive the use of absolute contribution margins for the determination of the optimal production programme. The competitive relations must find their way into the **decision criteria**. For this to occur, the following consideration can be employed: if it is known that the multiple-product restriction resource i is limited, it becomes a matter of finding the most productive use for it, and the contribution margin attainable per unit of the resource i (e.g. per machine hour) for the production of product type j becomes relevant. This is called the **specific contribution margin** $\widehat{cm}_{ij}$ and it arises from the division of the absolute contribution margin cm_j by the consumption of the limited resource i:

$$\widehat{cm}_{ij} = \frac{cm_j}{v_{ij}} \quad j = 1, \ldots, J \tag{2.7}$$

The product type with the **highest specific contribution margin** has first **priority** since it is the most profitable per unit of the used capacity, and production should be expanded until either the resource i or the appropriate sales limit restricts it. Provided that the latter occurs first, the product type with the second highest specific contribution margin can be included in the production programme, and so on, until full exhaustion of the limited capacity occurs.

In the above example, the specific contribution margins are as follows:

$$\widehat{cm}_{11} = \frac{cm_1}{v_{11}} = \frac{40}{2} = 20 \text{ and } \widehat{cm}_{12} = \frac{cm_2}{v_{12}} = \frac{80}{1} = 10$$

Now, the results are the reverse of the previous situation. According to the specific contribution margins, Product 1 earns twice as much as Product 2 and, therefore, Product 1 should be produced first, up to the consumption of the capacity or its sales limit (as in the case of the example). The available 1000 machine hours of Resource 1 are first used by Product 1 to the extent of 300·2 = 600 machine hours, and 400 machine hours then remain for Product 2, which facilitates the production of 50 units of it and with it considerably less than the appropriate sales limit.

The **optimal policy** is as follows:

$$x_1^* = 300; \quad x_2^* = \min\{200;(1000-300\cdot 2)/8\} = \min\{200;50\} = 50; \quad x_3^* = 0$$

A total contribution margin CM = 16,000 and a profit Π = 12,000 result. Obviously, this production policy is also located on the corner of the area of feasible solutions because at least one multiple-product restriction is fulfilled in the form of an equation.

Solution Structure

The general procedure for one effective multiple-product restriction in linear form is as follows: with linear relations and i as the index of one effective multiple-product restriction, the products with $cmj > 0$ are to be ordered according to their **specific contribution margins** $\widehat{cm}_{ij}$ and to be assigned to the scarce capacity according to this order, considering their respective sales limits, until all of the available capacity is exhausted.

The case of **one effective multiple-product restriction** is present when:

- The initial production programme '$x_j = \overline{x}_j$ for all products j with $cm_j > 0$' leads to the fact that the supply of exactly one multiple-product restriction (e.g. machine capacity) is lower than the demand.
- Several effective restrictions exist with identical rankings of products according to their specific contribution margins for all restrictions (*Special Case 1*, see below; in which the restriction ultimately limiting production is determined using the optimal solution).
- One identical restriction for all products limiting the production amounts of each equally below their respective sales limits and other multiple-product restrictions (*Special Case 2*, see below).

Provided that **lower limits** exist for individual products, this procedure should be followed: first, the products with their respective minimum production amounts are included in the production programme. Then, the available capacities of the restrictions are reduced by the capacities required for these minimum amounts. The production programme decision remains to be found for the *additional* capacities and can be solved on the basis of the above procedure.

Special Cases

The **approach** described **above** is not only appropriate with one effective multiple-product restriction for the initial policy '$x_j = \overline{x}_j$ for all products j with $cm_j > 0$' but also in the special cases with several effective restrictions as mentioned above. These cases will now be clarified.

Special Case 1: If the specific contribution margins lead to an **identical order** for all effective multiple-product restrictions, any of them can be chosen. In the example shown in ◘ Table 2.4, this is the case (changes against the initial situation from ◘ Table 2.2 are again emphasised).

Now, with the initial policy of x_1 = 300 and x_2 = 200, the second restriction is also effective. The specific contribution margins for i = 2 amount to:

Table 2.4 Data of the special case

Product	$j = 1$	$j = 2$	$j = 3$
Price p_j	200	480	1,100
Variable costs c_j	160	400	1,170
Contribution margin cm_j	40	80	−70
Sales limit $\bar{x}_j$	300	200	600
Consumption v_{1j}	2	8	5
Consumption v_{2j}	1	3	1
Machine		$i = 1$	$i = 2$
Capacity $\bar{V}_i$		1,000	630

$$\widehat{cm}_{21} = \frac{cm_1}{v_{21}} = \frac{40}{1} = 40 \text{ and } \widehat{cm}_{22} = \frac{cm_2}{v_{22}} = \frac{80}{3} = 26.67$$

The **sequence** of the products according **to their specific contribution margins** is identical for *both* restrictions. Their production will begin again with 300 units of Product 1. Then Product 2 will be introduced into the programme and *three* restrictions are to be fundamentally considered. In addition to the two restrictions outlined above, the restriction of $i = 2$ also needs to be considered. Also, 330 machine hours are available, which would allow a production of 110 units of Product 2. Therefore, the restriction shown at the top is tighter, and the optimal policy of 50 units for product $j = 2$ remains unchanged.

There is actually only **one effective multiple-product restriction**; yet it is not known a priori which one it will be. However, this does not play a role because the order of the products to be produced according to their specific contribution margins is identical for all possible restrictions.

Special Case 2: The approach described is also appropriate if there is exactly one identical restriction $\bar{i}$, for all product types, that **limits** the **production** of *every* product more than the respective sales limit and all other effective multiple-product restrictions.

Example: The above limitation for $i = 2$ is $\bar{V}_2 = 240$ (ceteris paribus). Assuming that only one product is to be produced, then it could be either 240 units of $j = 1$ or 80 units of $j = 2$. Both are below their respective sales limits; consequently, these upper limits and the restriction $i = 1$ are irrelevant, although $i = 1$ also restricts the initial policy on the basis of the sales limits. In this situation, only the second production restriction is effective for the determination of the optimum production plan. The optimal policy is the production of the product with the highest specific contribution margin for $i = 2$, and the maximum number of Product 1 is $x_1 = 240$.

► Example with a Non-linear Profit Function

Three product types and the following contribution margins are given:

$$cm_1(x_1)\cdot x_1 = 80\cdot x_1 - 2\cdot x_1^2$$

$$cm_2(x_2)\cdot x_2 = 640\cdot x_2 - 16\cdot x_2^2$$

$$cm_3(x_3)\cdot x_3 = 100\cdot x_3 - 2.5\cdot x_3^2$$

The sales limits and production restrictions of the initial example (◘ Table 2.2) and Production Restriction 1 apply with:

$$2\cdot x_1 + 8\cdot x_2 + 5\cdot x_3 \leq \overline{V} = 2{,}500$$

The unlimited optima of all three products amount to 20. As a result, 300 (280) machine hours of the Production Restriction 1 (2) are needed. All sales limits and the Production Restriction 2 are ineffective.

With $\overline{V} \leq 300$ it is the case of one effective multiple-product restriction and the **specific marginal contribution margins** for $i = 1$ of the different products are relevant:

$$\widehat{cm'}(x_1)_{11} = 40 - 2\cdot x_1$$

$$\widehat{cm'}(x_2)_{12} = 80 - 4\cdot x_2$$

$$\widehat{cm'}(x_3)_{13} = 20 - x_3$$

Starting with production amounts $x_j = 0$ ($j = 1, 2, 3$), Product 2 would evidently be first, as it has the highest specific marginal contribution margin. It decreases successively and reaches a value of 40 with the amount $x_2 = 10$, which corresponds to the specific marginal contribution margin for Product 1 at $x_1 = 0$. At $x_2 = 10$, 80 machine hours are needed, so it follows that:

For $\overline{V} \leq 80$ the optimal programme is: $x_1^* = 0; \quad x_2^* = \overline{V}/8; \quad x_3^* = 0.$

If $\overline{V} > 80$, both Product 2 and Product 1 are produced. The volumes of these products are to be increased simultaneously under the condition of identical specific marginal contribution margins:

$$40 - 2\cdot x_1 = 80 - 4\cdot x_2 \quad \Rightarrow \quad x_1 = -20 + 2\cdot x_2$$

Inserted in the restriction $i = 1$ shows:

$$2\cdot(-20 + 2\cdot x_2) + 8\cdot x_2 = \overline{V} \quad \Rightarrow x_2 = \frac{\overline{V} + 40}{12}$$

This simultaneous increase takes place until the amounts of both products have reached a value of 20 for the respective specific marginal contribution margin and correspond with the specific marginal contribution margin of Product 3 at $x_3 = 0$. These amounts are $x1 = 10$ and $x2 = 15$. Also, 140 machine hours are needed, and as another result shows:

For $80 < \overline{V} \leq 140$ follows: $x_1^* = -20 + 2\cdot x_2^*; \quad x_2^* = \dfrac{\overline{V} + 40}{12}; \quad x_3^* = 0.$

Finally, for $140 < \overline{V} \leq 300$ all products are produced. Their amounts are to be found (analogously to the above case) under the condition of the identical specific marginal contribution margins. For x_1^* the above function can be applied; for x_3^* follows analogously:

2

$x_3^* = -60 + 4 \cdot x_2^*$

Inserting both functions in $i = 1$ shows $x_2^* = \frac{\overline{V} + 340}{32}$.

With it the optimal solutions arise as a function of the severity of the first production restriction. The capacity of $\overline{V}$ dictates whether certain products are contained in the production programme or not.

This is also responsible for the fact that the optimal programme cannot simply be determined by the use of a *Lagrange* operator solved by setting the partial derivatives to zero. The relevant *Lagrange* function would be:

$$LG(x_1, x_1, x_1, \lambda, \overline{V}) = \sum_{j=1}^{3} cm_j(x_j) \cdot x_j - \lambda \cdot \left(\sum_{j=1}^{3} v_{1j} \cdot x_j \right) \cdot \overline{V}$$

If this function is maximised by forming the first derivatives of LG to xj ($j = 1, 2, 3$) and λ, setting them to zero, and solving the resulting equation system, the results appear as shown above for the case of $140 < \overline{V}$ (the reader is invited to check this).

Implicitly a certain area is subordinated for $\overline{V}$, and the solution is not applicable to other intervals. Basically, the a priori knowledge of products contained or not contained in the programme with a certain capacity of machine hours is required. Only for the products contained in the programme, the solution can be found by setting the first derivatives to zero; for the products not contained, the first derivative of LG regularly is negative, on the contrary, at $x_j = 0$ (the *Lagrange* multiplier λ is responsible for this). This is shown in the so-called *Kuhn-Tucker condition* regarding the products for the above *Lagrange approach*:

$$x_j^* > 0 \text{ and } \frac{\partial LG^*}{\partial x_j} = 0; x_j^* = 0 \text{ and } \frac{\partial LG^*}{\partial x_j} \le 0$$

The *Lagrange* approach can be used *iteratively*: in the first step the *Lagrange* function LG can be maximised by setting the first derivatives for *all* products and the *Lagrange* multiplier to zero. As a result, the solution of the third case described above, which depends on the central supply $\overline{V}$, rises. For a given value of $\overline{V}$ (for instance, 90), the non-negativity of the solution can be easily examined. Provided a negative amount for at least one product is displayed, the whole solution is inadmissible (with $\overline{V} = 90$, Product 3 shows a negative result). The optimisation can be restarted in the second step, while the products with negative amounts a priori are set to 0. This procedure can be applied until a feasible optimum arises. ◀

■ *Stepwise Linear Contribution Margins*

The case of stepwise linear contribution margins to a certain extent lies 'in the middle' between linear and non-linear profit functions. It is characterised by the fact that there are intervals of production amounts for the individual products, which in each case has constant but different contribution margins. It can arise, for instance, from a **discount** that is offered for purchasing a certain volume of a raw material needed for production. Ceteris paribus, the variable costs drop (the contribution margin rises) for this product but only from a particular production volume onwards. The reverse case is also possible, in which the contribution margins from a certain production volume decrease, due to, for example, sales-price reductions used to achieve sales increases.

- *Solution with Declining Contribution Margin Jumps (Virtual-Product Rule)*

The determination of the optimum production decision under these conditions can be carried out in the same way as the standard case of linear contribution margins described above, if **declining contribution margin jumps** occur. Then, every product can be split into as many **virtual products** as there are contribution margin jumps. All virtual products of all product types can then be ordered according to their specific contribution margins and assigned successively to the limited capacity. Because lower specific contribution margins can appear for the virtual products of a product type with declining jumps only for higher production volumes, the above allocation rules for the standard case remain valid.

Example: A modification of the example will serve for clarification. It is assumed for Product Type 1 that 200 units can be sold at a price of 200. However, to sell an additional 100 units, the sales price must drop to 170 for the additional units. Product Type 1, therefore, is split into the two virtual Products 1a and 1b to which ceteris paribus different contribution margins apply. ◘ Table 2.5 shows the new situation (with Product Type 3 neglected).

The sales limit for Product Type 1 remains at 300 units, but only 200 units can be sold for the higher price. The sequence according to the specific contribution margins with regard to $i = 1$ is as follows:

$$\widehat{cm}_{11a} = \frac{40}{2} = 20;\ \widehat{cm}_{11b} = \frac{10}{2} = 5;\ \widehat{cm}_{12} = \frac{80}{8} = 10$$

Therefore, the optimal programme for $\overline{V}_1 = 1{,}000$ is as follows:

$$x_{1a}^* = 200;\quad x_{1b}^* = 0;\quad x_2^* = 75$$

◘ **Table 2.5** Declining contribution margin jumps

Product	$j = 1a$	$j = 1b$	$j = 2$
Price p_j	200	170	480
Variable costs c_j	160	160	400
Contribution margin cm_j	40	10	80
Sales limit $\overline{x}_j$	200	100	200
Consumption v_{1j}	2	2	8
Consumption v_{2j}	9	9	4

With regard to the separate product types, the **solution structure** shows a similar result as did the non-linear profit functions: the programme can comprise of several product types that are not produced to their maximum amounts (in the linear case this is only possible if one effective multiple-product restriction is larger than all sales limits so that actually only one product type is included in the production programme). With regard to the **virtual products**, the conclusions drawn are completely analogous to those of the standard linear scenario.

- *Solution with Progressive Contribution Margin Jumps*

In contrast to the solution with declining contribution margin jumps, progressive contribution margin jumps prevent the use of the standard-allocation rules. The reason is due to the fact that the limited capacity is first to be used with products that have the highest specific contribution margins. However, this is impossible in the present situation because the higher contribution margins assume that a certain production volume with lower contribution margins must be produced first.

In this case, only a **comprehensive analysis of the total programme** leads to the optimal solution where **specific contribution margins** can still be applied.

Example: With regard to the contribution margins of Product Type 1, the above declining jumps are simply reversed (◘ Table 2.6).

The specific contribution margins are as follows:

$$\widehat{cm}_{11a} = \frac{10}{2} = 5; \widehat{cm}_{11b} = \frac{40}{2} = 20; \widehat{cm}_{12} = \frac{80}{8} = 10$$

In order to achieve the lower variable unit costs of Product 1 (e.g. resulting from a specific discount), 100 units must first be produced with less favourable conditions. The limited capacity $i = 1$ with 200 machine hours would be exhausted by it. If this capacity $i = 1$ is limited to no more than 200 machine hours, Product Type 2 would be produced instead because a more profitable utilisation of the capacity would be achieved with it. Therefore, the production of Product Type 1 can only be considered in the case of a minimum range of the limited capacity. With the fictitious use

◘ **Table 2.6** Progressive contribution margin jumps

Product	j **= 1a**	j **= 1b**	j **= 2**
Price p_j	200	200	480
Variable costs c_j	190	160	400
Contribution margin cm_j	10	40	80
Sales limit $\bar{x}_j$	100	200	200
Consumption v_{1j}	2	2	8
Consumption v_{2j}	9	9	4

of the whole limited capacity $i = 1$ for Product Type 1 (up to the sales limit), *on average* the **specific contribution margin** is as follows:

$$\widehat{cm}_{11}^{\varnothing} = \frac{\overline{x}_{1a} \cdot v_{11} \cdot \widehat{cm}_{11a} + \left(\overline{V}_1 - \overline{x}_{1a} \cdot v_{11}\right) \cdot \widehat{cm}_{11b}}{\overline{V}_1} = \widehat{cm}_{11a} - \left(\widehat{cm}_{11b} - \widehat{cm}_{11a}\right) \cdot \frac{\overline{x}_{1a} \cdot v_{11}}{\overline{V}_1}$$

$$= 20 - 15 \cdot \frac{200}{\overline{V}_1} \left(\text{for } 200 \le \overline{V}_1 \le 600\right)$$

Typically, Product Type 1 becomes the **more profitable option** with the **more capacity that becomes** available. The critical central supply with which Product Type 1, on average, shows a profitable capacity allocation equal to Product Type 2 arises from:

$$20 - \frac{3,000}{\overline{V}_1^{\circ}} = \widehat{cm}_{12} = 10 \Rightarrow \overline{V}_1^{\circ} = \frac{3,000}{10} = 300$$

The **solution** depends on the limited capacity:
- $0 \le \overline{V}_1 \le 300$: only Product Type 2
- $300 \le \overline{V}_1 \le 600$: only Product Type 1
- $600 \le \overline{V}_1$: Product Type 1 produced up to sales limit, Product Type 2 depending on the capacity

With progressive contribution margin jumps, the **sequence** of the product types cannot be indicated **independently of the available capacity**. A specific sequence, therefore, only applies *locally* in relation to the available capacity in the specific situation under review. Changes in capacities can affect the order of the allocation of product types within the limited capacity.

▪ *Evaluation of the Solution*

For the evaluation, the (purely linear) standard case is referred to again, and the **optimal solution** of the production allocation or scheduling decision problem provides valuable insights for other analyses. It particularly allows the estimation of **restriction change effects**. This contains the gross profit change if a restriction is reduced or expanded by one unit and, therefore, characterises the **marginal price of this unit** as the amount that could be paid without a change to the profit obtained in the initial situation. The following examples show that these values depend on the respective level of the capacity restrictions and the optimal solution connected with it.

Based on the initial solution (◘ Table 2.3) of 300 units for Product 1 and 50 units for Product 2, a **short-term expansion of the production capacity** of Machine 1 may be considered. Every additional production hour would be used for the production of Product 2 and would result in a specific contribution margin improvement of 10. Due to the second product's sales limit of 150 units for the current period, ceteris paribus, no more than 1200 additional production hours should be made available, as with them, exactly 150 units of Product 2 could be produced. An extra 1000 machine hours would be attained by an additional shift and would lead to additional salary costs of 8000 along with a **net improvement** of 10,000 – 8000 = 2000. Sales policies that expand the sales limits within the available production capacities could further increase profits. With these considerations, the capacity of the second machine would seem to be a possible bottleneck.

With regard to **influencing the sales limits**, similar considerations can be employed, for example, appropriate multiple-product restrictions. An increase in the sales limit of Product 1, for instance, coincides with a decrease in the amount of Product 2 due to competitive reasons. As a result, an increase of one unit in the sales limit does not lead to an increased profit of 40, rather only 20, as every additional unit of Product 1 decreases sales of Product 2 by 0.25 units (the increase in the sales limit of Product 2 is unimportant as the previous limit cannot be achieved due to the production restrictions), and thus the profit changes by 40 – 0.25 · 80 = 20, up to additional sales of 200 units (potential integrity restrictions are not considered).

These considerations can also be employed in reverse. For instance, **losses** connected with **capacity decreases** can be analysed, for example, what are the 'costs' of one machine hour of Machine 1. Such considerations are important for **supplementary orders** received during the current period but not considered in the original plan (see also ▶ Chap. 3). With limited capacities, such supplementary orders claim limited resources, which must be taken away from other uses. Therefore, the supplementary orders can only be profitable if they produce at least as much profit as was attainable with what the capacity was used for (this equals the meaning of the specific contribution margin, which therefore is relevant again). Every lost production hour from Machine 1 would be taken away from the production of Product 2, and therefore would result in a loss of 10 for the first 400 machine hours. After that, the production of Product 1 will be limited with losses of 20 per hour.

Analogously, the 'costs' of a **decrease in the sales potential** of Product 1 could be determined. Every unit of Product 1 not produced would permit *the additional* production of 0.25 units of Product 2; therefore, the resulting loss only amounts to 40 – 0.25 · 80 = 20.

2.2.4 Several Effective Multiple-Product Restrictions

For the following analysis, the machine hours available for the second machine are decreased. The new scenario is represented in ◘ Table 2.7.

Product 3 can be neglected because of its negative contribution margin, so a two-product case will be analysed. With the initial policy of 300 (200) units for Product 1 (2) *both* **production restrictions** are violated; in fact both sales limits are redundant as the production restrictions are stronger than them, and even the exclusive production of Product 1 (2) will not attain them (Product 1: 1,620/9 = 180 can be produced because of $\bar{V}_2 = 1{,}620$; Product 2: 1,000/8 = 125 units because of $\bar{V}_1 = 1{,}000$).

Table 2.7 Data for several effective multiple-product restrictions

Product	$j = 1$	$j = 2$	$j = 3$	
Price p_j	200	480	1,100	
Variable costs c_j	160	400	1,170	
Contribution margin cm_j	40	80	−70	
Sales limit $\bar{x}_j$	300	200	600	
Consumption v_{1j}	2	8	5	
Consumption v_{2j}	9	4	1	
Machine			$i = 1$	$i = 2$
Capacity $\bar{V}_i$			1,000	1,620

Therefore, in this **case both production restrictions are effective.** This can be represented in the form of a linear equation system:

$$2 \cdot x_1^* + 8 \cdot x_2^* = 1,000$$

$$9 \cdot x_1^* + 4 \cdot x_2^* = 1,620$$

The second equation solved towards x_2^* leads to:

$$x_2^* = \frac{1,620}{4} - \frac{9}{4} \cdot x_1^* = 405 - 2.25 \cdot x_1^*$$

Used in the first equation it follows:

$$2 \cdot x_1^* + 8 \cdot \left(405 - 2.25 \cdot x_1^*\right) = 1,000 \Rightarrow x_1^* = 140$$

From it again arises $x_2^* = 405 - 2.25 \cdot 140 = 90$. The contribution margin of this policy amounts to 12,800 and the period profit is 8,800. Based upon all of the conditions, no other production programme will yield a higher period profit.

- *Solution Structure and Linear Programming*

In the current example, the solution can be found easily because of the low number of products and restrictions. However, this changes with the (realistic) expansion of product and restriction numbers. Possibly, in these cases, all restriction combinations may need to be calculated explicitly, but this is quite time-consuming and, in such cases, it is better to use **linear programming** procedures, particularly the **Simplex method**.

The **solution structure** can be summarised as follows: if *linear dependencies* and at least *two* effective multiple-product restrictions exist, an optimal solution to the

2

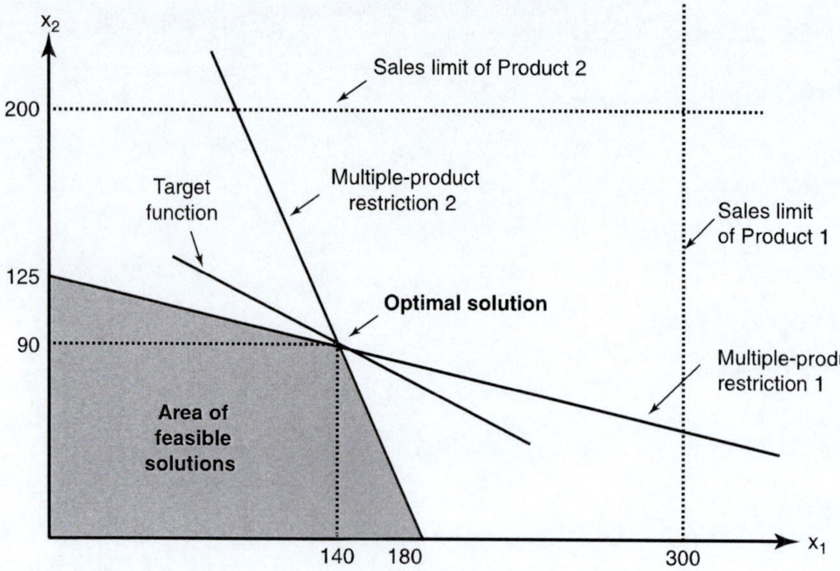

Fig. 2.1 Graphical solution of the linear programme

production allocation decision problem can always be found among the **corner points** of the area of feasible solutions (For this *corner theorem* of linear programming and for the proof, see Bol (1980, p. 57–59). Corner points can be specified by a *formal definition*. A corner point of a [convex] set is a point [element of the set] that cannot be represented as a convex combination of two other points of this set; according to this definition, for example, all points of the marginal curve of a circle are corner points. See Bol (1980, p. 49–51)). Figure 2.1 shows the graphical solution of the linear programme for the above example.

If **lower limits** exist for products, a similar procedure as in the case of only one appropriate multiple-product restriction can be applied, and all products are to be placed first on the level of their respective lower limits; afterwards the capacities must be reduced by the respective demands. The remaining optimisation problem concerns *additional* amounts and *remaining* capacities. The above solution structure is applied to this remaining problem analogously.

- *Simplex Method*

Since the optimal solution is a corner point of the area of feasible solutions, it is possible to determine all corner points and their contribution margins; the point with the highest contribution margin represents the optimal solution. This procedure can be very time-consuming.

The Simplex method is a procedure that searches the corner points with the search criteria and stop criteria provided. For the **solution**, *non-negative* **slack variables** w are introduced as a first step, in order to change the set of inequations that represent the restrictions into a set of equations. In the example, $N = I + J = 4$, restrictions exist, which can be represented after the introduction of these slack variables w_n ($n = 1, ..., N$) as follows:

$$2 \cdot x_1 + 8 \cdot x_2 + 1 \cdot w_1 + 0 \cdot w_2 + 0 \cdot w_3 + 0 \cdot w_4 = 1{,}000$$

$$1 \cdot x_1 + 0 \cdot x_2 + 0 \cdot w_1 + 0 \cdot w_2 + 1 \cdot w_3 + 0 \cdot w_4 = 300$$

$$0 \cdot x_1 + 1 \cdot x_2 + 0 \cdot w_1 + 0 \cdot w_2 + 0 \cdot w_3 + 1 \cdot w_4 = 200 \quad (2.8)$$

$$x_1, x_2 \geq 0; w_1, w_2, w_3, w_4 \geq 0$$

The slack variables indicate the **capacity** is not exhausted, that is, still available; for instance, $w_1 = 200$ shows that 200 machine hours of the first machine are not needed by the production programme.

A linear equation system with J **structure variables** x_j, N **slack variables** (altogether $M = J + N = 2 \cdot J + I$ variables) and N **restrictions** arises. For the determination of the corner points for $M - N = J$ variables (so-called **non-basis variables**) usually a starting value of 0 is assumed and the remaining equation system of the **basis variables** is solved. **Non-negative** solutions of these basis variables represent a corner point of the area of feasible solutions.

The definition of the search and stop criteria is achieved by **a specific integration of the target function**. It is added as an additional equation to the previous system and is subject to the same procedures as the coefficient matrix. In addition, in the initial step, the target function is supplemented by the slack variables. However, as these produce no contribution, they get a contribution margin of zero in each case. In the example it follows:

$$CM = 40 \cdot x_1 + 80 \cdot x_2 + 0 \cdot w_1 + 0 \cdot w_2 + 0 \cdot w_3 + 0 \cdot w_4 \quad (2.9)$$

This **target function** can also be written as:

$$-40 \cdot x_1 - 80 \cdot x_2 - 0 \cdot w_1 - 0 \cdot w_2 - 0 \cdot w_3 - 0 \cdot w_4 + CM = 0 \quad (2.10)$$

In this form, an additional element of the equation system by way of a new, fictitious variable CM is introduced whose coefficients are zero in the other equations. Therefore, it plays no role in the relevant transformations (for this reason, the matrix column for the variable CM is regularly left out, although it is included in the following text for clarification purposes).

- *Iterations with the Simplex Method*

The **starting point** is the trivial basis solution with the J **structural variables** x_j set to zero. Here, the complications become obvious through the potential existence of multiple-product lower limits because in this case, the initial solution is inadmissible. Only the slack variables are in the basis by which a contribution margin $CM = 0$ is achieved. Now, the equation system is represented by the following initial tableau (the head column BV represents the **basis variables**, the *RS column* represents the values of the '**right side**' of the equation system, that is, the available capacities or the upper limits, and the last line indicates the target function):

2

Initial tableau

BV	x_1	x_2	w_1	w_2	w_3	w_4	*CM*	*RS*
w_1	2	8	1	0	0	0	0	1,000
w_2	9	4	0	1	0	0	0	1,620
w_3	1	0	0	0	1	0	0	300
w_4	0	1	0	0	0	1	0	200
	−40	−80	0	0	0	0	1	0

The value below the *RS* column in the last line indicates the contribution margin of the respective basis solution (initially, this is set to zero).

This initial solution is not optimal, because it can be improved upon by starting production of either Product 1 or Product 2. On the basis of the contribution margins, such improvement possibilities are generally shown by **negative coefficients** of the respective **non-basis variables**. As a rule, the non-basis variable with the highest negative target function coefficient is used for a basis exchange (here x_2); it enters the basis, and the connected column of the tableaus is named the **pivot column**.

Now the variable, which leaves the previous basis, is to be determined. For this, one considers which restriction limits the range of this basis variable the most. This can be determined by division of the values of the *RS* column by the respective coefficients of the **pivot column**. The lowest (positive) quotient marks the severest restriction. In the example, the lowest (positive) quotient is found in the first line of the tableau. Negative quotients are not considered because they violate the non-negativity restriction. Coefficients in the pivot column with a value of zero are also not considered, as their quotient is not defined here, because the new basis variable is not connected with the restriction and such non-existing capacity demands do not need to be considered. The line (with the strongest binding restriction) is called the **pivot line**, and the **pivot element** can be characterised through the *pivot column* and the *pivot line* (in the example this is $v_{12} = 8$). Therefore, w_1 leaves the basis because the capacity of the first machine is completely exhausted.

The new basis solution is determined by transforming the **pivot column** (including the element in the target function line) into the **unit vector**. All elements of the **pivot line** are divided first by the **pivot element**. Afterwards, the usual rules for transforming equation systems are applied to produce a unit vector *in the* x_2 *column* (pivot column). This first iteration is presented in the following tableau:

Tableau after the first iteration

BV	x_1	x_2	w_1	w_2	w_3	w_4	*CM*	*RS*
x_2	1/4	1	1/8	0	0	0	0	125
w_2	8	0	−1/2	1	0	0	0	1,120
w_3	1	0	0	0	1	0	0	300
w_4	−1/4	0	−1/8	0	0	1	0	75
	−20	0	10	0	0	0	1	10,000

The **coefficients** in the columns of both **non-basis variables** x_1 and w_1 can be interpreted intuitively as **change factors** for the restrictions and indicate changes in the basis variables connected with the respective line if *one unit* of the non-basis variables is introduced into the basis:

- If x_1 was integrated into the basis, x_2 would be reduced by 0.25 units because the first machine is fully exhausted. Accordingly, 8 *additional* production hours on Machine 2 would be demanded: 9 machine hours for one unit x_1 less $0.25 \cdot 4 = 1$ hour due to the decrease in x_2. As a result, a value arises for the first column in the target function line. Every additional unit x_1 results in an immediate contribution margin of 40; however, a contribution margin loss of $0.25 \cdot 80 = 20$ (for the reduced production of the second product) follows as well, that is, a net overall increase of 20.
- If w_1 were to be integrated into the basis, it would mean free capacity is created again for Machine 1 (i.e. reduced use of this machine). Every unit of capacity given up equals 0.125 units of Product 2, and with it a decrease in Machine 2's usage capacity by $0.125 \cdot 4 = 0.5$ machine hours. The resulting *contribution margin loss* (indicated in the target function line) amounts to $0.125 \cdot 80 = 10$.

Negative target function coefficients of the non-basis variables indicate possibilities for an increase in the contribution margin (and therefore, the profit), with **positive coefficients** for losses. This will also be clear from the target function's description, which after the first iteration, can be written as:

$$-20 \cdot x_1 + 10 \cdot w_1 + CM = 10{,}000$$

$$\Rightarrow CM = 10{,}000 + 20 \cdot x_1 - 10 \cdot w_1 \quad (2.11)$$

Therefore, another improvement can be achieved by the inclusion of Product 1 into the basis. In the next step, Column 1 becomes the pivot column, Line 2 the pivot line and w_2 leaves the basis. The required steps are completely analogous to the first iteration and the new tableau is:

2

Tableau after second iteration (= final tableau)

BV	x_1	x_2	w_1	w_2	w_3	w_4	*CM*	*RS*
x_2	0	1	9/64	−1/32	0	0	0	90
x_1	1	0	−1/16	1/8	0	0	0	140
w_3	0	0	1/16	−1/8	1	0	0	160
w_4	0	0	−9/64	1/32	0	1	0	110
	0	0	8.75	2.5	0	0	1	12,800

This now concludes the procedure as the **optimal solution** is found; the target function line shows only positive coefficients of the non-basis variables. Any change would only lower the profit achieved in the calculated solution:

$$8.75 \cdot w_1 + 2.5 \cdot w_2 + CM = 12{,}800$$

$$\Rightarrow CM = 12{,}800 - 8.75 \cdot w_1 - 2.5 \cdot w_2$$

The interpretation of the **coefficients** in the columns of the **non-basis variables** is completely analogous to the tableau after the first iteration. The contribution margin loss from w_1 arises from the fact that every free production hour leads to a decrease in production from x_2 to the amount of 9/64 and to an increase in the production from x_1 to the amount of 1/16. The profit change amounts to 1/16 · 40 – 9/64 · 80 = –8.75. Similarly, the loss from w_2 can be explained.

The **Simplex method** can also be applied for situations of one effective multiple-product restriction or for situations without such restrictions. However, the optimum can be found, as shown, with much simpler procedures.

Procedural Decisions

The approach shown can also be applied with the inclusion of procedural decisions. To illustrate its use, the example in the text is modified so that both appropriate multiple-product restrictions now refer to two optional procedures, which are available for every product (every product now only faces one production step for which the two procedures are available).

The variable costs and therefore the contribution margins of the products depend on the chosen procedure. For every product j = 1, 2, 3, there are two production alternatives n = 1, 2 and, therefore, two possible contribution margins cm_{nj}. Every product can now be expressed in the form of virtual products – the number of different virtual products equals the production (procedural) options. The total amount of a product corresponds to the sum of the amounts produced with these combinations in each case, and may not exceed the product-specific sales limit. Therefore, in the example the following value is calculated:

$$\max_{x_{nj}} \sum_{j=1}^{3}\sum_{n=1}^{2} cm_{nj} \cdot x_{nj}$$

With the restrictions (it is assumed that procedure $n = 1$ (2) concerns the multiple-product restriction $i = 1$ (2)):

$$2 \cdot x_{11} + 8 \cdot x_{11} + 5 \cdot x_{13} \leq 1{,}000$$

$$9 \cdot x_{21} + 4 \cdot x_{11} + 1 \cdot x_{23} \leq 1{,}620$$

$$x_{11} + x_{21} \leq 300 \quad x_{12} + x_{22} \leq 200 \quad x_{13} + x_{23} \leq 600$$

This approach uses the linear programming technique. Evidently, the problem structure is completely analogous to the procedure described in the text as only the number of the structure variables increases because many possible combinations are under consideration.

- *Evaluation of the Solution*

The result shown in the final tableau can be used to answer a number of questions. The relations expressed in it can be summarised as follows:

$$x_2 = 90 - \frac{9}{64} \cdot w_1 + \frac{1}{32} \cdot w_2$$

$$x_1 = 140 + \frac{1}{16} \cdot w_1 - \frac{1}{8} \cdot w_2$$

$$w_3 = 160 - \frac{1}{16} \cdot w_1 + \frac{1}{8} \cdot w_2$$

$$w_4 = 110 + \frac{9}{64} \cdot w_1 - \frac{1}{32} \cdot w_2$$

$$CM = 12{,}800 - 8.75 \cdot w_1 - 2.5 \cdot w_2$$

The discussion of the **Simplex method** showed how the coefficients in the columns of the non-basis variables can be interpreted as **change factors**. It was compared to the previous situation when non-basis variables were introduced into the basis. With regard to the exemplary final tableau, slack variables were introduced, that is, indicating **a decrease in the production capacity**. If, for any reason, the capacity was reduced by *one* production hour for Machine 1 (2), ceteris paribus, the affected production amounts and sales potentials would have to be reduced in the above manner from which a contribution margin loss of 8.75 (2.5) would result.

Non-linear Profit Functions

In the non-linear case, the optimum does not necessarily lie at the corner of the area of feasible solutions. Therefore, searching the corner points offers no guarantee of finding the optimal solution, and generally the optimum can only be described as regards its *necessary conditions*, which correspond with the *KUHN-TUCKER* conditions. A *LAGRANGE* function is set up:

$$LG=\sum_{j=1}^{J}cm_j\left(x_j\right)\cdot x_j-\sum_{i=1}^{I}\lambda_i\cdot\left(\sum_{j=1}^{J}v_{ij}\cdot x_j-\bar{V}_i\right)-\sum_{j=1}^{J}\mu_j\cdot\left(x_j-\bar{x}_j\right)$$

λi and μj are *LAGRANGE* multipliers for the multiple-product restrictions or the sales limits. They are positive if the respective restriction is fulfilled as an equation, or else they have a value of zero. The optimal solution must fulfil the following first-order conditions:

$$x_j^* > 0 \text{ and } \frac{\partial LG^*}{\partial x_j}=0; x_j^*=0 \text{ and } \frac{\partial LG^*}{\partial x_j}\leq 0$$

$$\lambda_j > 0 \text{ and } \sum_{j=1}^{J}v_{ij}\cdot x_j=\bar{V}_i; \lambda_j=0 \text{ and } \sum_{j=1}^{J}v_{ij}\cdot x_j\leq\bar{V}_i$$
$$\mu_j > 0 \text{ and } x_j=\bar{x}_j; \mu_j=0 \text{ and } x_j\leq\bar{x}_j$$

Based on this structure, it is always: $LG^*=CM^*$. The above conditions are applied when presenting a (local) optimum; they are sufficient if the contribution margin function CM is *concave*. Provided that CM is *strictly concave*, the optimum marked at the top is *unambiguous* because a strict concave function can only have one maximum. The conditions should not be mistaken for an algorithm – a concise procedure for the determination of the optimum that can only be derived in certain cases from them.

The values of the *LAGRANGE* multipliers correspond *at the optimum* to the (marginal) contribution margin changes caused by (marginal) changes to the limitations of the restrictions:

$$\lambda_j=\frac{\partial LG^*}{\partial\bar{V}_i}=\frac{\partial CM^*}{\partial\bar{V}_i}; \mu_j=\frac{\partial LG^*}{\partial\bar{x}_j}=\frac{\partial CM^*}{\partial\bar{x}_j}$$

Because linear target functions represent a special case of *LG*, the target function coefficient of the *slack variables* shown in the final tableau of the Simplex method can be interpreted as appropriate multipliers.
In general, the solution of non-linear production programme decision problems has to be found applying *non-linear programming* methods (i.e. Künzi and Krelle 1979; or Luptácik 1981).

As shown in both previous decision situations, these values cannot be used for **arbitrary changes**, as they only apply as long as the non-negativity conditions for the basis variables are not violated. For example, an increase in w_1 leads to the decrease in x_2 and w_3; and w_1 can only be increased as long as neither x_2 nor w_3 become 0. The condition $w_2 = 0$ indicates a maximum value of 640 machine hours for w_1 and analogously for w_2 a maximum value of 1120. Thus, the **structure of the optimal solution** expressed by the above equations applies only to capacities of 1000 – 640 = 360 machine hours for Machine 1 and 1620 – 1120 = 500 machine hours for Machine 2 (in each case ceteris paribus under the assumption of an unchanged capacity of the other restriction).

The equation system of the final tableau can also be used in reverse and for both previous decision situations for potential **expansions of the production capacities** and/or **sales limits**. Therefore, a capacity increase of 100 machine hours for Machine 1, for instance, would mean *a negative* value $w_1 = -100$. From the target function line, a profit improvement of 875 is derived from a decrease to x_1 of 6.25 and an increase to x_2 of 14.0625. Analogously, a value of $w_2 = -100$ causes a profit improvement of 250 on the basis of an increase in x_1 by 12.5 and a decrease in x_2 by 3.125. These relations cannot be considered arbitrarily, because again attention must be paid to the non-negativity conditions of the basis variables. From these considerations (in each case ceteris paribus), a lower limit for w_1 of $-782.\overline{2}$ and for w_2 of -1280 can be derived. The structural relations of the final tableau apply to production capacities from a maximum of $1000 + 782.\overline{2} = 1{,}782.\overline{2}$ machine hours for Machine 1 and 1620 + 1280 = 2900 machine hours for Machine 2 (in each case ceteris paribus under the assumption of the unchanged capacity of the other machine). Increases in sales potential, with given production capacities, evidently have no impact in the short run because sales potential does not present a bottleneck.

Additionally, **profit changes** as a result of **short-term price changes** could be discussed for the different products. Changes would affect the respective contribution margins and, therefore, the target function coefficients. Graphically, this leads to a change in the upward slopes of the iso-contribution margin lines. Changes in the previous optimal solution must not necessarily be connected with it; this solution remains valid as long as the previous corner point remains a tangential point of the new iso-contribution margin lines.

2.3 Opportunity Costs and Decision-Making

2.3.1 Conceptual Bases

Opportunity costs refer to **costs** in the sense of '**missed opportunities**' when undertaking a certain action or alternative: the opportunity for taking another action is given up and its target contribution is also lost. To assess the profitability of the planned action alternative, these lost target contributions can be considered 'costs' of the planned alternative. Accordingly, opportunity costs can be defined for various target functions; however, in accordance with the assumptions set here, the following examples refer only to the profit-related target.

The above characteristic focuses on the lost alternatives as an essential feature. However, the **opportunity costs concept** is multi-layered. The different **types are** shown in ◘ Fig. 2.2.

Input-related opportunity costs refer to input factors used during the production process, for example, machine hours and raw materials. They indicate the attainable marginal profit assuming the *optimal* use of the factor under consideration. In contrast to the purchase price of an input factor, the optimal marginal profit of a factor is not known a priori, but rather depends on the specific decision problem and the scarcity of the situations pertaining to it.

Output-related opportunity costs refer to units of the final products. As **optimal costs**, they equal the resources required for one unit of a product valued at its respective **input-related marginal profit** of these resources. On the contrary, **as alternative costs** they correspond to the **profit of the best, unused application**.

The intention of the opportunity costs' use for decision-making lies in the **description of the factor scarcity** of the resources used along with the inclusion of factor limitations. For example, modified contribution margins of the final products could be used to consider scarcity; and the restrictions would not be explicitly included for decision-making in the ideal case, as the optimal decision could simply be determined by a comparison of these modified contribution margins.

This intention and the idea to register lost profit due to missed opportunities appear intuitively plausible, yet the following analysis will show in detail that the supposed advantages are rather small, or, in fact, that opportunity costs will contribute **no contribution** to the solution of the decision problems treated in this chapter. In all cases, **linear dependencies** are assumed.

◘ **Fig. 2.2** Types of opportunity costs

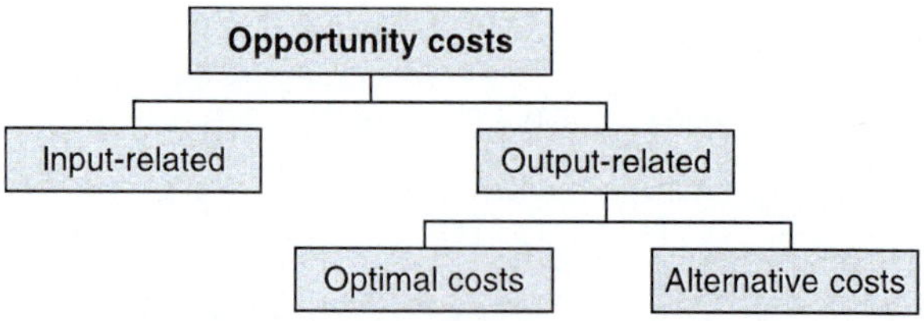

2.3.2 Input-Related Opportunity Costs

The definition of this cost category implies that these costs are calculated on the basis of the optimal use of the respective resource. The **marginal profit per factor unit** with assumed **optimal factor use** – that is, the profit change that arises, if one unit of the resource is utilised more or less – is analysed, while their optimal use is assumed. This definition reflects the fact that input-related opportunity costs are only known with the optimal solution of the underlying decision problem; the marginal profit arising from the resources' optimal use can only be derived from the solution.

For the decision situations considered in this chapter, the **input-related opportunity costs** can be retrieved from the respective solutions:

1. *Without effective multiple-product restriction.* The marginal profit of the I resources is **zero** in each case because they are sufficiently available. Additional resource units would be worthless because the available sales limits represent the actual bottleneck; and decreases in the available resources would be without effect for the same reason (unless these decreases become more important than the sales limits, with the impact of a single multiple-product restriction arising as a result).
2. The **sales potentials** can be understood as input factors as well. Every product unit sold decreases the resource 'sales potential' by one unit. Because the sales potentials are scarce, their input-related opportunity costs are not zero and correspond to the contribution margin cm_j per unit of the respective product.
3. *One effective multiple-product restriction.* In this case, one resource i is scarce. Therefore, for every additional factor unit, more (less) availability would be valuable (harmful): it increases (decreases) the **specific contribution margin** of the product type finally accepted into the programme. The input-related marginal profit is **zero** again.
4. For a particular case this statement must be modified: should the sales potential of the product type that was finally accepted into the production programme also be exhausted by coincidence due to the capacity limit of the restriction i, additional factor units of the resource i would flow into the product type of the next best profitable specific contribution margin.

   The input-related opportunity costs of the sales potentials of the products included in the programme are positive if they are completely exhausted; otherwise they are also zero. However, they are not identical to the contribution margins cm_j of the products. Due to the limited restriction i, increased production of a product can only be achieved by a reduction in the production of the other products. If a product j's sales potential is increased by one unit, the contribution margin cm_j is to be decreased by the amount that arises from the specific contribution margin of the **next best product** multiplied by the capacity needed for the production of one unit of product j. In the initial example of the case of one effective multiple-product restriction, this was already determined for $\overline{x}_1$ within the evaluation of the following solution:

$$cm_1 - \frac{v_{11}}{v_{12}} \cdot cm_2 = cm_1 - v_{11} \cdot \frac{cm_2}{v_{12}} = cm_1 - v_{11} \cdot \widehat{cm_1} = 40 - \frac{2}{8} \cdot 80 = 40 - 2 \cdot 10 = 20$$

5. *Several effective multiple-product restrictions.* Here, the input-related opportunity costs can be derived from the Simplex's final tableau. They correspond to the **coefficients of the slack variables** in the target function line. The optimal use of additional factor units is indicated by the *change coefficients* in the columns of the slack variables.
6. In all cases, the input-related opportunity costs are defined as **a by-product of the optimal solution**. Therefore, they cannot contribute to the determination of the optimal solution. This observation also becomes relevant as regards the output-related form of the opportunity costs.

2.3.3 Output-Related Optimal Costs

Now, the input-related opportunity costs of the I resources and the J sales potentials are given. λ_i is the input-related marginal profit of the resource $i = 1, ..., I$ and μ_j the input-related marginal profit of the sales potential for product $j = 1, ..., J$. Then, the output-related optimal costs c_j^* of the product j are as follows:

$$c_j^* = \sum_{i=1}^{I} v_{ij} \cdot \lambda_i + \mu_j \; j = 1, \ldots, J \tag{2.12}$$

The **modified contribution margin** cm_j^m is as follows:

$$cm_j^m = cm_j - c_j^* = p_j - c_j - c_j^* \; j = 1, \ldots, J \tag{2.13}$$

The measures used in (2.12) and (2.13) show some interesting characteristics, which can be clarified on the bases of the initial example. At first, the case of *one effective multiple-product restriction* is examined. There, $i = 1$ was the limited restriction, and the optimal solution was 300 (50) units of Product 1 (2). The following data can be derived from the solution:

$$\lambda_1 = \widehat{cm12} = 10; \; \lambda_2 = 0; \; \mu_1 = cm_1 - v_{11} \cdot \widehat{cm12} = 20; \; \mu_2 = 0 \tag{2.14}$$

From it results the following **optimal costs** and modified contribution margins:

$$c_1^* = 2 \cdot 10 + 20 = 40; \; cm_1^m = 40 - 40 = 0 \tag{2.15}$$

$$c_2^* = 8 \cdot 10 = 80; \; cm_2^m = 80 - 80 = 0 \tag{2.16}$$

Both products have a **modified contribution margin** of zero. This result is also applied in the case of *several* effective multiple-product restrictions. From the final tableau follows:

$$\lambda_1 = 8{,}75; \; \lambda_2 = 2{,}5; \; \mu_1 = \mu_2 = 0 \tag{2.17}$$

The optimal costs and modified contribution margins are then:

$$c_1^* = 2 \cdot 8.75 + 9 \cdot 2.5 = 40; \; cm_1^m = 0 \tag{2.18}$$

$$c_2^* = 8 \cdot 8.75 + 4 \cdot 2.5 = 80; \; cm_2^m = 0 \tag{2.19}$$

All products contained in the optimal programme had modified contribution margins of **zero**, provided that *linear dependencies* exist. They follow from the general structure of the optimal solution (as indicated above) and are shown together with the relations for non-linear profit functions in the case of several effective multiple-product restrictions. For all products contained in the optimal programme, the following applies:

$$x_j^* > 0 \text{ and } \frac{\partial LG^*}{\partial x_j} = 0 \tag{2.20}$$

The derivation of the LAGRANGE function LG^* is in the linear case:

$$\frac{\partial LG^*}{\partial x_j} = cm_j - \sum_{i=1}^{I} v_{ij} \cdot \lambda_i - \mu_j = cm_j - c_j^* = cm_j^m \tag{2.21}$$

Therefore, all **modified contribution margins** of products included in the optimal programme are **zero**; usually all products not included in the optimal programme are **negative**. The **extent to which** the products with modified contribution margins of zero are to be produced, however, is not explained by it.

Another interesting result is seen when (2.21) is written as follows:

$$cm_j = \sum_{i=1}^{I} v_{ij} \cdot \lambda_i + \mu_j \left(\text{for } x_j^* > 0\right) \tag{2.22}$$

Both sides of (2.22) multiplied by x_j^*, and then cumulated for all products j (for products not contained in the optimal programme: $cm_j \cdot x_j^* = 0$), and considering that only limited restrictions possess input-related opportunity costs unequal to zero, result in:

$$\sum_{j=1}^{J} cm_j \cdot x_j^* = CM^* = \sum_{i=i}^{I} \overline{V}_i \cdot \lambda_i + \sum_{j=1}^{J} \overline{x}_j \cdot \mu_j \tag{2.23}$$

The input-related marginal profit of all restrictions (capacities and sales limits) corresponds to the total contribution margin of the optimal production programme. In this respect, the two sides of the coin are revealed, which yield the same contribution margin: on the one hand, the optimal contribution margin can be determined directly from the production programme; on the other hand, the optimal contribution margin can be determined using the resources' input-related factors, which result from their optimal use and thus implicitly from the optimal programme. The **above Simplex' final tableau** can easily be checked for this. The factors prove that:

$$1{,}000 \cdot 8.75 + 1{,}620 \cdot 2.5 + 300 \cdot 0 + 200 \cdot 0 = 12{,}800 = CM^* \tag{2.24}$$

In summary, several difficulties arise with the use of opportunity costs. First, their exact knowledge assumes a knowledge of the optimal solution, which makes its determination unnecessary. Secondly, **no sequence** of the products arises with the examples of the modified contribution margins; it is only known that *both* products are included in the programme but nothing precisely is known about their amounts. The input-related opportunity costs show both production restrictions as limited, so that under *explicit use of these restrictions* an equation system is to be solved. Even an omniscient management accountant, who, by pure coincidence, uses the correct opportunity costs without knowledge of the optimal programme, needs to explicitly include the assumptions for supporting the decision-making process.

2.3.4 Output-Related Alternative Costs

For the inclusion of output-related alternative costs, the initial example (◘ Table 2.2) is modified according to the information in ◘ Table 2.8 (changes are marked).

Product 3 now has a positive contribution margin; there are no sales limits temporarily, and *only* the production restriction of the first machine is effective, so that with the consumption coefficients, the restriction index can be omitted to simplify matters. It is now the case of *one effective multiple-product restriction*, in which the

◘ **Table 2.8** Changed example

Product	$j = 1$	$j = 2$	$j = 3$
Price p_j	200	480	**1,100**
Variable costs c_j	160	400	**1,090**
Contribution margin cm_j	40	80	**10**
Sales limit $\bar{x}_j$	$+\infty$	$+\infty$	$+\infty$
Consumption v_{1j}	2	8	5
Consumption v_{2j}	**0**	**0**	**0**

Machine	$i = 1$	$i = 2$
Capacity $\bar{V}_i$	**1,000**	**0**

optimal production programme arises from the sequence of the specific contribution margins. This sequence corresponds with the indices of the product types:

$$\widehat{cm_1} = 20 > \widehat{cm_2} = 10 > \widehat{cm_3} = 2 \tag{2.25}$$

However, due to missing sales limits, *only* Product 1 with 1000/2 = 500 units is produced:

$$x_1^* = 500; x_2^* = x_3^* = 0; CM^* = 20{,}000 \tag{2.26}$$

The output-related alternative costs κ_j of a product equal the profit of the best unused application (i.e. the product not produced). If a certain product j is produced, one excludes the production of the next best product; the contribution margin lost is charged to the product j as a cost factor.

In the example, the next best option arises for every product from the sequence of the **specific contribution margins**. The production of Product 1 prevents the production of Product 2, and the production of either Product 2 or 3 prevents the production of Product 1. From this, the following output-related alternative costs and the appropriate modified contribution margins $cm_j^m = cm_j - \kappa_j$ can be found as:

$$\kappa_1 = v_1 \cdot \widehat{cm_2} = 2 \cdot 10 = 20 \qquad cm_1^m = 20 - 20 = 20$$

$$\kappa_2 = v_2 \cdot \widehat{cm_1} = 8 \cdot 20 = 160 \qquad cm_2^m = 80 - 160 = -80$$

$$\kappa_3 = v_3 \cdot \widehat{cm_1} = 5 \cdot 20 = 100 \qquad cm_3^m = 10 - 100 = -90$$

Abiding by the **decision rule** that only products **with non-negative modified contribution margins** should be produced, the modified contribution margins now indicate that the correct decision is that only Product 1 is to be produced, with the other two products renounced.

Therefore, the output-related alternative costs could *apparently* be applied for decision-making purposes, while the optimal costs – as shown above – are problematic. Yet, this is a rash conclusion. Optimal costs could also be used in the above example as they correspond to the alternative costs for Products 2 and 3 because the input-related marginal profit is identical to the specific contribution margin of the first product. Product 1 has a modified contribution margin of zero. With it, the optimal decision would be found as well as the alternative costs. **Decision-making using alternative costs** is not less complicated than using optimal costs since in both cases information (ranking the products according to the specific contribution margins) is required, which could also be used for the direct determination of the optimum solution.

These illustrations may indicate that the initial positive features of the alternative costs are caused by the special structure of the example. This is confirmed by the inclusion of the sales limits of the initial example as an additional restriction again. Then, the optimal production programme is as follows:

2

$$x_1^* = 300; \quad x_2^* = 50; \quad x_3^* = 0 \tag{2.27}$$

Now the **alternative costs** can only be unambiguously decided for Product 1 because Product 1 still prevents Product 2 from being manufactured. But which product type is prevented by Product 2? If the optimal solution in (2.27) were not known, Product 1 would be preferred. A modified contribution margin of –80 would arise for Product 2, by which the actual optimal policy would be missed.

The **correct alternative costs** – like the optimal costs – are only known with knowledge of the **optimal solution** of the production programme decision problem. Then, the production of Product 2 does not impact Product 1 but Product 3 because the production of Product 1 does not need to be limited. Now Product 2's alternative costs are 8 · 2 = 16; they are lower than cm_2, the modified contribution margin of Product 2 is 80 – 16 = 64, and thus positive. Appropriately, Product 3 prevents the production of Product 2, which would lead to a modified contribution margin of 10 – 50 = –40. The modified contribution margins indicate that the correct decision is to produce Products 1 and 2 only. Because of the limited production restriction – in this example – the sequence of both products is shown by their specific modified contribution margins in which again Product 1 (+10) is slightly preferred to Product 2 (+8).

This simple example shows that the **dilemma** of the optimal costs also exists for the alternative costs: *the optimal solution must be known if the decisions made on the basis of the alternative costs are to be optimal.*

Therefore, in **summary**, it can be stated that opportunity costs do not support or simplify decision-making for finding the optimal programme. Instead, they represent a **side result** in which their application becomes relevant for the subsequent analysis. These issues will be further explored in the next chapter in the context of lowest sales-price limits.

2.4 Summary

The solution of production programme decisions in the short term is based on costs and revenues; the exclusive use of **variable profit measures is sufficient** but not necessary. The optimum solution can also be found based on **full costs**. Yet, if these are applied to unit costs under the assumptions given, short-term decision problems are regularly wrong.

The **'pure' production programme decision** assumes that production methods (e.g. machines) for the final products are decided a priori. Then, only the optimal production amounts and sales volumes of the final products can be determined, and **contribution margins** play a dominant role in decision-making when linear dependencies are assumed. With **excess capacity**, all products with positive contribution margins are to be produced to the extent of their respective sales limits. With **one effective multiple-product restriction**, specific contribution margins (contribution margins per unit of the bottleneck) are used to assign the sequence of products until their individual sales limits are exhausted. With **several effective**

multiple-product restrictions in a simultaneous approach, linear programming is used to solve the decision problem. With linear dependencies, the optimum is a **corner point** – always at the *border* of the area of feasible solutions. These relations do not apply in the case of non-linear profit functions; here, for example, the optimum can also lie inside the area of feasible solutions. The additional inclusion of **procedural decisions** can be treated by analogous application of the principles found by the 'pure' production programme decision.

Opportunity costs appear in the form of **input- and output-related types**. All types assume a **knowledge of the optimal solution** of the production programme decision problem. Therefore, they cannot provide any real contribution to the determination of the optimum solution; their importance arises with the subsequent analysis.

2.5 Assessment Material

Review Questions

1. Which general conditions characterise the problems of production programme decisions? Which preference types thereby become dispensable?
2. When may absorbed costing lead to wrong decisions?
3. What is the contribution margin per unit, and how can it be interpreted?
4. How can the restrictions of a production programme decision problem be classified?
5. Why is the distinction of the planning problems important according to their effective multiple-product restrictions?
6. How can the optimal production policy be generally characterised without an effective multiple-product restriction?
7. Why are specific contribution margins used in the case of one effective multiple-product restriction?
8. What is the so-called *Virtual-product rule*?
9. Why cannot the *Virtual-product rule* be used in the case of progressive contribution margin jumps and one effective multiple-product restriction?
10. How can the optimal production policy be determined with at least two effective multiple-product restrictions? What characteristic features of the solution structure are utilised?
11. How do the solution structures of linear and non-linear problems of the production programme decision differ?
12. How can opportunity costs be classified?
13. In which way can opportunity costs be helpful to support decision-making?
14. How can the basic approach of 'pure' production programme decisions be modified for the inclusion of the procedural decisions?

Exercises

1. **'Pure' production decisions and opportunity costs**. With fixed costs of 1000, a company can produce three products with the following data for its two existing machines:

2

Product	$j = 1$	$j = 2$	$j = 3$
Price p_j	400	560	2,100
Variable costs c_j	370	502	2,120
Sales limit $\overline{x}_i$	100	100	600
Consumption v_{1j}	10	20	5
Consumption v_{2j}	3	8	1

Production capacity for the two machines is as follows:

Machine	$i = 1$	$i = 2$
Capacity $\overline{V}_{im}$	4,000	1,200

We shall assume that all of the assumptions for short-term decision problems are effective.

(a) What is the optimum production programme?

(b) Now assume that the maximum sales limits have changed as follows:

Product	$j = 1$	$j = 2$	$j = 3$
Sales limit $\overline{x}_j$	**300**	**500**	**800**

What is the optimum production programme under these conditions? What is the maximum amount that the company could pay for 200 (50) additional machine hours of Machine 1 (2)?

(a) Now assume that the machine hour consumption required in the case of the second machine has also changed so that overall (with the same capacities) the following situation arises:

Product	$j = 1$	$j = 2$	$j = 3$
Price p_j	400	560	2,100
Variable costs c_j	370	502	2,120
Sales limit $\overline{x}_j$	**300**	**500**	**800**
Consumption v_{1j}	10	20	5
Consumption v_{2j}	**5**	**2**	1

Calculate the new optimum production programme. How high are the input-related opportunity costs of the two machines and how high are the output-related optimum costs for the three products? Is it worth extending the maximum sales limits by additional advertising? How would the optimum production volumes change if there were 30 more hours available for the first machine?

2. **Output-related opportunity costs**. Let us modify the situation given in Problem 1 as follows:

Product	$j = 1$	$j = 2$	$j = 3$
Price p_j	400	560	2,100
Variable costs c_j	370	502	**2,090**
Sales limit $\overline{x}_j$	$+\infty$	$+\infty$	$+\infty$
Consumption v_j	10	20	5

Only the first manufacturing restriction is effective (with a capacity of 4000), and there are currently no maximum sales limits.

(a) How high are the output-related opportunity costs for the three products?

(b) Assume that there is a maximum sales limit of $\overline{x}_1 = 200$ for product $j = 1$. Calculate the new output-related opportunity costs for the three products.

3. **Production and procedural decisions**. A company manufactures three products in two working sequences $i = 1, 2$, whereby there are two (three) choices of procedures for the first (second) sequence. Also, assume that one of the raw materials ($i = 3$) used in all of the products is only available in limited quantities at specific times. The relevant data follow (the figures are in respect of time requirements and sets of costs for the two sequences $i = 1, 2$ as well as the maximum sales limits and are taken from an example in Kilger et al. (2012, p. 664); note that the raw material requirements v_{3j} do not depend on the procedural decisions).

The capacity $\overline{V}_i$ for $i = 3$ is 160,000 (amount of raw materials initially available). Otherwise, assume that the assumptions for a short-term production programme decision are applicable. You are asked to formulate the decision problem on the basis of a linear programme optimisation.

Product	$j = 1$	$j = 2$	$j = 3$
Sales limit $\overline{x}_j$	10,000	12,000	8,000
Consumption v_{11j}	5	5	7
Consumption v_{12j}	4	3	6
Consumption v_{21j}	8	5	5
Consumption v_{22j}	5	5	5
Consumption v_{23j}	3	3	4
Consumption v_{3j}	5	3	6

Sequence	$i = 1$		$i = 2$		
Procedure	$m = 1$	$m = 2$	$m = 1$	$m = 2$	$m = 3$
Capacity $\overline{V}_{im}$	120,000	120,000	120,000	120,000	120,000

Accounting Information and Pricing Decisions

Inhaltsverzeichnis

P. Schuster et al., *Management Accounting*,
Springer Texts in Business and Economics,
https://doi.org/10.1007/978-3-030-62022-6_3

Learning Objectives
After studying this chapter, you should be able to:
- Identify the relevant costs of price limits
- Determine lowest-price limits and highest-price limits
- Derive optimisation criteria and conditions for pricing decisions
- Analyse the influence of fixed costs on price setting
- Understand the influence of competition on prices

3.1 Costs as a Basis for Pricing Decisions

In setting prices, companies generally use a broad spectrum, particularly for differentiated products in which the company has a *virtual* monopolistic position. Even when the price has to be negotiated or is suggested by a customer (e.g. in the case of an inquiry for an order), decisions must be made, such as whether or not to actually offer the product for sale.

Questions concerning the optimal production programme with *given* prices were already discussed in the previous chapter. In this chapter, the required level of production based upon the sales price achievable is examined. Essentially, it deals with determining the **lowest-price limits** for the products on sale and determining the **highest-price limits** for the required input factors. These are typical decisions that the management accounting system aims to support. The second part of this chapter discusses the determination of **optimal prices**. Pricing decisions cannot be made on the basis of costs *only* but must include other internal circumstances (e.g. production capacity and financial situation) as well as external circumstances, such as customer behaviour, competition and legal restrictions (e.g. laws prohibiting restricted competition). Additionally, setting prices must be done in tandem with all **other marketing variables**, such as sales terms and conditions, product quality, promotion, distribution channels or levels of customer service. The enforceability of the price, price elasticity concerns and competitor's prices also need to be considered.

Costs, however, form an *important* aspect of the pricing decision. The economic models for the determination of optimal prices use costs as a critical influencing factor. Costs serve not only as a reference point for lowest-price limits but also for the **justification** of higher prices or for **tender prices** of public orders. Therefore, in the area of price setting, marketing and accounting cooperate closely in practice.

The **scenario used** in the previous chapter is adopted here again. Short-term pricing decisions are predominantly considered as the management accounting system is mainly used for short-term decision-support, for example, the introduction of new products will not be covered here but will instead be examined in ▸ Chap. 5. A given capacity and certainty (i.e. particular expectations) will both be assumed here, but these assumptions will not apply in analysing certain special problems (in this chapter uncertainty will be limited to a decision-maker who is neutral towards risk but will be expanded to other situations in ▸ Chap. 4).

Within the framework of the decision support function of the management accounting system, the **maximisation of profit for a particular accounting period** is aimed for. For some analyses, the maximisation of net present value is used, whereas when other targets are devised, such as the maximisation of market share, other results can arise.

In a way, the **question posed in this** third chapter is reversed from that considered previously. Instead of production amounts leading to *given* prices, the question to be answered here relates to **prices correlating with certain production amounts**. Therefore, it is no surprise that many of the considerations outlined in the second chapter remain valid here. This will become particularly evident when considering the lowest-price limits, as for example, opportunity costs can play an important role.

From the perspective of the management accounting system, the **manifestation of the price** is irrelevant, as this is a marketing decision. Parameters used in marketing are discounts, bonuses, package size, components and differentiation of customers. In the following, ***price*** is seen as the actual return or the equivalent to the company's input realised through sales of their products.

3.2 Price Limits

3.2.1 Overview

Price limits are **critical values** at which the company is **indifferent** between two forms of actions the company could follow. Price limits encompass highest-price limits and lowest-price limits.

The **lowest-price limit** is the **minimum price** of a (final) product at which it will still be offered for sale either at all, or in a certain quantity.

The **highest-price limit** is the **highest price of an input factor** that the company needs for its production at which it is still willing to buy the factor either at all, or in a certain quantity.

Price limits are applied for decision support in a number of situations, including the following:

- The **acceptance or rejection of a supplementary order**. The lowest-price limit forms the border, that is, the minimum price for negotiations about the supplementary order. With a given price for the supplementary order, the highest-price limit for a required input factor forms the decision criterion for its acceptance or refusal.
- The **elimination of a product from the production programme**. In the short term, if the price falls below the lowest-price limit (i.e. if the price of a required input factor rises above its highest-price limit), the production of this product would be discontinued.
- The **change of the composition of the production programme**. With a price below a certain price limit or with a price of an input factor above a certain price limit, the production quantity of the product is reduced and the increased capacity can be used for increased production of other products. It is also referred to as the **relative price limit**.

It should be noted that these different decisions do not necessarily require the *same* price limit. **Price limits form decision criteria,** which can be applied only in a specific decision situation.

The **fundamental procedure** to determine price limits is via the comparison of the contribution margin achieved by the continuation of the *status quo* with the contribution margin which arises by changing the *status quo* due to a certain decision. It is assumed that the contribution margin increases as a result of a rise in the product price and drops with a rise of the procurement price of an input factor, as otherwise the price limit would not be unambiguous. This contribution margin depends on the sales price of the product or on the procurement price of a required input factor. Then, the price limit corresponds to the price at which the contribution margin is identical to the *status quo* after the change. This implies that the refusal of the supplementary order will *not* induce costs. Yet, a negative reaction from the customer seems possible (e.g. he could be annoyed by the refusal which could affect other orders). Such changes of the *status quo* would then have to be considered separately.

This simple procedure can become relatively complex in specific situations because *all* effects on costs of the changed decision must be considered (i.e. the principle of **relevant costs**). Therefore, the following analysis is based on typical examples of price limit situations.

3.2.2 Short-Term Lowest-Price Limits

At first, a supplementary order that consists of a single unit of a product not currently produced is analysed. The **bases for the lowest-price limit** are the **marginal costs** of its production. For a single unit, the marginal costs correspond to the variable costs if no interdependence exists towards the previous production programme decision, for example, no bottlenecks: the lowest-price limit $\underline{p}$ equals the variable costs c of the supplementary order. Apart from the costs required for the input factors, they also include the variable costs of production, administration and sales. In practice, difficulties often arise when determining the variable costs because they contain overhead costs, which are direct costs treated like indirect costs and therefore require a proportionate allocation.

Even in a company that only produces one product (the supplementary order would consist of an additional unit of that product) there are costs that are indirect costs at the level of single units (for example, fixed costs in relation to batches of the order) whose exact change would need to be considered with regard to the supplementary order.

- **Relevant costs**

The **valuation** of the variable resource consumption depends on the possible alternatives (relevant costs).

Example: a supplementary order results in costs of 120 and also needs $v = 2$ units of an input factor, of which 100 units are still available. The purchase price of these units was 30 per unit. The prevailing price at the time of the decision about the supplementary order is 35. The company is considering whether to use these two units from its storage should the supplementary order be accepted. Calculate the lowest-price limit.

The valuation of two units of the input factor depends on the **planned alternate use** of the units if the supplementary order is not accepted. If they are used for regular production (as might be expected), the lowest-price limit can be seen in the **current price**, provided no transaction costs arise, that is,

$$\hat{p} = 120 + 2 \cdot 35 = 190$$

The stock is thereby replenished in the original condition, otherwise regular production would be affected by the **acceptance** of the supplementary order.

If the stored input factors are **remaining stock** that, apart from the unexpected supplementary order cannot be used for regular production, the lowest-price limit equals the (net) **sales value**. If the remaining stock possesses no sales value in the market, and possibly even warehouse charges or disposal costs, they can be saved by the **acceptance** of the supplementary order in the amount of 2, in which case the lowest-price limit arises as

$$\hat{p} = 120 - 2 = 118$$

A lowest-price limit below the variable costs is achieved here because to a certain extent, the *status quo* has changed. If the supplementary order is not accepted, certain costs will result in the future. Therefore, these need to be considered for the decision. As a result, the initial acquisition costs might have no meaning for *short-term* lowest-price limits.

If the **acceptance** of the supplementary order has effects on the core business, the **lost contribution margins** have to be charged to the supplementary order. Examples are bottlenecks in production or the substitution of another product on the basis of demand changes caused by the supplementary order.

Example: A customer places a one-time order of 100 units of a product, which differs from Product 1 only by a special colour. The variable costs of the special product exceed the cost of Product 1 (which costs $c_1 = 42$) by 2. The (net) list price of Product 1 is $p_1 = 60$. The lowest-price limit for the supplementary order based on the assumption that the customer would fully substitute 100 units of Product 1 is

$$\hat{p} = (42 + 2) + (60 - 42) = 62$$

If the customer rejects this price and goes to a competitor if a price of more than 60 is demanded (he would not even buy the 100 units of Product 1), the lowest-price limit drops to $c = 44$.

Under certain circumstances, **complementary** (instead of **substitutional**) **effects** can appear which would decrease the lowest-price limit appropriately. *Example*: the customer requires other products from the company when the supplementary order is accepted.

Occasionally, an order appearing to be a typical supplementary order is only a test sale and is repeated with satisfaction until finally becoming part of the seller's **regular business**. If a price is initially offered for the supplementary order close to the short-term lowest-price limit, it will later be very difficult to convince the customer that a higher price would actually be justified because the supplementary order slips into the normal business activity.

■ Non-linear Cost Functions: Experience Curve

With linear cost functions, marginal costs always equal variable costs. For a supplementary order consisting of several units, the lowest-price limit is therefore independent of the number of units considered. In contrast, the situation changes for nonlinear cost functions. This is the case with the **experience curve**.

Example: a company receives an inquiry for the production of $x = 30$ units of a product not currently produced. An estimate by the technical engineers based on a prototype demonstrates that marginal costs of the first unit at $C' = 270$ might decrease by 15% due to production experience based upon an experience curve with a learning rate $\alpha = 15\%$. Calculate the lowest-price limit.

The **experience curve** assumes that the unit costs decrease in each case with a duplication of the accumulated production amount by a certain factor: the learning rate α. It is an extension of the **learning curve**, which was specifically formulated for labour costs. $C'(X)$ *show* the marginal costs of the Xth unit, that is, an accumulated production amount of X *exists*. They are the following:

$$C'(X) = C'(1) \cdot (1-\alpha)^z \tag{3.1}$$

and $C'(1)$ are the marginal costs of the first unit. The number of the duplications is z, that is $X = 1 \cdot 2^z$. To determine marginal costs for any X, the following procedure can be used: from $X = 2^z$ arises by taking the logarithm:

$$z = \frac{\log X}{\log 2}$$

Take the logarithm from $(1-\alpha)^z$

$$z \cdot \log(1-\alpha) = \frac{\log X}{\log 2} \cdot \log(1-\alpha) = \log X \cdot \frac{\log(1-\alpha)}{\log 2} = \log X \cdot \kappa$$

and $(1-\alpha)^z = X^\kappa$ follows from it. The parameter κ is called the **cost elasticity** (relative reduction in costs by increasing the production amount) and results from the learning rate α as follows:

$$\alpha = 1 - 2^{\kappa} \text{ or } \kappa = \frac{\log(1-\alpha)}{\log 2} \tag{3.2}$$

and for the logarithm an arbitrary (identical in the numerator and denominator) basis can be taken. A learning rate of $\alpha = 0.15$ results in (3.2) $\kappa = -0.2345$.

Fig. 3.1 Experience curve

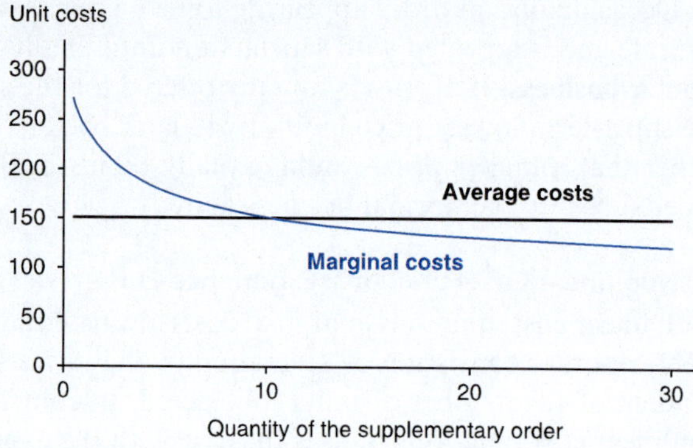

The **marginal cost function** then is the following:

$$C'(X) = C'(1) \cdot X^k. \tag{3.3}$$

In the example, the marginal cost of the first unit produced is 270. With the second unit, there is the first duplication of the accumulated amount (1 + 1 = 2 · 1) and the marginal costs decrease to 270 · (1–0.15) = 229.50, the marginal cost of the fourth unit amounts to 229.50 · (1–0.15) = 195.08 (rounded), and by repeating this process, the 30th unit only costs

$$C'(X = 30) = 270 \cdot 30^{-0.2345} = 121.63$$

The trend of the marginal costs for the order of 30 units is represented in Fig. 3.1. The **lowest-price limit** corresponds to the **average unit costs** c, which is

$$c = \frac{\sum_{X=1}^{30} C'(1) \cdot X^{-0.2345}}{30} = 153.82.$$

An **approximation** of this can be determined by integration instead of by summation in the following manner:

$$c = \frac{1}{30} \cdot \int_1^{30} C'(1) \cdot X^{-0.2345} dX = \frac{1}{30} \cdot \left[\frac{270 \cdot 30^{1-0.2345}}{1-0.2345} - \frac{270}{1-0.2345} \right] = 147.12$$

3.2.3 Short-Term Lowest-Price Limits with Potential Capacity Restrictions

In determining lowest-price limits, one must consider the existence of capacity restrictions. Fundamentally, there are two possibilities from a *short-term perspective*:

1. The **expansion of the available capacity**. *Example*: the production department is already operating at full capacity. The supplementary order, however, could be fulfilled by the use of overtime. A machine already runs during the entire available production time. The supplementary order would require an increase in the capac-

ity (adaptation of the capacity above the optimal capacity). As a result, **increased variable costs** have to be allocated to the supplementary order. Other capacity adaptations are discussed in the context of long-term lowest-price limits.

2. The **restricted production of the previous product**. If the capacity is not expanded, the previous product's production must be limited in order to be able to execute the supplementary order. Subsequently, previously achieved contribution margins are lost and have to be charged to the supplementary order as **opportunity costs**. The lowest-price limit increases accordingly. This is shown in the following example.

Example: the initial example in the second chapter was examined with the following data (■ Table 3.1). An optimal production programme containing upper sales limits of product $x_1^* = 300$ and $x_2^* = 200$ resulted because both contribution margins were positive *and* the capacities of both machines with $\bar{V}_1 = 2{,}500$ or $\bar{V}_2 = 3{,}700$ were not fully exhausted.

■ Lowest-Price Limit Without Effective Restrictions

If the supplementary order (product indexed 0) consists of only one single unit, both machines remain unrestricted:

$$v_1 + 2,200 + 1 \cdot v_{10} = 2,203 < 2,300$$

$$v_2 + 3,500 + 1 \cdot v_{20} = 3,505 < 3,700$$

Therefore, the previous production programme would be unchanged and the **acceptance** of the supplementary order is based upon relevant costs of $c_0 = 270$; consequently, the lowest-price limit is as follows:

$$\hat{p} = c_0 = 270$$

This remains valid for a supplementary order with additional units, as long as no bottleneck appears.

■ Table. 3.1 Data of the example

Product	$j = 1$	$j = 2$	Supplementary order $j = 0$
Price p_j	200	480	$\hat{p}$
Variable costs c_j	160	400	270
Contribution margin cm_j	40	80	$\hat{p} - 270$
Upper limit $\bar{x}_j$	300	200	–
Consumption v_{1j}	2	8	3
Consumption v_{2j}	9	4	5

3

▪ Lowest-Price Limit with One Effective Restriction

Assuming now that the supplementary order is for 60 units, an examination of the extent of machine utilisation demonstrates that the required capacity of the machine $i = 2$ exceeds that available by 100 hours:

$$v_1 = 2,200 + 60 \cdot v_{10} = 2,380 < 2,500$$

$$v_2 = 3,500 = 60 \cdot v_{20} = 3,800 > 3,700$$

Therefore, in contrast to the *status quo,* the previous production programme must be limited when the supplementary order is accepted. The **optimal production programme** is to be found for the products $j = 1, 2$ based upon the capacity limitation of $\bar{V}_2 = 3400$ (from the existing capacity of 3700, the supplementary order is reduced by 300 hours). Since only one bottleneck exists, it is sufficient to consider the specific contribution margins:

$$\widehat{cm}_{21} = \frac{40}{9} = 4.\bar{4} \text{ and } \widehat{cm}_{22} = \frac{80}{4} = 20.$$

Product $j = 1$ produces the lower specific contribution margin and is partially crowded out by the supplementary order. The required 100 hours affects the production of product $j = 1$ and reduces its contribution margin by the following:

$$100 \cdot \widehat{cm}_{21} = 100 \cdot 4.\bar{4} = 444.\bar{4}$$

now equalling the (input-related) **opportunity costs** that have to be charged to the supplementary order. The lowest-price limit increases with it to

$$\hat{p} = \frac{c_0 \cdot x_0 + 100 \cdot \widehat{cm}_{21}}{x_0} = 270 + \frac{444.\bar{4}}{60} = 277.41(\text{rounded})$$

Product $j = 1$ is restricted by $100 / v_{21} = 100 / 9 = 11.\bar{1}$ units (a nonintegrity assumption applies, that is, not only completed units of a product can be produced within a period, but partially finished products can also be used. With an integrity condition, as in the example, 12 units would be crowded out, the opportunity costs would be $12 \cdot 40 = 480$ and the lowest-price limit is 278). The opportunity costs are: $11.\bar{1} \cdot \widehat{cm}_1 = 11.\bar{1} \cdot 40 = 444.\bar{4}$

The **capacity utilisation** for machine $i = 2$ is at its maximum of 3,700 hours. The crowding out of the previous production programme becomes noticeable with machine $i = 1$, and the capacity is now

$$V_1 = 2,200 - 11.\bar{1} \cdot v_{11} + 60 \cdot v_{10} = 2,200 - 11.\bar{1} \cdot 2 + 60 \cdot 3 = 2,357.\bar{7} < 2,500$$

▪ Lowest-Price Limit with Two Effective Restrictions

If several (potential) bottlenecks appear, the required **procedure essentially** consists of the following two steps:

1. The existing capacities are decreased by those required for the supplementary order.

2. The optimal production programme is determined for the reduced capacities. The difference between the originally attainable contribution margin and the contribution margin with reduced capacities is to be charged to the supplementary order as opportunity costs.

Continuation of the example: if the amount of the supplementary order rises further, additional units of the product with the lower specific contribution margin (in the example $j = 1$) are crowded out, as long as one of **two conditions** apply:
1. Product $j = 1$ has completely disappeared from the production programme.
2. Another machine becomes the bottleneck.

Case 1: In the example, the second condition applies. To show the consequences that arise while applying the first condition, it is assumed here that machine $i = 1$ causes no bottleneck (i.e. $\overline{V}_1 = 10{,}000$). The condition arises in the example with a supplementary order in excess of 580 units and is calculated as follows: Product $j = 1$ needs $x_1 \cdot v_{21} = 300 \cdot 9 = 2{,}700$ hours. Due to the fact that in the *status quo* 200 hours are available, the supplementary order will require 2700 + 200 = 2,900 hours. From it results $x_0 = 2{,}900/v_{20} = 2{,}900/5 = 580$ units. With $x_0 > 580$, the next best product (i.e. with the next highest specific contribution margin) must be limited; in this example, this is the product $j = 2$. This is because it has a specific contribution margin of 20 (per machine hour), and accordingly the opportunity cost for every unit about the 580th unit increases by $20 \cdot v_{20} = 100$ each.

Case 2: Condition 2 can only become effective, if, as in the example, the consumption coefficient of the supplementary order exceeds the released hours caused by the substitution of the crowded-out product, that is, $v_{10} > v_{11} \cdot v_{20}/v_{21}$. Otherwise, with increasing amounts of the supplementary order, Machine 1 would show no bottleneck. Condition 2 is fulfilled with $x_0 > 135$ (rounded). This occurs as follows: first, the required consumption for $j = 2$ is subtracted from the respective capacities of the machines; these are $x_2 = 200$; $200 \cdot 8 = 1600$ hours of machine $i = 1$ and $200 \cdot 4 = 800$ hours of machine $i = 2$. As $x_0 > 40$ machine, $i = 2$ becomes the bottleneck, and the following arises:

$$9x_1 + 5x_0 = 3{,}700 - 4\overline{x}_2 = 3{,}700 - 800 = 2{,}900$$

or

$$x_1 = \frac{2{,}900 - 5x_0}{9}$$

The appropriate consumption restriction for machine $i = 1$ is

$$2x_1 + 3x_0 \leq 2{,}500 - 8\overline{x}_2 = 2{,}500 - 1{,}600 = 900$$

and, finally, for x_1 becomes $x_0 \leq 2300/17 = 135$ (rounded). For larger supplementary orders **both** previous products **must be limited**. Then, the opportunity costs per unit correspond to the supplementary order using the coefficients multiplied by the consumption coefficient of the **slack variables** in the target function line of the appropriate simplex final tableau.

Continuation of the example: Assuming that the supplementary order is x_0 = 150 units, the available capacities of both machines can then be calculated:

$$\bar{V}_1^{\text{neu}} = 2,500 - 150 \cdot v_{10} = 2,500 - 450 = 2,050$$

$$\bar{V}_2^{\text{neu}} = 3,700 - 150 \cdot v_{20} = 3,700 - 750 = 2,950$$

The solution can be determined with the help of the simplex method (in performing this calculation, the redundant upper sales limits in addition to the *dummy column* were omitted from the target function, as they have no effect on the solution):

Initial tableau

BV	x_1	x_2	w_1	w_2	*RS*
w_1	2	8	1	0	2,050
w_2	9	4	0	1	2,950
	−40	−80	0	0	0

Tableau after first iteration

BV	x_1	x_2	w_1	w_2	*RS*
x_2	1/4	1	1/8	0	256.25
w_2	8	0	−1/2	1	1925
	−20	0	10	0	20,500

Tableau after second iteration (final tableau)

BV	x_1	x_2	w_1	w_2	*RS*
x_2	0	1	9/64	−1/32	196.09375
x_1	1	0	−1/16	1/8	240.625
	0	0	8.75	2.5	25,312.5

The opportunity costs for the last unit of the supplementary order amount to the following:

$$8.75 \cdot v_{10} + 2.5 \cdot v_{20} = 8.75 \cdot 3 + 2.5 \cdot 5 = 38.75$$

The extent of these opportunity costs *only* depends on the fact that both machines become restricted. However, within a certain range, they do not depend on the **amount** of the supplementary order. This can be simply shown by the fact that identical coefficients of the slack variables were already determined in the example contained in the final tableau of the second chapter. Therefore, the opportunity costs for every unit of the supplementary order in excess of x_0 = 135 (rounded) are identical (as long as the solution structure remains unchanged from the final tableau).

Now, for both products: to produce an (additional) unit of the supplementary order, 3 hours of the machine i = 1 and 5 hours of the machine i = 2 must be released. From the final tableau, the crowding out of both products can be seen. Product 1 is reduced by

$$3\cdot\left(-\frac{1}{16}\right)+5\cdot\left(\frac{1}{8}\right)=\frac{7}{16}$$

and Product 2 by

$$3\cdot\left(\frac{9}{64}\right)+5\cdot\left(-\frac{1}{32}\right)=\frac{17}{64}$$

It can be easily seen that a supplementary order of 700 units eliminates the production of Product 1. From this point on, only Product 2 can be reduced. This applies until one of the two bottlenecks i = 1, 2 is fully utilised by the supplementary order. In the example, this is the case for machine i = 2 with x_0 = 3700/5 = 740 units (machine i = 1 allows 2500/3 = $833.\overline{3}$ units). Then, the whole previous production programme is crowded out and only the supplementary order is produced.

Generally, it can be said: with an increasing **amount** x_0 of the supplementary order, the **lowest-price limit rises** (weakly) monotonously. The first $200/v_{20}$ = 200/5 = 40 units can be produced without crowding out effects from the *status quo*, that is, the lowest-price limit remains constant at 270. Then, it must be distinguished between Cases 1 and 2.

Case 1: for an amount of $40 < x_0 \leq 580$ a continuous amount of the product j = 1 is replaced with each unit of the supplementary order, that is, every additional unit costs

$$c_0+5\cdot\widehat{cm_{21}}=270+5\cdot4.\overline{4}=292.\overline{2}$$

For $580 < x_0 \leq 740$ an amount of the product j = 2 must be replaced, that is, the lowest-price limit increases to

$$c_0+5\cdot\widehat{cm_{22}}=270+5\cdot20=370$$

Case 2: for an amount of $40 < x_0 \leq 135$ (rounded) every unit again causes marginal cost of $292.\overline{2}$. For $135 < x_0 \leq 700$ marginal costs increase to

$$270+8.75\cdot v_{10}+2.5\cdot v_{20}=270+8.75\cdot3+2.5\cdot5=308.75$$

For $700 < x_0 \leq 740$ only product j = 2 is substituted, and the lowest-price limit increases to 370.

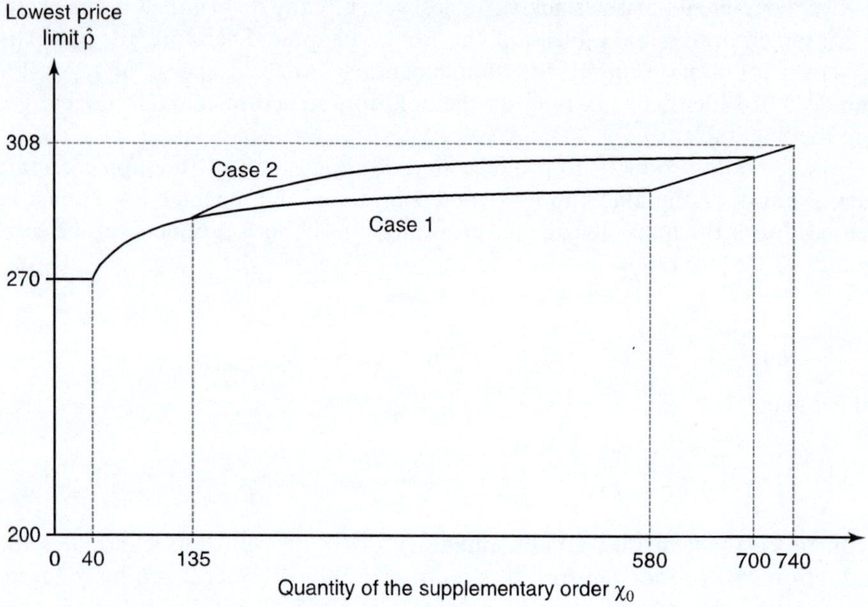

Fig. 3.2 Development of the lowest-price limit

This shows that the **lowest-price limit is a function of the amount** of the supplementary order (as shown in Fig. 3.2 for both cases). The consequences are: (i) the better the state of the company's business, the higher the lowest-price limit; the worse the state of the company's business, the lower the lowest-price limit; (ii) a price reduction (e.g. a discount) for an extensive supplementary order can only be considered with a price essentially above the lowest-price limit.

The analysis shown in the example determining the lowest-price limit of a supplementary order can be transferred analogously to the question of the (short term) **crowding out,** and eventually, the **elimination** of a product contained in the production programme. By changing the product's price, the target function changes due to the fact that the contribution margin per unit also changes. The optimal production arises and the total contribution margin can be determined in the usual manner again. Assuming both products j = 1, 2 and Product 0 of the supplementary order in the example would adhere to the existing production programme, then the determined lowest-price limits (270, $292.\overline{2}$, 308.75, 370) form the decision positions for the production levels of the three products, as long as no upper limit exists for Product 0.

In summary, the determination of the lowest-price limit in a situation with several effective restrictions equals a **sensitivity analysis** (or **parametric programming**). To a certain extent, the opportunity costs arising as a by-product within the determination of the optimal production programme can be used as long as the solution structure (i.e. in the simplex tableau, the same corner point) remains unchanged.

3.2.4 Long-Term Lowest-Price Limits

- **Lowest-Price Limits and Fixed Costs**

In the short term, many fixed costs appear as variable costs. A typical example is direct labour costs, which are allocated on the basis of manufacturing hours to the individual product units, and thus, qualify as being variable. However, they are not changeable, and such costs are not relevant for the determination of the lowest-price limits because they arise independent from the decision about the supplementary order, subject to not being a bottleneck. In the event of this latter scenario occurring, opportunity costs correspond to the lost contribution margin, but not on the basis of the hours multiplied by the costs per hour.

If the supplementary order causes so-called **order-fixed costs**, they should be considered in their full amount. The order-fixed costs are variable with regard to the order, but fixed in the context of the units of the order. Because the lowest-price limit generally is expressed per unit, it requires the unitising of order-fixed costs. Increasing the amount of the supplementary order **gradually decreases** the order-fixed costs pertaining to the lowest-price limit per unit.

Example: a supplementary order of 10 units of a product that is not part of the regular production programme results in unit variable costs of $c = 120$. A mould is required for production which causes costs of 500. The mould is unusable after production has finished. The lowest-price limit then is

$$\hat{p} = c + \frac{500}{10} = 170$$

With a supplementary order of 20 units, the lowest-price limit drops to $c + 500/20 = 145$.

- **Lowest-Price Limits with Long-Term Supplementary Orders**

If the execution of a supplementary order requires investment, which can be de-installed after completion, it (i.e. the investment) is to be considered in the lowest-price limit.

Example: a long-term supplementary order for 50 units (ten units per year) of a product not currently part of the regular production programme is received. By accepting the order, an investment in a special machine is required, with an initial investment outlay I and a residual (liquidation) value LQ after 5 years. The customer prefers an agreement based on a fixed price per unit. The variable unit costs are estimated at c. Although a future increase of the unit costs is expected, it is believed that they can be balanced out through learning effects, so that c remains constant throughout all periods.

If no discounting of future cash flow surpluses is assumed, then the lowest-price limit is simply the following:

$$\hat{p} = c + \frac{(I - LQ) \cdot 0.2}{10}$$

The initial investment outlays reduced by the residual value is simply allocated evenly throughout the years and afterwards is calculated per unit.

With a discount rate $i > 0$ ($\rho = 1 + i$) the **net present value** *(NPV)* of the whole cash flow profile is determined and is set to zero for the determination of the lowest-price limit. For the preceding example, it follows:

$$NPV = \sum_{t=1}^{5} 10 \cdot \left(\hat{p} - c\right) \cdot \rho^{-t} - I + LQ \cdot \rho^{-5} = 0$$

Considering the fact that

$$\sum_{t=1}^{5} \rho^{-t} = \frac{\rho^5 - 1}{i \cdot \rho^5} = \frac{1}{CRF\left(\rho, T = 5\right)}$$

with CRF as a capital recovery factor or annuity factor, the lowest-price limit follows as

$$\hat{p} = c + \frac{\left(I - LQ \cdot \rho^{-5}\right) \cdot CRF\left(\rho, T = 5\right)}{10} \tag{3.4}$$

From this, two results are recognisable: instead of $I - LQ$ the higher amount $I - LQ \cdot \rho^{-5}$ is distributed leading to an increase of the lowest-price limit. Also, the application of the capital recovery factor shows an effect in the same direction, as with a discount rate of $i = 0.1$ the $CRF(1.1; T = 5) = 0.2638 > 0.2$. Both results increase with a rise in the discount rate i, and, therefore, the **lowest-price limit rises with higher discount rates**. If the variable costs rose (against the assumptions made in the example), the lowest-price limit would be further increased.

Lowest-Price Limits with Unused Capacities

If a supplementary order is rejected, very often the possibility exists to either sell or shut down parts of the unused capacity. This alternative changes the *status quo*, and therefore, is relevant for the determination of the lowest-price limit.

Then, however, the problem arises as to what extent the **saved fixed costs** can be allocated to the *order*. In addition, the question of why the capacity reduction was not done previously needs to be answered first. If the argument is used, for example, that the refusal of the supplementary order was the initiating event to reduce the capacity, it remains open as to how many periods the fixed costs of the order can be allocated to. This equally concerns the question as to how to allocate the liquidation value from selling capacities.

Typically, the closure or sale of unused capacities is *not the optimal* alternative to the acceptance of an order. **Capacities** are created to be able to produce profitable products. Therefore, the alternative to the acceptance of an order is the hope for another order; however, this alternative contains some uncertainty. The following is a simple example, which applies the mathematical expected value (for a risk neutral decision-maker) within the framework of a sequential model as a decision criterion.

▶ Example

A contract manufacturer has an unchangeable capacity and for simplicity it is assumed that the capacity is exactly one order. The variable costs *c* are known with certainty. An additional order has been offered to him on three occasions, which he has to either accept or decline. If he accepts one, he must fulfil it *and* cannot accept other orders because of his given capacity.

The distribution of the contribution margins *cm* of the possible orders is as follows:

$cm_L = 30$ with the probability $\phi = 0.2$

$cm_M = 60$ with the probability $\phi = 0.4$

$cm_H = 90$ with the probability $\phi = 0.4$

and remains unchanged during every period. The decision tree for this situation is represented in ◘ Fig. 3.3. The blue arrows mark the sequential decisions that are optimal in the respective situation. ◀

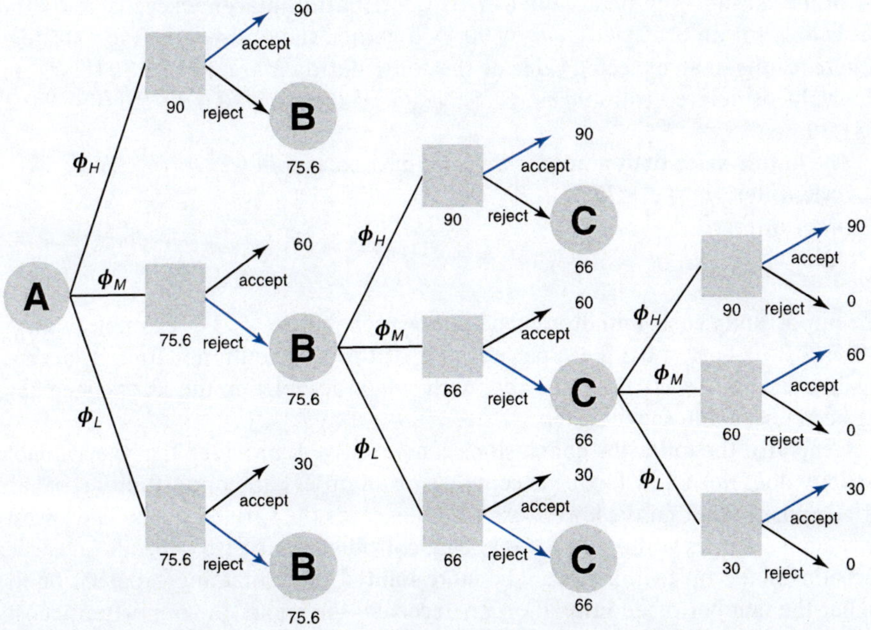

◘ **Fig. 3.3** Decision tree

Such a sequential decision situation is solved by starting with the final sequence. First, the optimal decision is determined assuming that both of the first two offers were rejected. Then a step back is taken and the preceding decision problem for all situations is solved. This follows the **optimality principle of dynamic programming** (*roll back procedure*).

For the decision situation in Knot *C*, the solution is simple: with a refusal, a contribution margin of 0 is achieved, therefore, it is optimal to accept *every* order in this situation. The expected value amounts to

$$\sum_{j=L,M,H} \phi_j \cdot cm_j = 66$$

Next, the decision is searched for, given that the first order was rejected. If an order with $cm_H = 90$ is placed, it will be accepted because its contribution margin exceeds the expected contribution margin that would have been earned had it been refused, namely 66. If an order with $cm_M = 60$ or with $cm_L = 30$ is received, it will be rejected for the same reason. The lowest-price limit as a deciding factor in the acceptance or refusal of an order corresponds to the variable costs *c* plus the opportunity costs of 66.

The expected value of the optimal decision strategy in the second step (Knot *B*) amounts to $90 \cdot \phi_H + 66 \cdot \phi_M + 66 \cdot \phi_L = 90 \cdot 0.4 + 66 \cdot (0.4 + 0.2) = 75.6$. This equals the opportunity cost of the decision concerning the first order received. An order should only be accepted if its contribution margin exceeds 75.6, and this is only for an order with $cm_H = 90$. Altogether, the optimal decision strategy ***ex ante*** results in an **expected value** of the contribution margin of 81.36 (Knot *A*). This value is derived from $90 \cdot \phi_H + 75.6 \cdot \phi_M + 75.6 \cdot \phi_L = 90 \cdot 0.4 + 75.6 \cdot (0.4 + 0.2) = 81.36$.

The lowest-price limit amounts are summarised as follows:

1. Order offer: $\hat{p} = c + 75.6$
2. Order offer: $\hat{p} = c + 66$
3. Order offer: $\hat{p} = c$

The opportunity costs initially depend on the **probabilities** ϕ_j. For example, with $\phi_L = 0.4$, $\phi_M = 0.4$, $\phi_H = 0.2$ the expected value of the contribution margin by accepting an order is 54 < 60, thus, an order with cm_M is accepted in the second step having been rejected in the first step.

Generally, the following conclusions can be derived: provided that the available capacity does not allow for the acceptance of all orders, the opportunity costs are strictly positive in that the **lowest-price limit exceeds** the variable costs. The lowest-price limit changes within the period being considered and also depends on earlier decisions made up to this time. The **more limited** the remaining capacity, or the higher the number of additional orders received, the **higher** the opportunity costs and by implication, the lowest-price limit.

An order with a high contribution margin will always be accepted. For an order with a medium contribution margin, the consequences between its acceptance and rejection are compared, and an order with a low contribution margin will only be accepted if there are no capacity restrictions. The lowest-price limit exceeds the marginal costs whenever there is a positive probability of capacity restrictions. This then becomes an argument for the use of full costs.

3.2.5 Highest-Price Limits

The highest-price limit is the highest **price** a company is **willing to pay** for a required **input factor**. The procurement of the input factor is only one of several possibilities available to the company. Other **possibilities** are the following:

- Direct **substitution** of the input factor by another input factor
- **Substitution** of the input factor by a change to the production process
- **Making instead of buying** the input factor

Here, it is assumed that only one (final) product requires this input factor. For the determination of the highest-price limit, the contribution margin that this product can achieve is used as the starting point for the analysis. The highest-price limit then corresponds to the highest amount that the input factor can cost and with which the contribution margin of the final product becomes zero.

Assuming that the retail price of the final product j is p_j, and the variable costs are $\overline{c}_j$ with the exception of the costs of the input factor whose highest-price limit is to be determined; a unit of the product j needs v_j units of the input factor. The total unit **variable costs** of the product j are

$$c_j = \overline{c}_j + v_j \cdot r$$

and r is the price of the input factor. Then, the **highest-price limit** results in

$$p_j - \left(\overline{c}_j + v_j \cdot \hat{r}\right) = 0 \text{ and } \hat{r} = \frac{p_j - \overline{c}_j}{v_j}, \text{respectively} \tag{3.5}$$

► **Example**

The product $j = 1$ needs $v_{11} = 4$ units of Input Factor 1. The sales price p_1 is 200 and the variable unit costs without the costs of the input factor are $\overline{c}_j = 140$. The highest-price limit is

$$\hat{r}_1 = \frac{200 - 140}{4} = 15$$

If, instead of using Input Factor 1, another Input Factor (i.e. 2) with a procurement price of $r_2 = 10$ could be applied (**substituted**), of which $v_{21} = 5$ units are needed, the unit contribution margin of Product 1 would be

$$cm_1 = p_1 - \left(\overline{c}_j + v_{21} \cdot r_2\right) = 200 - (140 + 5 \cdot 10) = 10$$

Then, the highest-price limit for Input Factor 1 with a direct **substitution possibility** is

$$\hat{r}_1 = \frac{p_1 - \bar{c}_1 - cm_1}{v_{11}} = \frac{200 - 140 - 10}{4} = 12.5$$ ◄

❯ The highest-price limit equals: the preliminary contribution margin, this is the contribution margin of the next best alternative divided by the consumption of the input factor, with the preliminary contribution margin therefore equalling revenues less preliminary variable costs.

If the price rises above 12.5, it would be cheaper for the company to use Input Factor 2 instead of 1. The upper price limit $\hat{r}_1$ can also be determined by the appropriate marginal productivities of the factors from the least cost combination: $\hat{r}_1 / r_2$ which equals the marginal productivity of Factor 1 divided by the marginal productivity of Factor 2: (1/4)/(1/5), that is, $\hat{r}_1 = r_2 \cdot 5/4$.

Additionally, a further assumed **procedure** (indexed with *I*) may exist for the production of the product *j* = 1 which requires *both* Input Factors 1 and 2. A unit of Product 1 requires v_{11}^I = 1 unit of Input Factor 1 and v_{21}^I = 2 units of Input Factor 2. Then, the product can be produced via **three different procedures**:

1. Input Factor 1 solely with the variable unit costs

$$\bar{c}_j + v_{11} \cdot r_1 = 140 + 4r_1$$

2. Input Factor 2 solely with the variable unit costs

$$\bar{c}_j + v_{21} \cdot r_2 = 140 + 5 \cdot 10 = 190$$

3. Procedure I (both input factors with variable unit costs)

$$\bar{c}_j + v_{11}^I \cdot r_1 + v_{21}^I \cdot r_2 = 140 + 1r_1 + 2 \cdot 10 = 160 + r_1$$

It can be easily proven that Procedure *I* is **efficient** because it is the cheapest option for certain values of r_1, namely, $6.\bar{6}$ " r_1 " 30. The upper limit corresponds to the highest-price limit. For $6.\bar{6} \le r_1 < 30$ procedure *I*, which requires Input Factor 1, is preferred. For $r_1 > 30$, Input Factor 1 is substituted entirely by Input Factor 2. If the procurement price r_1 drops below $6.\bar{6}$, then using only Input Factor 1 is the preferred choice. In connection with the highest-price limit, this means that at this price, more (i.e. quadruple) of Input Factor 1 is purchased.

The comparison of the first and second possibilities (with the highest-price limit of 12.5) is obsolete because it does not compare efficient production procedures in this area. As in this case the highest-price limit cannot exhaust the whole contribution margin of Product 1 as a contribution margin of at least cm_1 = 10 per unit remains.

Often the possibility exists to **produce (make)** the required Input Factor 1 instead of buying it. In this case, the input factor becomes an intermediate product and its lowest-price limit has to be determined. This then is the boundary for the highest-price limit of the input factor.

Table 3.2 Data of the example

Product	$j = 1$	$j = 2$	$j = 3$
Price p_j	200	480	320
Variable costs c_j	160	400	270
Contribution margin cm_j	40	80	50
Consumption v_j	4	5	8
Sales volume x_j	300	200	40
Preliminary variable costs $\overline{c}_j$	140	375	230
Highest-price limit $\hat{r}_j$	15	21	11.25

Now, it is assumed that the **input factor** is used for **several final products**. Then **a product-specific highest-price limit** can be found for every individual product and the highest of these price limits is the **absolute highest-price limit**. Once a procurement price exceeds it, nothing is produced. For a price under one of the product-specific highest-price limits, the corresponding product is included in the production programme, otherwise it is omitted.

Example: the initial data of an earlier example has been modified. The (potential) production programme consists of three products $j = 1, 2$ and 3. The relevant data are outlined in Table 3.2. The variable costs including the (current) costs of the input factor $r = 5$ are initially provided. From this, the preliminary variable costs can be determined prior to the costs of the input factor:

$$\overline{c}_j = c_j - v_j \cdot r$$

The preliminary contribution margin per unit prior to the costs of the input factor is $p_j - \overline{c}_j$, and the product-specific highest-price limits are

$$\hat{r}_j = \frac{p_j - \overline{c}_j}{v_j}, j = 1, 2, 3$$

Therefore, the **absolute highest-price limit** is 21. The **demand** q for the input factor is dependent on price r as follows:

$$r < 11.25: \quad q = \sum_{j=1}^{3} v_j \cdot x_j = 4 \cdot 300 + 5 \cdot 200 + 8 \cdot 40 = 2{,}520$$

$$11.25 \le r < 15: \quad q = v_1 \cdot x_1 + v_2 \cdot x_2 = 4 \cdot 300 + 5 \cdot 200 = 2{,}200$$

$$15 \le r < 21: \quad q = v_2 \cdot x_2 = 5 \cdot 200 = 1{,}000$$

$$21 \le r: \quad q = 0$$

If products of the programme are **interdependent**, this must be considered within the determination of the highest-price limit.

Continuation of the example: Assume that Products 2 and 3 are offered exclusively in packages of 5 units of Product 2 and 1 unit of Product 3 (entirely complementary). Now, the product group-specific highest-price limit is

$$\hat{r}_{23} = \frac{(p_2 - \overline{c}_2)\cdot x_2 + (p_3 - \overline{c}_3)\cdot x_3}{v_2 \cdot x_2 + v_3 \cdot x_3} = \frac{105\cdot 200 + 90\cdot 40}{5\cdot 200 + 8\cdot 40} = 18.\overline{63}$$

In the example, this is also the absolute highest-price limit.

Should the **composition** of the existing production programme remain intact, the following (only) highest-price limit results:

$$\hat{r}_{123} = \sum_{j=1}^{3} \frac{(p_j - \overline{c}_j)\cdot x_j}{v_j \cdot x_j} = \frac{42,600}{2,520} = 16.905$$

The figure expressed as the numerator (in the example, 42,600) is also called the **upper cost limit** and it only has decision relevance when the above condition applies.

3.3 Optimal Prices

3.3.1 The Basic Model

Costs form *one* important component in determining sales prices. The analysis of optimal prices from a management accounting perspective is limited to cost effects assuming an unchanged marketing policy (ceteris paribus analysis). In this respect, the question of **which costs** should be included in determining optimal prices and how the **premium** applied to these costs should be determined is of essential interest.

A necessary requirement to undertake such an analysis is a knowledge of the **price demand curve**

$$x = x(p) \tag{3.6}$$

that is, the relationship between the price p and the sales volume x of a product whereby the price demand curve describes all market circumstances. In the following section, a monopoly situation is assumed; whereas the explicit consideration of competitive reactions will be considered later.

For 'normal' products, the following applies: $x' = dx/dp < 0$, that is, with an increasing price, demand for the product decreases. This simple relationship is assumed here. The price demand curve is defined only for positive amounts of x. **The price elasticity** (of demand) η shows the influence of the price on the sales volume:

$$\eta = \frac{dx}{x} : \frac{dp}{p} = \frac{dx}{dp}\cdot\frac{p}{x} \tag{3.7}$$

If $x' < 0$, the **price elasticity is negative**. η regularly depends on the price p (and also the price demand curve of x). With a multiplicative price demand curve $x(p) = \alpha \cdot p^{\beta}$ results $\eta = \beta < 0$ being constant. The price elasticity (as a function) contains the same amount of information as the price demand curve.

If a company **maximises** its **profit** Π, its revenues and costs must be compared, in the form of $C = C(x)$,

$$\max_{p} \Pi(p) = p \cdot x(p) - C(x(p))$$

A necessary **condition** for the maximisation of profit is that the first derivation is zero:

$$\Pi' = x(p) + p \cdot \frac{dx}{dp} - C'(x) \cdot \frac{dx}{dp} = 0 \tag{3.8}$$

As a result, the **above equation** is derived as follows: At the optimal price, **marginal revenues** (the first two terms in (3.8)) equal **marginal costs** (the third term). It is therefore assumed that the first derivation of the profit Π identifies only one maximum, that is, that the parameters to be maximised are strictly concave. A prerequisite is that sufficient capacity exists for the production of $x(p^*)$.

- **The Optimal Price**

This optimality condition multiplied by p/x and the expression $(dx/dp) \cdot (p/x)$ replaced by the price elasticity η, results in the so-called ***Amoroso Robinson* relation *as*** follows:

$$p^* = \frac{\eta}{1+\eta} \cdot C'(x(p^*)) \tag{3.9}$$

As the sales-maximising price, which can only be determined from the price demand curve lies at $\eta = -1$, the profit-maximising price p^* must lie in the area of $\eta < -1$. Otherwise, the optimal price would not cover the marginal costs and would even become negative. The *Amoroso Robinson relation* is derived from rearranging the optimality condition, and therefore, does not necessarily allow a direct determination of the optimal price p^* because this price also affects marginal costs.

Example: Assuming a **linear price demand curve**, that is, $x(p) = \alpha - \beta \cdot p$ (with $\alpha > 0$ and $\beta > 0$), and a linear cost function, that is, $C(x) = C^F + c \cdot x$, then a simplified profit equation is

$$\Pi = p \cdot (\alpha - \beta \cdot p) - C^F - c \cdot (\alpha - \beta \cdot p)$$

and the optimality condition is

$$p^* = \frac{1}{2} \cdot \left(\frac{\alpha}{\beta} + c \right) \tag{3.10}$$

Example: with a **multiplicative price demand curve** of the form $x(p) = \alpha \cdot p^{\beta}$ the optimal price is defined only for $\beta < -1$ and is due to $\eta = \beta$:

$$p^* = \frac{\beta}{1+\beta} \cdot C' \tag{3.11}$$

with a linear cost function $C(x) = c$ the optimal price can be directly derived.

This exemplary determination of the optimal price proves the simple relation: **marginal revenues = marginal costs**. This implies that costs only enter the model in the form of marginal costs, more specifically in the form of the **marginal cost *function***. Therefore, for linear cost functions, **variable costs** are relevant and **fixed costs** are irrelevant (see ►Chap. 4). The optimal price p^* does not guarantee the achievement of a sufficient contribution margin to cover the fixed costs.

> The link to the **lowest-price limit** is obvious: total marginal costs are relevant. The difference in the lowest-price limit lies only in the underlying amount: the lowest-price limit is the average of the relevant costs of the whole supplementary order, for the optimal price, the marginal cost function forms the basis. If the marginal cost function is constant, both concepts correspond to each other. If so, then the optimal price can be determined from the lowest-price limit plus a premium (contribution margin).

If full costs were used to determine the price, the actual optimal price could also result. However, it would only arise coincidently, if at the planned quantity, the full cost price exactly fulfils the *Amoroso Robinson* condition (3.9). Usually, however, (short term) pricing decisions result in subsequent decisions which miss the maximum profit by a considerable amount.

In the same way, **progressive price determination** based on costs and adding a profit surcharge do not lead to optimal prices, as they do not consider the market at all. Additionally, using full costs a **circular problem** arises, as to be able to determine the full costs, the sales volume must already be known. However, this depends on the required price and the corresponding costs. '**Calculation out of the market**' is a typical possible effect.

▪ 'Cost-Plus' Price Determination

With the 'cost-plus' price determination the price is based on

$$p = (1+\delta) \cdot c$$

and for c either the variable unit cost or the full unit cost is applied. Then, $\delta \cdot c$ should cover the remaining fixed costs and the profit.

This procedure has gained popularity for **trade price calculations** because it is a very **simple** and **schematic** procedure. The unit costs are the costs of goods purchased (i.e. the direct costs). Several rules of thumb exist for specific product groups and industries. A modification of this procedure is ***target pricing***, where a **targeted *return on investment (ROI)*** is used as the profit surcharge. The *ROI* is determined by the quotient of the profit including debt interest divided by total capital. This procedure is frequently applied in the United States, as the *ROI* is regarded as an essential measure for the management control of decentralised companies. The price determination results from the following:

$$p = c + i \cdot I$$

where *c* equals the full costs per unit (with all the relevant problems) and *i* symbolises the interest rate on the assigned capital *I* necessary for the production of the product. An **advantage** of this procedure is that the profit surcharge does not change with cost fluctuations, which therefore does not result in price increases. A **disadvantage** (apart from the use of full costs per unit) is that the problems associated with the allocation of Capital *I* to individual products appears.

An Experiment

- Within a (long distance) business game, *Franzen* (1984) divided a total of 1,280 participants from companies into two groups. Within the two groups, the teams got quarterly information in addition to sales statistics, financial data, capacity utilisation and stock levels. The first group's information was based on *full costs*, while the other group's information was based on *marginal costs*.
- The teams with the full cost information made rather 'peculiar' decisions. A relatively new product was loaded with high (fixed) overhead costs, and to become profitable (apparently), the teams raised the price with the result that sales dropped and high stock resulted. As a reaction, production was reduced, which resulted in a decline of capacity utilisation and an increase of unit costs (at full costs). To diminish this sales failure, an 'old' product was promoted mainly through a price war. The old product's sales volume expanded. The result of these actions was an obsolete product range and a misallocation of resources.
- The teams with marginal cost information achieved essentially better results and the often-anticipated danger of prices set too low were not realised in the experiment.

Only under very **special assumptions** does the 'cost-plus' price determination lead to *optimal* prices, these are the following:

1. Only **variable costs** may be used, and these must be **constant** per unit.
2. The price demand curve must have a **constant elasticity**. Then, a profit surcharge of $\delta = \eta/(1 + \eta) - 1$ proves the optimal price (see (3.11)).
3. With a *linear* price demand curve, the profit surcharge is $\delta = [\alpha / (\beta \cdot \kappa) - 1]/2$ which is not dependent on the sales volume *x* but on the variable costs (with higher *c* the profit surcharge drops).

Additionally, neither temporal nor product interdependences must exist.

3.3.2 Optimal Prices in the Long Run

Optimal prices in the long run require a differentiated analysis to be outlined with regard to capacity costs and dynamic price strategies.

3

- **Capacity Costs**

The claim that fixed costs should not be considered for pricing decisions only applies when determining **optimal prices in the short term**. From a long-term perspective, building sufficient capacity requires costs to be incurred (from a short-term perspective, these are fixed costs). *Example*: Series-type production by a car manufacturer frequently requires new investments to sustain long-term orders.

The costs of building capacity in the future must, however, be considered for the *ex ante* price determination. These will be fixed for the longer term and cannot be influenced thereafter. They represent **relevant costs** for determining the optimal price in the long-term; whereas in the *short term,* they have to be treated differently. The following situation demonstrates this (adapted from *Banker* and *Hughes*, 1994):

The production of a product causes variable costs per unit of c (in the short term). It requires v **units of a resource**, which cannot be adapted to capacity changes at short notice. Examples of it would be a machine with a certain unchangeable capacity for the period under consideration. Once the capacity $\bar{V}$ is determined, it cannot be reduced. In contrast, a short-term expansion is possible, although it induces relatively high costs. For the above examples, this would mean a production intensity increase or overtime work. This expansion is assumed to have limitless possibilities (for simplicity reasons so as not to have to consider capacity limitations).

Specifically, **capacity** $\bar{V}$ causes total (fixed) **costs** in the amount of $c_0\ \bar{V}$ per period. One unit of the capacity $\bar{V}$ costs $c_1 > c_0$. Other fixed costs of the company are included in C^F. The total costs of producing x units after the determination of the capacity are

$$C\left(x,\bar{V}\right) = C^F + c \cdot x + c_0 \cdot \bar{V} + \begin{cases} 0 & \text{if } v \cdot x \le \bar{V} \\ c_1 \cdot \left(v \cdot x - \bar{V}\right) & \text{if } v \cdot x > \bar{V} \end{cases} \qquad (3.12)$$

If the future demand x is known with **certainty,** the decision about the capacity is trivial, as only $\bar{V}$ in the required *amount* $v \cdot x$ will avoid additional costs. The *ex ante* profit function then is

$$\Pi = p \cdot x - \left(c \cdot x + c_0 \cdot \bar{V} + C^F\right) = p \cdot x - \left(c \cdot x + c_0 \cdot v \cdot x + C^F\right).$$

With a linear demand curve $x = \alpha - \beta \cdot p$ ($\alpha, \beta > 0$, that is, $x > 0$ is guaranteed) the necessary condition of the profit maximum is

$$\frac{\partial \Pi}{\partial p} = \alpha - 2\beta \cdot p + \beta \cdot c + \beta \cdot c_0 \cdot v = 0$$

and

$$p^* = \frac{1}{2} \cdot \left(\frac{\alpha}{\beta} + (c + v \cdot c_0) \right) \tag{3.13}$$

It is apparent that the optimal price treats the costs of capacity as if they were variable costs; that is, the costs of capacity are relevant for the price determination *ex ante*. Yet, once the capacity is determined, the relevant costs decrease to c and the capacity costs are '*sunk*'. However, the *ex post* optimal (short term) price remains unchanged because at this price p^* the capacity is fully utilised and a reduced (short term) price would result in a higher amount. This could only be covered by producing in excess of the capacity $\bar{V}$ and would result in unit cost of $c + v \cdot c_1 > c + v \cdot c_0$. This cannot be optimal due to the optimality condition for p^*. The difference between c and p^* equals the contribution margin of one unit (to be crowded out) and corresponds exactly with the opportunity costs of the limited capacity. Short-term and long-term prices therefore fall together.

▪ Uncertainty About the Sales Volume

Now, the capacity decision is met in a way that will never lead to additional costs c_1. Therefore, these are not included in determining the costs of the price decision. In the following, a **stochastic price demand curve** is assumed in the form:

$$x = \alpha - \beta \cdot p + \varepsilon$$

with ε as a random variable with a mathematical expected value $E[\varepsilon] = 0$. Accordingly, a price p leads to an expected sales volume of $E[x] = \alpha - \beta \cdot p$. The density function of the (random) variable x is $f(x) > 0$ and the distribution function $F(x)$.

The **expected profit** for a certain capacity $\bar{V}$ and a price p is

$$E\left[\Pi(p,\bar{V})\right] = (p-c) \cdot E[x] - C^F - c_0 \cdot \bar{V} - \int_{\frac{\bar{V}}{v}}^{\infty} c_1 \cdot (v \cdot \xi - \bar{V}) \cdot f(\xi) \mathrm{d}\xi \tag{3.14}$$

The first expression is the expected contribution margin. It is reduced by the fixed costs C^F, the fixed costs of the resource with the capacity $\bar{V}$ and the expected value of the additional costs as a result of the missing capacity (ξ is the integration variable for x). These additional costs are each $x > \bar{V}/v$ (implicitly $p^* > c + v \cdot c_1$ is assumed, that is, that the additional costs are not excessive as otherwise the company would produce at (normal) capacity and increased demand could not occur).

The company has to make two decisions: the optimal capacity $\bar{V}^*$ and the optimal price p^*. The necessary conditions arise from the partial derivatives of (3.14) towards both measures. First, the **capacity decision** follows from:

$$\frac{\partial E[\Pi]}{\partial \bar{V}} = -c_0 + c_1 \cdot \underbrace{\int_{\frac{\bar{V}}{v}}^{\infty} f(\xi)\,\mathrm{d}\xi}_{=1-F\left(\frac{\bar{V}}{v}\right)} + \frac{1}{v} \cdot c_1 \cdot \underbrace{\left[v \cdot \frac{\bar{V}}{v} - \bar{V}\right]}_{=0} \cdot f\left(\frac{\bar{V}}{v}\right) = 0$$

The optimal capacity $\bar{V}^*$ is implicitly determined by

$$1 - F\left(\frac{\bar{V}^*}{v}\right) = \frac{c_0}{c_1} \tag{3.15}$$

The higher the additional costs c_1 in relation to c_0, the higher $F(\bar{V}^*/v)$, that is, the larger the capacity $\bar{V}^*$. Assuming $F(\cdot)$ is symmetrical, then $c_1 > 2c_0$ even increasing capacity to which the mathematical expected value of the sales volume corresponds.

The optimal price p^* arises by setting the partial derivative of (3.15) to zero:

$$\frac{\partial E[\Pi]}{\partial p} = E[x] + (p-c) \cdot E'[x] - c_1 \cdot \frac{\partial}{\partial p}\left(\int_{\frac{\bar{V}}{v}}^{\infty} (v \cdot \xi - \bar{V}) \cdot f(\xi)\,\mathrm{d}\xi\right)$$

$$= (\alpha - \beta \cdot p) + (p-c)(-\beta) + c_1 \cdot v \cdot \beta \cdot \left[1 - F\left(\frac{\bar{V}}{v}\right)\right]$$

and, first, x is replaced by the price demand function. The last term of this expression arises as follows: if the density function $f(x) = f(\alpha - \beta \cdot p + \varepsilon)$ is transformed into the density function $f_0(\varepsilon)$:

$$\frac{\partial}{\partial p}\left(c_1 \cdot \int_{\bar{V}/v}^{\infty} (v \cdot \xi - \bar{V}) \cdot f(\xi)\,d\xi\right) =$$

$$\frac{\partial}{\partial p}\left(c_1 \cdot \int_{\bar{V}/v - \alpha + \beta \cdot p}^{\infty} \left[v \cdot (\alpha - \beta \cdot p + \varepsilon) - \bar{V}\right] \cdot f_0(\varepsilon)\,d\varepsilon\right) =$$

$$= -c_1 \cdot v \cdot \beta \cdot \int_{\bar{V}/v - \alpha + \beta \cdot p}^{\infty} f_0(\varepsilon)\,d\varepsilon - c_1 \cdot \beta \cdot \underbrace{\left[v \cdot \left(\alpha - \beta \cdot p + \frac{\bar{V}}{v} - \alpha + \beta \cdot p\right) - \bar{V}\right]}_{=0} \cdot$$

$$f_0\left(\frac{\bar{V}}{v} - \alpha + \beta \cdot p\right)$$

A simplification of the condition using the optimality condition (3.15) for $\bar{V}^*$ proves

$$\frac{\partial E[\Pi]}{\partial p} = \alpha - 2\beta \cdot p + \beta \cdot c + \beta \cdot c_1 \cdot v \cdot \frac{c_0}{c_1} = 0$$

and, finally

$$p^* = \frac{1}{2} \cdot \left(\frac{\alpha}{\beta} + (c + v \cdot c_0) \right). \tag{3.16}$$

A surprising **result** emerges: the optimal price p^* corresponds to the optimal price in the certainty situation (see (3.15)). Furthermore, it does *not* depend on the additional costs c_1 of the overtime work but only on the variable costs c and the cost per unit of the resource $v \cdot c_0$. The additional costs c_1 play a prominent role in the determination of the optimal capacity, but they are not relevant for the optimal price. The optimal capacity already considers the whole effect of c_1. Naturally, this result depends on the model specifications from the costs of capacity's function.

The costs of the capacity $c_0 \cdot \bar{V}$ are allocated evenly to the sales volume $x = \bar{V}^* / v$ that can be produced at the full utilisation of normal capacity. This 'cost per unit' $(c + v \cdot c_0)$ does not correspond to the average costs of the resource use. These are higher because the additional costs $v \cdot c_1$ are certainly relevant for it. With a probability of $1 - F(\bar{V}^* / v) > 0$ optimal capacity is exceeded and with it additional costs per unit are incurred.

The long-term optimal price and the corresponding capacity are simultaneously decided upon. If these two decisions fall apart and **new information** becomes available between determining the capacity and the price, the capacity determination will be affected, which again must be solved within the framework of a sequential decision model. If, for example, ε becomes known **before** setting the price, the price will vary between the two extreme condition-dependent cases: if the capacity is sufficient with certainty, the optimal price in the short term will be

$$p = \frac{1}{2} \cdot \left(\frac{\alpha + \varepsilon}{\beta} + c \right)$$

If the capacity is exceeded with certainty, the price will be

$$p = \frac{1}{2} \cdot \left(\frac{\alpha + \varepsilon}{\beta} + (c + v \cdot c_1) \right)$$

The price decision reacts to this information, but it does not have a *retroactive* influence on the capacity decision. In such a case, it cannot be determined by the use of (3.15) and a sequential model has to be established instead. The reason for this lies in the fact that ε is not integrated into the model in a linear form, but in a multiplicative way by $p \cdot x(p)$. Therefore, a varying ε does not have an even effect on the expected value considered.

3.3.3 Dynamic Price Strategies

Prices often cannot be changed arbitrarily in every period but are influenced by the prices from previous periods. A price strategy is a number of prices $\{p_1, p_2, \ldots, p_T\}$ for the time period under consideration of $t = 1, \ldots, T$. In contrast to a static analysis, variables from different periods are included here.

There are various **reasons for the interdependence** between the prices and the sales volumes from different periods. They can result from market and production circumstances. Examples include:

- **Price expectations**. The price in a period forms the price expectations of later periods, which may induce, for example, speculation. As the price increases, price reductions may not change the demand behaviour symmetrically, so pulsation strategies can be utilised.
- **Carry-over effects**. for example, brand loyalty, availability of alternatives and imitations, the influence of word-of-mouth.
- **Product life cycle**. This determines the demand and competitive effects.
- **Costs dynamics**. The unit cost for a period depends on the production amount (and with it the sales volume) of previous periods (e.g. experience curve or learning curve, wear effects). In this context, *skimming strategies* (absorption) and *penetration strategies* (market penetration) are known.
- **Targets**. Interdependences due to the company's targets (see ▶ Chap. 2).

Temporal interdependences can be shown with a **dynamic price demand curve** in the following form:

$$x_t = x_t\left(p_1, p_2, \ldots, p_t\right) \text{or } x_t = x_t\left(x_1, x_2, \ldots, x_{t-1}, p_t\right). \tag{3.17}$$

The sales volume in period t depends not only on the price p_t of the current period but also on one or several prices in the past. As previous prices and sales volumes are linked through the price-demand curve, this dependence can also be assumed for previous sales volumes.

Simplistically, considering only two periods, the sales volume of the second period is formulated as $x_2 = x_2(x_1, p_2)$. The net present value of the profit for both periods using the discount factor $\rho = 1 + i$ is

$$\Pi = \left[p_1 \cdot x_1 - C\left(x_1\right)\right] \cdot \rho^{-1} + \left[p_2 \cdot x_2 - C\left(x_2\right)\right] \cdot \rho^{-2}$$

This shows that the optimal price of the second period (generally, the period considered last) does not differ structurally from the optimal price in the short term. All previous period's data disappear at the formation of the first derivation as a necessary condition for profit maximum.

The optimal (dynamic) price in the **first period** arises by

$$\frac{\partial \Pi}{\partial p_1} = \left(x_1 + \left[p_1 - C'\left(x_1\right)\right] \cdot \frac{\mathrm{d}x_1}{\mathrm{d}p_1}\right) \cdot \rho^{-1} + \left[p_2 - C'\left(x_2\right)\right] \cdot \frac{\partial x_2}{\partial x_1} \cdot \frac{\mathrm{d}x_1}{\mathrm{d}p_1} \cdot \rho^{-2} = 0. \tag{3.18}$$

Compared to the optimal price in the short term *in* $t = 1$, namely (see also (3.8))

$$x_1 + \left[p_1 - C'(x_1)\right] \cdot \frac{dx_1}{dp_1} = 0$$

they differ by the discounted contribution margin of the second period. The optimal price appears as a trade-off between short-term and long-term profit.

The **effect** of the difference on the optimal price p_1^* depends on the algebraic sign of the partial derivative $\partial x_2/\partial x_1$. Under the usual assumptions of $dx_1/dp_1 < 0$ and $p^* - C'(x) > 0$ arises:

Case 1: $\partial x_2/\partial x_1 > 0$. The difference is negative. The optimal price p_1^* *is lower* than in the short-term case for a plausible reason: higher sales (relatively) in the first period cause an increase in the sales in the next period. Increased sales in Period 1 can be achieved by lowering the price.

Case 2: $\partial x_2/\partial x_1 < 0$. The optimal price p_1^* is higher than in the short-term case.

The decision about the price in the first period shifts the price demand curve, which will be relevant for the next period. The effect will be stronger (ceteris paribus) if the marginal cost function reaches a lower level in the subsequent period compared to the first period, which is the case with learning effects. In other words, for the determination of the optimal *price strategy*, later costs become relevant. If the effects are very strong in the following period, even a starting price below marginal cost may be sensible.

In an analogous way, **cost interdependences** can be considered on the basis of $c_t = c_t(x_1, x_2, ..., x_{t-1}, x_t)$. Examples include **learning effects** resulting in a decrease of the production costs per unit and increasing accumulated production amounts (see the discussion at the beginning of this chapter). Another example is **wear effects**. With expansion of production, more frequent and/or increased maintenance activities may be required due to material defects and machine wear. Resource consumption can therefore change due to extensive use. On a unit product basis, these effects lead to an increase in the production costs per unit produced due to the expansion of production.

To illustrate these relations, **basic unit cost** bc_t of a period t are considered only if *no* production took place in earlier periods. Now, the dependences on the accumulated production amounts are considered by **change factors** $k_t(x_t)$ of the costs per unit (cash outflows) and indicate to what extent *future* (periods $t + 1$, $t + 2$, ...) costs per unit change if the production amount x_t is selected in period t. The resulting cost per unit c_t are

$$c_1 = \left[\prod_{\tau=1}^{t-1} \left(1 + k_\tau(x_\tau)\right)\right] \cdot bc_t \quad t = 1, \ldots, T, c_1 = bc_1 \tag{3.19}$$

The costs per unit in $t = 4$, for example, would be

$$c_4 = \left(1 + k_1(x_1)\right) \cdot \left(1 + k_2(x_2)\right) \cdot \left(1 + k_3(x_3)\right) \cdot bc_4$$

This exemplifies the effects of earlier production amounts on the costs per unit of later periods. Standardised change factors $k_t(0) = 0$ lead to the following:
- $k'_t(x_t) < 0$ in the case of **learning effects.**
- $k'_t(x_t) > 0$ in the case of **wear effects.**

3

At the beginning of period $t = 1$, for which the optimal production programme and the optimal prices are to be determined, the production for periods $t = 2, \ldots, T$ given on the basis of certain expectations is $x_t = \bar{x}_t$ for $t = 2, \ldots, T$. With this, all change factors $k_t(x_t)$ are also given for the following periods. A modified factor arises from it for the cash outflows per unit of

$$\bar{c}_t = \left[\prod_{\tau=2}^{t-1}\left(1+k_\tau\left(\bar{x}_\tau\right)\right)\right]\cdot bc_t \quad t = 2,\ldots,T, \bar{c}_2 = bc_2 \tag{3.20}$$

The net present value of the cash outflows NPV_o is as follows:

$$NPV_o = c_1 \cdot x_1 \cdot \rho^{-1} + \left(1+k_1\left(x_1\right)\right)\cdot\sum_{t=2}^{T}\bar{c}_t \cdot \bar{x}_t \cdot \rho^{-t} + \sum_{t=1}^{T} COF_t^F \cdot \rho^{-t}$$

with $\rho = 1 + i$ as the compounding factor and COF_t^F as the fixed cash outflows of the respective period. Under this set of assumptions, the net present value of the cash outflows only depends on the **production amount of the first period**, that is, $NPV_o = NPV_o(x_1)$. The **marginal cost** of a unit x_1 corresponds to the first derivation of the function of the net present value of the cash outflows towards x_1:

$$NPV_o'\left(x_1\right) = c_1 \cdot \rho^{-1} + c'_1\left(x_1\right)\cdot\sum_{t=2}^{T}\bar{c}_t \cdot \bar{x}_t \cdot \rho^{-t} \tag{3.21}$$

The **'dynamic' marginal cost** shown in (3.21) differs from the 'static' marginal cost c_1 (without interest effect) or $c_1 \cdot \rho^{-1}$ (with interest effect) of the first period by the extent of the impact on the future production's cash outflows. With the existence of learning effects, the 'dynamic' marginal costs are lower; with the existence of wear effects, they are higher than the 'static' marginal cost.

The optimal production programme is derived from the net present value NPV, the difference between NPV of cash inflows, and the NPV of cash outflows. Current cash inflows are considered at $CIF_t = p_t(x_t) \cdot x_t$ with $p_t'\left(x_t\right) < 0$. Due to the assumption of given amounts for $t = 2, \ldots, T$ and the absence of temporal interdependences of revenues cash inflows for all $t = 2, \ldots, T$ arise. The setting of the first derivation of NPV towards x_1 to zero produces the following **condition** on the **optimal** $\hat{x}_1$ amount now as

$$\left[p_1'\left(\hat{x}_1\right)\cdot\hat{x}_1 + p_1\left(\hat{x}_1\right) - c_1\right]\cdot\rho^{-1} - k_1'\left(\hat{x}_1\right)\cdot\sum_{t=2}^{T}\bar{c}_t \cdot \bar{x}_t \cdot \rho^{-t} = 0$$

or

$$p_1'\left(\hat{x}_1\right)\cdot\hat{x}_1 + p_1\left(\hat{x}_1\right) - c_1 - k_1'\left(\hat{x}_1\right)\cdot\sum_{t=2}^{T}\overline{c}_t\cdot\overline{x}_t\cdot\rho^{-(t-1)} = 0 \tag{3.22}$$

Formally, the relation '**marginal revenue = marginal costs**' remains valid, but now the marginal costs contain a dynamic aspect. With x_1^* and p_1^* as the optimal solution; from a 'traditional' cost and management accounting perspective and assuming a static view, (3.22) considers the following consequences:

- With the existence of **learning effects,** $\hat{x}_1 > x_1^*$ and with it $\hat{p}_1 < p_1^*$, as the basis of $k_1'\left(\hat{x}_1\right) < 0$, the additional term in (3.22) is positive. Therefore, it is worthwhile to reduce the price considering the 'dynamic' effects in order to **produce** (and sell) **more** than by exclusive consideration of the current period. This may be regarded as an '*investment in experience*'. The surplus in the first period is consciously reduced (by a short-term over-production) to be able to use the advantages of the experiences gained in the long-term in the form of lower future production cash outflows.
- With **wear and tear effects**, it is $\hat{x}_1 < x_1^*$ or $\hat{p}_1 < p_1^*$ and here a higher price is preferable taking into account the 'dynamic' effects to **produce less** as for each unit produced in $t = 1$, the cash outflows for the future production programme increase. Therefore, current production is limited so as not to allow disadvantages to become too large.

Important

The **intensity of the respective effects** depends on the following factors: Expectations or determinations in regard to the *future production programmes* are important. In the case of wear effects, higher future production volumes also induce higher costs. Unambiguously, higher negative cash flow consequences arise even for the current production decision leading to a lower optimal amount in the first period. Certainly, with the learning effects, higher future production amounts strengthen the intensity of the current learning effect (because the accumulated experiences have an effect on a larger number of future products). On the other hand, they lower the costs due to the learning effect of the *future production amounts*. The combined effect is unknown *a priori*.

Furthermore, the **economic life** (or: useful life) T is also important. The longer the considered project is used, the more important the learning or wear effects become. Finally, the **discount rate** i plays a role also. The larger the capital market interest rate (*ceteris paribus*), the larger the effect caused by discounting and the less important the future cash flow consequences of current decisions.

In the previous assumption of given amounts *for* $t = 2, \ldots, T$ it served to clarify the fundamental relation. However, it is obviously restrictive. **Future amounts and prices** are part of the **same inter-temporal optimisation considerations** as the decisions of the first period. Therefore, the production volume of subsequent periods depends on the production volume chosen initially, which by themselves, are affected by these future amounts. Therefore, an extensive optimisation requires a *simultaneous* determination of the total production strategy over a period of time.

3.3.4 Interdependence Between Products

All of the previous analyses about optimal prices referred to a *single* product only. As long as no interdependences with other company products exist, this does not appear to be a problem. If a particular company offers only a single product for sale, then no issue arises. However, usually a number of different interdependences exist between products:

- **Substitutional relations**. *Example*: a customer buying a BMW 525 will not buy a BMW 325 (full substitution).
- **Complementary relations**. *Example*: a memory card is bought with the purchase of a digital camera.
- **Product bundling**. *Example*: toothpaste and mouthwash are packaged together.
- **Costs interdependences**. *Example*: with the joint production of two products, the sum of the costs is reduced (*economies of scope*, synergies) or increased (cost of complexity and cost of product variety) when compared to the situation when only one product is produced.

If such interdependences exist, they refer to the so-called **product lines**.

From the perspective of the management accounting system, cost interdependences are particularly important. As previously mentioned, in determining price limits they lead to issues in calculating marginal cost functions as they generally cannot be allocated to individual products. Therefore, one of the most important factors for optimal price determination is distorted as costs can only be considered for products together (particularly in joint production scenarios); however, the dilemma remains that marketing considerations may need a separate perspective on individual products.

The effects of **market interdependences** resemble those of dynamic price strategies. The connection between product $j = 1$ and product $j = 2$ is given by the following price demand curve:

$$x_j = x_j\left(p_1, p_2\right) \text{or}\; x_j = x_j\left(p_j, x_i\right) \text{for}\; i, j = 1,2; i \neq j \tag{3.23}$$

The total profit is

$$\Pi = \left(p_1 \cdot x_1 - C\left(x_1\right)\right) + \left(p_2 \cdot x_2 - C\left(x_2\right)\right)$$

The necessary **condition** of the optimal price p_1 arises by the partial derivation of Π towards

$$\frac{\partial \Pi}{\partial p_1} = x_1 + \left(p_1 - C'\left(x_1\right)\right) \cdot \frac{\partial x_1}{\partial p_1} + \left(p_2 - C'\left(x_2\right)\right) \cdot \frac{\partial x_2}{\partial p_1} = 0 \tag{3.24}$$

In contrast to the optimal price of Product 1, while disregarding the interdependences, a **difference** (the last term in (3.24)) results again. On the condition of $p_2 - C'(x_2) > 0$ the algebraic sign depends on the partial derivative $\partial x_2/\partial p_1$.

Case 1: $\partial x_2/\partial p_1 > 0$. If the volume of product $j = 2$ rises when the price of product $j = 1$ is increased, a **substitutional relationship** exists. Then, the difference is positive with the optimal price p_1^* lying above the price to be determined and without considering substitution. The sales volume of product $j = 1$ is thereby reduced, while at the same time the sales volume of product $j = 2$ is increased. In the optimum, the contribution margin gains and losses balance each other out.

Case 2: $\partial x_2/\partial p_1 < 0$. This reflects a **complementary relationship**. The difference term is negative with the optimal price p_1^* lying below the price to be determined and without considering the complement. The sales volume of product $j = 1$ is thereby increased, which also increases the sales volume of product $j = 2$.

The necessary condition (3.24) can be written as follows:

$$\frac{\partial \Pi}{\partial p_1} = x_1 + \frac{\partial x_1}{\partial p_1} \cdot \left[\left(p_1 - C'(x_1) \right) + \left(p_2 - C'(x_2) \right) \cdot \frac{\partial x_2}{\partial x_1} \right] = 0 \tag{3.25}$$

The above statements apply appropriately – with $\partial x_2/\partial x_1 > 0$ indicating complementarity and $\partial x_2/\partial x_1 < 0$ substitutionality.

There is a difference in the optimal price when the relationship among the products is considered and when it is neglected. This difference depends on the other product's marginal contribution margin and on the strength of the relationship. With interdependences between products, the optimal price can *undercut* the marginal costs if the indirect effects are strong enough (for example, with substitutional relationships among several products).

The statements about the effects of market interdependences on the optimal price are based on a *ceteris paribus* assumption, that is, particularly under the assumption that the price of the other product $j = 2$ is kept constant. If the prices of *both* products are to be optimised simultaneously, the statements may not necessarily apply.

▪ Calculatory Balance and Fixed Cost Allocation

The mutual influence of prices with interdependences between products is achieved by the so-called **calculatory balance** or combined costing. In principle, this refers to the subsidisation of low (or even negative) contribution margin products which are offered based on marketing considerations (i.e. lure products) by high contribution margins gained from other products (e.g. prestige products). In determining the optimal price, this feature is not very helpful. When the management accounting system is applied to balance these differences, a higher proportion of fixed costs (or overhead costs) are often allocated to those products with a higher contribution margin than to those products with a lower contribution margin. A decision-maker considering these products in isolation should attempt to avoid making wrong decisions.

The **allocation of fixed costs** is an **unsuitable** instrument for pricing decisions when product interdependences exist as illustrated in the following example.

Example: a company produces two substitute products $j = 1$ and 2 with the following price demand curves and variable costs:

$$x_1 = 100 - 2p_1 + p_2 \text{ and } c_1 = 4$$

$$x_2 = 200 - 2p_2 + p_1 \text{ and } c_2 = 5$$

Total fixed costs are 5096.5. The contribution margin function is (fixed costs are not relevant):

$$CM = (p_1 - 4)\cdot(100 - 2p_1 + p_2) + (p_2 - 5)\cdot(200 - 2p_2 + p_1)$$

$$\frac{\partial CM}{\partial p_1} = 100 - 2p_1 + p_2 - 2\cdot(p_1 - 4) + p_2 - 5 = 103 - 4p_1 + 2p_2 = 0$$

$$\frac{\partial CM}{\partial p_2} = 200 - 2p_2 + p_1 - 2\cdot(p_2 - 5) + p_1 - 4 = 206 - 4p_2 + 2p_1 = 0$$

The optimal prices $p_1^* = 68.\overline{6}$ and $p_2^* = 85.8\overline{3}$, the sales volumes $x_1^* = 48.5$ and $x_2^* = 97$ as well as a contribution margin $CM = 10{,}977.1\overline{6}$ result from it.

For illustration: by *isolated* optimisation of CM_1 and CM_2 the following equation arises

$$\frac{\partial CM_1}{\partial p_1} = 100 - 2p_1 + p_2 - 2\cdot(p_1 - 4) = 108 - 4p_1 + p_2 = 0$$

$$\frac{\partial CM_2}{\partial p_2} = 200 - 2p_2 + p_1 - 2\cdot(p_2 - 5) = 210 - 4p_2 + p_1 = 0 \tag{3.26}$$

As a result, $p_1 = 42.8$ and $p_2 = 63.2$ arise, with isolated contribution margins of $CM_1 = 3{,}010.88$ and $CM_2 = 6{,}774.48$, and in sum $CM = 9{,}785.36$. The prices undercut the optimal prices, and the **contribution margin** achieved decreases by about 11%.

If the variable costs c_j are left as parameters in the contribution margins CM_j of (3.26), the (isolated) optimal prices p_j follow:

$$p_1 = 25 + \frac{p_2}{4} + \frac{c_1}{2} \text{ and } p_2 = 50 + \frac{p_1}{4} + \frac{c_2}{2}$$

The application of full costs instead of variable costs appears to be meaningful because the isolatedly determined prices are too low and the use of higher costs results in an increase in prices.

For this, the following procedure should be used: the fixed costs in the amount of 5,096.5 are allocated between the two products $j = 1$ and $j = 2$ in the ratio of 38.46%/61.54% = 1,960.2/3,136.3 (the only reason for these relations and amounts of fixed costs is that they were constructed based on the solution, and they lead to optimal prices with fixed cost allocation). 48.5 units of Product 1 are produced, that is, unit 'costs' are 4 + 1,960.2/48.5 = 44.416, 'costs' per unit of Product 2 are 5 + 3,136.3/97 = 37.33. As Product 1 is produced in about half the volume of Product 2, one unit of Product 1 contains more fixed costs than one unit of Product 2, despite the fact that Product 2 generates a higher unit contribution margin ($cm_2 = 80.8\overline{3}$). If this cost information is used to replace c_j in the determination equation (3.26), the isolated optimal prices (with rounding errors) become the (actual) optimal prices of $p_1^* = 68.\overline{6}$ and $p_2^* = 85.8\overline{3}$, and the optimal amounts stay unchanged.

However, with such a procedure an important detail is disregarded: the allocation of the fixed costs could not occur if the optimal sales volumes were not already known, and this requires a knowledge of the optimal prices. Therefore, the 'solution' of the interdependence problem by the allocation of fixed costs is based on a circular problem: *after* knowledge of the optimal prices and quantities, (usually a partial) allocation of the fixed costs can be *constructed* and isolated optimal prices can then be found.

In summary, for the optimal price decision with product interdependences, only variable costs are relevant. Fixed costs, no matter how allocated to products, lead to incorrect decisions. However, with substitutional relations, the (partial) allocation of fixed costs to variable costs results in 'better' pricing decisions *if* (either wrongly or simplistically) the isolated optimisation of every product is assumed. As regards complementary products, this does not work as the optimal prices are lower than the isolated optimal prices. On the contrary, this interpretation is possible when the optimal price of one product increases relatively and the price of the other product drops relatively. This is possible under certain conditions with substitutional products as well as complementary products where a product would have to carry the other product's costs.

3.3.5 Competitive Reactions

So far, a price demand curve has been assumed. This typically applies to a monopoly situation or if the company possesses a certain monopolistic position as a result of an imperfect market. Then, competitive reactions have no noticeable effect on the company and therefore do not have to be considered for price setting.

In the case of an **oligopolistic market**, this assumption does not apply. Here, a low number of competitors closely observe mutual prices in order to enable immediate reactions (e.g. raising or dropping their own prices). Therefore, competitors' strategic reactions are essential for a company's individual pricing decisions. Consequently, a classic duopoly situation (*Bertrand's* equilibrium) will be now discussed, followed by the pricing of an offer.

▪ A Classic Duopoly Situation

The following section shows the influence of competitor reactions when addressing a particular market situation. The so-called ***Bertrand*** **equilibrium** is most suitable for modelling a price decision in this context.

Example: two Companies 1 and 2 produce a homogeneous product. The cost functions are linear with identical variable costs of $c_1 = c_2 = c$. Both companies announce their prices p_j at the same time and they cannot alter them during the period under consideration. The demand for the products is divided based upon the price-demand curve of the market for this homogenous product $x(p_1, p_2)$; the companies have to fulfil this demand with the sales volumes x_1 and x_2. Assume also that both companies have sufficient production capacity.

Customers will buy from the company with the lower announced price, and the other company will not sell anything. With identical price offers, the demanded quantity is divided according to a certain rule (for example, identical sales for both); however, this assumption is not essential for the following reason.

Assume that Company 1 knew that Company 2 offered p_2. Then its optimal price decision would be to offer a price infinitely below it, $p_1 = p_2 - \varepsilon$, since their sales will equal the total demand. However, as both companies, will only offer a price $p_j \geq c$ (as otherwise they would make a loss), the **only equilibrium** is $p_1^* = p_2^* = c$. In every other case, the other company may possibly undercut the price, just like the company itself would have an incentive to undercut the price of their rival. However, this solution is relatively unsatisfactory because no company achieves a contribution margin. Therefore, it does not matter how the demand is distributed between them.

If **fixed costs** exist, both companies suffer a loss exactly equal to these fixed costs. Both would have an incentive to offer (at least) a price covering their fixed costs in the hope that they can sell a certain amount. Yet, as their fixed costs are sunk costs, every company has an incentive to underbid the other and to thereby capture the entire demand and to achieve at least a positive contribution margin, even if not by the amount of their total fixed costs. Here, the balance $p_1^* = p_2^* = c$ remains again as the single solution.

What happens if the **variable costs** of both companies are **different**, for example at $c_1 < c_2$? In this case the optimal price of Company 1 is just below c_2, that is, $p_1^* = c_2 - \varepsilon$ (unless, the monopoly price is lower, as then this would be optimal). At this price, all of the demand goes to this company and it achieves the maximum profit taking into account the fact that Company 2 must offer a price of at least c_2 to avoid a loss. In this case, the optimal price of Company 1 *only* depends on the variable costs of Company 2.

Now, the 'pure' ***Bertrand*** **situation** is certainly extreme since the companies compete exclusively on price. Assuming that the products at least differ a little, a different result emerges. The same applies to the situation whereby the companies have limited capacities, so that they cannot satisfy all of the demand. Not completely realistic is the assumption that the companies are bound to maintain their prices once they are announced. The companies could engage in price collusion and agree to divide the market between them. However, in every case, the competitor's costs influence the company's own optimal price.

The solution to this competitive situation essentially depends on the fact that the companies **know** the **mutual costs** in advance. Typically, this is not the case. A company may estimate their competitor's costs relatively well, but it will hardly have certainty about it. In the case of a new product, the producing company may not even know its own costs precisely. Such an **uncertainty** is discussed in the following section concerning public tenders.

Pricing a Tender

A public tender (submission) is a special auction procedure (i.e. *competitive bidding* for an order). A typical form of a public tender is a *closed bid*. Each offer is delivered in a sealed envelope, and the contractor opens all received offers at a certain point in time and then decides which offer is the best. Tenders are frequently used among public contractors but can also be used by private companies in deciding upon large investments.

The **best offer** depends on the quality, the offered price and other further considerations such as reliability or previous experiences with the company. For example, if the offers show identical qualities and no other considerations play a role, the best offer corresponds with the lowest price. This is the assumption in the following section.

The offering company hopes to offer the highest price p at which it will just receive the order, provided that this price exceeds its relevant costs c, with $\Phi(p)$ as the probability that the company wins the tender at the offered price p, the **target function** of the company when assuming *risk neutrality* is

$$\max_p \mathrm{E}[\Pi] = (p - c) \cdot \Phi(p) \tag{3.27}$$

The trade-off for the optimal price determination becomes evident: the higher the offered price, the higher the contribution margin $p - c$, but the lower the probability $\Phi(p)$ of getting the order. The problem with this price decision lies in the estimation of the probability. Information about the competitors' cost situation is valuable. Assuming that there is only one other company that will offer the product for sale, and assuming the competitor's costs are estimated to exceed 300,000, the probability of getting the order for a tender price below 300,000 is 100% provided the competitor will not bid below its own costs.

In principle, the **optimal tender price** is higher than the costs c, and a positive contribution margin is achieved with it. The **surcharge** on the costs depends on the circumstances of the offer, particularly:

- Type of order selected, for example, lowest price, the *Vickrey* rule (i.e. a procedure in which the lowest bidder gets the offer but receives the price of the next-highest bidder. This procedure has the interesting quality in that, as a dominant strategy, a price is offered in the amount of their own costs c with optional changes later to the tender.
- Relations between the company's own costs and their competitors' costs.
- The number of competitors.

The Winner's Curse

- The winner's curse denotes the paradox that getting an offer often makes the bidder unhappy. The reason: if the tender is connected with identical costs for all bidders and these are unknown to the companies, they must be estimated. The company, which estimated the costs the lowest, gets the offer because it can offer the lowest price. The fact, however, that all other companies have estimated the (same) costs higher may indicate nothing else other than the cost estimation was too low. That means that the price will not bring the expected contribution margin. This is the '*bad news*' arriving after getting the order.
- *Rational* companies will consider this for their bid and will demand a higher price. If they get the order, they do not have to regret this; if they do not get the order, they will not have to 'suffer' any additional costs. If all companies were to consider this appropriately, the tendering procedure would remain unchanged.

Costs of preparing the bid are not relevant for the optimal offer price because they result from the decision to make the bid and are independent of the final decision made. Instead, the decision *whether* to make a bid arises from a comparison of the expected contribution margin against the costs of the bid.

3.4 Summary

Price limits are **critical values**, which cause certain decisions. **Lowest-price limits** are required for decisions about the acceptance or rejection of a one time-only special order or the removal of a product from the production programme. **Highest-price limits** support the decision regarding the purchase of goods. **Relative price limits** lead to a change of the production programme's composition.

For the determination of price limits, the **relevant costs** have to be determined. These are the costs which arise from the decision when compared to the original cost situation. For a special order, they always include the **marginal costs** (of the whole order, not just the last unit) and all other costs which may be **affected by the decision**. These other costs may include **opportunity costs**, which appear when an order affects the previous production programme. This can also concern **fixed costs** (in the short term), that is, with an optional increase or decrease in capacities when an order is accepted or rejected.

Price limits are critical values at which a decision changes. This does not imply that the real prices must correspond to these price limits. Particularly, costs can also be applied for **determining optimal sales prices**. However, they are not isolated, but instead have to be treated in connection with all **marketing variables**.

The **optimal price in the short-term** results from the fundamental equation: **marginal revenue = marginal costs**. Fixed costs therefore do not play a role. This implies that typical procedures for determining prices in general (e.g. job costing, *target pricing*) do not result in optimal prices. However, if fixed costs are influential (from a short-term perspective), they are relevant. This is the same consideration for the **lowest-price limit**; as according to the production's time dimension, fixed costs may need to be considered. For example, as most costs are influential for a long-term manufacturing order, the price decision is based on full costs. However, the allocation problem of (the variable) overhead costs among a number of orders remains. The optimal price depends not only on the period's **product costs** under consideration but also on; **future costs** (dynamic price strategies), **interdependences** to other products and with it, on their costs as well as on the **competitors' costs** when they have a noticeable influence on the decisions of the company.

The result of the analysis of how optimal prices depend on costs has shown that there are **various relations** to which attention should be paid. A formal analysis can be limited to one or two products and to one or two periods (ceteris paribus). However, in the **practical application** of the results, difficulties appear, as **very complex relations** exist. Additional **problems** with the application of the model's results lie in the required **data** themselves. For example, the estimation of the price-demand curve is not easy. Difficulties also lie in the product and market definitions, the consideration of product interdependences and the influences of other marketing instruments that cannot sufficiently be isolated from the price as an impact factor.

3.5 Assessment Material

Review Questions

1. How do price limits differ for the buyer and the seller of a product?
2. Under what circumstances is it meaningful to use the replacement costs of required raw materials for the lowest-price limit of a product?
3. How do marginal costs differ from relevant costs?
4. For the determination of the lowest-price limit of a supplementary order with limited capacity, why must the *optimal* production programme be compared with the *status quo*?
5. What are the cost elasticity and the learning rate in the context of the experience curve?
6. How does the lowest-price limit (per unit) of a supplementary order behave with higher order amounts if the production costs per unit are constant and only potential capacity limitations exist?
7. Which types of substitutional or complementary effects exist between products? How do these have an effect on lowest-price limits and (cost-based) optimal prices of these products?
8. How does the consideration of interest effects change the lowest-price limit of long-term orders?
9. For what type of pricing decisions are decision trees applied?

10. What must be considered for the determination of the highest-price limit of an input factor?
11. Under which conditions do cost-plus price determinations lead to optimal prices?
12. What effects do market form and competition have on a company's price setting? How can these effects be recognised?
13. Which consequences arise from dynamic cost relations for the determination of production strategies?

Exercises

1. **Lowest-price limit and learning curve.** *Har&Vester plc* produces tractors. *ASA* approaches the company with a supplementary order of five units of a rarely sold type of tractor. *Har&Vester* expects that the assembly hours decrease in each case with a duplication of the accumulated production amount by a certain percentage. Four units of that type were produced some time ago; the learning rate α is estimated at 0.12. Determine the short-term lowest-price limit for the supplementary order of the five (additional) tractors. The following data are available:

Direct materials per tractor	360,000
Material overheads	25% of direct materials
Direct labour per hour	800
Manufacturing overheads	40% of the labour costs
Average assembly hours per tractor (on the basis of the first four tractors)	434 hours
Variable administration overhead costs	5% of the variable production costs
Order-fixed costs	125,000

2. **Cost-plus into and out of the market.** A company determines its sales price for a particular product on the basis of full costs plus a percentage profit surcharge of 10%. The variable unit costs for the product are $c = 200$ and fixed costs of $C^F = 20{,}000$ are assumed for calculation purposes. These cost figures are assumed to be constant for the following periods.

The conditions in the market are characterised by a straight-line price-demand curve of the type $p(x) = 520 - x$ for all periods. However, the company is unaware of this formula. It adjusts its calculations and therefore its prices to the respective current demand.

(a) Assume that the company initially sets its price on the basis of a sales volume of $x = 120$. Follow movements in demand and prices over several periods.

(b) Assume now that the company initially sets its price on the basis of a sales volume of 170. Pursue the demand and price development over at least ten periods. Against which value do the movements converge?
(c) Assume that the company knows that the market conditions are characterised by a straight-line price-demand curve valid for all periods; it just does not know the formula's parameters. After how many periods, at the latest, should it give up the procedures used in Parts a) and b) of the assignment? How will the genuinely optimal price and the genuinely optimal sales then look? Will this combination ever be achieved with the above procedure?

3. **Pricing an offer.** The municipal refuse disposal department has invited tenders for eight refuse disposal lorries. The company could fulfil the order without any bottlenecks. It estimates the variable costs of a refuse disposal lorry to be 45, whereby it would need to add on a further 3 per lorry for specific requirements. At current levels of capacity, the full costs are 125. The sales price for similar lorries is in the range of 140–190 each. It estimates the conversion costs of squeezing this order into its normal production, resulting from changes to equipment especially in the paint shop, to be 16. The costs for preparing the offer are 10. Based on its previous experience, both on the prices achieved for earlier orders from the refuse disposal department as well as on their competitors' behaviour, the company believes that it may assume the following probability distribution for the proposed order:

$$\Phi(p) = \begin{cases} 0 & 250 < p \\ 1 - p/250 & 0 \leq p \leq 250 \\ 1 & p < 0 \end{cases}$$

How high is the optimum tender price (the company is neutral to risk)? How much higher would the optimum tender price be if the variable costs were 50 higher?

4. **Pricing an offer with simplified job costing.** A road construction company is tendering for five tunnel projects. *Trench&Dig* and *Bust&Drill* are bidding for these projects. The lowest offers in each of the five projects will be successful. The current overall order-related costs for *both* companies to undertake one tunnel project j are: $C_j = 100 + 20M_j + 40L_j$, whereby M_j represents machine hours and L_j also represents labour hours. Undertaking an average tunnel project takes up 40 machine hours and 20 machine hours, respectively.

These are the following machine and labour hours for the five tunnel projects:

Tunnel project no.	Machine hours	Labour hours
1	21	8
2	17	10
3	24	11

Tunnel project no.	Machine hours	Labour hours
4	20	12
5	19	7

Trench&Dig use a simplified job costing system in which all costs are charged based on labour hours. The total costs of an average project are 1,700 giving an average marginal rate of 85 per labour hour. *Bust&Drill,* on the other hand, *only* use machine hours in their calculation; resulting in average costs per machine hour of 42.5. Both companies add a fixed profit of 60 to the costs.

(a) Calculate the two offers for each project, the actual (expected) costs and determine which company would be awarded each project.

(b) Is there a difference between the profit expected on the basis of a) and the projected profit in the calculation? If so, by how much and why?

5. **Lowest-price limits.** Under the terms of its regular policies, a company produces three products with a machine $i = 1$. In addition, it can produce a fourth product that is rarely demanded. Therefore, the company does not include it in its standard periodical planning of its production and sales programme but instead waits for actual customer inquiries. The three standard products require raw material ($i = 2$) that is only available in limited quantities in the current period. The following data for the current period relating to the three standard products $j = 1, 2, 3$, machine and raw materials capacities apply:

Product	$j = 1$	$j = 2$	$j = 3$
Price p_j	500	750	90
Variable costs c_j	460	725	55
Maximum sales Volume $\bar{x}_j$	800	1,000	200
Consumption v_{1j}	4	1	2
Consumption v_{2j}	5	5	3

	Machine $i = 1$	**Raw material $i = 2$**
Capacity V_i	1,000	1,800

You may ignore the discreteness stipulation (integrity assumption) in all of the following questions. There are fixed costs amounting to 6,000 and the company's objective is to maximise profits in each period. You should assume the usual hypotheses relating to a short-term decision problem.

(a) Directly after the beginning of the period but *before* realising the optimum programme for the three standard products, the company receives an inquiry from a customer for a special order of product $j = 4$. The customer wants 150 pieces of the special product, production of which requires 3 machine hours and 2 units of the raw material (in each case per piece of the special product). The variable unit costs are $c_4 = 50$. Assume that the company is completely free to decide to what extent it satisfies the customer's order (e.g. it may supply only one piece of the special product). How high is the lowest-price limit for the special product?
(b) Assume that the customer is willing to pay a maximum price of 74 for the special product and that the company is still free to decide the extent to which it satisfies the customer's order. How many pieces of the special product, and at what price, will it take into its programme? How would you answer this question if taking the special product into the programme involved additional costs for converting the machinery of 200?
(c) Now assume that the company can only accept the order in its entirety. How high is the lowest-price limit for the special product?

6. **Lowest-price limits and the sequential acceptance of an order.** Consider a company that manufactures to contract. Existing capacity allows acceptance of exactly *two* contracts during the forthcoming planning period but expects a total of *three* potential contracts of which the conditions are uncertain. For each of the contracts, the company expects three possible outcomes of the order's contribution margin with the following probabilities:

$$cm_L = 40\,;\text{probability}\ \phi_L = 0.3$$

$$cm_M = 70\,;\text{probability}\ \phi_M = 0.2$$

$$cm_H = 100\,;\text{probability}\ \phi_H = 0.5$$

The variable costs of a contract are $c = 400$. Every contract accepted must be fulfilled.

(a) Determine the development of the lowest-price limits and the opportunity costs in each sequence. How high is the expected contribution margin that the company can receive for the planning period? Upon completing certain steps, assume the company could expand their capacity to three contracts. What is the most that it could pay for these steps?
(b) How would the questions in Part a) of the assignment have to be answered if there were not three but *four* potential incoming contracts?
(c) How would the questions in Part a) of the assignment have to be answered if there were four potential incoming contracts and $cm_L = -10$ and $cm_H = 130$?

7. **Cost dynamics and intertemporal strategies.** A company acquires a production machine at a price of 60,000 whose economic life amounts to *three* periods and will not be replaced thereafter. With it one product type can be produced. The sales prices and variable costs per unit are as follows ($t = 1, 2, 3$; $x_0 = 0$):

$$p_t(x_t) = 2{,}300 - 4 \cdot x_t$$

$$c_t = 1{,}500 - c \cdot x_{t-1};\quad c \geq 0$$

The fixed cash outflows amount to $COF_t^F = COF^F = 10{,}000$ in every period and the capital market interest rate is $i = 0.25$.

(a) Assume that $c = 0$. Determine the optimal production decisions for each period separately and the project's net present value arising from it. Is a 'traditional' cost accounting approach (periodic considerations) justified in the presented case?

(b) Now assume $c = 2$. What intertemporal costs interdependences exist? Determine the production amounts, sales prices, period surpluses and the net present value under the assumption of *successively isolated* period considerations.

(c) Determine the optimal production decision of the separate periods for $c = 2$ as well as the net present value of the project by full consideration of the interdependence effects (*hint*: There are two ways for solving this problem). How do production amounts and sales volumes, sales prices, period surpluses and net present value change when the uniform discount rate is changed to 0% or to 100%?

Decision-Making Under Uncertainty

Contents

P. Schuster et al., *Management Accounting*, Springer Texts in Business and Economics, https://doi.org/10.1007/978-3-030-62022-6_4

Learning Objectives

After studying this chapter, you should be able to:
- Present cost-volume-profit relationships
- Analyse the effects of uncertainty in production programme decisions
- Show the relevance of fixed costs in different situations

4.1 Introduction

Literature on decision-making in management accounting typically assumes **certainty (certain expectations);** this was also assumed in the previous chapters. There are several **reasons** for this, particularly the following two:

1. On the one hand, the management accounting system mainly serves as an instrument of information for the support of **short-term decisions** whose consequences are considered only for a specific period of time (e.g. a month, quarter or year). Here, it can generally be assumed that within such a time frame, forecast uncertainties are negligible, and therefore certain expectations are realistic.
2. On the other hand, management accounting data can explain the **fundamental principles** that remain valid under uncertainty.

Yet, both arguments are hardly convincing. Even from a short-term perspective, aspects of uncertainty cannot be excluded. For example, who already knows at the beginning of a quarter, a season or a year how the prices for both procurement and sales, or indeed, the firms' sales potential will actually develop? Whether such possibly negligible uncertainty exists can only be accurately determined after an explicit analysis of the decisions taken with the **inclusion of uncertainty**; that is, only then possible changes to optimal policies induced by uncertainty become obvious. Similarly, the second argument also has to be considered. Only by an explicit inclusion of uncertain expectations can an optimum be determined if these decision-making principles apply. Therefore, in the following section uncertain expectations within the framework of short-term decision problems are explicitly included.

It should be highlighted that uncertainty plays a role not just in decision-making. For example, a subsequent chapter dealing with variance analysis and control illustrates problems that assume uncertain expectations which will be analysed in a particular manner.

This chapter discusses approaches that can give the decision-maker a 'feeling for the meaning of uncertainty' with regard to the decision problem, that is, **cost-volume-profit relationships** with one or multiple products in addition to the 'stochastic' variations. At the centre of the analysis is the case of *risk*, that is, when the decision-maker knows (or assumes) subjective **probability distributions** for the parameters of the decision problem faced by them. During the course of this book's discussion, the question of the **decision relevance of fixed costs** is addressed. The answer to this question arises to a certain extent as a side result from the analysis of the individual problem structures.

4.2 Cost-Volume-Profit Relationships (Break-Even Analysis)

4.2.1 Introduction

Uncertain expectations are characterised by the fact that a decision problem's **parameters** (e.g. procurement prices, sales prices or sales potential) are not known in advance. The value of the parameter is known to lie within a certain range of values, but the precise value itself is not known a priori. For this, **sensitivity analysis** can be used in a number of different ways:

1. On the one hand, sensitivity analysis can examine for a given set of changes to particular variables, how sensitive the **target measure** is to **changes** in the original parameters. This leads to a range in the value of the target measure, which can be compared, for example, with a subjectively expected range of values.
2. On the other hand, a sensitivity analysis can question which combination of the uncertain parameters contained within the original **decision remains optimal**. In this case a **parameter range** arises and can then be compared with the expected parameter range. In an ideal scenario, the expected parameter range is a subset of the 'positive' range; that is, the uncertainty has no relevance for the existing problem. Additionally, the 'positive' parameter range does not necessarily present the optimal solution but can also reflect 'critical' results (e.g. minimum profits). In this case, the 'positive' parameter range describes all those parameter combinations which guarantee to at least attain the given 'critical' result.

In a break-even analysis (*BEA*), the second way is at the centre of attention. The **basic model** of *BEA* analyses the specific '*critical*' value of the **sales volume** with which the company achieves neither a profit nor a loss. By comparison with the expected changes to sales volumes during the course of a particular period, the profit risk and possible necessary adaptations are covered (this shows that the connections of a *BEA* can finally be used for *both* of the above ways).

The following sections of this chapter specify and discuss some important cases of break-even analysis. For this to occur, structural relations between the target measures (a period's profits) and the parameters or variables of the problem are outlined. In the following and analogously to the previous chapters, linear functions are assumed, but later on exceptions from linearity are discussed.

4.2.2 Single-Product Break-Even Analysis

The simplest situation exists if only one product is produced. Then the period's profit is as follows:

$$\Pi = (p - c) \cdot x - C^F = cm \cdot x - C^F \tag{4.1}$$

with:

- *cm* contribution margin
- *c* variable cost per unit

- p sales price per unit
- x product units
- C^F fixed costs

The **break-even amount** $\hat{x}$ can be found by solving (4.1) according to the sales volume under the condition *profit* = 0:

$$\hat{x} = \frac{C^F}{cm} = \frac{C^F}{p - c} \tag{4.2}$$

Example With fixed costs of 120,000, a sales price of 100 and variable unit cost of 40 the break-even amount equals 120,000/(100 – 40) = 2000. For the given parameters (sales price, unit cost and fixed costs) at least 2000 units must be sold to reach the profit zone. Should the capacity allow only a production of (for example) 1700 units, the profit zone can never be reached. This would be similar to a market situation that makes reaching this break-even volume impossible. On the contrary, if the sales volume can vary in the range of [1000; 3000], both a profit and a loss situation are possible and the *basic model shown* cannot explain which situation is more relevant and/or more likely.

The **single-product case presented** does not strictly require a company that offers only one product since an *isolated* analysis (for each product type) can be undertaken. In this case, the *fixed costs* of the company must be allocated and divided among the different products. Amounts are then calculated according to (4.1) and (4.2). This examination does not register any compensational effects between the product types; that is, compensation from the loss of one product by profit gained from another product remains unconsidered. Moreover, dividing the fixed costs between the individual product types may lead to substantial problems or might even be impossible (e.g. in cases where the depreciation of a building which is being used for the production of several different product types).

◘ Figure 4.1 shows the relationships given in (4.1) and (4.2). The intersection of the revenue (sales) function R and the total cost function C indicates the break-even amount. If the revenues exceed the costs, the company is in the profit zone, otherwise it is in the loss zone.

The minimum value of *profit* = 0 is not the only possibility, as generally a **critical value** for the (minimum) profit $\underline{\Pi}$ can be characterised by the following break-even point:

$$\hat{x} = \frac{C^F + \underline{\Pi}}{cm} \tag{4.3}$$

With a given sales volume x, the **break-even price** $\hat{p}$ arises from it:

$$\hat{p} = c + \frac{C^F + \underline{\Pi}}{x} \tag{4.4}$$

Continuation of the Example Assuming x = 1800 and Π = 0, a break-even price of 106.67 is required to enter the profit zone. For example, with a previous sales price of 90 (ceteris paribus) a price increase of 16.67 is required. Potential reactions to sales

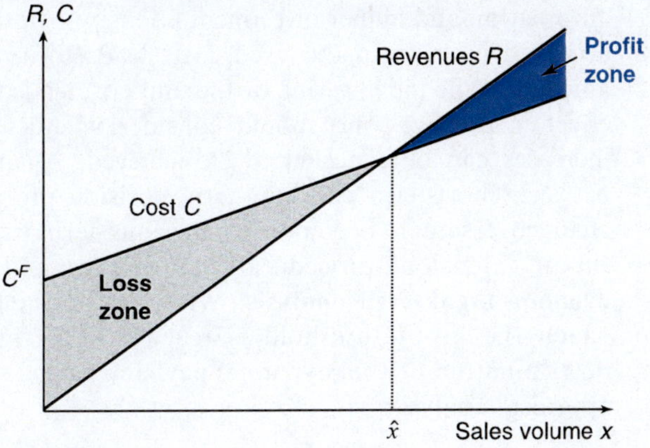

Fig. 4.1 Break-even model

volume might occur if the sales side is represented by a (bent) price demand curve. If a price increase is regarded as impossible, efforts may instead lead to cost reductions and subsequently the break-even unit cost may arise from:

$$\hat{c} = p - \frac{C^F + \underline{\Pi}}{x} \tag{4.5}$$

In the above example with $p = 90$ the allowable variable costs per unit are 23.33 to prevent a loss-making situation. For that to occur, investments might be necessary and therefore, the conditions required for a short-term decision problem are exceeded. Here, the results of the *BEA* can only have a *signalling function*.

- **Evaluation of the Results**
- By selecting a suitable $\underline{\Pi}$ and by appropriately applying the formula outlined many other **questions** can be answered, such as:
- How does a **change** to the proportional unit cost affect the sales price, fixed costs, minimum profit and break-even amount? If certain costs increase in future periods (e.g. on the basis of wage increases and other price increases on the procurement side) for both variable unit costs and fixed costs, the necessary sales volume increase needed to retain $\underline{\Pi}$ or the previous profit can be calculated (ceteris paribus).
- Assuming that **additional advertising** or the hiring of additional sales staff are being considered, this can be connected with an increase in fixed costs; and with the help of (4.3), the necessary sales volume required to reach at least the previous profit level can be determined.
- What sales volume is required to at least cover the **cash flow affecting parts** of the fixed costs? In this case $\underline{\Pi}$ is set to the amount of the (negative) cash flow of the ineffective fixed cost components. Additionally, it needs to be assumed that the sales prices and variable unit costs are fully cash flow effective in each case so as to gain information on the liquidity status.
- How does the *break-even amount* change by **procedural changeover** connected with lower variable unit costs but higher fixed costs (e.g. due to higher

automation and higher investment intensity)? In this example, contrary effects arise: an increase in the fixed costs leads to an increase of the break-even amount, while the lowering of the unit cost leads to a decrease of it. If the net effect is positive, one should consider whether the required sales volume increases can be expected to be achieved. Again, the issue of the division between short-term and long-term decision problems arises, and procedural changeovers might become a regular long-term issue.

- In an extension, procedural changeovers and capacity changes yield a **dynamic break-even analysis**. With it, the **point in time** is determined, at which the profit threshold is reached. This analysis corresponds to the determination of the (dynamic) **payback period** in the context of investment appraisal analysis.

4.2.3 Safety Coefficient and Operating Leverage

Two risk measures are used in the context of cost-volume-profit relationships: safety coefficient SC and operating leverage OL.

The **safety coefficient** indicates the percentage sales (in € or product units) may drop without entering the loss zone. With x being the starting level of the sales volume, it follows:

$$SC = \frac{p \cdot x - p \cdot \hat{x}}{p \cdot x} = \frac{x - \hat{x}}{x} = 1 - \frac{\hat{x}}{x} \tag{4.6}$$

With $\hat{x} < x$ and thus $SC > 0$, there is some room for falling sales volume. The higher the safety coefficient SC, the more certain it is of a profit during the period (or of reaching a certain profit $\underline{\Pi}$).

The initial amount x needs to be specified in this context. Often in the literature, x refers to the full utilisation of the production capacity. This can be based on the understanding that the desired production amount refers to the available capacity for all products with a positive contribution margin. If so, then the uncertainty of sales volumes can be measured by the safety coefficient.

Example With a capacity of $x = 4{,}000$ and a break-even amount of 3,000, the safety coefficient is $1 - 3000/4000 = 0.25$; the capacity utilisation can therefore be reduced by 25% before the loss zone is entered.

The **operating leverage** measures the variability of the profit Π as a function of a change in sales. The operating leverage is the **relative profit change** in relation to a **relative sales change** (sales = revenues = R):

$$OL = \frac{\frac{\Delta \Pi}{\Pi}}{\frac{\Delta R}{R}} \tag{4.7}$$

If the sales price and the unit cost are kept constant, profit and sales changes can be derived from changes in the quantities sold:

$$OL = \frac{\dfrac{\Delta x \cdot cm}{x \cdot cm - C^F}}{\dfrac{\Delta x \cdot p}{x \cdot p}} \tag{4.8}$$

This clarifies the **influence of fixed costs,** that is, higher fixed costs reduce the denominator and therefore cause a rise of this quotient, and with it, a rise in the operating leverage. Furthermore, the higher the fixed costs for a company, any proportional sales changes will inevitably induce bigger proportional profit changes. The variability of profit is thereby positively tied to fixed costs; a company is more susceptible to losses when sales decline, the higher that their fixed costs are.

Even though the original intent of the coefficient OL is to represent the scale of the profit variability, it really does not measure anything apart from the safety coefficient, which becomes obvious based upon the following transformations:

$$OL = \frac{\Delta x \cdot cm \cdot x}{\Delta x \cdot \left(x \cdot cm - C^F\right)} = \frac{x}{x - \dfrac{C^F}{cm}} = \frac{1}{\dfrac{x - \hat{x}}{x}} = \frac{1}{SC} \tag{4.9}$$

As can be seen, the OL is simply the **reciprocal value** of the safety coefficient. The higher the SC, the more certain is the sales situation and therefore the lower the OL and with it the 'risk'. Both SC and OL are often referred to as 'risk measures'. However, '**risk**' often refers only to 'negative' environmental states, with 'chance' as a counterpart. However, interpreting **risk** as a **probability distribution** of certain parameters, that is, with the possible inclusion of both positive and negative developments, then these SC and OL concepts are not covered by the measures at all which can lead to problematic consequences.

Example The operating leverage is often applied in connection with procedural changeovers that change cost structures (lower variable costs and higher fixed costs). Frequently, it is assumed that the procedure with the lower unit cost is riskier than the other procedure because – independent of the fixed costs – the lower variable unit costs are said to induce a bigger variability in profit. This statement can be understood if the risk is presented by the **profit variance**. With the sales volume $\tilde{x}$ as the only uncertain measure, the profit variance arises as follows:

$$\sigma^2\left(\tilde{\Pi}\right) = \sigma^2\left(\tilde{x} \cdot cm - C^F\right) = \sigma^2\left(\tilde{x} \cdot cm\right) = \sigma^2\left(\tilde{x}\right) \cdot cm^2 = \sigma^2\left(\tilde{x}\right) \cdot \left(p - c\right)^2 \tag{4.10}$$

Therefore, lower variable unit costs c lead to a higher contribution margin cm and to a higher profit variance; and on the contrary, the (constant) fixed costs have no consequences for the risk represented by that measure.

However, these relationships do not apply to the operating leverage. In accordance with (4.9), lower unit costs induce a higher contribution margin and thereby a lower break-even amount and a higher safety coefficient which results in a lower operating leverage. The effect of the unit costs works in exactly the **reverse direction** for OL. On the other hand, higher fixed costs cause a higher OL, while the profit variance remains unaffected.

► Example

The sales volume variance amounts to 150 and the sales price is 10. Two procedures with the following data are available:

$$C_1^F = 1000;\ c_1 = 8;\ \Rightarrow\ cm_1 = 2;\ \hat{x}_1 = \frac{1000}{2} = 500$$

$$C_2^F = 2000;\ c_2 = 6;\ \Rightarrow\ cm_2 = 4;\ \hat{x}_2 = \frac{2000}{4} = 500$$

The profit variances arise as follows:

$$\text{Variance of Procedure 1}: \sigma^2\left(\tilde{\Pi}_1\right) = \sigma^2\left(\tilde{x}\right) \cdot cm_1^2 = 150 \cdot 2^2 = 150 \cdot 4 = 600$$

$$\text{Variance of Procedure 2}: \sigma^2\left(\tilde{\Pi}_2\right) = \sigma^2\left(\tilde{x}\right) \cdot cm_2^2 = 150 \cdot 4^2 = 150 \cdot 16 = 2400$$

Based on the variance, Procedure 2 shows a higher risk even though both procedures have **identical break-even amounts** and with them **identical values for** *SC* and *OL*, no matter what initial amount x is chosen. ◄

Important

The qualities of *SC* and *OL* with regard to the representation of risk also depend on the measurement of risk. If the **variation coefficient** (as a relative measure) replaces the variance (as an absolute measure), the assessment changes.

The variation coefficient *VC* is defined as the relation between the standard deviation and the expected value:

$$VC = \sigma(\Pi) / \left|\mathrm{E}[\Pi]\right| \quad \left(\mathrm{E}[\Pi] \neq 0\right)$$

Transformed into:

$$VC = \frac{(p-c)\cdot\sigma(x)}{\left|(p-c)\cdot\mathrm{E}[x] - C^F\right|} = \frac{\sigma(x)}{\left|\mathrm{E}[x] - \hat{x}\right|}$$

With an expected positive profit, the risk measure *VC* rises (drops) with falling (rising) break-even amounts. However, a higher break-even amount also induces a lower value of *SC* (or a higher value of *OL*) and therefore a rise of the measured risk; in this case the assessments correspond to each other.

There is another reason for a cautious use of *SC* or *OL*, unless an explicit consideration of the probability distributions is assured: particularly, if the initial amount x is based on the capacity utilisation. If, for example, $x = 4000$ and $\hat{x} = 2000$ are assumed, the $SC = 0.5$. Therefore, a capacity utilisation of 50% is regarded as sufficient to avoid entrance into the loss zone. This might imply a good 'cushion' and a low loss risk, but this conclusion is absurd – for example, if the probability to reach sales of more than 2000 units is *zero*. This understanding has caused the development of the so-called **stochastic break-even analysis**. This will be considered in the next section.

4.2.4 Stochastic Break-Even Analysis: The Single-Product Case

An explicit examination of the company's profit probability distribution helps to better assess risk. As its distribution arises from the distributions of the individual factors determining the actual profit, the analysis must begin with these single distributions. Initially, the *basic model* of the cost-volume-profit relationship/break-even analysis was (4.1) related to the additional **risky sales volumes** while all other factors (prices, unit cost, fixed costs) were considered constant. An expected profit arises as follows:

$$\mathrm{E}[\Pi] = \mathrm{E}[x] \cdot cm - C^F \tag{4.11}$$

with E[·] as a mathematical expected value operator. Now the risk manifests itself in the **probability** that a certain **success level** $\underline{\Pi}$ is achieved:

$$\Pr\{\tilde{\Pi} \geq \underline{\Pi}\} \tag{4.12}$$

Pr[·] is the probability that the condition applies. For $\underline{\Pi} = 0$ the **break-even probability** can be derived as:

$$Pr\{\tilde{\Pi} \geq 0\} \Leftrightarrow Pr\left\{\tilde{x} \geq \hat{x}\right\} \tag{4.13}$$

If the distribution of the sales volumes corresponds to particular standard distributions, the profit probabilities can be determined analytically.

Example Assuming that the sales volume x has a uniform distribution in the interval $[\underline{x}, \overline{x}]$, the density function $f(x)$ and the distribution function $F(x)$ of the sales volumes are as follows:

$$f(x) = \frac{1}{\overline{x} - \underline{x}}; \quad F(x) = \frac{x - \underline{x}}{\overline{x} - \underline{x}} \quad x \in [\underline{x}; \overline{x}] \tag{4.14}$$

The **break-even probability** follows from (4.13) and (4.14):

$$Pr\{\tilde{\Pi} \geq 0\} = 1 - F(\hat{x}) \tag{4.15}$$

Analogously, appropriate probabilities can be derived for any level of $\underline{\Pi}$ by adding $\underline{\Pi}$ to the fixed costs.

► Example

The sales volumes have a uniform distribution in the interval [0; 10,000]. Then, the density function amounts to 0.0001 with a distribution function $F(x) = 0.0001x$ for all x in the given interval. With a contribution margin cm = 50 and fixed costs of 200,000, a **break-even amount** of 4,000 is found. The value of the distribution function at this point amounts to 0.4 with a **break-even probability** of 0.6; that is, in 60% of all cases a profit is expected. The probabilities for some other success levels are as follows:

$$Pr\{\tilde{\Pi} \geq \underline{\Pi} = -100{,}000\} = 1 - F(2000) = 0.8$$

$$Pr\{\tilde{\Pi} \geq \underline{\Pi} = 125{,}000\} = 1 - F(6500) = 0.35$$

$$Pr\{\tilde{\Pi} \geq \underline{\Pi} = 480{,}000\} = 1 - F(13{,}600) = 0$$

4

The distribution in general can be determined for different levels of profit as follows: the **break-even amount** for a profit $\underline{\Pi}$ is:

$$\hat{x} = \frac{200{,}000 + \underline{\Pi}}{50} = 4{,}000 + 0.02 \cdot \underline{\Pi}$$

Set into the expression $1 - F(\hat{x})$, it arises:

$$1 - F(\hat{x}) = \frac{\overline{x} - \hat{x}}{\overline{x} - \underline{x}} = \frac{10{,}000 - 4000 - 0.02 \cdot \underline{\Pi}}{10{,}000 - 0} = 0.6 - 0.000002 \cdot \underline{\Pi}$$

And it follows from it that:

$$\Pr\{\tilde{\Pi} \geq \underline{\Pi}\} = \begin{cases} 0 & \text{if } \underline{\Pi} \geq 300{,}000 \\ 0.6 - 0.000002\underline{\Pi} & \text{if } -200{,}000 < \underline{\Pi} < 300{,}000 \\ 1 & \text{if } \underline{\Pi} \leq -200{,}000 \end{cases}$$ ◄

For the determination of the distribution function at $\hat{x}$ it must be considered that the **break-even amount** does not necessarily have to lie within the interval of the possible sales volumes. If it is lower than the lower interval limit, a probability of 1 (100%) arises; if it is higher than the upper interval limit, the probability is 0. All other areas can apply the distribution function of the sales volumes, therefore:

$$Pr\{\tilde{\Pi} \geq 0\} = \begin{cases} 0 & \text{if } \hat{x} \geq \overline{x} \\ \frac{\overline{x} - \hat{x}}{\overline{x} - \underline{x}} & \text{if } \underline{x} < \hat{x} < \overline{x} \\ 1 & \text{if } \hat{x} \leq \underline{x} \end{cases} \tag{4.16}$$

Now, the previous question can also be reversed: by how much is the **maximum profit** exceeded with a **given probability**? That is, the profit $\underline{\Pi}$ is searched for with:

$$Pr\{\tilde{\Pi} \geq \underline{\Pi}\} = \overline{Pr} \tag{4.17}$$

Because of $Pr\{\tilde{\Pi} \geq \underline{\Pi}\} = 1 - F(\hat{x})$, for uniform distributions of sales volumes x follows:

$$1 - F(\hat{x}) = \frac{\overline{x} - \hat{x}}{\overline{x} - \underline{x}} = \frac{\overline{x} - \dfrac{C^F + \underline{\Pi}}{cm}}{\overline{x} - \underline{x}} = \overline{\Pr} \tag{4.18}$$

This can be dissolved towards Π, from which follows:

$$\underline{\Pi} = cm\left(\overline{x} - \overline{\Pr}\cdot\left(\overline{x} - \underline{x}\right)\right) - C^F \tag{4.19}$$

Evidently, both questions represent identical occurrences, as the given formula must only be solved towards one measure in each case.

Simulation Procedures

Simulation procedures work as follows (see for example Hertz 1964):

(a) First, the parameters (e.g. sales price, sales volume, unit cost) considered to be uncertain are selected.

(b) Then, an isolated probability distribution is estimated for every uncertain parameter.

(c) In the third step, the initial asset values are determined for a simulation run by producing random numbers in uniform distribution within the interval [0, 1]. Based on them and in accordance with the respective *distribution function* of the uncertain parameters, the specific parameter values are transformed (e.g. if $F(x)$ is the (constant) distribution function of the uncertain sales volume x and the random number is 0.4, then the sales volume for the simulation run arises from $x = F^{-1}(0.4)$). Stochastic dependences between parameters can be considered by successive procedures. If, for example, the distribution of the sales volumes depends on the sales price, the sales price is transformed in the first step and in the second step, the appropriate sales volume is generated from the sales volume distribution *conditional* on this price.

(d) With the parameters determined in the third step, the target measure is calculated.

(e) Steps (3) and (4) are repeated continuously (e.g. 10,000 times).

(f) The distribution function of the target measure is determined from its relative frequencies.

The case of the **normal distribution of random variables** is considered in the literature, as the data can be located in standard normal distribution tables. In addition, the assumption of a normal distribution has the advantage that in the case of additive linkages of several random variables of normal distribution (for example, in the multi-product case) the resulting total random variable shows normal distribution and can therefore be derived from the standard tables (uniform distribution is less 'friendly' in the multi-product case). Yet, even the normal distribution encounters difficulties if multiplicative linkages of random variables exist (e.g. if the contribution margin is also uncertain). Usually, a random variable arising as a product of two normally distributed random variables is not normally distributed anymore and the standard table procedure can only be regarded as a preliminary approximation of unproven 'quality'. In the case of more complex stochastic relations, **direct simulation procedures** must be used for the determination of the distribution function of the uncertain profit.

The previous analysis did not explain *how* to use the information about the probabilities within the decision-making framework. In general, information provided should 'fit' to the decision criteria to which they are applied. The information of the **stochastic break-even analysis** fits best for the following two decision theoretical **criteria**:

- **Probability maximisation with a given profit amount**: The alternative with the maximum probability that a certain result is at least reached is chosen. With a minimum profit of 0, this is generally the alternative with the maximum break-even probability. However, it is the alternative with the highest $Pr\left\{\tilde{\Pi} \geq \underline{\Pi}\right\}$.
- **Profit maximisation with a given probability**: The alternative with the highest profit achieved with a given probability is chosen. The maximum profit $\underline{\Pi}$ with the relation $Pr\left\{\tilde{\Pi} \geq \underline{\Pi}\right\} = \overline{Pr}$ is considered.

▶ Example

Assume the previous example (uniform distribution of sales volumes in the interval [0, 10,000] with fixed costs of 200,000 and a contribution margin of 50). Assume also additional capacity is at the firm's disposal. To hire additional sales staff, additional fixed costs of 90,000 are incurred and an increase of the upper limit of the sales volume distribution is 12,500 (with given uniform distribution assumed).

Probability maximisation with given profit amount

In the initial situation a given minimum profit of $\underline{\Pi} = 200{,}000$ would require a sales volume of at least 8000 achievable with a probability of 0.2. With additional staff and additional fixed costs, the amount required rises to at least 9800. The increased upper limit of the sales volume distribution is reached with the following probability:

$$1 - \frac{9800}{12{,}500} = 0.216$$

Therefore, hiring additional sales staff is the preferred choice.

Profit maximisation with given probability

With a given probability of $\overline{\text{Pr}} = 0.55$ the following profit results:

$$\underline{\Pi} = 50 \times \left[10{,}000 - 0.55 \times (10{,}000 - 0)\right] - 200{,}000 = 25{,}000$$

With additional sales staff this becomes

$$\underline{\Pi} = 50 \times \left[12{,}500 - 0.55 \times (12{,}500 - 0)\right] - 290{,}000 = -8{,}750$$

Now it is preferable to renounce the option of additional sales staff. ◀

▪ Value at Risk (VaR) and Cash Flow at Risk (CFaR)

The stochastic **break-even analysis** is closely related to specific risk measures which have attained a special importance in practical **risk management** during the past few years. Primarily financial institutions with their trading strategies in the capital markets have paid particular attention to 'useful' measures of risks. One typical measure is the ***Value at Risk*** (VaR) as a variant of the so-called **downside risk.** Here, the change ΔV of the value of a portfolio of financial securities in the course of a certain holding period (e.g. 10 days) is considered. Such value changes can be positive or negative and are associated with a probability distribution. For market-traded financial securities, such distributions can be estimated. For example, based on daily stock prices and on a probability distribution, the question about a certain loss not exceeded with a given probability $\overline{Pr}$ during the holding period under consideration can be answered. This amount is called **VaR**. Conversely, this means that the **incoming losses** will exceed the VaR only with the counterprobability (e.g. 5%).

Therefore, formally the VaR arises from:

$$Pr\{\Delta W \geq VaR\} = \overline{Pr}$$

The definition of the VaR is completely analogous to the problem definitions described in (4.17); that is, the determination of the maximum profit exceeded with a given probability.

VaR as a measure of risk is a popular measure in the financial industry (e.g. $RORAC$ as the *Return on Risk Adjusted Capital* with the VaR representing the 'capital' in the denominator). Its application in other industries is connected with **problems** as they prioritise the **volatility** of a company's surpluses. The distributions of these surpluses change from period to period depending upon the strategies pursued by the company and its competitors. Previous market data are not reliable bases for the risk measurement. The ***Cash Flow at Risk*** ($CFaR$) was promoted for these industries to consider their peculiarities. CF as the operational cash flow of a company within a period leads to the following **definition**, which is analogous to the VaR:

$$Pr\{CF \geq CFaR\} = \overline{Pr}$$

The distribution of the operational cash flows is based on the single distributions of the procurement prices, sales prices, exchange rates, sales volumes, etc. Basically, the $CFaR$ is a **variation of the stochastic break-even analysis** under application of a **simulation** as a method to determine the total distribution of surpluses. In this context, the stochastic break-even analysis, under a different name, is of special interest here.

4.2.5 Multi-Product Break-Even Analysis

The multi-product scenario opens up the same questions as the single-product scenario. However, the analysis is more complicated due to the **balancing effects** that may appear between the different product types, for example, certain product types might compensate for contribution margins not achieved by a particular product. The analysis depends solely on the aggregate production programme and whether the total desired results have been achieved or not.

Now, there is not only *one* break-even amount but a **multiplicity of product quantity combinations** that cover the fixed costs and the subsequent achievement of a minimum profit $\underline{\Pi}$. The following reverts to the deterministic model. $\hat{\mathbf{X}}$ as the quantity combinations of sales volumes of the individual product types $j = 1, \ldots, J$ and $\hat{\mathbf{x}} = (\hat{x}_1, \hat{x}_2, \ldots, \hat{x}_J) \in \hat{\mathbf{X}}$ as a (non-negative) sales volume vector, the quantity combinations are defined as follows:

$$\hat{\mathbf{X}} = \left\{ \hat{\mathbf{x}} \geq \mathbf{0} \middle| \sum_{j=1}^{J} \hat{x}_j \cdot cm_j = C^F + \underline{\Pi} \right\} \tag{4.20}$$

The **two products case** (4.20) can be presented in the form of straight lines:

$$\hat{x}_1 \cdot cm_1 + \hat{x}_2 \cdot cm_2 = C^F + \underline{\Pi} \Rightarrow \hat{x}_2 = \frac{C^F + \underline{\Pi}}{cm_2} - \frac{cm_1}{cm_2} \cdot \hat{x}_1 \tag{4.21}$$

However, with **more than two products** such dissolution is impossible (positive contribution margins are assumed for every product). Then, the following options arise: the *isolated break-even amount* $\hat{x}_j^i$ is calculated for *every* product, that is, it is implied that each product has to cover $C^F + \underline{\Pi}$. J different break-even amounts can be easily determined according to (4.2) or (4.3). These isolated sets indicate the respective upper limits of the individual product types in (4.20) and, at the same time, are elements of $\hat{\mathbf{X}}$ as vectors with the jth component being positive. These J vectors are *linearly independent* and mark the vector space of the dimension J. Every break-even vector from $\hat{\mathbf{X}}$ can be a **convex combination** of the isolated break-even vectors. The arbitrary component j of $\hat{\mathbf{x}} \in \hat{\mathbf{X}}$ simply arises by the multiplication of the *isolated break-even amount* $\hat{x}_j^i$ of the product j with a non-negative share α_j (with all products' shares adding up to 1).

With $\hat{\mathbf{x}}_\mathbf{j} = (0, \supset, \hat{x}_j^i \supset, 0)$, that is, the isolated break-even vector for the product j, it follows for each $\hat{\mathbf{x}} \in \hat{\mathbf{X}}$:

$$\hat{\mathbf{x}} = \alpha_1 \cdot \hat{\mathbf{x}}_\mathbf{1} + \alpha_2 \cdot \hat{\mathbf{x}}_\mathbf{2} + \cdots + \alpha_J \cdot \hat{\mathbf{x}}_\mathbf{J} = \sum_{j=1}^{J} \alpha_j \cdot \hat{\mathbf{x}}_\mathbf{J} \tag{4.22}$$

with $\alpha_j \geq 0 \quad \forall_j; \quad \sum_{j=1}^{J} \alpha_j = 1.$

- **Constant Sales Mix**

In situations of a constant **'sales mix'** of the product types, the multiple-products case can be related back to the one-product case, as the respective quantities of each product can be derived as a function of the leading product. In the following, the first product is chosen as the leading product, and β_j are the constants of the sales volumes of the products j towards the amount of Product 1:

$$\beta_j = \frac{x_j}{x_1} \quad \text{for } j = 1, \ldots, J \tag{4.23}$$

Now, the total contribution margin CM can be written as

$$CM = \sum_{j=1}^{J} x_j \cdot cm_j = \sum_{j=1}^{J} \left(x_1 \cdot \beta_j\right) \cdot cm_j = x_1 \cdot \sum_{j=1}^{J} \beta_j \cdot cm_j = x_1 \cdot \overline{cm} \tag{4.24}$$

The **break-even amount** of the leading product can be derived from:

$$\hat{x}_1 = \frac{C^F + \Pi}{\overline{cm}} \tag{4.25}$$

and then the amounts of the products can be easily found by use of (4.23) and (4.25).

With a constant sales mix a **break even sales** can be calculated as:

$$\hat{R} = \sum_{j=1}^{J} \hat{x}_1 \cdot p_j = x_1 \cdot \sum_{j=1}^{J} \beta_1 \cdot p_j = x_1 \cdot \overline{p} \tag{4.26}$$

(4.25) extended by $\overline{p}$ is as follows:

$$\hat{R} = \overline{p} \cdot \hat{x}_1 = \frac{C^F + \Pi}{\overline{cm} / \overline{p}} \tag{4.27}$$

In accordance with (4.24) $\overline{cm}$ is the sum of the weighted contribution margins of all products. The relationships of the total contribution margin CM_j of a product type j to the sales are as follows:

$$\frac{CM_j}{R} = \frac{x_j \cdot cm_j}{x_1 \cdot \overline{p}} = \frac{x_j \cdot \left(\beta_j \cdot cm_j\right)}{x_1 \cdot \overline{p}} = \frac{\beta_j \cdot cm_j}{\overline{p}} \tag{4.28}$$

Therefore, the relation between contribution margins and sales is given and constant for every product j. The *break-even sales* result from it:

$$\hat{R} = \frac{C^F + \Pi}{\sum_{j=1}^{J} \frac{CM_j}{R}} \tag{4.29}$$

▶ Example

There are $J = 4$ product types with the following contribution margins:

$$cm_1 = 50; \; cm_2 = 100; \; cm_3 = 80; \; cm_4 = 120$$

The fixed costs are 240,000. A minimum profit is not required and the 'pure' break-even case is considered. The resulting isolated *break-even amounts* are as follows:

$$\hat{x}_1^i = 4{,}800; \; \hat{x}_2^i = 2{,}400; \; \hat{x}_3^i = 3{,}000; \; \hat{x}_4^i = 2{,}000$$

Then, an arbitrary *break-even vector* can be written with the non-negative α_i adding up to 1 as follows:

$$\begin{bmatrix} \hat{x}_1 \\ \hat{x}_2 \\ \hat{x}_3 \\ \hat{x}_4 \end{bmatrix} = \alpha_1 \cdot \begin{bmatrix} 4{,}800 \\ 0 \\ 0 \\ 0 \end{bmatrix} + \alpha_2 \cdot \begin{bmatrix} 0 \\ 2{,}400 \\ 0 \\ 0 \end{bmatrix} + \alpha_3 \cdot \begin{bmatrix} 0 \\ 0 \\ 3{,}000 \\ 0 \end{bmatrix} + \alpha_4 \cdot \begin{bmatrix} 0 \\ 0 \\ 0 \\ 2{,}000 \end{bmatrix} = \alpha_1 \cdot \begin{bmatrix} \alpha_1 \cdot 4{,}800 \\ \alpha_2 \cdot 2{,}400 \\ \alpha_3 \cdot 3{,}000 \\ \alpha_4 \cdot 2{,}000 \end{bmatrix}$$

With, for example, $\alpha_j = 0.25$ follows for all j:

$$\hat{x}_1 = 1{,}200;\ \hat{x}_2 = 600;\ \hat{x}_3 = 750;\ \hat{x}_4 = 500$$

In the reverse way for any arbitrary *break-even vector*, the amounts can be determined, for example: the following *break-even vector* is given:

$$\hat{x}_1 = 2{,}000;\ \hat{x}_2 = 200;\ \hat{x}_3 = 0;\ \hat{x}_4 = 1{,}000$$

This vector can be represented as a convex combination of the isolated *break-even vectors* with the following shares:

$$\alpha_1 = \frac{2{,}000}{4{,}800} = 0.41\overline{6};\quad \alpha_2 = \frac{200}{2{,}400} = 0.08\overline{3};\quad \alpha_3 = 0;\quad \alpha_3 = \frac{1{,}000}{2{,}000} = 0.5$$

They sum to 100% again. ◀

The use of **break-even sales** in the multiple-products case is very popular as sales are **linear**, easily observable and one-dimensional. In contrast, the **multi-dimensional product mix** is more difficult to interpret and requires a comparison with the break-even vectors $\hat{\mathbf{X}}$. The rigid assumption of a constant sales mix is often forgotten with the obviously easy application of break-even sales. If this assumption is fulfilled, the observation of the leading product is sufficient, that is, the analysis of multiple products is not necessary at all. If it is not fulfilled, the observation of sales yields little information as the precise analysis depends again on *which* products have actually contributed to sales.

► Example

The last example is continued by assuming product relations of 1: 2: 3.375: 4. Then it follows:

$$\overline{cm} = 1 \cdot 50 + 2 \cdot 100 + 3.375 \cdot 80 + 4 \cdot 120 = 1{,}000.$$

The break-even amount of the leading product is as follows:

$$\hat{x}_1 = \frac{240{,}000}{1{,}000} = 240$$

The other quantities result from it as follows:

$$\hat{x}_2 = 240 \cdot 2 = 480;\ \hat{x}_3 = 240 \cdot 3.375 = 810;\ \hat{x}_4 = 240 \cdot 4 = 960$$

If the following prices are assumed:

$$p_1 = 110;\ p_2 = 200;\ p_3 = 160;\ p_4 = 220$$

follows: $\bar{p} = 1 \cdot 110 + 2 \cdot 200 + 3.375 \cdot 160 + 4 \cdot 220 = 1{,}930$

$$\frac{CM_1}{R} = \frac{50}{1{,}930};\ \frac{CM_2}{R} = \frac{200}{1{,}930};\ \frac{CM_3}{R} = \frac{270}{1{,}930};\ \frac{CM_4}{R} = \frac{480}{1{,}930}$$

The sum of these relations amounts to 1000/1930 and with it the *break-even sales* is calculated as:

$$\hat{R} = \frac{240{,}000}{\frac{1{,}000}{1{,}930}} = \frac{240{,}000 \cdot 1{,}930}{1{,}000} = 463{,}200$$

The reader can easily check that the resulting combination (240; 480; 810; 960) equals the sales. Moreover, because of the constant sales mix this combination is unambiguous. ◄

- **Pessimistic and Optimistic Variations**

To get a better understanding of the width of the profit zone to be expected in the context of an uncertain sales mix, it is possible to calculate a **pessimistic case** and an **optimistic case** with sales limits being observed. In the pessimistic case, products are sorted in ascending order based upon their individual relationships between contribution margin and sales relations CM_j/R_j, beginning with the product with the lowest relative contribution margin. It is assumed that the revenues are generated in accordance with this order. The first revenues are exclusively achieved by the product with the lowest relation CM_j/R_j up to its upper sales limit (or its otherwise budgeted amount) and is then followed by the second worst product, etc. In the case of a missing sales limit, only the 'worst' product is used in determining the break-even sales.

Conversely, the **optimistic case** ranks products in descending order of CM_j/R_j, beginning with the product with the highest individual contribution margin. ◘ Figure 4.2 shows both of these cases for three products.

Obviously, the break-even sales in the pessimistic case is essentially higher than that in the optimistic case. The result of the version with a constant sales mix lies between the two results achieved in the pessimistic and the optimistic cases.

Stochastic analysis has been developed for the multi-product case, for example, by Johnson and Simik (1971) or Miller and Morris (1985). The intentions of such analyses are completely analogous to those of the one product case, so a presentation is not shown here. Problems of stochastic interdependences between different product types are treated in the next section in detail.

4.2.6 Result

The above descriptions attempt to demonstrate that a break-even analysis serves, firstly of all, for getting a feeling for the meaning of **uncertainty**. Secondly, it can also fulfil an important **signalling function** that can lead to the procurement of

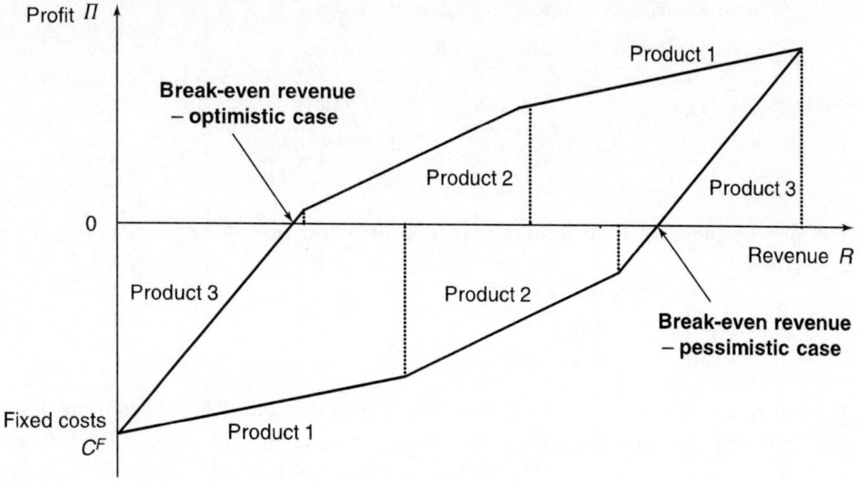

Fig. 4.2 Break-even sales variations with three products

further information and/or more extensive plans incorporating an explicit **inclusion of probability distributions**. Insights gained from a stochastic break-even analysis may contribute to the latter. The **problems** of a break-even analysis mainly relate to the fact that no practical implications follow as to how specifically its results should be implemented. The results of the stochastic break-even analysis are in accordance with—as shown—decision criteria under risk, but these are of a rather specialised nature. Therefore, it seems necessary to examine the planning problems under risk more closely with an explicit analysis of the consequences of different problem structures according to short-term company policy.

4.3 Summary

For decision-making with uncertain expectations, several approaches exist. Firstly, it can be meaningful to develop an understanding of the uncertainty's importance for the existing decision problem. The analysis of **cost-volume-profit relationships** (i.e. a **break-even analysis**) can contribute to that. Secondly, in its non-stochastic version, it shows production amounts (or combinations of production amounts) that neither achieve a profit nor a loss nor reach a certain minimum profit. The resulting formula can be used to answer various questions. In particular, 'risk measures' can be determined in the form of the **safety coefficient** and the **operating leverage**. Their problem is that they are calculated independently from the probability distributions. To better understand such distributions a **stochastic break-even analysis** can be introduced, which is currently discussed in practice under the name of **Cash Flow at Risk**. Ultimately, the problem with all different break-even analyses lies in the fact that it remains open about how to finally decide what the solution structure looks like under uncertainty.

4.4 Assessment Material

Review Questions

1. Why is it important to explicitly consider aspects of uncertainty even for short-term decision problems?
2. Which questions does a sensitivity analysis respond to, and which relationship exists between sensitivity and break-even analysis?
3. Can a break-even analysis in a single-product case be exclusively applied in a company with only one product?
4. Describe 'risk measures' derived from a break-even analysis. What are their problems?
5. How do the non-stochastic and the stochastic variations of the break-even analysis differ?
6. Which peculiarities must be considered for a multi-product break-even analysis?
7. An article by Miller and Morris (1985) deals with the conditions of a multi-product break-even analysis with uncertain contribution margins. The analysis takes place in two steps. In the first step, the 'optimal' production programme is determined on the basis of the maximisation of the expected profit. Then, in the second step, probability information is calculated for the 'optimal' production amounts now known for different profit levels. How do you assess such a procedure?

Exercises

1. **Break-even analysis of a single-product company**. A company produces one product, of which the sales price is $p = 120$ and variable costs are $c = 80$ per unit.
   (a) How large is the break-even volume with fixed costs of 10,000, 20,000 and 30,000? How would you answer the question if there was a required minimum profit of $\Pi = 35{,}000$?
   (b) The fixed costs for the current year are now set at 10,000. Assume that you can expect an annual rate of increase in the fixed costs of 5% and an annual rate of increase in the variable unit costs of 2% for the next 3 years. How must the volumes sold change if the company is to achieve an annual minimum profit of $\Pi = 20{,}000$? How would you answer this question if, for example, the minimum profit had to increase annually by 10%?
   (c) Using the information contained in Part (b) of the assignment, assume now that the company cannot achieve sales volumes above the break-even volume for the current year because this represents the maximum market demand. How high would the annual increase in sales prices (with sales constantly equivalent to the current break-even volume at any point in time) have to be to achieve the above minimum profit?
   (d) Using the information contained in Part (b) of the assignment, assume now that the company does not expect any increase in the variable unit costs, but that it is threatened with an annual drop in sales prices of 3%. How would the variable units costs (with the given sales amounting to the current break-even volume at any one time and with the other given data) have to

change in order to achieve the desired minimum profits given in Part (b) of the assignment?

(e) Assume fixed costs amounting to 20,000 and a desired minimum profit of $\underline{\Pi} = 40{,}000$. The current level of sales is 2000 units. How large is the safety coefficient and the operating leverage at this sales level? How can these figures be intuitively interpreted? How do they change if the variable costs per unit are 70, 60 or 50?

2. **Stochastic break-even analysis**. A single-product company has fixed costs of 100,000 and achieves a contribution margin of 5 per unit. The sales volumes are connected to risk and are evenly spread over the interval [2,000; 42,000].
   (a) Calculate the break-even probability with minimum profits of $\underline{\Pi} = 0$, 50,000 and 150,000? What is the probability of at least covering the cash flow relevant fixed costs if they amount to 8,000, 20,000 or 50,000?
   (b) What is the maximum profit that can be exceeded with a 70% probability?

3. **Break-even analysis of a multi-product company**. A company manufactures five products yielding the following unit contribution margins:

Product	$j = 1$	$j = 2$	$j = 3$	$j = 4$	$j = 5$
Price p_j	23	59	99	18	145
Variable costs c_j	13	44	69	13	95

The fixed costs amount to 400,000.

(a) Prepare a general presentation on all of the possible combinations of sales volumes that earn a minimum $\underline{\Pi} = 50{,}000$.

(b) Now, assume that the products are characterised by a constant sales mix with Product 1 as the leading product. The respective ratios of sales are as follows:

$$\beta_2 = 1;\ \beta_3 = 2;\ \beta_4 = 4;\ \beta_5 = 6$$

Under these conditions, calculate the break-even volumes for each of the products? What partial coefficients characterise these break-even volumes within the scope of the general presentation in Part (a)? Calculate the break-even revenues?

(c) What are the break-even revenues in Part (a) using both the optimistic and the pessimistic approach?

Cost Management

Contents

P. Schuster et al., *Management Accounting*,
Springer Texts in Business and Economics,
https://doi.org/10.1007/978-3-030-62022-6_5

Learning Objectives

After studying this chapter, you should be able to:

- Understand the range and contents of cost management
- Present value chain analysis and strategic cost analysis as elements of strategic management accounting
- Use activity-based costing for cost management
- Illustrate target costing
- Present life cycle costing

5.1 Contents of Cost Management

In previous chapters, costs were considered as given, and with it, their use for specific decisions, such as production programme or price decisions, were also considered. This chapter addresses the **management** of **costs** (and **revenues**). It deals with activities that **influence** costs for the improvement of the company's economic viability. This **influencing** includes

- **Cost Level**: Management of factor prices (e.g. by supplier selection or make-or-buy decisions) and of factor amounts (e.g. by quality management and rationalisation).
- **Cost Structure**: Changing the proportions of variable and fixed costs as well as direct and indirect costs (e.g. by capacity utilisation or outsourcing).
- **Cost Behaviour Patterns**: Avoidance of progressive cost patterns (e.g. by complexity reduction or increased use of identical components).

Cost management has recently focused on **long-term activities** to influence costs. Short-term cost management often cannot affect the actual causes of costs because they are regularly determined by strategic decisions such as company strategy, long-term production programme (e.g. the variety of variants), production technology (e.g. high complexity) or the degree of vertical integration.

New **manufacturing technologies** such as flexible manufacturing systems and *computer-integrated manufacturing* with several *computer-aided tasks* affect production costs in the long run. Empirically, it has been estimated to be in the range of 70–80% of current production costs. The on-going management of costs is not useful in such a situation, but mainly supports short-term decisions such as those about the organisation of the production process.

Applying new manufacturing technologies shifts **cost structures** to an increased proportion of **fixed costs** in relation to total production costs. The reason for this is a higher level of automation including higher depreciation, a higher cost of capital and a reduction (or even full elimination) of direct labour costs.

Increased **competition** forces rapid adaptation to short-term changes in customer demand and the introduction of new products and services. Therefore, **product life cycles** are substantially shortened, but preceding costs (e.g. research and development and the costs of the market launch) do not decrease. On the contrary, preceding costs rise relative to the total production costs. Similar observations can be made for the downstream costs (e.g. customer service or product disposal). A management accounting system strictly related to time periods cannot substantially support these decisions.

These environmental developments have effects on the **management accounting system** and its optimal **degree of complexity**.

- The rising **complexity** of economic relations and business performance requires a more complex management accounting system to sufficiently illustrate economic circumstances.
- The rising **dynamics** of the environment necessitates rapid adaptations of the management accounting systems. Once the operational structure is sufficiently modelled, it may change again.

The management accounting system must adapt to these competing requirements because cost-benefit considerations determine the optimal degree of complexity. For example, it has been suggested that the current management accounting system should only be used in a rough form with specific questions analysed in greater detail on a case by case basis.

The target of cost management is to influence the causes of costs as soon as possible (so-called **proactive cost management**). Starting points of cost management can be company's **products**, **processes** or **resources**. This chapter presents and discusses some of these concepts and instruments, with a focus on the shaping of the **information system**, which provides decision support for cost management. 'Traditional' management accounting systems are regularly accused of not being suitable for it without appropriate adaptations or without introducing other instruments, some of which will be analysed subsequently.

The relationship between cost management and company strategy is firstly discussed. In particular, value chain analysis, the consideration of non-company data and the stronger use of non-monetary measures will be discussed, followed by the application possibilities of activity-based costing to products, processes and resources. Finally, with their primary focus on products, target costing and life cycle costing will be considered.

This chapter deals with **information systems** that should enable better decisions for the management of costs. The use of **incentives** for responsible employees to reduce costs based upon predetermined targets is not covered. Such considerations of **behavioural control** are discussed in detail in subsequent chapters of this book.

5.2 Cost Management and Company Strategy

5.2.1 The Management Accounting System and Company Strategy

According to Porter (1980), **competitive strategies** can be based upon the following two options:

- Cost leadership
- Differentiation

In each case, they are related to either the firm's total market or separate market segments (concentration) in which the firm competes.

Cost leadership encompasses the strategies by which the company wants to become or remain the least expensive producer in their industry. With a product having similar features (customer's utility) as rival products, customers are generally willing to pay the same price (market price). Lower costs are the reason for the success of this approach as: the company with the lowest costs attains higher profits than their competitors (assuming the same sales price applies to all firms). Cost leadership works particularly well for standardised products that are mass produced.

With **differentiation**, the company seeks to produce a unique product. Every product can be regarded as a bundle of different qualities that contributes to fulfilling the customer's utility. If a product combines qualities that customers regard as important, they will be willing to pay a higher price for it. Examples of the use of a differentiation strategy include quality, longevity, image, customer service or fast delivery. A company achieves above-average success when the sales price increase exceeds the (additional) costs of the differentiation due to the additional utility.

The **decision** as to which principle strategy to follow requires cost and revenue information. Different information is required depending on the selected principle strategy that the company will follow. Table 5.1 shows some essential differences depending on the selected strategy (see also, for example, Shank and Govindarajan 1993, p. 18). Traditional management accounting instruments are more relevant for a cost leadership strategy than for a differentiation strategy.

Table 5.1 Competitive strategy and the management accounting system

Cost leadership	Differentiation
Cost leadership requires detailed budgeting and control of costs.	The primary focus is the additional utility of certain product features. With it, revenue budgeting and control become more essential than that of costs.
The optimisation of the production process and the reduction of overhead costs are the focus of operational decisions.	Marketing-political instruments are the focus of operational decisions.
Costs are a primary basis for pricing decisions.	The willingness of customers to pay for the additional utility is particularly relevant for pricing decisions.
Cost variance analysis and cost budgets are essential instruments to assess managers.	Revenue and contribution margin variances are essential instruments to assess managers.

5.2.2 Value Chain Analysis

The absolute and the relative costs of a company are essential for successful strategies. According to Porter (1985), the value chain builds a framework for use within the management accounting system as a basis for the discussion of the cost situation.

The **value chain** encompasses all strategic activities that are necessary for the manufacturing of a product, such as development, production, sales and support activities (e.g. procurement, human resource management, IT). Crucial areas for the creation of value can be identified as a basis for competitive advantage and can then be analysed in relation to all of the company's activities. There can be value chains for the industry in addition to the company or parts of it.

The **demarcation of activities** depends on individual firm circumstances based upon specific products and industry situations as well as the purpose to which the analysis will be subsequently used. The division of activities might be made based upon details using the following **criteria** relating to cost analysis and strategic relevance:

- **Different drivers**. They show (strategic) influences on costs.
- **Economic viability principle**. To examine costs of insignificant activities that should not be analysed separately.
- **Cost dynamics** and strong growth of costs. This points towards a future need for action.
- The products provide other solutions (for customers' requirements) than those of the **competitors**. This is a potential source of cost advantage or product differentiation.

Special attention is paid to the **relation between different activities.** There are three different forms:

1. Linkages of activities **within the value chain**. The cost of activities can be affected by the intensification of another activity. There may be synergetic effects.
2. Interweaving of certain activities with other activities in the **value chains of other company units**. Although strategic business units should be independent, some interweaving often cannot be avoided because they are necessary for business units connected with the company's organisation.
3. Linkages of certain activities with other activities in the **value chains of suppliers and customers** (vertical linkages). Suppliers' and customers' activities can influence the cost and benefits of the company's own activities, and synergies can arise. Strategies like *Just In Time (JIT)* or *Total Quality Management (TQM)* require the inclusion of the suppliers or customers to be successful.

The third form of relation is often not considered in a company's analysis, as it '*starts too late, and it stops too soon*' (Shank 1989, p. 51). There are very few practical examples relating to the application of value chain analysis (see Shank and Govindarajan 1992a, b). **One reason for this** relates to the fact that incumbent management accounting systems often cannot supply the required data. This is due to a variety of reasons. Firstly, the value-generating activities may not correspond with functions or activities in cost centres, which often include very different technologies, activities and business units. If this occurs, the interweaving among business units remains unconsidered. On the other hand, management accounting systems are typically too detailed and precise for strategic decisions, and it is questionable to what extent it is useful to install a separate management accounting component for strategic decisions.

5.2.3 Strategic Cost Analysis

The identification of relevant activities is a prerequisite for strategic cost analysis. The demarcation of the activities is already partially based on cost considerations so that the definition of the activities and the cost analysis are dependent on each other. In the following section, two additional **steps** are discussed. They are as follows:

- Allocation of costs and revenues to the activities
- Determination of cost drivers for the activities

Allocation of Costs and Revenues to the Activities

The allocation of costs is largely analogous to the cost accounting technique used in the cost centres: direct costs are directly related to the activities, indirect costs through the use of different allocation principles. Due to the length of the time period being considered, all costs can be considered as influenceable so that **full costs** are allocated onto the activities. Depending on the circumstances, it is also possible to allocate **revenues**. Presently, the **theoretical foundation** for both is still in its infancy. In the literature, the suggestion of Porter (1985) is typically used without any further consideration. The allocation principles for *ABC* will be shown later, so only two fundamental difficulties are shown here. Essentially, they deal with the following two questions:

1. **Which costs** should actually be allocated to the activities? Actual costs have been suggested, as they are supposed to best approximate long-term costs. Yet, from a strategic perspective, they don't appear to be particularly suitable. If (long-term) budgeted costs are not used, then at least the cost dynamics, which arise from industry growth or technological change, should be incorporated and explicitly considered.
2. How should the **indirect costs** (including fixed costs) be allocated to the activities? This can only be arbitrarily done, and the strong emphasis on linkages and interweaving of activities must have substantial consequences on the cost accounting concept.

Although **no great precision** is required for strategic decisions, the described difficulties can contribute to or detract from real strategic problems. Strategic attempts at cost reduction can lead to the wrong direction being pursued. However, it could be argued that 'modern' accounting systems better resolve this issue now than previous accounting systems did in the past.

- **Determination of Cost Drivers for Activities**

Cost drivers for activities can be:

- Company size: economies and diseconomies of scale
- Experience and learning effects
- Structure of the capacity utilisation
- Linkages within the value chain
- Vertical linkages to suppliers and customers
- Interweaving with activities in the value chains of the company's other strategic business units
- Vertical integration: extent of forward and backward integration
- Timing of strategies: pioneer, early or late market entry
- Other decisions: production programme and technology
- Location
- Institutional conditions: legal rules, taxes and labour unions

Usually, the costs of an activity are not only affected by one single **cost driver** but by **several** ones. The cost drivers are not independent of each other; it is possible that they increase mutually or react contrarily. Examples would be possibly the location and vertical linkages, which can mutually strengthen their effect on costs. A contrary effect could be caused by vertical integration and the timing of strategies (lower flexibility).

The analysis indicates crucial cost drivers. A **cost reduction programme** will start with these. Activities can be divided between value-adding and not value-adding ones. **Value-adding activities** cause a rise in the customer's utility while the **non-value adding activities** do not. They can result, for example, from time delays, waste or bad coordination of subdivisions. They cause activities such as for storage, multiple logistic transactions, quality controls, rework and warranty works. Cost reduction strategies will therefore focus on them.

The **subjective assessment** of the activities and the costs caused by them frequently deviates from each other. This forms a basis for cost reductions as well as for investment strategies in certain activities.

Another strategy is a **change of the value chain's composition**, such as changing the production technology, using another sales channel or alternative raw material, or deciding upon a relocation.

In the case of a **differentiation strategy**, the strategic cost analysis serves as the determination of the (additional) differentiation costs that need to be compared with the additional benefits (revenue analysis). Special emphasis has to be made towards the durability of the differentiation and its related costs.

Which Cost Drivers 'Drive' manufacturing Overhead Costs?
In their much noted article '*The Hidden Factory*', Miller and Vollmann (1985) claim that manufacturing overhead costs are driven less by production volume or direct labour costs than by transactions. They present four different forms of transactions:

- Logistics transactions: for example, receiving materials, transportation and storage
- Balancing transactions: for example, materials planning
- Quality transactions: for example, quality control, rework and repair
- Change transactions: for example, manufacturing changes as a result of new materials or construction changes

Banker et al. (1995) empirically tested this hypothesis and their results support the view that these four transaction types explain about 77% of manufacturing overhead costs. Their findings also support significance for all cost drivers, except for quality transactions. The cost drivers applied are usable factory space per unit (for logistics transactions), number of employees for purchases and manufacturing (for balancing transactions), number of employees occupied with quality transactions and construction changes (for change transactions).

The work by Banker et al. (1995) was among those using empirical correlation or regression analysis in connection with *ABC* at the beginning of the 1990s (see also Foster and Gupta 1990, or Banker and Johnston 1993). Such analyses *can be heavily criticised.* For example, Dopuch (1993) argues that these works contain only indications for the fact that the application of additional and/or other cost drivers leads to revised cost estimations. Whether these are 'better' than the previous ones cannot be clarified as long as the *real* cost function is unknown. The fact that an application of *ABC* cost drivers does not automatically lead to more exact cost estimates is empirically documented, for example, by Noreen and Soderstrom (1994, 1997).

5.2.4 Consideration of Information About Industry Structure

Strategic decisions should not be made on the basis of internal activities and cost analyses alone, as the strategic environment of the company is also important and therefore ought to be considered. Yet, such an **external focus** of the management accounting system is unusual. Therefore, an extension to the management accounting system would involve dealing with, for example, customers, suppliers, and competitors. The components of the industry structure in a model devised by Porter (1980) describe the company embedded in the competitive forces of the industry, and this largely determines the company's costs. These forces are described in the following section.

▪ Customers and Suppliers

Customer information is a crucial component of cost and revenue management (i.e. to which a market orientation of cost management is referred) along with information about suppliers. From a strategic management accounting perspective, **value chain analysis** for customers and suppliers is necessary to recognise the linkages or linkage possibilities. An extension to the transformation from raw materials until the final user receives the end product is suggested. This clarifies the company's own share in the creation of value as well as the share of total profits for all companies in the production chain. This information is helpful in estimating the negotiating power of suppliers and customers.

▪ Competitors

Information about the value chains of **competitors** is essential for several reasons:

- In general, competitors do not have identical value chains. Such differences may represent opportunities for **differentiation** and with it a competitive advantage.
- Information about competitors is also required for an estimation of their **reactions** to particular strategies. If a competitor has a sufficiently flexible value chain, the competitor can diminish the desired effects of cost reduction or differentiation strategies.
- For strategic decisions, not only is the absolute cost relation and position of a company important, but their **relative cost position in comparison to** the leading competitor, a direct competitor, the industry average or the 'best of the best' *(benchmark)* are also suitable bases for comparison purposes. Comparisons are often based on product costs to eliminate capacity utilisation or company size issues. With it, another cost allocation problem appears which can strongly impair the results of a comparison.

▪ Potential New Competitors

An additional cost analysis deals with **market entry** and **market exit barriers**. These barriers are essentially based on strategic cost drivers, such as experience, capacity utilisation, vertical integration and location.

The extension of management accounting data to include information about other companies typically leads to an **information procurement problem** (this is rather unusual for management accounting systems). The information cannot be adequately found directly (e.g. often the technology of the suppliers, customers and competitors is known), while the costs of other companies can only be estimated indirectly and approximately (e.g. based on annual accounts or published reports). It is sometimes (but not always) sufficient for strategic decisions to know the cost tendencies of competitors.

The following example illustrates the strategic effects of the production capacity development. The capacity serves as an influencing factor on the **competitive position and competition** as well as a **market entry barrier**. The company M as a monopolist in a product market fears the entrance of a competitor E. In order to produce, both companies must develop the production capacities V_M and V_E, which are then unchangeable. A unit of capacity leads to costs c and enables the production of one unit of the product. Subsequently, the companies determine their *production amounts* x_j within $[0, V_j]$, $j = M, E$. To simplify, the variable costs of production are assumed to be zero. Following on from that, both companies will fully use their developed capacities, that is, $x_j = V$ (as far as the revenue function rises in V_j).

The **market demand** is represented by the following price demand function:

$$p = a - x_M - x_E \tag{5.1}$$

Therefore, both companies compete by sales volumes. In the following, the simplification $a - c \equiv 1$ is used. The **profits** of both companies are then:

$$\Pi_M = \Pi_M \cdot (a - V_M - V_E) - c \cdot V_M = V_M \cdot (1 - V_M - V_E)$$

$$\Pi_E = V_E \cdot (1 - V_M - V_E)$$

Assume that the *capacity* developed by M is **reversible**, for example, by sales of machines or by renting free capacity to other companies. In this case, the situation is of identical strategic importance as one of a simultaneous decision about the capacities of the two companies M and E. Maximisation of profits leads to the following functions:

$$\frac{\partial \Pi_M}{\partial V_M} = 1 - 2V_M - V_E = 0 \Rightarrow V_M = \frac{1 - V_E}{2} \tag{5.2}$$

$$\frac{\partial \Pi_E}{\partial V_E} = 1 - 2V_E - V_M = 0 \Rightarrow V_E = \frac{1 - V_M}{2} \tag{5.3}$$

In a *NASH* **equilibrium**, no company may have an incentive to deviate from its chosen capacity, provided that the other company remains within its equilibrium capacity. Both balanced capacities are described by V_j^*. Then for $j = M, E$ applies:

$$V_j^* = \frac{1 - \frac{1 - V_j^*}{2}}{2} \Rightarrow V_j^* = \frac{1}{3}$$

The achieved profits in each case are 1/9.

Now, it is assumed that the capacity is **irreversible**, that is, the capacity costs $c \cdot V_j$ are **sunk**. In this case, the capacity decision taken has strategic effects because M can determine its capacity before the company acts in the market and E must react to it in an optimal way. The function of E in Eq. (5.2) remains unchanged, but M anticipates this **function** and uses it in its profit function, that is,

$$\Pi_M = V_M \cdot \left(1 - V_M - \frac{1 - V_M}{2}\right) \tag{5.4}$$

Maximisation of profit towards V_M leads to

$$V_M^S = \frac{1}{2},\ V_E^S = \frac{1}{4} \text{ and } \Pi_M^S = \frac{1}{8},\ \Pi_E^S = \frac{1}{16}$$

Company M can achieve a *higher* profit in comparison to a firm having a reversible capacity. The reason lies in the fact that M can convincingly **commit itself** to a higher capacity and E must accept this as given. Therefore, E gets only a smaller share of the market. This irreversibility or sunk capacity costs cause a **strategic advantage** for M. *Ex post* after E set its capacity on $V_E^s = 1/4$, the capacity choice of

M would not be optimal, as M would choose a capacity of 3/8. However, this is excluded by the irreversibility of the capacity.

M cannot prevent the **market entrance** of E by a rise in its capacity but can reduce the negative consequences. In a monopoly scenario, M would also choose a capacity of $V_M = ½$ and achieve a profit of $\Pi_M = 1/4$. This can change if the **market entry costs** of E are explicitly considered in the amount of $C_E > 0$. In the above equilibrium, E's expected profit after a market entrance is 1/16. As a result, E would not enter the market if $C_E > 1/16$.

If the entrance costs $C_E \leq 1/16$, the above considerations apply again, but M can consider whether it operates **'over-capacity'** with the only purpose to prevent the market entrance of E. E will enter if its profit with optimal capacity choice V_E is smaller than 1/16, that is,

$$\max_{V_E} V_E \cdot (1 - V_M - V_E) - C_E < 0$$

or

$$\left(\frac{1 - V_M}{2}\right)^2 - C_E < 0$$

Preventing market penetration requires a minimum capacity of M at

$$V_M^M > 1 - 2 \cdot \sqrt{C_E} > \frac{1}{2} \text{ for } C_E < \frac{1}{16} \tag{5.5}$$

If C_E is 'near enough' to 1/16, M would lose less operating over-capacity than if E actually enters the market. For example, assuming that $C_E = 0.04$, $V_M^M > 0.6$ were chosen, and the profit amounts to $\Pi_M^M = 0.24 > 1/8$ in the situation that E enters the market.

The amount produced does not lie above the *ex post* maximum profit. After the choice of capacity V_M and the non-entrance of E, the *ex post* profit function is $x_M \cdot (a - x_M)$ with $a = 1 + c > 1$, from which a production amount of $x_M = \min\{a/2; V_M\}$ arises.

5.3 The German Version of Activity-Based Costing

5.3.1 Introduction

An analysis of Grenzplankostenrechnung (*GPK*), the common German cost accounting system, shows that some **indirect (or overhead) costs** are treated in a rather neglected way due to the **focus** on the **determination of marginal costs relevant to decision-making** for final products. The differentiated treatment of indirect costs at cost pool level – although possible – is very questionable for non-production cost pools due to missing cost base factors with double functions. As perhaps the largest element of indirect costs, **fixed costs** are not considered to be **decision relevant in the short-term**. Therefore, the danger exists that they are treated as one block and with it less seriously, even though they have increased considerably in importance in the application of new manufacturing technologies and in the context of pre-production costs in connection with shorter product life cycles. Aimed especially at the management of indirect costs in areas apart from production, new instruments have been developed.

The **Prozesskostenrechnung** (*Activity-Based Costing* [*ABC*], *Activity-Based Management*, *Transaction-Based Costing)* is perhaps the most prominent system that has been developed, but national differences do exist. *Activity-Based Costing* was originally developed in the United States due to the dissatisfaction with the usual treatment of overhead costs' allocated using direct labour, a procedure that is common in the United States and is in accordance with US-GAAP. Therefore, the American version of *ABC* mainly deals with product calculations, while the German version (shown subsequently) focuses on the connection to the highly developed *GPK* in indirect (non-production) company areas.

The **Prozesskostenrechnung** is basically a **full cost system** aimed at showing detailed real **resource consumption** for all activities and/or products. It includes considerations relating to capacity utilisation and, therefore, is especially relevant for strategic decisions. Consequently, it is not suitable for **short-term decisions** as the total full costs, or at least large parts of them, are allocated to activities, and then, onto products. At short notice, fixed costs (as *per definition*) are not influenced by decisions taken; however, as a result of the procedure they appear to be, which may lead to potentially incorrect decisions.

The following section presents the **procedure of the Prozesskostenrechnung**.

5.3.2 Procedure of the Prozesskostenrechnung

The procedure consists of the following four steps which will be discussed presently:

- Determination of activities and allocation of costs
- Determination of cost drivers
- Computation of activity cost rates
- Combination into main activities

Determination of Activities and Allocation of Costs

The Prozesskostenrechnung is based on the given cost pool system of the company. An activity analysis determines the main **activities** ('Prozesse') of every cost pool. Typically, a rough analysis led by hypotheses based on previous experience is initially undertaken. Unstructured interviews and conversations with cost pool managers as well as an analysis of existing documents are used to identify the activities of each cost pool. This is followed by a detailed analysis, e.g. with semi-structured interviews. Approximately five to ten activities are identified, which should be able to explain the majority of resources consumed in each cost pool. A distortional effect may arise as a result of the fact that the analysis is based on individual employee's statements. Activities not yet illustrated by the computer system must be registered separately, thereby causing costs and possibly inaccuracies.

Activities are divided into repetitive and non-repetitive activities. **Repetitive activities** are often standardised and schematised. For example, in the financial accounting cost pool, the activities of classifying accounts, making a book entry and balancing accounts are repetitive. **Non-repetitive activities** are innovative, dispositive or creative (e.g. advertising, management, research and legal advice) and are not particularly suitable for the determination of activity cost rates.

In the next step, the cost pool's costs are allocated between each of the separate activities. Fundamentally, a decision between the use of budgeted versus actual costs has to be made. Cost allocation can be undertaken **directly using** analytic cost budgeting, in which all cost categories are examined separately and then assigned to the respective activities, which makes it a very expensive approach. Therefore, other base factors are frequently used to allocate the cost pool's costs (**indirect determination**). An example would be the allocation of workers 'man-years of work' to the relevant activities. The lower the inaccuracy of such a simplified determination, the higher the proportion of labour costs allocated to all cost pool costs.

Example The financial accounting cost pool has identified the following activities: classifying accounts, making a book entry, balancing accounts and management of the department. Total costs amount to 360,000. A division according to man-years of work or labour costs shows the following cost rates of activities (◘ Table 5.2).

- **Determination of Cost Drivers**

Now, the activities are divided into **'leistungsmengeninduzierte'** ***(lmi) (induced by volume)*** and **'leistungsmengenneutrale'** ***(lmn) (not induced by volume)*** activities. Leistungsmengeninduzierte activities depend on the volume of the cost pools, not necessarily in a proportional manner but according to demand. Leistungsmengenneutrale activities are not influenced by the volume of the cost pool. *Example*: the activity 'management of the department' is a typical *lmn activity*.

Cost drivers are searched for every single *lmi activity*. To simplify, only *one cost driver* is assigned to each activity, even in the case of heterogeneous cost causation. No cost drivers are used for *lmn activities*, as – *by definition* – they cannot be influenced by cost pool volumes.

◘ **Table 5.2** Distribution of the cost pool costs

Activity	Man-years of work	Labour costs	Costs
Classifying accounts	3	135,000	162,000
Making a book entry	2	50,000	60,000
Balancing accounts	2	55,000	66,000
Management of department	1	60,000	72,000
Total costs		300,000	360,000

The cost drivers usually relate to **amounts** or **volumes** and rarely to values. In many cases, it is directly the concerning activity amount. For example, 'making an inquiry for an offer' (number of offers), 'orders placed' (number of orders) or 'customer complaints handled' (number of complaints). The capacity utilisation of the company which is central to *GPK* has no important function.

- **Computation of Activity Cost Rates**

The cost of activities is computed by:

$$\text{Cost per activity} = \frac{\text{Total cost of activity}}{\text{Total volume of activity}}$$

The cost of activities can be distinguished between those which include ***lmn activity costs*** and those which do not. *Lmn costs* can be aggregated for the whole cost pool (e.g. remaining costs), and if so, then the corresponding cost rates only contain *lmi costs*. The *lmn costs* can be treated as a period cost in the accounts. Full costs can be allocated to the products using a proportional rate based on the activity costs, or the *lmn costs* of the cost pool can be allocated by a surcharge on the *lmi costs* of the cost pool's activities. The *lmn activities* are assumed to be related to the volume of each cost pool. Problems of inaccuracy arise when *lmn costs* dominate an activity in a cost pool containing a majority of non-repetitive activities, for example, the research and development department.

Example For the previous example, the following cost drivers and activity volumes were found. The *lmi* and *lmn activity cost rates* can be calculated as shown in ◘ Table 5.3.

The activity costs, irrespective of whether they are based on *lmi* or total costs, contain fixed costs, a lower proportion of which arise with a higher budgeted volume of activities. This problem corresponds to when budgeted full costs are used for

◘ **Table 5.3** *lmi* and total cost rates of activities

Activity	Costs	Costs after allocation of the *lmn* costs	Activity volume	*lmi* cost rate	Total cost rate
Classifying accounts	162,000	202,500	900,000	0.180	0.225
Making a book entry	60,000	75,000	1,200,000	0.050	0.063
Balancing accounts	66,000	82,500	132,000	0.500	0.625
Management of department	72,000	–	–	–	–
Total costs	360,000	360,000			

capacity variance analysis (see ► Chap. 6). The cost rate per activity thereby depends on the definition of the **activity volumes**. Several possibilities exist in this regard:

1. **Actual respectively normal capacity.** Here, cost rates change with current volume changes. For strategic decisions, this may not be meaningful. Product costs are based on (budgeted or actual) full costs.
2. **Bottleneck capacity plan.** Activity volumes are related to the maximum capacity that can be achieved under explicit consideration of the strongest restriction, and cost rates only change if capacity restrictions change. If actual capacity is below this, then products are not charged at full costs.
3. **Capacity plan.** Activity volumes are related to the maximum capacity of the respective activity. The cost rates for each activity are completely independent of actual capacity. Typically, products are charged below full costs. One advantage of this suggestion is that real resource utilisation becomes recognisable for every activity. Strategic decisions about the resource supply can be supported with it. High costs of unused activities draw attention to overcapacity along with an unfavourable coordination of the activities.

▪ Combination into Main Activities

A main activity is a combination of activities in different cost pools that affects the total indirect costs. This step is a peculiarity of the Prozesskostenrechnung and is presented in ◘ Fig. 5.1. Summing the individual cost rates combines all activities with identical cost drivers. Then, activities whose cost drivers are fixed in relation to each other (*law of the interchangeability of the influence factors*) are combined. Both steps are possible without loss of accuracy. Further combinations increase

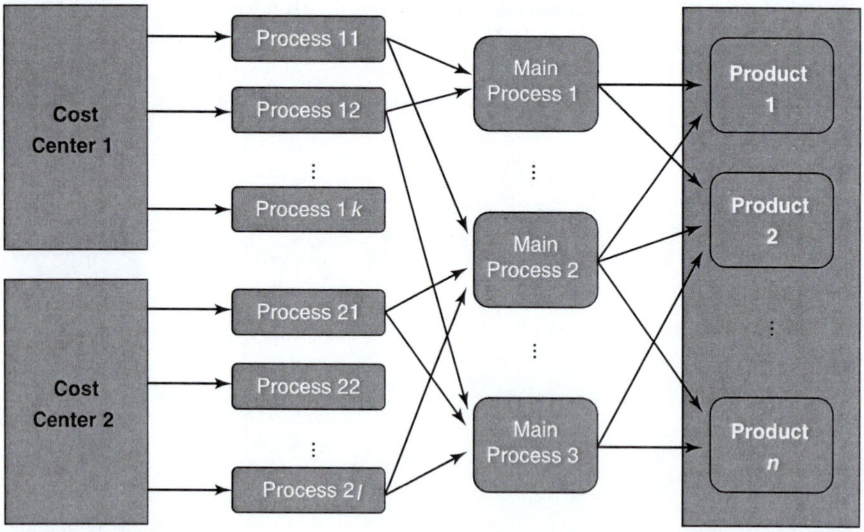

◘ **Fig. 5.1** Combination into main activities. (Slightly adapted from Troßmann 1992, p. 525)

Table 5.4 Combination of activities

Cost pool	Cost driver	Cost rate per activity
Purchasing department	Number of orders	3.52
Incoming goods department	Number of random examinations	5.70
Warehouse department	Number of deliveries	4.20

inaccuracy of the main activity cost rates and are based on assumptions about the (average) relation of the required cost drivers.

Example The activities shown in Table 5.4 should be combined into the cost driver 'number of orders'. It is assumed that the number of orders equals the number of deliveries and that 20% of the deliveries are examined at random for quality control purposes. The cost rate for the main activity 'procurement per order' is calculated as

$$3.52 + 5.7 \cdot 0.2 + 4.2 = 8.86$$

Collectively, the aim is to form approximately seven to ten **main activities**. This combination induces a reduction of information by the more inaccurate cost rates; however, the advantage is clarity of vision as it is immediately obvious within the company how high the cost of a particular activity is. For example, product diversification raises not only the variables costs, but also resource consumption in other areas, which leads to rises in costs, particularly of fixed costs. In practice 'traditional' cost accounting often overlooks this, but the Prozesskostenrechnung makes it obvious, changes mental structures and opens the 'view beyond one's own nose'.

Effects in Comparison to Job Costing

Allocation Effect: Change caused by the use of a volume based rather than a value-based cost allocation factor.

Example: A jeweller produces identical quantities of gold and silver bracelets. The material costs of a gold bracelet amounts to 100, of a silver bracelet to 10. In traditional job costing, a surcharge for material overhead is typically based on direct material costs. With a surcharge rate of 20%, indirect costs of 20 per gold bracelet and 2 per silver bracelet arise. In reality, warehouse costs and costs of logistical transactions are equal with the exception of the interest on the capital tied-up. Assuming that half of the overhead costs are independent of value, then the Prozesskostenrechnung determines that 10 + 11/2 = 15.5 of indirect costs be applied to the gold bracelets and 1 + 11/2 = 6.5 to the silver ones. Intensified mistakes arise in traditional job costing if other value-based surcharges are applied based upon the higher rates (e.g. for administration overhead and sales overhead costs).

Effect of Degression: Order or batch fixed costs are equally divided in traditional job costing to the product units. This assumes an average order or batch size, while in reality constant activity costs arise unaffected by the size of an order or a batch. In the Prozesskostenrechnung, this leads to a drop in unit costs with rising amounts.

Example: Assume that the unit cost of a product before order costs is 36. The activity costs of an order are 200. The average order size is 100 units. With it, average unit costs of 36 + 200/100 = 38 arise. Taking into account that the market price, for example, allows costs of up to 40, a minimum order size of 50 units can be determined (= 200/(40–36)). Smaller orders are not profitable.

Complexity Effect: The consideration of the complexity of the products leads to higher (lower) allocated costs to products with high (low) complexity.
Example: A company produces two types of printers in identical amounts. Printer A needs 3 manufacturing-hours; Printer B needs 4 manufacturing-hours. The overhead costs caused by the complexity of the products amount to 1400, of which 600 are allocated to Printer A and 800 to Printer B, provided that manufacturing-hours are used as the allocation base. For the complexity cost, the cost driver 'number of the parts' is determined with a cost rate of 70. Printer A consists of 5 parts and Printer B of 15 parts. Based on this information only 350 of the overhead costs are allocated to Printer A and 1,050 to printer B.

Relations Between *GPK* and Prozesskostenrechnung (*PKR*)

There are great similarities between the cost allocation bases applied in *GPK* for non-production cost pools (see **Table 5.1**) and the appropriate cost drivers of *PKR*. They are even partially identical.

The **differences** between both systems essentially lie in the manner in which the calculation is performed in the case of *single function cost base factors*. While *GPK* uses indirect cost base factors (often value-related), such procedures are rejected by *PKR* which uses volume-related factors. Similarities also exist, although *GPK* uses a far less dedicated system of cost base factors.

The character of the *PKR* as a **full cost accounting system** is unsuitable as a distinguishing feature, as *GPK* can also be transformed into a parallel full cost system. In addition, the combination of cost drivers throughout different cost pools is known in *GPK* (but is used as an approximation).

Resource Consumption Accounting presently discusses a system combining elements from *GPK* and *ABC*.

5.3.3 Assessment

The Prozesskostenrechnung (*PKR*) is a **full cost accounting system** and allocates all costs onto activities and then subsequently onto products. This is in accordance with the prevailing view of company practice: on the one hand, thinking in terms of full costs is strongly present there; while on the other hand, users mostly know the activity volumes well, which are applied as a basis for cost allocation in *PKR*. *PKR* experiences a **high acceptance rate**. In practice, direct costing systems have a lower acceptance rate.

Full costing systems have been subject to much theoretical discussion and criticism. For more than 40 years, theory tried to develop systems without (or with a reduced) an allocation of indirect costs. Indeed, *PKR* contains a repeated allocation of cost types:

1. Personnel costs to (partial) activities in the cost pool
2. Remaining overhead costs to (partial) activities
3. *lmn costs* to (partial) activities
4. Activity costs to activity amounts
5. Activity costs to products

Proportionality is assumed in each of the allocation steps. However, it has to be noted that long-term decisions must be made on the basis of **long-term costs**, provided that such costs are considered suitable. Long-term costs are full costs because in the long-term all costs are influenced by decisions and can, thus, be regarded as variable. The problem of cost allocation automatically appears with it. The assumption of proportionality is therefore based on the hypothesis that activity costs actually **approximate** the costs influenced by strategic decisions. However, a company with many products and activities can never precisely determine all of the relevant costs for every decision.

If this hypothesis does not lead to relevant costs, it must be adapted appropriately. Yet, this can be a very difficult issue. One option is the additional identification of time perspectives of fixed activity costs. Another option is to not allocate certain indirect costs analogously to a one-tier or a multi-tier contribution margin system. However, with this latter option, useful and simple (or at least appearing to be simple) unit product costs are affected.

Reasons for the Failure of Activity-Based Costing

Sharman (2004, p. 283 f), in a critical article about *ABC* being applied in the United States by only a small percentage of American companies, lists the following reasons for possible failure:

- The software used is not integrated into the operational electronic data processing system.
- *ABC applications* are not integrated into operational planning processes.
- Most applications were furnished with inadequate financial funds.
- Therefore, recent discussions in the United States turn to *GPK*, particularly because it is integrated as part of standard software (e.g. SAP).

5.3.4 Application Possibilities of Activity-Based Costing

Activity-based costing (*ABC*) was developed after dissatisfaction with the treatment of overhead costs in 'traditional' cost accounting. However, ABC is missing an effective instrument to support overhead cost management, and this becomes especially obvious in situations involving high proportions of overhead costs. Activity-based costing firstly dedicates its attention to **indirect company areas**, such as research and development, construction, logistics, planning and budgeting, production control, quality control, maintenance, administration, sales and services. In theory, it should influence attitudes towards overhead costs as they are not unwanted side effects of the production process but rather enable value-creating activities. According to ABC, the primary perspective should be shifted from a bare allocation of overhead costs towards understanding the **cost of the use of the resources**.

The activity-based costing approach described in this chapter relates to the *PKR* version, which is in wide use in German-speaking countries. It includes the following ideas about value chain analysis:

1. It divides the company into **activities** building on the given cost pool structure and tries to find cost drivers for them. Apart from operational cost drivers known from other management accounting systems (e.g. from *GPK*), some strategic cost drivers (e.g. complexity and wealth of variants) are also used.
2. It considers **linkages within the value chain** by the combination of activities throughout the company, excluding vertical linkages and interweaving with other business units (in as far as they have cost pools of their own).

Applications of *ABC* include: overhead cost management, strategic calculations, customer profitability analysis and the support of product design.

5.3.5 Overhead Cost Management

Overhead cost management is based on activity-based costs and activity cost rates. They enable the selection of important activities and cost drivers for the overhead costs and form a starting point for **rationalisation**.

1. An analysis of activities typically reveals that not all activities create value. Overhead cost management aims to **limit** or to **avoid** non-value activities without reducing the customer's utility (performance, function, quality, etc.). In the context of production, these *non-value activities* cause costs to be incurred, for example, waiting times during the production process, additional logistical transactions or quality control issues. Examples of cost determination factors for such activities are as follows:
   - Number of parts
   - Company structure and means of transportation for logistical transactions
   - Supplier's quality, qualifications of staff and production errors for quality control

However, the measurement of these cost determination factors using cost drivers is rarely possible.

Empirical Results

- Innes et al. (2000) examined the application of activity-based costing in the largest British companies using questionnaires. They found that the main use of *ABC* was in areas such as cost reduction (90.3%), pricing policies (80.6%), performance measurement (74.2%) and illustration of cost relations (64.5%). However, they also found that compared with a previous questionnaire administered in 1994 the proportion of *ABC* users (rather low at 17.5% of respondent companies) and companies occupying themselves with the introduction of this system had *fallen*. At the same time, the proportion of companies that had decided against using activity-based costing after an analysis of its possibilities had increased. While these proportional changes are not regarded as significant, there does appear to be a significant increase in the proportion of companies, which are not interested in the implementation of activity-based costing at all.

The reduction of *non-value activities* typically starts at the **cost driver level** by trying to reduce the amount of activities, for example via, an optimisation of the process structure, a change in the company structure or the introduction of flexible manufacturing systems or modern manufacturing methods such as *total quality management* and *just in time*. The introduction of minimal order amounts can also be beneficial. These actions support the view that **measures related to volumes** instead of values have increased importance for management control.

For the activities described above, the assumption that their reduction causes a decrease in overhead costs plays a prominent role, and the **amount** of costs saved is an essential decision criterion in choosing which areas of the company to begin with when initiating cost reduction activities. Activity-based costing delivers only limited information on the most effective areas as it determines the activity costs under the assumption that a decrease in the amount of activity (at least on average) causes a *proportional* decrease in the activity costs. The validity of this assumption determines whether or not the results can be simulated.

Cost savings by a decrease in the level of activity will work for the variable part of activity costs and will be revealed almost *automatically*. Additional savings require additional measures: '*Expenses are fixed only when managers fail to do anything to reduce them*'. (Cooper and Kaplan 1991, p. 135) Otherwise decreases in the level of activity only result in increased spare capacity but not in the desired cost reductions sought.

2. Is the **outsourcing** of activities preferred? This decision (vertical integration) is rarely short-term based and generally results in long-term effects. It has strategic importance that cannot immediately be expressed from a cost perspective (e.g. quality assurance, reliability and supplier dependence).

To make a suitable decision, it must be assumed (or better yet guaranteed) that the activity costs can actually be saved through the buy-in of activities, although this is often not the case. Certain fixed costs cannot be 'disinvested', and as activity-based costing does not include an analysis of synergies (*economies of scope* from activities) due to its approach to overhead cost allocation, higher costs for another activity may suddenly appear as a result of terminating a different activity.

▶ **Example**

In a building with 1,000 m^2 of space, three products are manufactured. Product 1 needs 200, Product 2 needs 300 and Product 3 needs 500 m^2. If Product 1 is bought in, the building costs (particularly depreciation) of 30,000 do not diminish proportionately. In this case, the two other products would face higher activity cost rates (the activity is 'to provide space appropriately') and higher building costs of 30,000/800 = 37.5 per m^2 (instead of 30,000/1,000 = 30 per m^2).

However, an alternative use of the free space could be found. For example, rented storage space might be moved into the building and then the saved rental costs (and perhaps carriage costs) become relevant for the buy-in decision of Product 1 but have *no* influence on the activity costs of the building's use. However, it is meaningful to include these rental costs in the activity 'to provide space'. If we assume it is 200 m^2 and costs are 6,000, then the activity cost rate is 36,000/1,200 = 30 per m^2 (and remains identical). With the storage move into the building, the rental costs can be saved. The space costs decrease to 30,000, and related to the 1,000 m^2 of space available, keep the activity cost rate constant at 30 per m^2. This is certainly a special case.

Imagining that there are many other possibilities for an alternative use of the free space, it is very expensive to just specify these alternatives (particularly if the buy-in decision is only one of many decisions that could be made). Activity-based costing **approximates** the average activity costs and with it the effects of an alternative. ◀

5.3.6 Strategic Calculation

Activity-based costing aims to determine **long-term product costs**, due to their importance for strategic decisions including the following:

- Determination or change of the *long-term* production programme: number of product variations, products selected or markets served, etc.
- Price setting or the introduction of a new product, cost of exotic variations, discounts granted, etc.

The use of activity costs for product calculation purposes is an attempt to approximate the **long-term resource consumption** owing to its production. For the calculation, an additional allocation step is introduced as the quantity of activities per unit of product must be measured, and unitisation is considered a necessary assumption. Therefore, the cost drivers have a double function: they are applied as proxy not only for the causation of overhead costs but also in determining the product cost. Furthermore, it is also a requirement that they should be able to indicate activity amounts that a certain product consumes. Only the cost drivers 'dependent on volume' (induced by volume) can be allocated to product units. On the contrary, the cost drivers not 'dependent on volume' (not induced by volume) can only be allocated at a higher level, for example, the production lot, the order, and the product group.

Compared with the usual **job costing** approach with relatively few cost factors, the calculation using activities leads to a detailed cost allocation, despite the allocation problems connected with a full cost system. Such information can change the (long-term) price setting of a firm.

The allocation of overhead costs is particularly inaccurate when a **diversification strategy is employed**, as this requires more allocations and considerations based on averages. An imprecise calculation leads to the fact that one product is allocated 'too much' in overhead costs with another product allocated 'too little'. A single-product company cannot face similar problems. A more specialised competitor automatically possesses more precise information that can be applied strategically. For example, he may offer a price that the company with the more imprecise cost information believes it may not be able to compete with due to being below its own production costs. In general, basic products produced in large amounts or simple products are typically allocated too many costs in traditional job costing, and a more exact calculation can induce the pushing of *these* products even if that is at odds with the strategic approach generally pursued.

Activity costing does not allocate more or less costs in comparison to traditional job costing (full cost); it just handles the allocation in a different way. This implies that for a product with costs determined to be 'too high' (compared with its demand for resources) others will be 'too low'. Such a product could be, for example, a complex special product with a low sales volume; and if so, it is subsidised to a certain extent (cross-subsidisation) by job costing. A more precise cost allocation helps to uncover this cross-subsidisation based on the activity costs. This is a fundamental advantage of *ABC*. A problem can arise from it; however, when *only* the costs, but no other circumstances are considered for strategic product decisions (e.g. the existence of a marketing alliance). Therefore, an improvement in cost precision can result in the opposite outcome without consideration of the group effects.

▶ Example

Deodorant spray and perfume with the same scent may be complimentary, with the perfume considered a 'specialty'. With cost information 'too exact', the deodorant spray may show costs of only 9 (instead of 10) and the perfume 200 (instead of 130). A perfume's sales price in the amount of 160 would lead to an incorrect cost accounting signal indicating perfume sales appear to be a loss maker. Actually, the perfume is the product providing and supporting the firm's image and once purchased induces a number of sales of deodorant spray afterwards. ◀

Another strategic implication arising is in relation to the **design of new products**. This is discussed in more detail in the next section covering *target costing*.

A special cost driver is the number of **product variations**. The number of variations causes overhead costs in the different company areas. From a strategic perspective, the question of how many specialties should be introduced in the production programme arises.

This cost driver, 'number of product variants', experiences difficulties due to the double function of the cost drivers: that is, 'to drive' the overhead costs whilst at the same time to be measurable for every product, based upon the mantra that products 'cause' activities. The idea that activities 'cause' costs does not work directly because the costs are incurred by a product variation and not by an individual unit. An **activity hierarchy** therefore appears, that is, costs 'are not driven' by individual product units. Another example is set-up costs that are caused by each set-up process.

5

- **Strategic Decisions with Activity-Based Costing**

The reasons for using activity-based costing for long-term decisions for product positioning and programming appear to be convincing but are hardly specific. For a better assessment, consideration of an **explicit long-term problem** can be used to examine whether and under what conditions the optimal solution can be found using activity-based costing.

The introduction of a new product and the instalment of the necessary production capacities required for it in $t = 0$ will now be considered as an *example*. Actually, this is an **investment problem**, with any future surpluses arising from an explicit **optimisation of the period-specific production programmes in operation**. The required initial investment outlay (in $t = 0$) I depends linearly on the period capacity to be installed $\overline{V}$ (in units of the product):

$$I = k \cdot \overline{V} \tag{5.6}$$

In it, k equals the cash outflows per unit of the period capacity. In every period, the product units are limited to a maximum of $\overline{V}$ units:

$$x_t \leq \overline{V} \quad \forall t \geq 1 \tag{5.7}$$

The economic life is given by T periods. Stock keeping is not considered, and in every period there is (possibly) a **period-specific** revenue function with the usual quality of decreasing marginal revenues:

$$R_t = R_t(x_t) = p_t(x_t) \cdot x_t \text{ with } R_t''(x_t) < 0 \tag{5.8}$$

The **variable unit costs** c^v are constant for every period and equal the cash outflows. To simplify, no other cash outflows are assumed. Therefore, the variable period costs (and cash outflows) are as follows:

$$C_t^v = x_t \cdot c^v \tag{5.9}$$

None of the **fixed costs for the period** equal cash outflows. They exist only by the (period-specific) **depreciation** D_t and the **imputed interest** (in the form of the uniform discount rate i) charged to the capital tied up at the end of the preceding period CT_{t-1}:

$$CT_t^F = D_t + i \cdot CT_{t-1} \tag{5.10}$$

The capital tie-up arises by

$$CT_{t-1} = I - \sum_{\tau=1}^{t-1} D_\tau \tag{5.11}$$

Activity-based costing in the present case would only have one **activity**, 'to supply production capacity', with the cost factor $\overline{V}$ already existing in unit numbers. For a given depreciation budget, the period-specific fixed cost rates per unit are as follows:

$$c_t^F = \frac{C_t^F}{\overline{V}} = \frac{D_t + i \cdot CT_{t-1}}{\overline{V}} \tag{5.12}$$

The **period-specific unit costs of activity-based costing** are

$$c_t = c^v + c_t^F \tag{5.13}$$

- **The Optimal Decision**

The company's target is the maximisation of the net present value

$$NPV = \sum_{t=1}^{T} \left(R_t - C_t^v\right) \cdot \rho^{-t} - I = \sum_{t=1}^{T} \left(R_t\left(x_t\right) - c^v \cdot x_t\right) \cdot \rho^{-t} - k \cdot \overline{V} \tag{5.14}$$

considering the constraints formulated in Eq. (5.7) for the separate periods. This problem can be disassembled in two steps:

1. For a *given* capacity $\overline{V}$, the **period-specific optimal amounts** are to be determined first. As a result, the revenues, variable costs and cash flow surpluses of this capacity arise.
2. Taking these into account, the optimal capacity dimension $\overline{V}$ is to be determined.

Due to the **absence of temporal interdependences** between the different periods, the optimum amounts determined in the first step can be decided for each period individually. The following *Lagrange* function is to be maximised for every period:

$$LG_t = R_t\left(x_t\right) - c^v \cdot x_t - \lambda_t \cdot \left(x_t - \overline{V}\right) \tag{5.15}$$

Assuming that the marginal revenues always initially exceed the variable costs per unit, there are positive **production amounts** in every period derived from Eq. (5.15) by the first derivation:

$$\frac{\partial LG_t^*}{\partial x_t} = R_t'\left(x_t^*\right) - c^v - \lambda_t^* = 0 \tag{5.16}$$

Based on the *Kuhn-Tucker* conditions the *Lagrange* multiplier is as follows:

$$\lambda_t^* \begin{cases} > 0 \text{ and } x_t^* = \overline{V} \\ = 0 \text{ and } x_t^* \le \overline{V} \end{cases} \tag{5.17}$$

Because of Eq. (5.17) the value of the *Lagrange* function always corresponds to the difference between revenues and variable costs at the optimal solution, that is, the contribution margin of the optimal solution: $LG_t^* = R_t\left(x_t^*\right) - c^v \cdot x_t^* = CM_t^*$.

This *LAGRANGE* multiplier can be interpreted at the optimum as a **marginal change of the target function** with a variation of the restriction:

$$\frac{dLG_t^*}{d\overline{V}} = \underbrace{\frac{\partial LG_t^*}{\partial x_t}}_{=0} \cdot \frac{dx_t^*}{d\overline{V}} + \underbrace{\frac{\partial LG_t^*}{\partial \lambda_t} \cdot \frac{d\lambda_t^*}{d\overline{V}}}_{=0} + \frac{\partial LG_t^*}{\partial \overline{V}} = \lambda_t^* \tag{5.18}$$

With this adaptation, determination of the **optimal capacity** follows in the second step. The net present value can be presented as

5

$$NPV\left(\overline{V}\right) = \sum_{t=1}^{T} LG_t^* \cdot \rho^{-t} - k \cdot \overline{V} \tag{5.19}$$

Differentiation from Eq. (5.19) towards $\overline{V}$ and observing Eq. (5.18) specifies

$$\frac{dNPV^*}{d\overline{V}} = \sum_{t=1}^{T} \lambda_t^* \cdot \rho^{-t} - k = 0 \tag{5.20}$$

The optimal **capacity** is exactly met when the net present value of the marginal surpluses achieved by a capacity increase (with optimal adaptation in the individual periods) corresponds exactly with the additional initial investment outlays.

Due to different **sales relations** of the individual periods (expressed by the period-specific revenue functions), the optimal amounts typically differ from period to period. In some periods, the capacity will be exhausted (the *LAGRANGE* multiplier according to Eq. (5.17) is regularly positive); in others, it is not exhausted (*LAGRANGE* multiplier is zero), depending on the respective sales conditions. By changing the variable costs per unit, these characteristics of the solution tend to increase over the course of time.

■ The Activity-Based Costing Solution

Literature about activity-based costing providing explicit information about long-term capacity and product programme planning is scarce. The concept of *ABC* is based on the idea that the activity cost rates **approximate long-term resource consumption** and that a knowledge of them is helpful for decision-making. Usually, the cost rates are based on averages of a **single individual period**.

Within the context of the above considerations, there are two possibilities:

1. **One period** is regarded as representative (e.g. the first period) and can be analysed using its revenues and costs, along with the determination of the **production programme** that **maximises the period profit**. A situation **without restriction** can be used according to the concept of *ABC*, and capacities can be adapted according to the level of demand (this is *virtually* considered in the costs rates). The capacity needed for the programme is determined which then induces the investment outlays.
2. Alternatively, this could be derived **for every period**. **Different capacity** needs result from different optimal programmes in each period due to the changing sales situations. The **maximum** period-specific capacity needs must be determined at the outset in order to achieve the production strategy.

Whatever variation is chosen, it always focuses on the **maximisation of profits based on *ABC* full costs**, and the cost rates per unit are given according to Eq. (5.13):

$$\Pi_t = R_t(x_t) - c_t \cdot x_t = R_t(x_t) - \left(c^v - c_t^F\right) \cdot x_t \tag{5.21}$$

Differentiation of (5.21) towards the amount specifies

$$\frac{\partial \Pi_t^p}{\partial x_t} = R_t'\left(x_t^p\right) - c^v - c_t^F = 0 \tag{5.22}$$

while p denotes the optimal figures in this case.

If Variation 1 was chosen, the optimal capacity would arise for the choice of the period t by:

$$\bar{V}^p = x_t^p \tag{5.23}$$

Instead with Variation 2, it is

$$\bar{V}^p = \max_t \left\{x_t^p\right\} \tag{5.24}$$

This indicates the problem: with Variation 1, the installed capacity depends on the (arbitrarily chosen) **period**; therefore, this solution can potentially agree with the actual optimal solution *by chance*. With Variation 2, the capacity choice is based on a **maximum requirement**, which in the extreme case is only relevant in one period, meaning that it will hardly be worth installing high capacities for such rare cases.

- **Conditions of Application of ABC**

The application of *ABC* only seems meaningful if the choice of a certain period plays no role, as then problems of the maximum requirement are not effective (even in Variation 2, the periods do not differ). This can be formally proven. To do so, it is assumed that the sales relations are identical for all periods:

$$R_t(x_t) = R(x_t) \quad \forall t \geq 1 \tag{5.25}$$

From condition (5.16), the optimal amount of a period follows by

$$\frac{\partial LG_t^*}{\partial x_t} = R'\left(x_t^*\right) - c^v - \lambda_t^* = 0 \tag{5.26}$$

From Eq. (5.26), the optimal amounts that are **identical in every period** and the **identical** *Lagrange* multipliers arise

$$\lambda_t^* = \lambda^* \tag{5.27}$$

This can be interpreted intuitively: with **static relations** any period can be used and seen as representative, meaning that the capacity decision can be made for it. If the capacity is too high (too low) for one period, then it is also too high (too low) for all other periods. Therefore, the production restriction Eq. (5.7) is always binding, and for every period an accurate **adaptation of production amounts and capacity** exists. Due to the static relations, the profit increase must be identical to a capacity expansion in every period.

Set into Eq. (5.27), the **condition** relevant for the **capacity decision** (5.20) results in:

$$\lambda_t^* \cdot \sum_{t=1}^{T} \rho^{-t} - k = 0 \Rightarrow \lambda^* = k \cdot CRF(\rho, T) \tag{5.28}$$

CRF is the capital recovery factor (i.e. the reciprocal value of the annuity value factor). In accordance with Eq. (5.28), the *Lagrange* multiplier corresponds to the optimum of the **annuity of the cash outflows per unit** *c* per capacity unit. The capacity is to be extended since (the same applies for every period) the **induced marginal contributions** just equal the **annuity of these cash outflows per unit**.

5

A comparison of Eq. (5.26) with the conditions relevant for *ABC* Eq. (5.22) shows that with static relations both solutions correspond if the following applies:

$$c_t^F = \lambda^* = k \cdot CRF(\rho, T) = \frac{I \cdot CRF(\rho, T)}{\overline{V}} \tag{5.29}$$

A **method of depreciation** must be chosen in such a way that a constant rate of fixed costs occurs, considering the capital invested and the related imputed interest as per the annuity of cash outflows per unit and per capacity unit. With the decreasing capital tie-up over time and the corresponding impact on the cost of capital, **progressive depreciations will occur**. Then, Eq. (5.22) leads to the same optimal production policy as the original model, and due to the **static relations** and the **periodic full capacity utilisation** in the real optimum, the capacity requirement arising for *ABC* can be used in making the capacity decision.

Certainly, in this respect **conditions of application** can be formulated for *ABC* and long-term decisions, but a closer consideration shows that these scenarios are not really '**strategic**'. The required static relations neglect strategic aspects and a hidden, operational, short-term problem arises for which a management accounting system is always recommended as a possible solution. The scenario considered above was consciously very simple, and this relates very well to *ABC*. The inclusion of dynamic cost developments and stochastic revenues and cost relations would intensify the negative conclusion reached.

▶ Example

The cash outflows per capacity unit are $c = 5$ and the installed capacity is assumed to be $\overline{V} = 2{,}000$. An initial investment outlay of $I = 10{,}000$ results. For a uniform discount rate of $i = 0.1$ and an economic life of $T = 4$, the following capital recovery factor arises (rounded):

$$CRF(\rho = 1.1; T = 4) = \frac{i \cdot (1+i)^4}{(1+i)^4 - 1} = 0.315471.$$

The **total annuity** according to Eq. (5.29) is:

$$I \cdot CRF(\rho = 1.1; T = 4) = 10{,}000 \cdot 0.315471 = 3{,}154.71$$

The **depreciation** and the **cost of capital** are found successively: the cost of capital for $t = 1$ arises from 10,000 · 0.1 = 1,000. If the above annuity is subtracted, the depreciation of the first period is determined. The residual value follows from it and is used as the basis for the cost of capital in $t = 2$, etc. The following depreciation and cost of capital plan arises:

	Cost of capital	Depreciation	Residual book value
$t = 1$	1,000.00	2,154.71	7,845.29
$t = 2$	784.53	2,370.18	5,475.11
$t = 3$	547.51	2,607.20	2,867.92
$t = 4$	286.79	2,867.92	0.00

The unit cost rate for the fixed costs is as follows:

$$c_t^F = \frac{I \cdot CRF}{\overline{V}} = \frac{3{,}154.71}{2{,}000} = 1.577355$$ ◄

5.3.7 Customer Profitability Analysis

Activity-based costing can also be used for the allocation of sales overheads, which then enables an analysis of sales regions, customer segments or individual customers. From a cost-based perspective, **customers** differ according to their order sizes, extent of special requirements, number of past order changes, demand for specialties, type of delivery, order volume, etc., and all of these affect overhead costs, not only in the sales area but also for the whole company. For example, there is a difference whether a customer buys 18,000 units of a product as one order or irregularly in 12 orders of approximately 1,500 units each.

A detailed cost allocation using *ABC* enables **customer profitability analysis to be undertaken** that might form the basis for future strategic sales decisions. Interesting revelations often appear, such as proof of the old 80:20 rule: 80% of revenues are generated by 20% of customers. ◘ Figure 5.2 shows a more moderate possible result from such an analysis.

Often large customers are among the loss-makers as they demand lower prices as well as a preferred influence on the product. This might be compensated for by additional charges for the additional services requested. Other means could be to try and create incentives to induce ordering larger amounts.

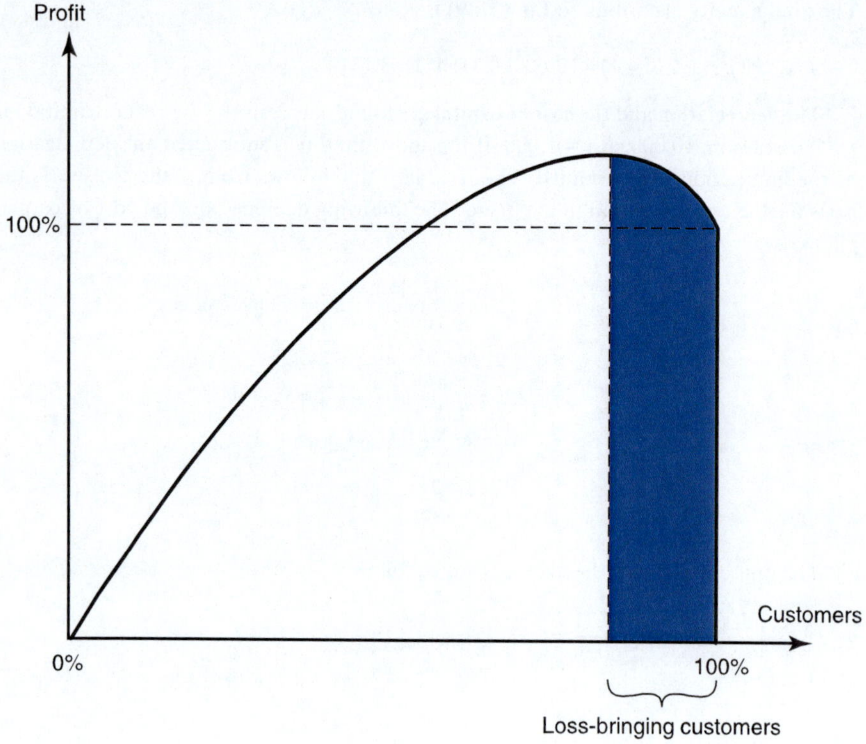

Fig. 5.2 Distribution of customer profitability

What Is the 'Gain' of Activity-Based-Costing?

The fact shown in the text and demonstrated by the empirical evidence is that cost allocation using *ABC* does not necessarily lead to the **higher economic achievement** of the company. To prove this, the relation between company value creation (as a degree of economic achievement) and the application of activity-based costing has to be confirmed (very few empirical studies about this exist thus far).

Gordon and Silvester (1999) examined unusual stock price effects after the announcement of the application of an activity-based costing system. The sample consisted of ten companies implementing *ABC* in 1988 (during a time of euphoric discussion about *ABC* in the United States) and was announced in an article in *Business Week* (this article included a detailed discussion of the intentions and qualities of the system). The stock price reactions of these ten companies were compared to those of *ABC*-free companies of comparable industry and company size. No significant stock price changes were found.

Other results appeared in a similar study by Kennedy and Affleck-Graves (2001) for the British market. They considered 47 companies that introduced *ABC* between 1988 and 1996 and compared them to a control group of non-users. The choice of companies was made based on their individual questioning rather than a public announcement of the *ABC* implementation. Stock price developments were compared for a period of 3 years after the introduction of the *ABC* system. The authors found significantly more *positive* stock price developments for the group of *ABC* users. However, the results should be interpreted with caution, due to the high number of factors relevant for stock price movements.

The results from Kennedy and Affleck-Graves (2001) do not support another empirical study from Great Britain by Innes et al. (2000), who found only 17.5% of *ABC* users in their research. This figure should be significantly higher if *ABC* (apparently) leads to such advantages. Such discrepancies are also addressed by Gosselin (1997, p. 105), who mentioned: '*This is the essence of the ABC paradox: if ABC has demonstrated benefits, why are more firms not actually employing it?*'

Additionally, these activities require attention as the activity costs suggest that **giving up a customer** (e.g. one who generates a loss) actually reduces the (activity) costs by this amount. Apart from other cost considerations, much more important is that the customer could represent, for example, a speculative market expected to achieve future profits, and therefore current losses may be acceptable.

5.4 Target Costing

5.4.1 Target Costs and Their Determination

Target costing (**target cost management**) is a method originally developed in Japan (*genka kikaku*) relating to the planning and introduction of new products and services. Its primary characteristic is that of a **consistent market orientation**. It requires an existing product idea and then deals with a decision about the product's introduction to market. Specifically: 'How much *may* the product cost?' instead of 'What *will* the product cost?' The **target costs** are the allowable costs of a product and are determined solely by market circumstances and company targets; that is, the product's technical feasibility is not the primary consideration.

Target costing's main application is as an instrument of cost management. Once the target costs have been determined, the objective becomes not to surpass them. *Target costing* begins very early during the product planning and development stage. During that phase, the majority of product costs (both production and overhead) is determined.

From a strategic perspective, target costing is an instrument of decision support within a **differentiation strategy** as it requires the customer's utility achieved by the product, noting that every product consists of a number of elements which also cause costs to be incurred. Differentiation makes sense if the new product leads to the desired profit, that is, if the target costs have not been exceeded.

The **target costs** are determined as follows:

$$\text{Target costs} = \text{budgeted sales price} - \text{budgeted target profit} \quad (5.30)$$

From a market perspective, it equals the maximum costs at which the product can be introduced successfully. The calculation corresponds to a **subtraction method**. The main innovation of *target costing* lies in its objective: *target costing* aims at developing the product in line with the market. Based on that philosophy, an orientation towards full costs and the consideration of a target profit naturally follow.

The **practical determination** of target costs seems simple at first glance. However, both the setting of the future sales price and the amount of the required target profit may prove difficult.

The **sales price** of the new product can be estimated, for example, based on market research data about the customer's expected utility, experiences with similar products or products to be substituted on account of the new product. However, problems may arise such as:

- The sales price will hardly remain **constant** for the lifespan of the product and the company may also decide to adopt dynamic price strategies. The sales price could also be affected by the reactions of future competitors. Therefore, in practice, an average sales price is frequently used.
- The sales price is only one of many **marketing instruments** and must be seen in the context of the marketing mix which needs to be determined in advance.

The determination of the **target profit** is also problematic due to other considerations. The following measures are suggested as examples (Sakurai 1989, p. 43):

- **Return on sales** (*ROS*)
- **Return on investment** (*ROI*)

The *ROI* is applied less frequently as it is difficult to estimate for firms with a multiplicity of different products. In addition, it also requires an allocation of investments or capital.

For the percentage of the return on sales, or the discount rate of the return on investment, there are no general recommendations. Typically, it will be derived from the company's targets, the alternatives and the competitive situation. Similarly, for the sales price, it is also very questionable to what extent a constant percentage could be considered for the target profit.

A fundamental problem exists due to **the subtle relation** amongst all three components of Eq. (5.30)

$$\text{Target costs} = \text{budgeted sales price} - \text{budgeted target profit}$$

If an autonomous price range is assumed (otherwise the determination of the market price would be trivial), the three components relate closely to each other. An illustration is the COURNOT model whereby the determination of the sales price and profit is made based on a cost function and a price-demand function. If the costs are not yet known for *target costing*, neither the sales price nor the profit can be determined in the first instance. In other words, if the sales price and target profit are determined in advance and used for the determination of the target costs, the result will only randomly be optimal for the company (cf. Ewert 1997). Therefore, *target costing* has to be considered rather **heuristically** in optimisation procedures.

5.4.2 Achieving the Target Costs

In the initial step target costs are to be compared with so-called **standard costs**. The target costs equal those costs that would arise for a new product using existing technology based on a first, initial draft of the product. As a rule, target costs are less than standard costs, with the difference indicating **cost savings** for the future product – the main purpose of this technique is to initiate changes to the product design and production leading to cost savings considered early, even in the product development stage, to enable a successful introduction of the product to market (in the following referred to as '*reduced standard costs*').

For strategic decisions, the (original and reduced) standard costs at a level of **full costs** are suitable under the assumption that the full costs can again serve as an approximation of the relevant costs in the long-term. However, this is very restrictive. For example, the experience curve can influence the unit cost with rising accumulated production amounts, but they cannot be precisely considered in the standard costs. Standard costs should also contain development costs, market construction costs and other non-current product costs. This idea is discussed in the following section about life cycle costing.

Product developers and technical designers are required to find ways and means of lowering the present standard costs in order to meet the target costs. This often requires a very good team spirit within the company. In a simplified view, the production process of a product consists of input factors (direct costs) and activities. The direct costs can be calculated in a simple way using **traditional costing**, and ***ABC*** can be used for the corresponding activities.

Cost Reduction Activities

The efficiency of such activities depends on each individual case. Examples can be:
- Influencing physical features of the product, such as size or weight, which later cause logistical costs
- Substitution of materials
- Use of identical or standardised parts
- Inclusion of suppliers in the planning process
- Change of working processes
- Buy-in instead of self-manufacturing

The time required for the initial product design allows a higher degree of freedom for locking in costs and revenues than during the detailed construction.

Cost reduction activities often change individual product functions and with it product qualities and the **market segment**. Strictly speaking, the whole process would need to be started anew because product qualities and the market segment serve as a basis for sales price determination.

In general, target costs equalling the difference between the retail price and the target profit are too rough a measure to use them directly for cost reduction purposes. Target costs apply to the whole bundle of product functions that can be marketed, and for detailed information that a product designer might find meaningful, the **division** of target costs into **individual functions**, and afterward to **components** that should fulfil these functions, is helpful. One procedure is the weighting of the functions according to their importance to the customer and in comparing the standard costs within an *ABC* analysis. Resources (with costs) should be used according to the functions desired by the customer. The proportion of target costs (in percentage terms) should correspond to the degree of importance of the function being considered (in percentage terms). Action is needed if these pairs of percentages fall considerably apart.

- **Product Launch Decisions**

When all possible cost reduction activities are considered, the reduced standard costs cannot be improved any further. Only if they are equal to or below the target costs, should the product be launched.

Product developers often try to avoid disappointment by considering the technical possibilities for the determination of target costs. The literature suggests a **two-tier procedure** for the determination of target costs: first, (market) 'allowable' costs are determined by subtraction of the sales price for the new product from the target profit. Then, target costs are assumed to be between the 'allowable' costs and the (original) standard costs (costs by use of existing technology) depending on the technical options and the competitive situation of the company. With the second step, there seems to be leeway for the target costs; yet, the question can be raised as to why 'allowable' costs and the target profit do not already include these considerations.

Target costs are not then used for decision support but rather as a **motivational instrument** for product developers and technical designers. Standard costs are applied to show the effects of their construction on the company's costs. Target costs could be set in such a way that is attainable but only with substantial effort. As **behavioural control** is addressed here, asymmetric information and conflicts of interest should also be explicitly considered. Consequences for the target costs and for the information reporting which arises are addressed later in this book.

5.4.3 Discussion

The *target costing* procedure outlined seems very appealing by solving very complex problems in a compact form. Some difficulties with it were already addressed during the description of the method. In the following section, the problem of a single period view of *target costing* will be explicitly discussed.

In general, *target costing* is a **multiple period problem**, which should be solved using investment appraisal methods. **Critical costs** are determined, which may not be exceeded so as to keep the investment profitable. In this regard, all aspects of capital budgeting problems are included in the simple equation of *target costing*: target costs = sales price – target profit. The question then arises as to what extent **investment appraisal considerations** can be explicitly derived.

For this, the net present value (*NPV*) of a project is used. To determine the *NPV*, assumptions are made which correspond to the typical procedure used in *target costing*: sales volumes x, sales prices p, variable unit costs c_v and fixed costs C^F all of which are constant for every period. A typical consideration of full costs (per unit) applies, and it is assumed that prices and costs are cash flow-effective at the end of the respective period.

Additional specific investments for the product can be explicitly considered by their initial investment outlay I and a liquidation value LQ. Given an economic life of t periods, the net present value follows as:

$$NPV = \sum_{t=1}^{T}\left[\left(p-c^{v}\right)\cdot x-C^{F}\right]\cdot\rho^{-t}+LQ\cdot\rho^{-T}-I \tag{5.31}$$

Using the annuity value factor (*AVF*) this is

$$NPV = \left[\left(p-c^{v}\right)\cdot x-C^{F}\right]\cdot AVF\left(\rho,T\right)+LQ\cdot\rho^{-T}+I \tag{5.32}$$

An absolutely profitable product requires $NPV \geq 0$. Analogous to the investment-theoretical calculation of the long-term lowest price limit (see ▶ Chap. 4), this leads to

$$p \geq \underbrace{c^{v}+\frac{C^{F}}{x}+\frac{\left(I-LQ\cdot\rho^{-T}\right)\cdot CRF\left(\rho,T\right)}{x}}_{\hat{c}} \tag{5.33}$$

with CRF as the capital recovery factor and $CRF = 1/AVF$.

On the right side of Eq. (5.33), there is a **'dynamic' full cost rate** $\hat{c}$. For the consideration of critical values, Eq. (5.33) must be fulfilled, so it follows

$$p = \hat{c} \tag{5.34}$$

Seen from the subtraction method's perspective, it implies that a profitable investment project only requires the **identification of sales price and full costs per unit** under the set premise. A target profit, in whatever form derived, cannot be explained. This would be required to change the profitability criterion, and the condition for a profitable project is a **severely positive minimum net present value** $\underline{NPV}$

$$p-\frac{\underline{NPV}\cdot CRF\left(\rho,T\right)}{x}=\hat{c} \tag{5.35}$$

Now, the critical full cost rate per unit (target cost) arises from the sales price less a size interpretable as a 'target profit', which can be represented as a unitised annuity of the minimum net present value. The problem then is how to find such a minimum net present value, and it is hardly possible within the described scenario. Therefore, in general, *target costing* from an **investment theoretical view** is 'too compact' to determine the profitability of a project with it.

One form of reasoning about a minimum net present value could be based on a reference to a **situation of limited financial means**. Then, only such projects with a certain minimum profitability can be realised. However, such considerations are usually integrated in the investment appraisal and capital budgeting process by an increased uniform discount rate, and therefore integrated in the true 'pure' net present value. The suggested procedure would lead to a double inclusion.

Another possibility would be to consider aspects of the **temporally optimal utilisation of real options**. This suggestion can be illustrated by the following simple example: Assume that a project can either be undertaken today or in one year's time. Future sales are uncertain but can be better estimated in one year than today, and the optimal decision is easier if the investment is not started immediately. Therefore, in some conditions the investment will be renounced (the net present value of this 'omission' is zero), whilst in other conditions the project will be undertaken (the net present value of this investment is positive because undertaking an investment cannot be enforced). The alternative to 'wait for a year and optimal adaptation at year 1', has a positive expected net present value. Should today's investment be preferred, its net present value must be at least as large as the expected net present value when waiting a year. Based on that understanding, a minimum (positive) net present value can be explained.

- **Intertemporal Trade-offs in Costs**

Other problems of *target costing* arise from the following simple observation: cost reductions are always profitable for a company ceteris paribus. Why should **cost reduction considerations** be stopped when the target costs are reached? Why should this be a 'good' or even 'optimal' cost policy?

An answer to this question can only be found by considering the fact that cost reductions in the early phases of product design and product development are not free. Construction improvements and product design changes induce various resource consumptions, for example, pre-launch trials, tests and examinations. Insofar as early cost management contains an **intertemporal trade-off,** the additional costs of planning and construction must be compared with the cost reduction enabled for future production and sales.

From this perspective, **target costs** and **target profit** appear as a result of an **optimisation process** based on cost substitution effects between different phases in the product life cycle. Not only does this prove the close connection to product life cycle costing presented in the next section, but it also appears that the sales price, the target profit and the target costs within the subtraction method are at best a formal structure whose completion must depend on optimisation considerations that need to be specified further.

It appears that the approach to adjust the future cost structures towards the market conditions using *target costing* and to therefore guarantee a profitable investment does not really succeed. Finally, it is crucial for the **application of *target costing*** whether these conceptual disadvantages are outweighed by other advantages (e.g. to change employees' attitude to a certain extent with a simple and easily understood instrument).

5.5 Life Cycle Costing

Life cycle costing (or *product life cycle costing*) tries to identify and allocate all costs occurring during the entire life cycle of a product. The subsequent information gathered can be used to manage costs and revenue at the following stages: **product development**, timing of the **product launch** and **product market retreat**, long-term **pricing policies and** for the allocation of costs between different life cycle phases. Like *target costing*, it assumes that the influence is greater at the beginning of a product's life, whereas, the state of information is weaker at this stage.

It is a perspective **spanning all periods** ('from the cradle up to the grave' of the product), and through this, dynamic cost and price developments can be illustrated. Costs and revenues are only explicitly shown in certain phases of the product life cycle. There is a tendency towards shortening product life cycles, and cycle times of between 2 and 5 years are no longer a rarity. Pre-production costs (e.g. research and development) are increasing and with it the parts of the costs that are not allocated to products in 'traditional' cost accounting.

5.5.1 Product Life Cycles

Typically, the life cycle of a product equals the **market cycle** and is divided into the launch stage, growth period, ripening phase, saturation stage and degeneration phase. These phases can generally be identified for every product.

The **production cycle** has to be distinguished from this market cycle. It begins with the conceptualisation of the product, followed by product development, detailed construction, production and sale. The first three phases conclude temporally after each other. However, for production and sale, these only apply when considering each individual product unit, as the market cycle overlaps with the production and sale phases.

In life cycle costing, the production cycle is the focus of attention, particularly the costs in each of the five phases which occur very differently. The first three phases (product design, development and construction) cause the so-called **pre-production costs**. These are costs that are incurred as a result of investments, research and development as well as marketing for the products launch. Occasionally, there are also **pre-production revenues accruing** such as subsidies or promotional allowances.

The production cycle is followed by the **consumer's cycle**. It begins with the purchase of a unit of the product, followed by the utilisation phase, with additional company services in demand, such as maintenance or repairs. The consumer's cycle ends with disinvestments, sales and finally, with the disposal of the product. In every phase, the consumer's cycle relates to an individual product unit.

During the consumer's cycle, further costs and revenues result for the company. **Post-production costs include** guarantees, customer service, maintenance, repair and stock-holding costs for spare parts and finally, product disposal. Parallel extensive **post-production revenues** often accrue from maintenance and repairs as well as from spare part sales.

5.5.2 Different Concepts of Life Cycle Costing

The starting point for life cycle costing begins with the budgeting and/or recording of separate life cycle costs over a period of time. To aid **budgeting**, it supports several decisions in the optimisation of costs in separate life cycle phases. Based on **actual costs and revenues**, it does not help most strategic decisions (e.g. the payback time can be determined irrespective of whether the price structure has changed or the efficiency can be increased). All of this information can be useful for adaptation decisions.

5

Life cycle costing is based on cash flows in which **investment appraisal is integrated** and considered in the context of the temporal structure of the cash flows, which are meaningful and necessary for long-term decision support. However, in practice, such life cycle costing concepts are only useable in the pre-production phase before the market cycle begins. As with mass production, current cash flows are typically no longer registered separately but instead costs and revenues are used.

The periodic cost accounting system considers pre-production and post-production costs only in special cases. As an example, depreciation on investments made before the start of production can be recorded and applied. **Cost accounting** collects the periodic costs and assigns them to the amounts produced or sold during the period. There are two **possibilities** for the allocation of pre-production and post-production costs, depending on how extensive the allocation should be.

1. One option is not to allocate them to a **cost object** but rather to treat them as the period's indirect costs.
2. The second option is to record them in auxiliary cost pools and then allocate them to the main cost pools via the cost rates of traditional job costing or of activity-based costing, and from there to the products produced in the respective period.

Both possibilities show the disadvantage that the pre-production costs and post-production costs are not **allocated** to the products, which really **cause** these costs (partially in a wider sense) to be incurred. Pre-production costs would need to be allocated to *future* products, post-production costs partially to discontinued products. A renunciation of the separate consideration of both cost types can be sufficient when their relative importance in terms of total costs of production and sales is low, or if their amounts are similar for all of a company's products *and* remain relatively consistent in proportion over the years. Otherwise product costing for a single period would be distorted for strategic decisions and **product success** could no longer be represented by the measurement of (short-term) costs and revenues.

Example The production of software predominantly causes pre-production costs, whereas the actual production costs are a minor part of total costs. Without the developmental costs, price calculations would be seriously distorted.

A possibility for multi-period life cycle costing consists of the **'capitalisation'** of pre-production costs and their subsequent allocation to the respective products.

For the (expected) post production costs, the same procedure applies apart from the fact that the allocation is done before any costs are incurred.

▫ Figure 5.3 shows typical **cost and revenue development during a product's life cycle**. The upper part shows costs and revenues with their periodical incurrence. It is obvious from this that the sole consideration of costs and revenues during an arbitrary period within the market cycle provides little information. The lower part of the figure shows the extensive presentation of costs and revenues during the market cycle. It is assumed that pre-production revenues reduce pre-production costs and likewise that post-production revenues reduce post-production costs.

An extensive allocation spanning multiple periods leads to several theoretical and practical **problems**.

- Many of the pre-production and post-production costs are not product-specific but instead represent a combination of product groups (**indirect costs**).
- A practical problem relates to the **allocation of all costs** between the products that cause them, with a strong deviation from financial accounting results.
- A problem exists in the **estimation** of the allocation basis for the respective costs. For the allocation of the pre-production costs, the total number of future products produced is required (if the allocation is made based on sales, then future prices also have to be forecasted). Vice versa, proportionate post-production costs must be allocated at the beginning of production.
- The **success rate** of pre-production costs is difficult to forecast in many industries. For example, the pharmaceutical success rate of research often amounts to less than 5%, that is, of 1000 projects researched, only 50 actually lead to marketable products. To allocate the research costs onto future products seems difficult and a 'correct' allocation therefore impossible. Therefore, unsuccessful research must be seen as a necessary condition for successful research and this must be allocated further. Alternatively, an average percentage of unsuccessful research can be regarded as period costs.

5.5.3 Shifting Costs Between Life Cycle Phases

Life cycle costing based on **budgeted costs and revenues** over the entire life cycle serves as a basis for cost management. It illustrates in a simple way how costs can be shifted between separate life cycle phases. Cost reduction in one phase of the life cycle typically also impacts on costs in later phases. Similarly, additional costs in early phases may be substantial for cost reductions in later phases. A cost accounting system focused on a single period will leave those inter-periodic effects unconsidered. Two typical examples will now be shown.

▪ Shifting of Production Costs and Sales Costs to Pre-Production Costs

Life cycle costing can show the impact of achieving a far greater cost reduction in later production and sales by virtue of an increase in costs incurred during the phases *before* the product launch. A commonly described rule of thumb mentions that an additional monetary unit in product design, product development and construction saves eight to ten monetary units in production and sales costs. The

5

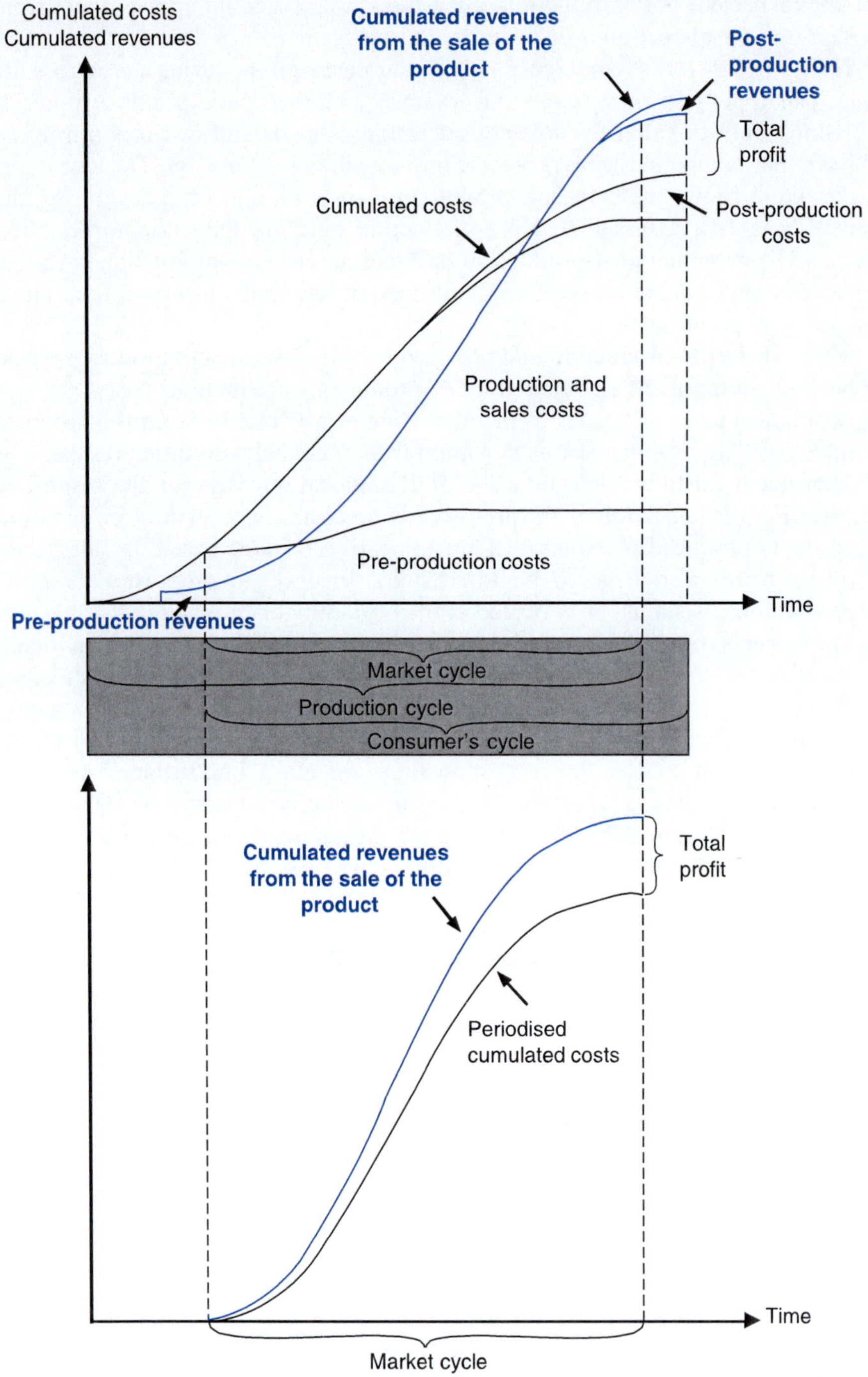

Fig. 5.3 Accumulated costs and revenues in life cycle costing

advantage of a well-designed product is a decrease in its product costs (e.g. by reduced production times) or an increase in its quality or flexibility. Life cycle costing supplements *target costing* by an economic viability analysis of the activity of the *target costing* itself.

Shifting of Costs in the Consumer's Cycle to the Production Cycle

For the **differentiation strategy**, an additional utility for the customer can be created by two strategies: (1) an improved performance or a reduced cost for the customer, and (2) via the strong support afforded by the use of life cycle costing.

5.6 Summary

Cost management aims to **influence** costs in regard to cost level, cost structure and cost development for the purpose of improving the economic viability of a company's production. Cost management activities relate to **strategic decisions**, such as the determination of company strategy, the long-term production programme, the use of manufacturing technology and vertical integration. The focus of cost management can be on a company's **products**, **activities** and **resources**. In this chapter, some concepts and instruments of cost management were represented and discussed. At the centre is the construction of the **information systems** that provide decision support for cost management. The **cost and management accounting system is based** on many simplistic **assumptions** that often appear only implicitly. Not considered are competitors' behaviour, risk of competition, or long-term effects caused by certain decisions. To enable 'good' decisions, the management and cost accounting system must be **adapted** appropriately.

The concept of a **strategic management accounting system** is based on **value chain analysis**. The company or a part of it is divided into **activities** that raise customer's utility. Costs are assigned to activities, and their **strategic cost drivers** are identified. Then, strategies can be determined based on their impact on the costs and benefits of the aforementioned activities.

The ***PKR*** (Prozesskostenrechnung), the German version of activity-based costing, focuses on the treatment of indirect costs – typically built on existing structures in relation to cost pools – and delivers a specified analysis of a company's activities. (Full) costs are assigned to these activities, and **activity cost rates are generated** for the corresponding **activities**. They are also analysed company-wide by considering the **main activities** that consist of partial activities within several cost pools. The *PKR* contains numerous **allocations** and assumes **proportionality**. Due to its characteristic as a full cost system, it has an explicitly long-term perspective, including capacity adaptations in its considerations and should therefore serve as a basis for strategic decisions.

PKR is **widely used in company practice** within German speaking countries. An essential reason for it lies in its schematic character and specific recommendations. For the decision models described in this text, the quality of the data naturally has an essential impact on the **quality of the solutions** of the models. Essentially, the problem of optimal **complexity** has to be solved again.

General **recommendations** to answer this question are difficult to provide and it is questionable whether the described procedures may be sufficiently accurate.

Activity-based costing, in general, is a pragmatic instrument that is directed towards the **indirect areas of a company** supplying the resources for business activities. **Applications** of *ABC* can be overhead cost management, strategic calculations, customer profitability analysis and product design support. However, more detailed considerations show a limited usability. For example, strategic calculations and long-term product design are only meaningful if **static circumstances** exist. Then, however, there is no real 'strategic' relation.

Target costing specifically aims at supporting **product design, product development** and **construction**. The target costs arise from the future sales price less the target profit. A product having higher costs than these target costs will not be launched. With the help of activity cost rates, the permitted long-term costs can be shown to product developers and technical designers. The weakness of this instrument lies in its single periodic view and its assumed constancy of sales price, target profit and costs.

Life cycle costing tries to record product costs from the initial design up to the end of use by the last consumer. Over this time span, the system should avoid incorrect cost signals that show up in a more or less periodic costing system. Life cycle costing can particularly steer the allocation of costs within the different life cycle phases.

In principle, all elements of a strategic management accounting system are based on a number of calculations that at most can be considered as an **approximation** of the real effects of strategic decisions. Often they are based on full costs, either actual or budgeted, without any consideration of its temporal structure. The approximations are used due to the fact that single analyses are too **extensive** and **uneconomical**, but in any application of these procedures, it should always be considered whether this is really meaningful for the specific decision or whether a single analysis really could or should be performed.

The suggested cost management instruments leave many questions unanswered. Their benefits need to be compared with those of other strategic decision instruments. These are often very rough or superficial, mainly due to the long-term perspective of the required data. Compared to the cost and management accounting system, which is highly developed for short-term decision-making, at present an **instrument deficit** has to be noted.

5.7 Assessment Material

Review Questions

1. Why is the cost accounting system often used for strategic decisions rather than investment appraisal?
2. How do the requirements of the cost and management accounting system relate to the strategic position of a company?
3. What are the advantages of a value chain analysis compared to the 'traditional' cost and management accounting system?

4. How do strategic cost drivers differ from ('traditional') cost allocation factors?
5. What type of external information is meaningful for a company's cost management?
6. How is complexity measured as a cost driver in activity-based costing?
7. What are the effects of a diversification strategy on the determination of product costs?
8. In which decision situations can the use of *target costing* be meaningful, and why?
9. Can *target costing* support optimal decisions about prices and sales volumes of a product to be newly launched?
10. What are the different methods to allocate pre-production and post-production costs, and for which situations are they suitable?

Exercises

1. **Strategic cost analysis.** *Scotch AG* manufactures city and mountain bikes. The company has already implemented an *ABC* system based on the following data:

Division	Cost driver	City bike	Mountain bike	Costs of activities
Incoming logistics	Number of orders	150	220	370,000
	lmn costs			150,000
Manufacturing	Direct materials (per unit)	1,900	4,000	5,330,000
	Direct labour (per unit)	1,200	1,400	2,240,000
	lmn costs			1,800,000
Administration and sales	Number of customer inquiries	350	500	900,000
	Number of customer orders	120	160	850,000
	lmn costs			1,400,000
Customer service	Number of units sold	700	1,000	51,000

The *lmn* costs are allocated on the basis of the *lmi* costs, whereby the basis is the direct labour costs in manufacturing, while for administration/sales it is the number of customer inquiries.

(a) Ascertain the total cost per unit for city and mountain bikes. Which products should the company produce if the sales price for city bikes is 6,500, for mountain bikes 12,500, and the company wants to charge a premium of at least 10% on the total costs? Benchmark cost structures with the best competitor whose total costs amount to 5,500 (cost distribution, 5% inward logistics, 33% production materials, 37% production time, 23% administration/sales and 2% customer service).

(b) Ben Miller, Junior Management Accountant at *Scotch plc,* is outraged by the total costs calculated by his superior, Richard Smith, who, despite knowing better, omits the following information from his calculations 'so as not to complicate matters'. The *lmn* costs for incoming logistics include 70,000 for market research that was carried out for the mountain bikes. In production, there are 700,000 of quality control costs, for which 90% (10%) are attributed to mountain (city) bikes and which are shown under *lmn costs.* Marketing costs of 800,000 are contained within administration/ sales' total *lmn* costs, whereby the activities are allocated in a ratio of 8:2 for mountain: city bikes. What are the undistorted total costs that Ben can present to the board?

2. **Activity-based costing.** *Winter Ltd* produces window frames from plastic granulates and plastic frames for balcony and veranda doors as special products. There is currently tremendous competitive pressure on the market and increases neither in price nor in volume seem to be possible, so management tries to get a better grip on costs in an attempt to improve profits. Until now, *Winter's* practice has been to use a traditional job costing system, but they are now considering introducing an activity-based costing system. It has already determined a number of cost drivers. Available data are given in the following tables.

Cost	Cost driver	Windows	Doors	Total costs
Manufacturing materials	Volume of materials (kg per item)	1	3	2,380,000
Material overheads	Number of stock movements	6	6	300,000
Production	Hours of production (per item)	1	3	1,360,000
	Machine hours (per item)	2	5	1,780,000
	Set-up processes	4	6	368,000
Administration/sales	Number of orders	250	300	500,000

	Windows	Doors
Production volume = sales volume	5,000	600
Selling price	1,200	3,300

(a) Determine the total costs per window (door) using a traditional job costing system with the usual references to manufacturing materials, manufacturing wages and production costs, and then using the activity-based costing system. How do you judge the relative advantages of each of the products?

(b) As a seller, *Winter* is already positioned in the higher price segment. Thus far, their customers have accepted this mainly because they can obtain the veranda doors from the same supplier, which is often not the case with the less expensive suppliers. The head of marketing estimates a drop in the window business at either 180 or 600 windows in the event that *Winter* ceases door production. Determine the effects of these two estimated losses of business on the net profits for the period using both job costing and the activity-based costing system.

(c) At 550 orders, capacity is limited in the administration and sales departments. Total costs of 500,000 represent the absorption costs at full (practical) capacity. Ascertain the total costs for 330 orders applying the principles of activity-based costing. In the period being studied, how high are the 'actual' costs if only 50% of the total costs behave in a variable manner to the number of orders and the remainder are considered as fixed? How do you explain the difference?

3. **Costs of utilising resources.** Four equally qualified employees work in the invoicing department, in which there is no division of labour. Each employee simply works on tasks according to the time required. Work studies have shown that each of these employees is capable of allocating 400,000 transactions to accounts, recording 500,000 book entries and making 4,000 reconciliations of accounts in the period being studied. The company expects reduced sales due to the poor economic situation, and consequently this department will only be working at a maximum capacity of 80%. The department also has a manager who does not do any of the day-to-day work. A study yielded the following breakdown of costs for the employees for each process.

Process	Process costs
Allocation to accounts	207,000
Recording entries	72,500
Reconciliations	80,000
Management	72,500

(a) For a single period, ascertain the costs of utilising the resources and the costs of the unused capacity if there were actually 1,100,000 allocations to accounts, 1,400,000 book entries recorded and 10,000 reconciliations during the time period studied. To do so, use the department's capacity first and then the expected bottleneck in the sales market as the starting point in your determination of the budgeted activity volume. How does this result change if you allocate the *lmn* costs on the basis of the *lmi* costs or, alternatively, without this allocation?

(b) What connection do the costs of utilising resources have with the costs of used and idle capacity?

4. ***Target Costing***. The Innovative Star Plc is considering the launch of a new product called 'Newcomer'. Extensive market research has been undertaken for 'Newcomer' and has determined the following price demand function:

$$x = \alpha - \beta \cdot p \text{ with } \alpha = 200 \text{ and } \beta = 1$$

On the basis of a previous product design and the currently available technology a linear cost function arises for the production of 'Newcomer':

$$C(x) = c \cdot x$$

The unit cost c depends on the production conditions, represented by a variable θ. They can be reduced by efforts a of the technical designers, and the following relation is assumed:

$$c = \frac{k}{\theta} - a$$

For the construction activities, costs of $V(a)$ estimated as a square function occur:

$$V(a) = a^2$$

The Innovative Star plc strives to maximise profit.

(a) First of all, present the problems that arise in general if the fundamental Eq. (5.30) of *target costing* is to be found in the present scenario.

(b) Occasionally, the suggestion can be made to use the budgeted sales of *target costing* by the amount of the sales-maximum price when the existence of a price demand function is assumed. With such an approach, what is the budgeted sales price, the optimal construction efforts, the target profit and the target costs? (Assume $c = 140$ and $\theta = 2$.)

(c) Now determine the answer to question (b) when all interdependences are considered. How do these measures depend on the production conditions? What fundamental problems arise if these conditions are known only to the technical designers but not to company management?

5. **Life cycle costing.** From next year onwards, a car component supplier's spoiler division wants to offer the 'TUP' model in addition to its existing 'XVC' model. The new model is more aerodynamic as a result of better materials. It has already recorded the costs for this period.

Materials: 400,000

Material overheads: 48,000, of which 8,000 have already been incurred in preparation for obtaining material for XVC

Manufacturing costs I: 600,000, whereby 76,000 have been for XVC (test runs for new production)

Manufacturing costs II: 880,000, of which 100,000 are for XVC (also test runs)

Administration: 460,000, whereby the costs of construction drawings and obtaining official permits for XVC are 180,000

Distribution: 18,000

Special sales costs: 24,000 for special packing

A total of 500 TUPs were manufactured. The company uses material costs as the basis for charging material overheads. For manufacturing (cost centres F I and F II), it takes machine hours in each case. TUP needs 1.6 (1.4) hours of **Life cycle costing** machine time in F I (F II); 100 (150) hours have been taken up for test runs for XVC. Administration and distribution costs are charged as a premium based on the costs of production.

(a) Using a job costing system, ascertain total costs for TUP when you allocate the pre-production costs for XVC to TUP. How do allocated costs change when these pre-production costs are not allocated to TUP?

(b) Calculate total costs for XVC, firstly including and then excluding its pre-production costs. There are 900 direct material costs for each unit and the budget foresees a 12% premium for material overheads. The budget has hourly rates for machinery usage in the production items corresponding to those for TUP (without pre-production costs). In F I (F II), XVC takes up 2 (2.1) hours. The rate of the premium for administration (distribution) costs is 20% (9%) and the special sales costs are 50 per item; 400 XVCs are due to be made in the next period. Overall, it is estimated that 4,000 will be made.

Variance Analysis and Control

Contents

P. Schuster et al., *Management Accounting*,
Springer Texts in Business and Economics,
https://doi.org/10.1007/978-3-030-62022-6_6

Learning Objectives

After studying this chapter, you should be able to:
- Analyse the functions of cost and revenue controls
- Present the different methods of variance analyses and their corresponding explanations
- Determine and discuss typical cost and revenue variances
- Present the analysis and evaluation of variances in a coherent manner

6.1 Causes of Variances and Functions of Control

Control is a specific management function that follows planning, decision-making and execution. To fulfil this function, certain budgetary measures are compared with actual measures and the resulting difference is denoted as a *variance*.

6.1.1 Causes of Variances

Firstly, variances can be analysed according to their controllability. *Uncontrollable variances* arise from unpredictable random events; and are influenced by the fact that within an organisation, the result of any activity depends on environmental developments. Typical examples include external occurrences (e.g. economic crises or interest rate increases), intercompany occurrences (e.g. unexpected competition or inroads into the market) and inner-company occurrences (e.g. machine failure, loss of important workers or human error). Generally, *controllable variances* are avoidable variances and consequently receive most of management's limited attention.

Variances can occur for many diverse reasons, and Fig. 6.1 gives an overview of some possible causes.

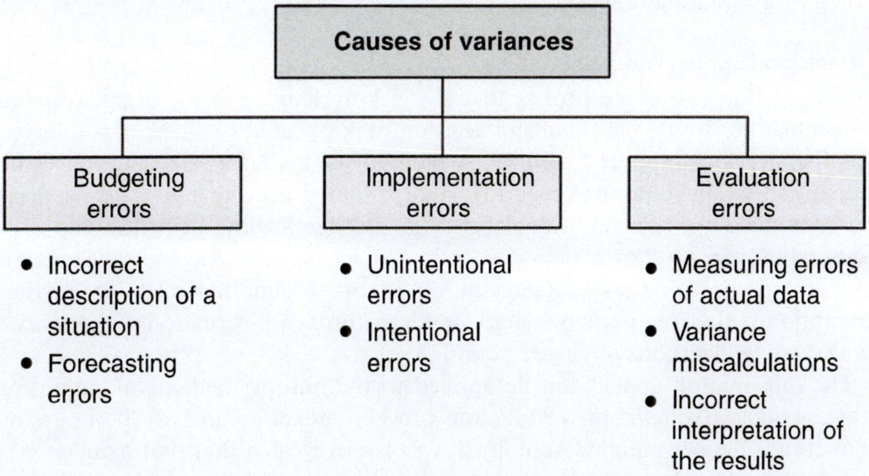

Fig. 6.1 Causes of variances

Budgeting errors can arise from an incorrect description of a situation, particularly the application of unsuitable decision models or wrong assumptions about the initial situation (e.g. an assumption of linear costs functions when costs are in fact non-linear). Planning and decision-making are regularly made under conditions of uncertainty (about the future environmental situation), and forecasting errors are the consequence of incorrect forecasts of environmental developments. While sufficiently precise previous experiences and/or expectations often exist, uncertainty may be reduced but cannot be completely avoided. The actual environmental situation causes differences in the results obtained in comparison to the original budget.

Implementation errors result from the incorrect execution of, for example, a task or activity. A distinction can be made between incorrect behaviour made unintentionally and intentionally. 'Unintentional errors' include, for example, machine failure, which could have been noticed and repaired by a detailed analysis. Intentional errors, on the contrary, are due to conscious decisions made by employees who can then consciously use the situation in the pursuit of their own self-interests.

The final cause of variances is due to *evaluation errors*. This predominantly includes measuring errors of actual data, such as incorrect notes or account recordings, variance miscalculations as well as an incorrect interpretation of the results, which can be either intentional or unintentional. Evaluation errors are not considered in the following sections as their avoidance must be achieved by organisational measures alone.

6.1.2 Functions of Control

The fundamental purpose of control is to uncover variances and to gather information to facilitate their evaluation. Control has two essential functions:
1. Decision support function
2. Behaviour-guiding function

▪ Decision Support Function

A primary function of control is to use the knowledge gained to assist in the improvement of future planning and decision-making processes, hereafter referred to as the 'decision support function'. A prerequisite is that it relates to a specific company situation containing repetitive and/or similar decisions. A one-time decision cannot be used for additional better knowledge leading to future improvements. However, as shown below, it is by no means necessary for the second function of control, that is, behavioural, to occur simultaneously. A further assumption is that the decisions made and environmental situations experienced are affected by decisions of earlier periods.

The information gained can be applied to the improvement of planning for future periods. *Example*: the production process budget assumes 1,900 hours of production time per annum. Actually, it was later revealed that this estimate was too optimistic because based upon normal maintenance procedures, production time is only 1,830 hours.

Additionally, the information gained can also be used to perform actions, with the aim of avoiding future variances, actions that can depend on processes, personnel or organisational type. For example, a production process that gets out of balance (with high rates of defective items) can be fixed.

■ Behaviour-Guiding Function

The second essential function of control is the *coordination* of decentralised company decisions. Control and coordination problems appear due to the existence of two conditions:

1. (Potential) target conflicts
2. Information asymmetry

Target conflicts occur when the targets and objectives of the decision-maker and the company's management differ.

Asymmetrically distributed information is typical within companies. Due to their activities and/or their expertise, divisional managers typically have better and more accurate information in comparison to senior company management located at head office. Usually, this is *the reason* to delegate decision-making. Had head office possessed all of the information themselves, rather than the divisions, there would be no reason for decentralisation. Regarding potential target conflicts, asymmetric information also exists due to the fact that the authority (the head office) cannot directly observe the decisions or the situation in which the particular behaviour was located.

If both conditions apply, a decision-maker can use their better information base for their own target achievements, which may possibly be to the detriment of head office. Senior management at head office may express a desired behaviour, which is non-verifiable. In the case of unfavourable results, the decision-maker can simply claim to have engaged in the correct behaviour, but that the unfavourable environmental situation prevented a better result. As a result, it is impossible for head office to recognise the causes of an observed variance.

Consequently, head office would like to guide the decision-maker's behaviour against such possible consequences (therefore, influencing *other people's* decisions). Direct behavioural control is often impossible or too expensive, so the control of results is used as a viable alternative. From previous decisions, conclusions on the real behaviour of the decision-maker can be made. Even though their behaviour cannot be changed retrospectively, a *future* incentive is constructed for the decision-maker to adapt his behaviour going forward (although generally not entirely in accordance with head office). Head office therefore controls the future behaviour of the decision-maker with the introduction of these controls (or threats). A consideration of previous decisions is not necessary (this will not apply if an employee does not immediately and fully understand and anticipate the function of control from the beginning but is still in a learning process. If so, several periods are then required, which enable them to adapt their behaviour according to the results of control). In a single-person company, this function plays no role.

Table 6.1 Functions of control

Periodicity context	Single decision problem	Repeated decision problem
One-person context	No function	Decision support function
Multi-person context	Behaviour-guiding function	Decision support function and behaviour-guiding function

Table 6.1 gives an overview of the two functions of control. Both functions can appear separately or simultaneously based upon the underlying situation. As discussed below, the fulfilment of both of these functions requires different control systems.

Relation to the Organisation

The application of control to guide the behaviour of decision-makers emphasises the need for a wider analysis of the problems of control. It is not enough to analyse control methods in isolation. The behavioural effect is relevant when considering assessment and incentive systems (e.g. profit-related payments, bonus plans, promotions) and, thus, relate to the organisation and, specifically, human resource management. Additionally, insights from the behavioural sciences imply that many people have a conscious or unconscious aversion to controls and when faced with them possibly react with dysfunctional behaviour.

Important

Unintended effects can arise, and managers can make their decisions in a way that optimises the measures by which they are assessed, for example, cost variances. If these do not register all of the effects of the decisions, two consequences can arise:

(i) Effects not registered will no longer be considered. *Example*: If only costs are analysed, quality or on-time delivery may not be evaluated for the purposes of the assessment.

(ii) Externalities, that is, effects on the other company areas, can arise without being considered as part of the initial decision-making. *Example*: A production manager reduces the profit in his area by procuring materials from the purchase department at short notice and with frequently changed specifications.

Incentive systems can have huge effects on budgeting if the superior knowledge of the decision-makers about the respective decision situation could be used in participative budgeting systems. The cooperation of the decision-makers in the planning process influences the selection of budgeting measures used in the determination of the variances and, with it, how the decision-makers are subsequently assessed.

6.1.3 Analysing Options

Variance analysis is less concerned with issues surrounding the determination and isolation of single variances than with *contextual* aspects. Causes for the variances need to be found as the amounts of the single variances are only symptoms of possible deeper underlying causes.

The availability of actual data for the influencing factors is simply a requirement, and, undoubtedly, in many cases it can be found easily. However, for other potential influencing factors they cannot be recorded at all, in general or for economic reasons, thereby ensuring that valuable information is lost.

Variance analysis addresses the question of whether additional influencing factors should be determined considering the corresponding evaluation costs. This evaluation should separate controllable and uncontrollable causes as only the former type can be affected. The selection of variances to be analysed is not only limited to those with conceptual relevance but also includes those with practical importance. With 20 to 30 cost types and 100 cost centres (this would not be considered an extreme case), between 2,000 and 3,000 monthly positions may arise. Due to the existence of evaluation costs, it is not meaningful to analyse all of these variances as a matter of policy.

In practice, rules of thumb are mostly applied. Most frequently, they are based on the following criteria:

- Absolute amount of the variance: that is, the amount of the negative or positive variance only; for example, further analysis is required if the variance is higher than ±100,000.
- Relative amount of the variance: related to the budgeted or the actual measure (e.g. if the variance is higher than ±5% of the original budgeted amount).
- A combination of both of the above criteria.

The *economic feasibility* of such rules will be analysed in this chapter. The evaluation of unintended variances provides decision support, while the intended variances (behavioural variances) are also relevant to the behaviour-guiding function. Evaluation models are different in regard to the two functions. Even though most examples come from the area of the execution or implementing of processes, identical considerations apply in relation to budgeting and evaluation errors.

6.2 Fundamental Concept of the Control Process

The control process can be divided into the following:

- Setting up the control field
- Determination of budgeted and actual measures
- Comparison of both measures and disaggregation of the total variance into separate variances
- Interpretation of the results

6.2.1 Setting Up the Control Field

The control field encompasses the definition of the control object, the extent of the control exerted and the control frequency. Control objects are activities or facts and circumstances (e.g. production costs divided into cost types within a cost centre; revenues earned by every product group and region).

The *control extent* marks the range of control exerted. For example, it is possible that all cost types for all cost centres or only certain cost types or costs centres are subject to control. In deciding between a complete and a partial analysis, costs and benefits need to be considered.

Due to the limited capacity of the employees executing the analysis and the lower costs of partial analyses, the latter are regularly chosen for economic viability reasons. Occasionally, this can lead to missing some necessary adaptation activities. On the other hand, a more extensive control extent requires more time, and a possible delay of the necessary adaptation activities.

The *control frequency* indicates in which intervals control activities are repeated (i.e. weekly, monthly, quarterly or annually). The economic viability principle is also to be considered here. It, too, is related to the control extent: the more extensive the analysis, the less frequently it has to be undertaken.

Practical optimisation models for the determination of control extent and frequency rarely exist, as the benefits of more extensive controls are difficult to quantify. Therefore, in practice, control fields are generally decided upon based on experience.

6.2.2 Determination of Budgeted and Actual Measures

The choice of a budgeted measure depends on the task it should fulfil. The following measures are especially worth consideration:

- Actual measures of the company from an earlier period
- Normalised measures as an average of actual measures of several earlier periods
- Actual measures of 'comparable' companies
- Budgeted measures from a forecast
- Budgeted measures as standardised measures: standard, optimal or behaviour-oriented measures

Actual Measures

Actual company data from an earlier period are applicable when making *time comparisons*. With this approach, changes to the respective measures can be well expressed over time. However, for both the decision support function and the behaviour-guiding function, past actual data are unsuitable as budgeted measures. As Eugen Schmalenbach (1934) stated, to do so would be to compare 'inefficiency with inefficiency'. For example, what insight does a variance generate that is calculated on the basis of a very unfavourable cost situation, possibly as a result of extreme inefficiency in the previous month? Yet, in accordance with the 'philosophy' of *continuous improvement* the comparison of actual data with actual data gains importance, as it depends on the changes that have occurred over the course of time.

- **Normalised Measures**

Normalised measures are an *average* of actual measures from several earlier periods, thereby ensuring that the problem of large fluctuations is reduced. This approach seems slightly more suitable but still does not fully solve the problem.

- **Actual Measures of 'Comparable' Companies**

Intercompany comparisons are important for competitive analysis. However, for the control process, such measures are not fully useable, as:

1. It is difficult to actually find comparable companies. In a strict sense of comparability of identical product groups and production technology, there is most likely no directly comparable company. In a reduced sense, there might be companies with similar characteristic features and if so, variances must be interpreted accordingly.
2. Generally, it is doubtful what insights can be gained from such variances. Is the actual performance of another company really a worthwhile target? In the context of the strategic positioning of the company, *differences* from other companies will instead be a critical success factor.
3. Another problem is being able to retrieve budgeted measures with identical definition and with identical details. The 'more comparable' the company whose actual data serve as the basis of the budgeted data, the less likely they will be known for reasons of competition. Both therefore weaken the insights gained from the control process.

- **Budgeted Measures from a Forecast**

The forecast here is based on the expected actual measure of a future account period. On the cost side, they can often be relatively exact and with low risk (e.g. failure of a machine). However, the forecast of future revenues is essentially more inaccurate.

One advantage is that these measures also simultaneously serve as items for company planning and budgeting and as a basis for operational decisions (e.g. in determining the optimum production and sales programme, procedural decisions). In contrast to an intercompany comparison, they are primarily focused on company strategy.

On the other hand, forecast measures also contain expected inefficiencies because they must be included in a company's plans. An incentive to avoid the 'average' inefficiencies is not induced by using such budgeted measures.

- **Budgeted Measures as Standardised Measures**

Budgeted measures as standardised measures *consciously* deviate from the forecast measures and are based on fixed prices, oriented more or less towards actual prices. There are three variations:

1. *Standard measures*. These are based on normal production conditions, such as normal capacity utilisation and an average consumption of input factors. Standard measures aim to simplify the budgeting process and can deviate from the normalised measures by using an average of earlier periods.
2. *Optimal measures*. Standard measures can be aligned based upon future optimal conditions. For example, standard costs are calculated on the assumption

of optimal capacity utilisation and optimal consumption of production factors, that is, without inefficiencies. However, budgeted measures determined on this basis are frequently demotivational, as the results can easily appear unfavourable.

3. *Behaviour-oriented measures*. Standard measures can also be derived from behaviour-oriented considerations (i.e. from behavioural science and from economic considerations).
   (i) Behavioural science uses psychological knowledge about typical behaviour patterns and situation-specific circumstances, which can then be applied to the behavioural control of decision-makers.
   (ii) Economic considerations are based on models assuming rational decision-makers. The behaviour arises from utility-maximising individuals with asymmetrically distributed information and potential conflicts of interests with other people.

Budgeted measures that serve as behaviour-guiding often do not comply with decision support. In this instance, two budgeted measures are required, one for each function. Moreover, the motivational effect is often only reached if the forecast is kept secret by the relevant decision-makers. Consequently, their superior knowledge of the decision situation cannot be utilised for corporate budgeting.

All options have specific advantages and disadvantages and as a result, a general recommendation for the determination of budgeted measures cannot be made.

▪ Determination of the Actual Measures

The actual measures of control must be identically defined as the chosen budgeted measures. Fixed costs are an additional problem, as the actual consumption does not distinguish between fixed and variable costs, and, as a result, the corresponding variance cannot be divided appropriately. In practice, a working hypothesis is often used to solve this problem, in that actual costs and budgeted costs are assumed to correspond to their fixed costs, and variances only appear in relation to variable costs.

6.3 Variance Analysis Options

6.3.1 The Reference System

Once the problems described above have been addressed, a comparison between budgeted and actual measures can occur. In the following section, we will firstly discuss costs under the working hypothesis mentioned above that variances only appear in relation to variable costs. Fixed costs are therefore ignored. The budget measures are therefore the budgeted variable costs and are indexed with b, in addition to the actual costs with a.

The difference between these two measures is the *total variance* and it can be constructed in two ways:

1. Actual-budgeted comparison: $\Delta C = C^a - C^b$.
2. Budgeted-actual comparison: $\Delta C = C^b - C^a$

The way chosen is largely a matter of preference, as both are equivalent. It could be argued that cost increases for budgeted costs should have a positive algebraic sign and this works for an actual-budgeted comparison.

A positive variance could be assessed as 'favourable' with a negative variance assessed as 'unfavourable'. In practice, it is not as simple as it seems as on some occasions a *cost* increase best serves the company's objective, for example, by recognising a strategic niche in which developmental efforts should be made so as to be successful in the long term. Assuming that a future higher profit than budgeted is viewed 'positively', it arises:

$$\Delta\Pi = \Pi^a - \Pi^b = \left[R^a - C^a\right] - \left[R^b - C^b\right] = \left[R^a - R^b\right] + \left[C^b - C^a\right]$$

Thus, in determining the relevant cost variances, a budgeted-actual comparison should be chosen. Conversely, with revenue, contribution margin or a profit variance, an actual-budgeted comparison should be used. By continuously using the negative algebraic sign in the definition of profit for cost variances, actual-budgeted comparisons are used for all partial variances:

$$\Delta\Pi = \Pi^a - \Pi^b = \left[R^a - R^b\right] - \left[C^a - C^b\right]$$

Another possibility would be to point out if each variance is a favourable or unfavourable one, which is common in many American textbooks by denoting either *F* (*favourable*) or *U* (*unfavourable*).

■ **Reference Basis**

The calculation of variances can be further structured by the reference basis chosen for the presentation of cost changes. *Reference bases* are either actual or budgeted costs. By applying the actual costs as a reference basis, changes are measured by reference to the actual costs. Budget costs arise from actual cost plus the appropriate change.
Reference system linked to actual measures: $y^b = y^a - \Delta^a y$
Reference system linked to budgeted measures: $y^a = y^b - \Delta^b y$
These two variations again only differ in the algebraic sign of the variance Δ.

However, essential differences arise with the disaggregation of the total variance into individual variances. This is because the change in an influencing factor is weighted by actual measures at one time and by budgeted measures at another time. In the case of a reference system linked to actual measures, the question underlying the subsequent variance analysis is how high the variance would be based on the actual situation. The scale for the variance amount is then the actual situation. With a reference system linked to budgeted measures, the question analogously would relate to how high the variance would be if, based on the planned situation, only one influencing factor would have encountered a variance. The choice of the reference base aims to determine to what extent the actual situation describes the (more) 'correct' situation (this would possibly be the case when the variances are based on uncontrollable causes) or when the planned situation represents the (more) 'correct' description of the situation (i.e. if variances are as a result of controllable causes).

Background Information

With emphasis on the decision support function, the use of actual reference bases could be promoted because they represent the most current manifestation of reality. The question would be: what effect on costs would it have if a factor had experienced *no* variance?

For the function of behaviour-guiding, budgeting factors are regarded as suitable, as they represent the desirable development that was not realised due to the existence of variances. In addition, the judgement would be impaired by actual uncontrollable developments.

According to the majority of the literature and company practice, actual-budgeted comparisons with the reference system linked to budgeted measures are to be applied in the following way. To shorten the manner of writing, Δ replaces Δ^b. The following example demonstrates the effects of different reference systems on particular variance amounts.

6

► Example: Effects of Different Reference Systems

A combination of the two types, the calculation of the variances and optional reference systems, formally leads to four possibilities for the calculation of variances.

To illustrate this, we assume the following factor prices r and factor quantity q: $r^b = 10$, $q^b = 21$; $r^a = 12$, $q^a = 20$.

From this results: budgeted costs $C^b = r^b \cdot p^b = 210$ and actual costs $C^a = r^a \cdot q^a = 240$.

Actual-budgeted comparison with the reference system linked to budgeted measures:

$$\Delta C = C^a - C^b = \left(r^b + \Delta^b r\right)\cdot\left(q^b \cdot \Delta^b q\right) - r^b \cdot q^b = \Delta^b r \cdot q^b + r^b \cdot \Delta^b q + \Delta^b r \cdot \Delta^b q =$$
$$= 2\cdot 21 + 10\cdot(-1) + 2\cdot(-1) = 42 - 10 - 2 = +30$$

Actual-budgeted comparison with the reference system linked to actual measures:

$$\Delta C = C^a - C^b = r^a \cdot q^a - \left(r^a - \Delta^b r\right)\cdot\left(q^a - \Delta^b q\right) = \Delta^b r \cdot q^a + r^a \cdot \Delta^b q - \Delta^b r \cdot \Delta^b q =$$
$$= 2\cdot 20 + 12\cdot(-1) - 2\times(-1) = 40 - 12 + 2 = +30$$

Budgeted-actual comparison with the reference system linked to budgeted measures:

$$\Delta C = C^b - C^a = r^b \cdot q^b - \left(r^b - \Delta^a r\right)\cdot\left(q^b - \Delta^a q\right) = \Delta^a r \cdot q^b + r^b \cdot \Delta^a q - \Delta^a r \cdot \Delta^a q =$$
$$= (-2)\cdot 21 + 10\cdot 1 - (-2)\cdot 1 = -42 + 10 + 2 = -30$$

Budgeted-actual comparison with the reference system linked to actual measures:

$$\Delta C = C^b - C^a = \left(r^a - \Delta^a r\right)\cdot\left(q^a + \Delta^a q\right) - r^a \cdot q^a = \Delta^a r \cdot q^a + r^a \cdot \Delta^a q + \Delta^a r \cdot \Delta^a q =$$
$$= (-2)\cdot 20 + 12\cdot 1 + (-2)\cdot 1 = -40 + 12 - 2 = -30$$

As shown above, two styles in each case lead to equivalent results: the amounts of the separate partial variances correspond, and the variations are based purely on different algebraic signs (+ or –). Therefore, the problem can be reduced to the two that seem the most meaningful: budgeted-actual comparison with the reference system linked to actual measures, and actual-budgeted comparison with the reference system linked to budgeted measures. ◄

6.3.2 The Fair Disaggregation of the Total Variance

Independent of the method chosen, the result is a total variance, which by itself provides little informational value. The total variance can be zero, even if there are several variances, provided that they offset each other. For example, a factor price increase can be offset by a lower consumption of that particular factor. Therefore, the real challenge of variance analysis consists of the disaggregation of each total variance into its single variances (or partial variances). This raises the question of whether this disaggregation is actually useful at all.

Fundamentally, all of the relevant information is contained in the change of the respective influencing factor Δy_i. For example, in the area of production, quantitative productivity reference numbers and not costs (valued amounts) serve as the essential control information for new manufacturing technologies.

The benefit of the variances in comparison to the value of the influencing factors predominantly serves as the quantification of the profit changes caused by changes to the influencing factor.

▪ Presuppositions for Disaggregation

Presuppositions for the disaggregation of the total variance into single variances are as follows:

1. An existing functional relationship exists between costs and certain influencing factors (cost and revenue determination factors) or that such a relationship can at least be assumed. The costs then can be represented as $C = C(y_1, y_2, ..., y_n)$ with y_i as the influencing factors.
2. Budgeted value y_i^b exists for these influencing factors.
3. Actual values y_i^a of the influencing factors are observed or measured.

In the case that no functional relation can be assumed, the impact of changes to an influencing factor on the costs cannot be measured at all. For cost functions, very precise functional relationships can often be found on account of technical circumstances; whereas for revenue functions, only an estimate of the connection can be guessed. Consequently, an inaccurate estimate can also result in variances (this will be examined later in this chapter).

▪ Disaggregation of the Total Variance

Assuming actual-budgeted comparison with the reference system linked to budgeted measures, the total variance is as follows:

$$\Delta C = C^a - C^b = C\left(y_1^a, y_2^a, \ldots, y_n^a\right) - C\left(y_1^b, y_2^b, \ldots, y_n^b\right) \tag{6.1}$$

A disaggregation of the total variance would be desirable in the way that the single variances in each case exactly relate to the change in an influencing factor $\Delta y_i = y_i^a - y_i^b$.

This presents no difficulties if the (marginal) costs based on the influencing factors are connected additively and are independent of each other. This possibly applies to many cost types within a cost centre (control object).

$$C\left(y_1, y_2, \ldots, y_n\right) = C\left(y_1\right) + C\left(y_2\right) + \ldots + C\left(y_n\right)$$

From it arises

$$\Delta C = \Delta C_1 + \Delta C_2 + \ldots + \Delta C_n$$

whereas $\Delta C_i = C\left(y_i^a\right) - C\left(y_i^b\right)$

However, non-additive linkages also regularly exist, mostly on the cost side where there are multiplicative linkages. Costs are the (input) factor prices multiplied by the factor amounts consumed. The factor amounts correspond to limited production processes with the capacity of the cost centre multiplied by the direct consumption coefficient, which indicates how many units are required per capacity unit.

6

In the special case of two cost-influencing factors, it follows that with multiplicative linkages of cost components no disaggregation of the total variance exists; and that all single variances are exclusively induced by changes to a single influencing factor (see ◘ Fig. 6.2). The costs are composed of the factor price r and the factor amount q, that is, $C(r, q) = r \cdot q$. Assuming an actual-budgeted comparison with the reference system linked to budgeted measures, the following variance arises:

$$\Delta C = C^a - C^b = r^a \cdot q^a - r^b \cdot q^b =$$
$$= \left(r^b + \Delta r\right) \cdot \left(q^b + \Delta q\right) - r^b \cdot q^b = \Delta r \cdot q^b + r^b \cdot \Delta q + \Delta q \cdot \Delta q$$

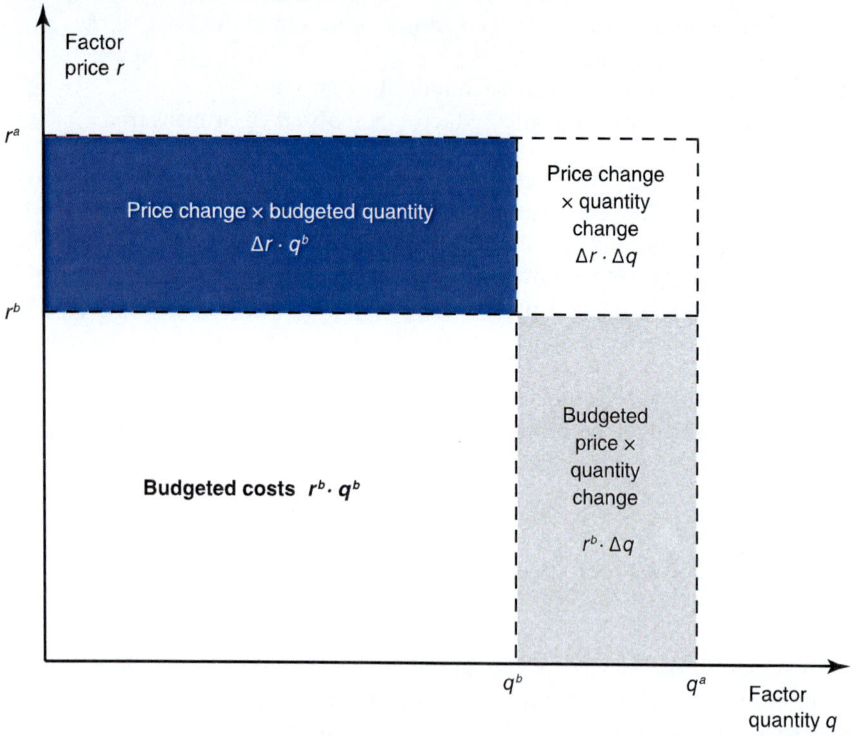

◘ **Fig. 6.2** Price and efficiency variances

The total variance consists of first-order variances, namely a price variance and an efficiency variance, in addition to a composite variance or second-order variance $\Delta r \cdot \Delta q$, caused by changes to both influencing factors.

The composite variance does not disappear if changes to the influencing factors are not additive but multiplicatively defined: $r^a = r^b \cdot \delta r$ with δr as the index of changes and $q^a = q^b \cdot \delta q$ analogously. The total variance is then: $\Delta C = r^b \cdot q^b \cdot (\delta r \cdot \delta q - 1)$.

An exact allocation of changes onto one of the two influencing factors is only possible without the existence of a composite variance; however, this can only be the case if either $\Delta r = 0$ or $\Delta q = 0$. If only one single influencing factor has changed, the disaggregation problem becomes irrelevant.

The total variance can be split up by the separation of the change caused by one influencing factor, with the impact on the other single variances also encompassing the composite variance. The two possibilities for it to occur are as follows:

$$\Delta C = \Delta r \cdot q^b + \Delta_1 (r,q)$$

$$\Delta C = \Delta_2 (r,q) + r^b \cdot \Delta q$$

If more than two influencing factors are multiplicatively tied together, additional composite variances will arise.

Example: $C = r \cdot v \cdot u$ and v equals the direct consumption coefficients for the considered input factor and u the capacity utilisation of the cost centres.

$$\begin{aligned} \Delta C = {} & \Delta r \cdot v^b \cdot u^b + r^b \cdot \Delta v \cdot u^b + r^b \cdot v^b \cdot \Delta u + && (\text{first-order variances}) \\ & + \Delta r \cdot \Delta v \cdot u^b + \Delta r \cdot v^b \cdot \Delta u + r^b \cdot \Delta v \cdot \Delta u + && (\text{second-order variances}) \\ & + \Delta r \cdot \Delta v \cdot \Delta u && (\text{third-order variances}) \end{aligned}$$

As a result, this indicates that a disaggregation of the total variance based upon causation is *only* possible if additive linkages of the costs exist based on the influencing factors alone, as multiplicative relations prohibit this. This is also true for subtler multiplicative linkages, as they can exist in revenue-influencing factors.

In more general terms: a disaggregation according to causation is impossible if the mixed derivatives (or difference quotients) of the costs after a minimum of two influencing factors do not disappear, that is,

$$\frac{\partial^2 C(y_1, y_2, \ldots, y_n)}{\partial y_i \cdot \partial y_j} \neq 0 \text{ for at least one pair } i, j = 1, 2, \ldots, n; i \neq j \tag{6.2}$$

Then, the effects of the change from y_i cannot be isolated from the change of y_j and vice versa.

Condition (6.2) also requires that the influencing factors are dependent on each other. This is often the case for the revenue side, but less so for costs. For example, the sales price depends on the amount of a product sold if a monopolistic range of the price-demand function exists. In determining the revenue variance based upon a price change, it must be considered that with the change in the sales price, the sales volume has also changed. Another example would be advertising activities, which affect the sales volume or the sales price. On the cost side, examples are higher repair costs that lead to lower energy costs or the use of an inferior production factor with lower costs simultaneously leading to higher amounts of waste or extended production times.

The disaggregation of the total variance must consider such interdependences to derive a meaningful result. In this example, the following simple cost function is assumed:

$$C(y_1, y_2) = y_1 + y_2(y_1)$$

If neglected, the functional relation of y_2 and y_1 leads to a (partly) unjustified allocation of partial variances to y_2, which is actually caused by a change to y_1. Therefore, another budgeted measure $y_2(y_1^i)$ is determined, which can extract these induced changes:

6

$$\Delta C = y_1^a + y_2^a - (y_1^b + y_2^b) = (y_1^a + y_1^b) + \left[(y_2^a - y_2(y_1^a)) + (y_2(y_1^a) - y_2^b)\right]$$
$$= \left[(y_1^a - y_1^b) + (y_2(y_1^a) - y_2^b)\right] + (y_2^a - y_2(y_1^a)) \quad (6.3)$$

$y_2^b = y_2(y_1^b)$ applies. The first component in (6.3) corresponds to the *direct* effect of y_1's impact on the costs, whereas the second variance corresponds to the *indirect* effect due to y_2. Only the third single variance can be allocated directly to the change in y_2.

N^{th}-Order Variances

- An nth-order variance is a variance in which the differences between actual and budgeted values are caused by n influencing factors. It inevitably appears when influencing factors are tied multiplicatively together.
- Only first-order variances (within the given framework of an actual-budgeted comparison with the reference system linked to budgeted measures) are accurately allocated; all higher variances appear from changes to several influencing factors together.
- If different people are responsible for two influencing factors, the responsibility of the second-order variance $\Delta y_1 \cdot \Delta y_2$ cannot be precisely assigned. Each is individually responsible as, if one had kept to its factors (i.e. $\Delta y_1 = 0$ or $\Delta y_2 = 0$), there would be no composite variance. Alternatively, a division of the responsibility would be problematic as for example, if a variance doubles, let us assume Δy_1, the composite variance also doubles, and with it the part allocated to the person not directly responsible for it.

Allocation according to causation can be sufficiently solved in this way. However, difficulties with the disaggregation appear when the functional relationship does not correspond to the underlying causal dependences. Often it is known that two influencing factors are related to each other, but not how this is so and which one is the driving force. Both influencing factors may depend on an unspecified (or unobservable) third factor. In continuation of the above *example*, this means that the functional connection of y_1 and y_2 could be also represented in the form of $y_1(y_2)$. The change in y_2 also includes the induced (partial) variance of y_1 and it arises:

$$\Delta C = \left(y_1^a - y_1\left(y_2^a\right)\right) + \left[\left(y_2^a - y_2^b\right) + y_1\left(y_2^a\right) - y_1^b\right]$$

This obviously deviates from (6.3). Thus, without knowledge of the causal chain of influencing factors, a disaggregation according to causation is impossible.

6.3.3 Methods of Variance Analysis

Different methods of variance analysis that have been developed by both theory and company practice will be outlined presently. According to the statements in the section above, they are a *more or less appropriate* solution to the problem of multiplicatively tied influencing factors. The distinction between them lies in how, and to what extent, they allocate the higher-order variances to the first-order variances.

The main methods are as follows:

- Method of differentiation.
- Method of alternatives.
- Cumulative method.
- Symmetric method.
- Min method.

Method of Differentiation

With this method, the higher-order variances remain unallocated to the first-order variances but are revealed separately, *en bloc* in total or separately. Thus, the allocation problem is not solved.

Method of Alternatives

The method of alternatives calculates single variances based upon the assumption that exactly one influencing factor is changed from actual value to budgeted value, with the remaining influencing factors unchanged (i.e. ceteris paribus). Two possibilities therefore arise depending on whether it originates from budgeted or actual costs:

$$\Delta C_i^{(1)} = C\left(y_1^a, y_2^a, \ldots, y_i^a, \ldots, y_n^a\right) - C\left(y_1^a, y_2^a, \ldots, y_i^b, \ldots, y_n^a\right)$$

$$\Delta C_i^{(2)} = C\left(y_1^b, y_2^b, \ldots, y_i^a, \ldots, y_n^b\right) - C\left(y_1^b, y_2^b, \ldots, y_i^b, \ldots, y_n^b\right)$$

in each case for $i = 1, 2, \ldots, n$. In the first case, every single variance $\Delta C_i^{(1)}$ encloses all higher-order variances, which contain Δy_i. Therefore, the variances of higher order are repeatedly considered. In the second case, no single variance $\Delta C_i^{(2)}$ contains variances of higher order. Generally, these results depend on the chosen reference system. They are considered for an actual-budgeted comparison with the reference systems linked to budgeted measures and vice versa for a budgeted-actual comparison linked to actual measures.

In both cases, the sum of the single variances no longer corresponds with the total variance. In general, it cannot be said that one method generates (calculates) *too small* single variances and another *too large* since the variances of higher order can be either positive or negative.

▪ Cumulative Method

The cumulative method assigns variances of higher order differently in comparison to single variances. The aim is to produce the sums that equal the single variances and the total variance. It proceeds as follows: first, an order of the influencing factors is decided upon. With an actual-budgeted comparison, the first single variance is determined analogously to the method of alternatives:

6

$$\Delta C_1 = C\left(y_1^a, y_2^a, \ldots, y_i^a, \ldots, y_n^a\right) - C\left(y_1^b, y_2^a, \ldots, y_i^a, \ldots, y_n^a\right)$$

In contrast to the method of alternatives, the other single variances are no longer calculated by the same comparison basis (here C_i) but rather by the last differential value used for determining the previous single variance. These intermediate measures as target figures are sequentially numbered. Therefore, for the second and subsequent influencing factors, the following arises:

$$\Delta C_2 = C\left(y_1^b, y_2^a, y_3^a, \ldots, y_n^a\right) - C\left(y_1^b, y_2^b, y_3^a, \ldots, y_n^a\right)$$

$$\Delta C_i = C\left(y_1^b, \ldots, y_{i-1}^b, y_i^a, y_{i+1}^a, \ldots, y_n^a\right) - C\left(y_1^b, \ldots, y_{i-1}^b, y_i^b, y_{i+1}^a, \ldots, y_n^a\right)$$

etc.... The last single variance again corresponds to the one calculated using the method of alternatives, here assuming (12):

$$\Delta C_n = C\left(y_1^b, y_2^b, \ldots, y_{n-1}^b, y_n^a\right) - C\left(y_1^b, y_2^b, \ldots, y_{n-1}^b, y_n^b\right)$$

It is easy to recognise that the sum of the single variances corresponds to the total variance. However, it is also problematic due to the fact that the amount of the single variances calculated for the different influencing factors depends on the order of their calculation.

▪ Symmetric Method

This method attempts to achieve an equal split of the higher-order variances, thus avoiding the order problem referred to above.

In the case of two multiplicatively tied influencing factors (and only in this context), this can be interpreted relatively easily as a weighting of the respective variance multiplied by the average of the budgeted and actual value of the other influencing factor. We assume $C = r \cdot q$ with r as a factor price and q as a factor amount. The price variance and the efficiency variance are calculated according to the symmetric method as:

$$\Delta C_r = \Delta r \cdot q^b + \frac{\Delta r \cdot \Delta q}{2} = \Delta r \cdot \frac{2q^b + \left(q^a - q^b\right)}{2} = \Delta r \cdot \frac{q^b + q^a}{2} = \Delta r \cdot \overline{q}$$

$$\Delta C_q = r^b \cdot \Delta q + \frac{\Delta r \cdot \Delta q}{2} = \Delta q \cdot \frac{2r^b + \left(r^a - r^b\right)}{2} = \Delta q \cdot \frac{r^b + r^a}{2} = \overline{r} \cdot \Delta q$$

The problem with the symmetric variance, however, is that no convincing explanation can be provided for the arbitrary subdivision of the higher-order variances with an equal allocation given to both. Decision theory uses a comparable assumption with the *Laplace rule*. Less convincing is the argument that the composite variance behaves directly proportional to every change amongst the single variances.

► Example

In a production department, the budget for an input factor assumes a factor price r^b of 240 and a factor amount of $q^b = 350$. The actual data are a factor price $r^a = 270$ and a factor amount $q^a = 400$.

The total variance based on an actual-budgeted comparison amounts to

$C^a = 270 \cdot 400 =$	108,000
$C^b = 240 \cdot 350 =$	84,000
$\Delta C =$	24,000

Method of differentiation:

Price variance: $\Delta r \cdot q^b = 30 \cdot 350 =$	10,500
Efficiency variance $r^b \cdot \Delta q = 240 \cdot 50 =$	12,000
Variance of second order: $\Delta r \cdot \Delta q = 30 \cdot 50 =$	1,500

Method of alternatives:

(1)	Starting with the actual costs C^a:		
	Price variance: 108,000 – 240·400 =	12,000	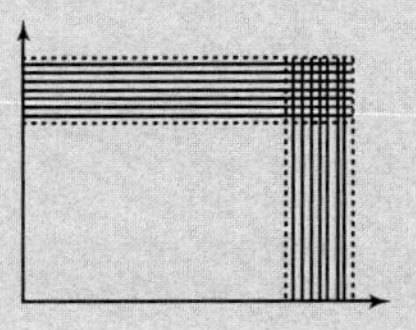
	Efficiency variance: 108,000 – 270·350 =	13,500	
(2)	Starting with budgeted cost C^b:		
	Price variance: 270·350 – 84,000 =	10,500	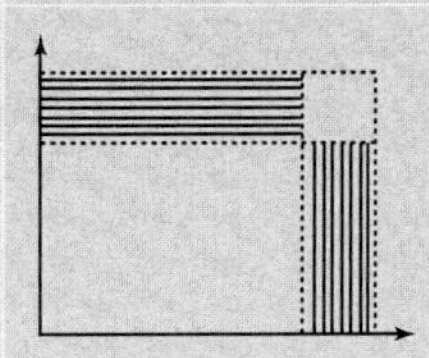
	Efficiency variance: 240·400 – 84,000 =	12,000	

Cumulative method:

(1)	Firstly splitting off the price variance:		
	Price variance: 108,000 – 240·400 =	12,000	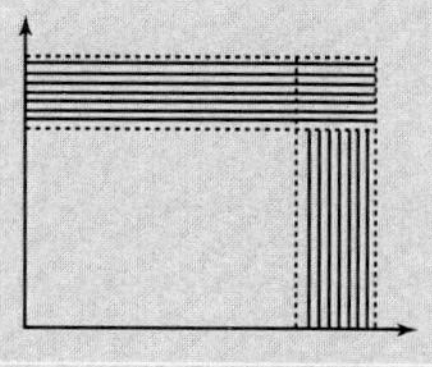
	Efficiency variance: 240·400 – 84,000 =	12,000	
(2)	Firstly splitting off the efficiency variance:		
	Efficiency variance: 108,000 – 270·350 =	13,500	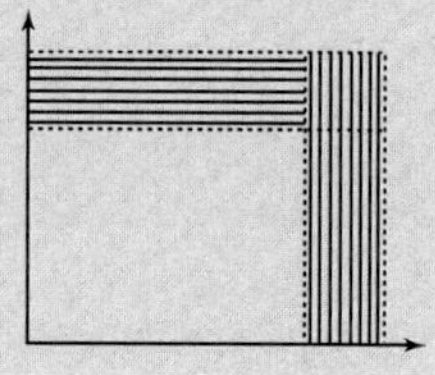
	Price variance: 270·350 – 84,000 =	10,500	

Symmetric method:

Price variance: $\Delta r \cdot q^b + \Delta r \cdot \Delta q/2$ =	11,250	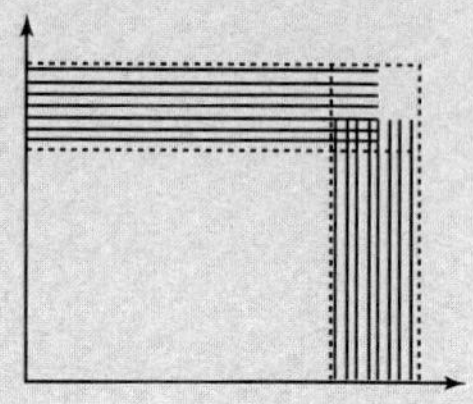
Efficiency variance: $r^b \cdot \Delta q + \Delta r \cdot \Delta q/2$ =	12,750	

◄

- **Min Method**

The min method, like the method of differentiation, generally includes an explicit identification of higher-order variances. However, it differs from that method by having a specific rule for the choice of base factors from which the cost changes are weighted. The weighting of Δ measures depends on the minimum of the remaining cost-influencing factors. Since no standardised definition of cost-allocation factors exist, this approach can have consequences for the explicit identification of partial variances including several Δ measures.

In the example of two influencing factors $C = r \cdot q$ with r as a factor price and q as a factor amount, the following approach is shown. The total variance is:

$$\Delta C = C^a - C^b = r^a \cdot q^a - r^b \cdot q^b$$

Case 1: All actual measures exceed the budgeted measures. With first-order variances, only partial variances with Δ measures are shown. The sum of these variances is

$$\Delta r \cdot \min\left\{q^a;\ q^b\right\} + \Delta q \cdot \min\left\{r^a;\ r^b\right\} = \Delta r \cdot q^b + \Delta q \cdot r^b$$

These variances correspond to the first-order variances according to the method of differentiation based upon the *budgeted measures*. The total variance arises by addition (with separate identification) of the variances of higher order $\Delta r \cdot \Delta q$.

Case 2: All actual measures are below the budgeted measures. Here, the sum of the first-order variances according to the min method is:

$$\Delta r \cdot \min\left\{q^a; q^b\right\} + \Delta q \cdot \min\left\{r^a; r^b\right\} = \Delta r \cdot q^a + \Delta q \cdot r^a$$

The separate Δ measures are now weighted using the *actual reference figures*. This implies that the variances of higher order $\Delta r \cdot \Delta q$ are to be *subtracted* so as to achieve the total variance.

Case 3: Different changes amongst the influencing factors. In the following example we assume that the actual price exceeds the budgeted price ($r^a > r^b$), while the actual quantity is below the budgeted quantity ($q^a < q^b$). According to the min method, the following first-order variances arise:

$$\Delta r \cdot \min\left\{q^a; q^b\right\} + \Delta q \cdot \min\left\{r^a; r^b\right\} = \Delta r \cdot q^a + \Delta q \cdot r^b$$

This sum corresponds to the total variance (it actually equals the partial variances based upon a cumulative variance analysis, with firstly, the price variance and secondly, the efficiency variance calculated):

$$\Delta r \cdot q^a + \Delta q \cdot r^b = \left(r^a - r^b\right) \cdot q^a + \left(q^a - q^b\right) \cdot r^b = r^a \cdot q^a - r^b \cdot q^b$$

Therefore, *no* variances of higher order need to be allocated, and the sum of the partial variances equals the total variance.

In the case of two influencing factors, the approach of the min method can generally be given as follows (with $sign(\Delta y_1) = 1$ for $\Delta y_1 > 0$ and $sign(\Delta y_1) = -1$ for $\Delta y_1 < 0$; with more than two influencing factors analogous, very different expressions arise for the variances of higher order):

$$\Delta C = \Delta y_1 \cdot \min\left\{y_2^a; y_2^b\right\} + \Delta y_2 \cdot \min\left\{y_1^a; y_1^b\right\} +$$
$$sign\left(\Delta y_1\right) \cdot \Delta y_1 \cdot \Delta y_2, \text{if } \Delta y_1 > 0 \text{ or } \Delta y_1 < 0 \text{ for all } i, \text{otherwise } 0$$

► Min Method Example

The three cases in the text are represented by the following data:

	Case 1	Case 2	Case 3
r^a	110	90	110
r^b	100	100	100
q^a	250	160	160
q^b	200	200	200
$C^a - C^b$	7,500	−5,600	−2,400

Case 1:

Price variance:	$\Delta r \cdot \min\{q^a; q^b\} = 10 \cdot 200 = 2{,}000$	=	2,000
Efficiency variance:	$\Delta q \cdot \min\{r^a; r^b\} = 50 \cdot 100$	=	5,000
Second-order variances:	$\Delta r \cdot \Delta q = 10 \cdot 50$	=	500

Case 2:

Price variance:	$\Delta r \cdot \min\{q^a; q^b\} = -10 \cdot 160$	=	−1,600
Efficiency variance:	$\Delta q \cdot \min\{r^a; r^b\} = -40 \cdot 90$	=	−3,600
Second-order variances:	$-\Delta r \cdot \Delta q = -(-10) \cdot (-40)$	=	−400

6

Case 3:

Price variance:	$\Delta r \cdot \min\{q^a; q^b\} = 10 \cdot 160$	=	1,600
Efficiency variance:	$\Delta q \cdot \min\{r^a; r^b\} = -40 \cdot 100$	=	−4,000

◄

6.3.4 Choosing an Appropriate Method

The appropriateness of the different methods must be judged according to their fulfilment of the required calculative tasks. For the decision support function, it is essential that no single variance remains unrecorded and that all information is used. An uneven determination of variances must be prevented so as to keep information comparable. According to the logic of the behaviour-guiding function, only the calculation of variances whose results are understandable as well as (a priori) acceptable (to prevent a discussion of the formal calculation of variances) should be considered. However, as discussed above, all methods are open to criticism.

The criteria to be considered in terms of selecting the most appropriate method are as follows:

- Completeness.
- Invariance.
- Fair representation without arbitrariness.
- Coordination ability.
- Economic viability and practicability.

Completeness

Completeness is one of the most important criteria. Completeness requires that the sum of the single variances should equal the total variance. This addresses the problem of the allocation of variances of higher order to changes amongst the influencing factors. Without an explicit identification of the variances of higher order, problems of acceptance arise, in a similar way to when the variances of higher order are allocated to all first-order variances. Consequently, the method of alternatives does not fulfil this criterion. Using the method of differentiation, the variances of higher order are explicitly provided with the requirement to therefore explain them. This also occurs with the min method. The cumulative method and the symmetric method both fulfil the completeness criterion.

▪ Invariance

The invariance criterion for single variances should ensure that the order of determining the single variances has no influence on their reported amounts. Otherwise, the decision support function would be endangered because it is unclear which order provides the best information. Using this approach, the behaviour-guiding function is impaired because acceptability problems may appear.

Invariance is fulfilled by all methods with the exception of the cumulative method. Nevertheless, this is the method most widespread in company practice. Heuristic rules for a certain order of determination were established to reduce acceptability problems.

- First, variances are determined whose influencing factors are exogenously determined and cannot be controlled. This is typically the (real) capacity utilisation variance and the factor price variance on the cost side.
- Subsequently, the less important variances are calculated. In this regard, 'important' variances are those that produce a high justification pressure on the person responsible.
- Once determined, this order remains unchanged.

The first two rules use the fact that the single variances determined later include less (or no) variances of higher order. The third rule creates a psychological barrier: casting doubt on the potential promise of the calculation method and, therefore, ensuring that people are more inclined to refrain from using it.

▪ Fair Representation without Arbitrariness

This criterion is based on the view of acceptability. According to it, the amount of the single variances should not be arbitrarily allocated to other influencing factors outside of the area of responsibility. The fair representation without arbitrariness has close relations with the principle of *controllability*, which is derived from organisational theory, that is, that an employee should only be judged on the basis of factors that are controllable. Even within this argument, the use of a reference system linked to actual measures is problematic. Only those influencing factors that can be directly affected by the manager's activities are seen as 'controllable'. Provided that changes to these measures are weighted by actual measures of the influencing factors, controllability would be violated.

As a result of the fair representation without arbitrariness criteria, implications arise for the allocation of partial variances and the choice of reference system. Firstly, it follows that variances of higher order, insofar as they also contain uncontrollable factors, should *not* be allocated to the relevant first-order variances. This criterion is fulfilled by all methods, which require a separate identification of variances of higher order: that is, the method of differentiation and the min method. It is also fulfilled by the method of alternatives based upon budgeted costs (with the given reference system). It is violated by the remaining methods.

From the perspective of the fair representation without arbitrariness criteria, the min method is problematic because of its situation-specific choice of reference system. As it lacks a systematic explanation for cases of all actual values being below all budgeted values, it therefore violates the aforementioned criteria.

▪ Coordination Ability

6

This criterion addresses the evaluation of single variances. The scale of the variance is often seen as a gauge about what extent a deeper analysis is worthwhile. Therefore, the variances should not contain mutually compensating effects. Insofar as variances of higher order are contained in single variances, this criterion is violated.

This does not necessarily mean that no *overlaps* can exist within the first-order variances. This is exemplified in ◘ Fig. 6.3 containing an actual-budgeted comparison with the reference system linked to budgeted measures, in which an

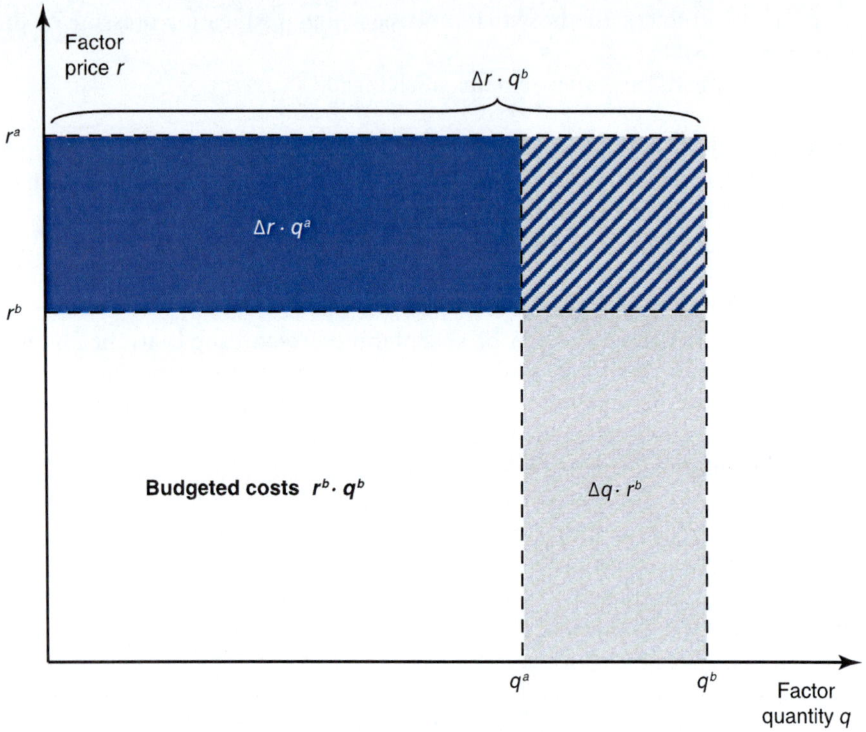

◘ **Fig. 6.3** Price and efficiency variances and different algebraic signs

increased actual price ($r^a > r^b$) induces a rise in costs, while the reduced quantity ($q^a < q^b$) results in a decrease in costs. Total cost differences amount to:

$$\Delta C = C^a - C^b = \underbrace{\Delta r \cdot q^a}_{<0} + \underbrace{\Delta q \cdot r^b}_{<0}$$

The first-order price variance with the reference system linked to budgeted measures is:

$$\Delta r \cdot q^p > \Delta r \cdot q^i > 0$$

▪ Figure 6.3 provides evidence that this variance contains the hatched area at the top right, which basically represents *no real* variance in the present constellation. The rising-costs effect of the price increase is therefore overestimated, and subsequently corrected within the full consideration of an actual-budgeted comparison with the reference system linked to budgeted measures by the (negative) second-order variance. Therefore, in the present case, the variance of higher order *compensates* an implicit overestimation of a first-order variance. Provided that both actual values are lower than the respective budgeted values, the area to the top right of ▪ Fig. 6.3 exists, but covered twice within the first-order variances based on a reference system linked to budgeted measures. Here, the variance of higher order again has a compensating effect. Only when the actual values always exceed the budgeted values, and in cases of an actual-budgeted comparison with the reference system linked to budgeted measures, no implicit compensation effects will exist.

The total variance ΔC considered in ▪ Fig. 6.3 shows that both partial variances equal those according to the min method. Therefore, the real intention of this method consists of releasing all variances with only one Δ measure from implicit compensational effects. Certainly, this approach appears plausible at first but has its problems. Besides the problems already mentioned in connection with fair representation without arbitrariness and behaviour-guiding, aspects of information gathering are also relevant to the decision support function. First-order variances document information about potential cost changes if all other influencing factors achieved their budgeted values. Similarly, the first-order variances with the reference system linked to actual measures show cost changes *in view of the current situation* (represented by the actual measures of the other influencing factors), if the considered factors are close to their budgeted values. Accordingly, the partial first-order variances of the min method either include or exclude this information depending on the data set.

▪ Economic Viability and Practicability

The criterion of *economic viability* attempts to balance costs and benefits in the calculation of single variances according to the different methods. *Practicability* refers to the costs of the method. In view of the possibilities afforded by electronic data processing, it should provide no fundamental problem for either method. Costs, however, can differ when the various methods require different amounts of time for explanation and understanding. Benefits relate to the extent that the methods serve the management control function. In this context, both the costs and the benefits can be difficult to quantify.

In summary, the method of differentiation best fulfils the above-mentioned requirements. It may be surprising to note that the cumulative method is the most widely used in practice because it was introduced earlier than the method of differentiation and therefore was not constantly questioned. However, it could also indicate that the disadvantages of the method of differentiation, that is, the separate identification of the variances of higher order, could lead to additional problems of understanding than previously assumed.

6.4 Typical Variances in Cost and Revenue Control

In the following section, some examples of cost and revenue controls corresponding to the above descriptions are discussed. The primary focus is at the *conceptual level*, and an overview of some specific characteristics with examples is provided.

6.4.1 Cost Control

The cost function is generally:

$$C = C(y_1, y_2, \ldots, y_n) + C^F$$

C^F symbolises the fixed costs, that is, the part of the total costs C that remains unchanged by any of the influencing factors $y_1, y_2, \ldots, y_n$. Therefore, no variance can be determined in regard to the fixed costs. This is the reason why fixed costs typically remain unconsidered in variance analysis (see our former 'working hypothesis' that the actual fixed costs equal the budgeted fixed costs). Cost centres as well as certain cost types within a cost centre regularly become the control object.

- **Capacity Utilisation Variances**

If an absorption costing system is used, budgeted costs also include fixed costs. Once the actual capacity utilisation does not correspond with the budgeted capacity utilisation, an auxiliary measure is determined in practice, *absorbed budgeted costs* C^v. It can be derived from

$$C^v = C^b \cdot \frac{u^a}{u^b} = \left[C(\mathbf{y}^b) + C^F\right] \cdot \frac{u^a}{u^b} = c(\mathbf{y}^b) \cdot u^a + C^F \cdot \frac{u^a}{u^b} \tag{6.4}$$

with u as the capacity utilisation of the cost centre and $\mathbf{y}$ as the vector of the influencing factors that are assumed to be *proportionally* related to the capacity utilisation u. This assumption is considered for limitational production processes of the form

$$C = \sum_{m=1}^{M} C_m = \sum_{m=1}^{M} r_m \cdot q_m = \sum_{m=1}^{M} r_m \cdot v_m \cdot u$$

with m as one of M factor types in the cost centre, r as factor prices, v as direct consumption coefficients and u as capacity utilisation of the cost centre (the determination of the absorbed budgeted costs requires these assumptions).

Obviously, the absorbed budgeted costs are gained by unitising the fixed costs and the actual budgeted costs at actual capacity utilisation are as follows:

$$C^s = C\left(\mathbf{y}^b\right)\cdot\frac{u^a}{u^b} + C^F = c\left(\mathbf{y}^b\right)\cdot u^a + C^F$$

The difference between the budgeted costs at actual capacity C^s and the absorbed budgeted costs C^v is the (so-called) capacity utilisation variance and it is determined at an actual-budgeted comparison as follows:

$$\text{Capacity utilisation variance} = C^S - C^V = \left[1 - \frac{u^a}{u^b}\right]\cdot C^F$$

It is proportional to the utilisation shown in ◘ Fig. 6.4. If $u_a < u_b$ then the absorbed budgeted costs do not include sufficient fixed costs and the capacity utilisation variance is positive, and vice versa.

(True) capacity utilisation variances are caused by a change in the capacity and are not typically the responsibility of the cost centre manager. Particularly in relation to production, the available capacity is almost exclusively determined externally. Production aims to produce the quantity required based on market demand at costs as low as possible. In practice, and by applying the cumulative method, the capacity utilisation variance has already been excluded at the beginning, while the remaining budgeted costs are relieved of all higher-order variances, which contain Δu.

Locating Responsibility for Price Variances and Negative Effects

The head of a purchasing department who is judged on the basis of price variances can also achieve a positive variance due to the fact that he procures extremely high amounts so as to earn high discounts or by frequently changing suppliers to use marginal differences in prices. Yet, both can have negative effects on other areas: High procurement amounts increase storage costs (for which usually the head of the purchasing department is not responsible). A frequent supplier change can require changeover costs in the production department. Low factor prices often result in lower quality. If this is not directly measurable, it will only be noticed during production, for instance, by higher levels of waste, which is again not the responsibility of the purchasing department but rather of the production manager. In such cases, it is important to enrich the analysis of price variances by other suitable criteria like quality indexes or by extending areas of responsibility.

- **Price Variances**

Price variances result from changes in the factor prices Δr. Often it is seen as appropriate and meaningful that the price variances are no one's responsibility,

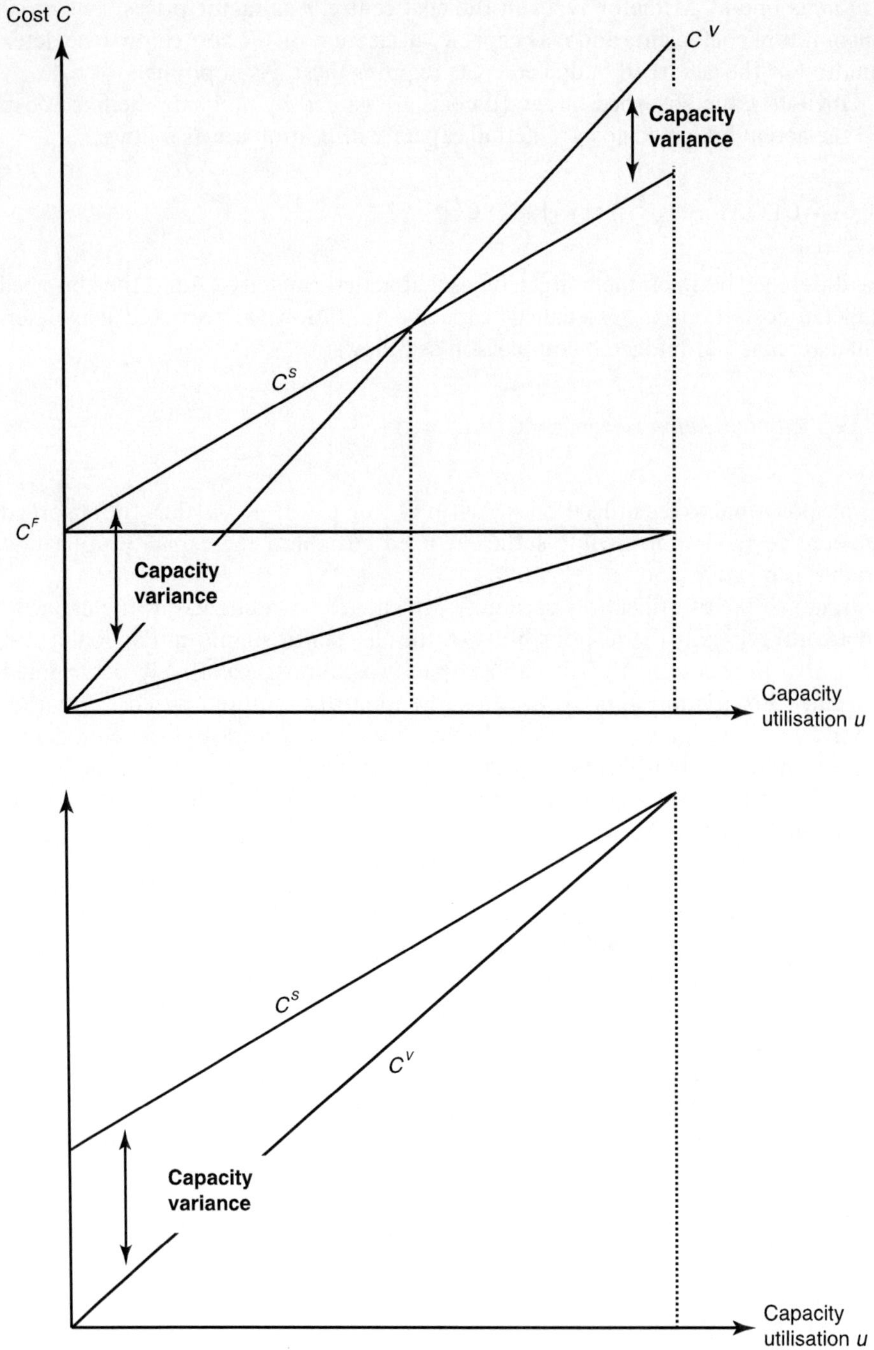

Fig. 6.4 Capacity utilisation variance

especially when the prices of the input factors vary significantly or are exclusively under external (uncontrollable) influences. Then, a forecast is often used rather than budgeted values. However, possibilities often exist to influence purchase prices and, in this case, price variances are certainly important for the performance measurement of the responsible person. For example, the purchase price might be reduced by the negotiating ability of a certain employee, the search for better supply sources or by the timing of orders in the case of price fluctuations, but even then, it remains doubtful to what extent the disadvantages of the responsibilities predominate.

If discounts are given, the price variance can be split into a *discount variance* and a (remaining) price variance. There is the problem of dependent influencing factors, that is, the effect from changes on price due to the amount procured. With a higher amount procured compared to the original budget, the discount also changes. This element of the total price variance is uncontrollable by the responsible person if someone else decides upon the procurement amounts.

Efficiency Variances

Efficiency variances result from changes to the direct consumption coefficient Δv and can have multiple causes depending on the production technology used. Examples include the following:

- Inefficiency (e.g. careless use of materials).
- Material quality deviations (e.g. reduced quality of the input factor).
- Order-dependent deviations (e.g. subsequent changes due to the customer's wishes or as a result of technical requirements).
- Mix variances (e.g. substitutive production processes).

Variances based on changes to production are also called *special variances*. Amongst them are as follows:

- Changes to the relationship between make and buy-in.
- Usage of other production plants.
- Changes in batch sizes.
- Changes in production intensity.

► Example of the Discount Variance

The cost budget for March included the procurement of 4,500 tons of a raw material with an expected price of 100 per ton. Furthermore, it is known that the supplier grants discounts according to the following plan:

Purchase of more than 1000 tons:	5% of the total price
Purchase of more than 5000 tons:	10% of the total price

Therefore, the budgeted costs amount to 4,500·95 = 427,500. Actual costs in March were 506,000 for 5,500 tons.

The actual price is 506,000/5,500 = 92. The budget was a price of 95 per ton and a lower discount was expected. Actually, as a result, each ton should have cost only 90.

With this information, the total variance can be divided into a discount variance and a (remaining) price variance.

Actual costs:	506,000	
Budgeted costs:	427,500	
Difference:		78,500
Budgeted costs of 5,500 tons without consideration of the discount change: 5,500·95 =	522,500	
Efficiency variance (capacity utilisation variance): 427,500 – 522,500 =		–95,000
Total variance: 506,000 – 522,500 =		–16,500
Budgeted costs of 5,500 tons with consideration of the discount change: 5,500·90 =	495,000	
Discount variance: 495,000 – 522,500 =		–27,500
(Remaining) price variance: 506,000 – 495,000 =		11,000

6

Do variances of higher order exist, and if so, where are they hidden?

The mutual dependence of price r and quantity q can be considered by the method of differentiation through the introduction of an additional additive variance, which corresponds to the change in price due to the changed discount:

$$\Delta r = \left(r^a - r^s\right) + \left(r^s - r^b\right) = \Delta^2 r + \Delta^1 r$$

with $r^s = r(q^a) = r^b + \Delta^1 r$. Therefore:

$$\Delta C = C^a - C^b = \left(r^b + \Delta^1 r + \Delta^2 r\right)\cdot\left(q^b + \Delta q\right) - r^b q^b =$$
$$= r^b \cdot \Delta q + \Delta^1 r \cdot q^b + \Delta^2 r \cdot q^b + \left[\Delta^1 r \cdot \Delta q + \Delta^2 r \cdot \Delta q\right] = \Delta^1 r \cdot \Delta q$$
$$= 95 \cdot 1{,}000 + (-5)\cdot 4{,}500 + 2\cdot 4{,}500 + \left[(-5)\cdot 1{,}000 + 2\cdot 1{,}000\right] = 78{,}500$$

The composite variances are contained in the discount variance (–5,000) and in the (remaining) price variance (2,000). A more detailed analysis of these dependences can be found in the forthcoming revenue control sections. ◄

The *batch size variance* results from changes to the relationship between set-up time and production time (set-up relation). There is often an average set-up time assumed if several products are produced together. Problems occur when several unconnected control objects are judged together.

The *intensity variance* is an example of a non-linear influence on costs. Although up to now only linear influences have been analysed, this particular variance essentially brings no additional complexity into the process of variance analysis.

A more detailed treatment of the special variances is presented here and it should be stressed again that practical options for the determination of single variances strongly depend on the technical characteristics of the company and on their ability to budget and report upon influencing factors.

Induced Variances

The previous variances referred to a separate control object, typically a cost centre with a responsible manager. However, variances of a control object can also have effects on the variances of other control objects. Such variances are called induced variances.

Induced variances appear because control objects are not isolated in a company but are organisationally tied together. Often these effects are blurred and hardly measurable, thus, difficult to record. This applies particularly for decentralised decisions when the decision-makers are assessed by their (individual) divisional success.

Induced variances in multi-level production processes are detectable. Figure 6.5 shows part of such a multi-level production process with two production centres. Production Centre 1 supplies an intermediate product (amongst other things) to Production Centre 2. For simplicity reasons, it is assumed that there are no variances with the exception of a single input factor for Production Centre 1, so in the following example only this input factor is considered. The respective costs of Production Centre 1 are

$$C_1 = r_1 \cdot v_1 \cdot u_1$$

with r as the factor price, v as the direct consumption coefficients and u as the capacity.

Production Centre 2 buys the intermediate product at a price of $c_1 = r_1 \cdot v_1$. The subsequent costs are

$$C_2 = r_2 \cdot v_2 \cdot u_2 = c_1 \cdot v_2 \cdot u_2 = r_1 \cdot v_1 \cdot v_2 \cdot u_2$$

If a price variance Δr_1 or an efficiency variance Δv_1 appears within Production Centre 1, a secondary price variance Δr_2 is induced in Production Centre 2.

Variances within a production centre can also induce variances in *preceding* centres. The capacity in Production Centre 1 u_1 depends (amongst other things) on the demand for the intermediate product by Production Centre 2, that is, $u_1 = v_2 \cdot u_2 + \dots$. From it results that a consumption variance Δv_2, just like a capacity utilisation variance Δu_2, induces a capacity utilisation variance in Production Centre 1.

A principal reason for the determination of induced variances lies in the idea of clearly showing the consequential effects that certain variances have in aggregate

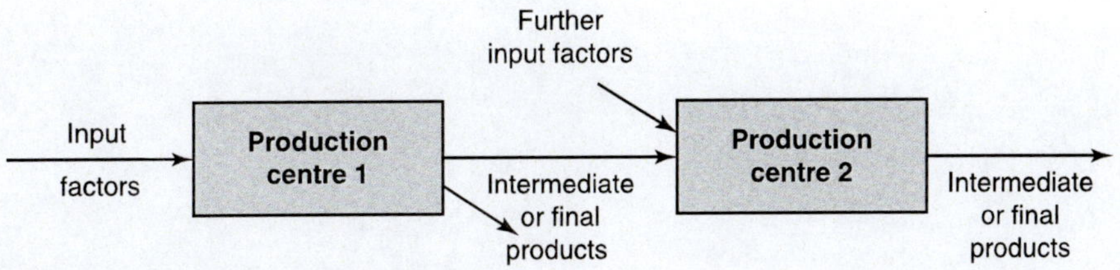

Fig. 6.5 Part of a multi-level production process

form. However, attention also has to be paid to the fact that no double counting of variances should occur, which could happen if the single variances of all cost centres were allocated to the appropriate managers responsible. In practice, it is extremely difficult to communicate the fact that adaptation decisions can induce variances.

6.4.2 Revenue Control

Influencing factors on revenue are the sales volume and marketing variables, particularly the sales price, advertising or distribution activities, customer segments etc. The main difference in comparison to cost control lies in the fact that the cost function is largely based on technological conditions whereas there is no comparable relation or setting in terms of revenue. Certainly, higher advertising activities will cause an increase in revenue; however, the extent of the increase cannot be precisely stated but can only be estimated based on previous experiences.

- **Interdependence of Influencing Factors**

Another difference when compared to cost control is the fact that the influencing factors typically are dependent on each other. A price increase causes a decrease in sales volume; a rise in advertising activities causes an increase in revenue and so on. In the following section, this is discussed using an example with a bent price-demand function.

Example: The budget assumes the following situation: a cost function of

$$C = 2 + x$$

and the price-demand function estimated in the relevant sales volume range at:

$$x = 20 - 2p$$

(It would be formally correct if the price-demand function was $x = 20 - 2p + \varepsilon$ with ε as a random size and $E[\varepsilon] = 0$. Then the following budgeted data arise from the maximisation of the expected revenue function). Therefore, the (optimal) budgeted values are a price $p^b = 5.5$ and a sales volume of $x^b = 9$, which results in budgeted revenues of $R^b = 49.5$.

At the end of the period, the following actual values are observed: an actual price $p^a = 6.6$, a sales volume $x^a = 7.7$ and actual revenues $R^a = 50.82$. The total revenue variance is $\Delta R = R^a - R^b = +1.32$. A disaggregation without consideration of the mutual dependences of price and quantity would lead to the following result (using the method of differentiation):

Price variance: $\Delta p \cdot x^b = (6.6 - 5.5) \cdot 9 =$	+9.90
Efficiency variance: $p^b \cdot \Delta x = 5.5 \cdot (7.7 - 9) =$	−7.15
Variance of second order: $\Delta p \cdot \Delta x = (6.6 - 5.5) \cdot (7.7 - 9) =$	−1.43
Total variance	+1.32

This result cannot be meaningfully interpreted because it does not consider the relationship expressed in the price-demand function. If the marketing department manager was assessed only on the controllable (isolated) price variance, he could achieve positive results with arbitrary price increases.

If it is assumed that the company firstly decides the price and subsequent quantity according to market demand, a price increase from 5.5 to 6.6 leads to a drop in demand from $x^b = 9$ to

$$x^s = x(p^a) = 20 - 2 \cdot 6.6 = 6.8$$

The total difference in quantities, $\Delta x = x^a - x^b$, must be divided using x^s into *two* different variances, a variance induced by a change in the price, $\Delta^1 x$, and a remaining variance $\Delta^2 x$, which includes the additional change. A parallel shift in the price-demand function is assumed, that is, constant changes in absolute amounts.

$$\Delta x = x^a - x^b = (x^a - x^s) + (x^s - x^b) = \Delta^2 x + \Delta^1 x$$

This disaggregation introduces an intermediate size x^s in the form of an additive linkage, which therefore causes no additional variances of higher order. In the example, these measures are $\Delta^1 x = 6.8 - 9 = -2.2$ and $\Delta^2 x = 7.7 - 6.8 = +0.9$.

The total variance with the method of differentiation is now:

$$\begin{aligned} \Delta R &= (p^b + \Delta p) \cdot (x^b + \Delta^1 x + \Delta^2 x) - p^b \cdot x^b = \\ &= [\Delta p \cdot x^b + p^b \cdot \Delta^1 x] + p^b \cdot \Delta^2 x + [\Delta p \cdot \Delta^1 x + \Delta p \cdot \Delta^2 x] \end{aligned} \tag{6.5}$$

The expression in the first square bracket describes the whole revenue change caused by the change in price. The efficiency variance above this is $p^b \Delta^2 x$, and the term in the second square bracket in (6.5) indicates the second-order variances. For this example, it is:

Price variance: (6.6 – 5.5)·9 + 5.5·(6.8–9) =	–2.20
Efficiency variance: 5.5·(7.7–6.8) =	4.95
Variance of second order: (6.6 – 5.5)·(6.8 – 9) + (6.6 – 5.5)·(7.7 – 6.8) =	–1.43
Total variance:	+1.32

This result gives a disaggregation of the total variance according to causation, provided that the direction of the relation expressed in the price-demand function is a true approximation. Due to the change in price, a negative influence on revenue arises. This may not always be the case. The price chosen in the example was done so as to try and maximise profits. Only with a maximum sales price, the price variance *must* always be negative. The (remaining) efficiency variance is positive, which could be interpreted as the positive effect of the application of the other marketing variables. The second-order variance remains unchanged by this procedure.

External and Internal Variances

Another peculiarity in comparison to cost control is the essentially stronger influence of uncontrollable measures on actual revenues as they depend on economic factors, market trends, customer behaviour and competition. Variance analysis can try to distinguish between uncontrollable (external) variances and internal factors. Internal variances can also be uncontrollable. In addition, information on industry price and market size is required. The company price p is related to the (uncontrollable) industry price p_m and a relative price is calculated:

$$p_r = p / p_m.$$

The variances affected by a change in the industry price are deducted from the total variance. In continuation of the above *example*, the following additional information is used:

$$p_m^b = 5 \Rightarrow p_r^b = \frac{p^b}{p_m^b} = \frac{5.5}{5} = 1.1 \text{ and } p_m^a = 5.5 \Rightarrow p_r^a = \frac{p^a}{p_m^a} = \frac{6.5}{5.5} = 1.2$$

Analogously, the sales volume x can be related to the market size x_m. The quotient of these is the market share x_r. A change in the market size is uncontrollable; however, the market share of the company can be influenced by marketing instruments. In the example, the following data are used:

$$x_m^b = 72 \Rightarrow x_r^b = \frac{x^b}{x_m^b} = \frac{9}{72} = 0.125 \text{ and } x_m^a = 77 \Rightarrow x_r^a = \frac{x^a}{x_m^a} = \frac{7.7}{77} = 0.1$$

Set into the revenue function, it is

$$R = p \cdot x = (p_r \cdot p_m) \cdot (x_r \cdot x_m) = \underbrace{(p_r \cdot x_r)}_{\substack{\text{internal} \\ \text{influencing factors}}} \cdot \underbrace{(p_m \cdot x_m)}_{\substack{\text{external} \\ \text{influencing factors}}}$$

In the example:

$$\begin{aligned}\Delta R &= (p_r^a \cdot x_r^a) \cdot (p_m^a \cdot x_m^a) - (p_r^b \cdot x_r^b) \cdot (p_m^b \cdot x_m^b) = \\ &= (1.2 \cdot 0.1) \cdot (5.5 \cdot 77) - (1.1 \cdot 0.125) \cdot (5 \cdot 72) = \\ &= 0.12 \cdot 423.5 - 0.1375 \cdot 360 = 1.32\end{aligned}$$

The total revenue variance can now be disassembled by standard methods into an internal part and an external part. For the method of differentiation, the result is

$$\Delta R = \underbrace{(0.12 - 0.1375) \cdot 360}_{\substack{-6.3 \\ \text{internal} \\ \text{variance}}} + \underbrace{0.1375 \cdot (423.5 - 360)}_{\substack{+8.73125 \\ \text{external} \\ \text{variance}}} + \underbrace{(0.12 - 0.1375) \cdot (423.5 - 360)}_{\substack{-1.11125 \\ \text{variance of the second order}}} = 1.32$$

Evidently, the internal variances together are negative and the positive total variance is due to external reasons such as a positive market situation.

Both variances can be further disassembled. The external variance can be divided into an industry price variance Δp_m and a market size variance Δx_m. The independence of these two influencing factors can usually be assumed as follows:

Industry price variance:

$$\left(p_r^b \cdot x_r^b\right)\cdot\left(p_m^a - p_r^b\right)\cdot x_m^b = 0.1375\cdot(5.5-5)\cdot 72 = +4.95$$

Market size variance:

$$\left(p_r^b \cdot x_r^b\right)\cdot p_m^b \cdot\left(x_m^a - x_m^b\right) = 0.1375\cdot 5\cdot(77-72) = +3.4375$$

Variance of higher order: 0.34375

This disaggregation is of interest only for the decision support function of management control but not as a basis for behaviour-guiding.

The disaggregation of the internal variance must consider the price-demand function (in the monopolistic area) of the company. In the example, the target measure for the market share based on the price change is as follows:

$$x_r^s = x_r\left(p_r^a\right) = \frac{x^s}{x_m^b}$$

The size x^s arises (as before) based on the use of the actual price p^a in the price-demand function at $x^s = 6.8$. The internal single variances are:

Marketing efficiency variance:

$$\left(p_r^a \cdot x_r^a - p_r^a \cdot x_r^s\right)\cdot\left(p_m^b \cdot x_m^b\right) = (0.12 - 0.11333)\cdot 360 = +2.4$$

Price efficiency variance:

$$\left(p_r^a \cdot x_r^s - p_r^b \cdot x_r^b\right)\cdot\left(p_m^b \cdot x_m^b\right) = (0.11333 - 0.1375)\cdot 360 = -8.7$$

This analysis arrives at a result similar to the previous variance analysis conducted: the price setting was very unfavourable, and other marketing strategies partly compensated for this. Further effects, for example of advertising, could potentially be isolated.

▪ Contribution Margin Variances

Variance analysis often relates to contribution margins as they provide more meaningful results than either isolated cost or revenue variance analysis. This assumes that certain revenues are – by causation – connected with certain costs. For example, marketing activities have an influence on revenues and costs simultaneously. Specifically, an increase in advertising activities will practically always result in additional revenues but to a certain extent will be counterbalanced by additional costs. Therefore, decisions about the optimal use of marketing variables and the evaluation of the marketing manager must include its costs. Another example is the direct impact that an increase in sales volume can have on production costs. Examples include *economies of scale* or learning (or experience) curve effects.

A peculiarity in determining contribution margin variances is that the actual and budgeted values can have *different* algebraic signs. Obviously, this cannot occur for costs and revenues. Even though it has no effect on the formal calculation of variances, interpretation difficulties frequently arise, which are mostly clarified only after an explicit consideration of the specific situation.

Example: For a product, production and sales are budgeted at $x^b = 3{,}000$ units. The budgeted contribution margin is $cm^b = -15$. The actual values are: $x^a = 2{,}400$ pieces and $cm^a = +3$. According to the method of differentiation, the single variances amount to:

6

Contribution margin variance: $(cm^a - cm^b)\cdot x^b = (3 + 15)\cdot 3{,}000 =$	54,000
Efficiency variance: $cm^b\cdot(x^a - x^b) = -15\cdot(2{,}400-3{,}000) =$	9,000
Variance of second order: $(cm^a - cm^b)\cdot(x^a - x^b) = (3 + 15)\cdot(2{,}400-3{,}000) =$	−10,800
Contribution margin variance:	52,200

Interpretation difficulties appear in the case of the efficiency variance as it is positive. The quantity sold was actually about 20% *below* the budget. Is the efficiency variance, therefore, unsuitable for judgement? The inconsistency can be resolved simply: the budgeted contribution margin was negative. This in isolation implies that from a short-term perspective, it would be optimal not to produce this product at all. By doing so, the efficiency variance would be maximised with $x^a = 0$, namely 45,000. Interestingly, the actual contribution margin in the example is positive.

However, the problem has another root originating from the question as to *why* a product *with a negative contribution margin* was considered at all. There are several possible reasons for this (for example, a product at the beginning of its life cycle trying to capture market share using a low-price strategy). If the responsible manager has not reached the target set, their evaluation based on the amount would be more meaningful. Another reason could be that this product is complementary to another product (main product and eye catcher), which by itself produces high contribution margins. In this case, only the two products together can be meaningfully analysed.

6.5 Budgeting Control

Variances can result from an incorrect description of a (planned) situation. Therefore, budgeting should also be an object of control, to prevent the resulting variances from being the sole responsibility of the person in charge of their implementation.

To determine budgeting variances a so-called *ex post* budget figure C^s can be calculated, and with it, the total variance split into a budgeting variance and a remaining implementation variance (evaluation mistakes are not considered here). It follows:

$$\Delta C = C^a - C^b = \underbrace{\left[C^a - C^s\right]}_{\text{implementation variance}} - \underbrace{\left[C^b - C^s\right]}_{\text{budgeting variance}} \tag{6.6}$$

The budgeting variance corresponds to the difference between the (original) budget measure and *the ex post budget measure*. A positive budgeting variance is connected to an unfavourable interpretation. The implementation variance is the difference between the actual measure and the *ex post budget measure* and can be further divided according to the influencing factors. On account of the additivity of the dismantling in (6.6), no composite variance appears.

► Example

The budgeted price of an input factor is 320. Due to an unpredictable shortage of this input factor, the market price rises in the budgeting period to 365. The purchase department can buy the input factor in a very favourable deal for 360. It is obvious that the entire change in price, from 360 to 320 = 40, is misleading because it does not meaningfully show the activity of the purchase department and their very successful work. Divided in accordance with (6.6), the following arises: an implementation variance of 360–365 = –5; and a budgeting variance of 365–320 = 45. ◄

The *ex post budget measure* is determined according to the hypothesis that the state of information already existed at the time of budgeting after an observation of the actual situation. A completely new budget is therefore established that differs from the *ex ante budget* by the use of the *realised* budgeting parameters, in addition to the application of a more suitable budgeting procedure. The *ex post budget measure* is the best possible budget measure that would have been attainable under the actual circumstances. However, no general statements about the algebraic signs can be made about the budgeting or implementation variances. The budgeting variance can be both positive and negative. In determining the direction of the implementation variance, it is important to know what bases were used in its calculation.

This hypothesis sets a very rigid measuring tool, as the quality of budgeting is measured by the extreme case of a perfect forecast. However, this is not really optimal because budgets are also subject to the economic viability principle in that the costs connected with improved budgeting accuracy should not exceed the benefits. This sets limits to the accuracy of budgeting despite the fact that a perfect forecast is usually not possible. The assignment of budgeting responsibilities can only be meaningful for variances that the responsible person can avoid. The search for information within the forecasting element is subject to the economic viability principle. Therefore, a perfect forecast does not build a meaningful basis.

The disaggregation of the total variance into the (additive) budgeting variance and implementation variance in accordance with (6.6) is problematic for the interpretation of both variances. Typically, it cannot be meaningful to hold the budgeting department responsible for the budgeting variance *and* the operational departments for the implementation of the (remaining) implementation variance. The differentiation depends on the state of information that the respective decision-makers have (or potentially could have). The assignment of the responsibility for the implementation variance assumes that the manager responsible for implementation knows *exactly* those environmental conditions before all his decisions are made, whereas in actual fact the state of information of the person responsible for budgets and of the person responsible for the implementation will usually differ.

The implementation variance contains an important incentive for the person in charge of the implementation when a better state of information exists: *only* through this can the person responsible be expected to actually utilise this better state of information and not to adhere to a budget that is already outdated. However, in this case, the *ex post budget measure* must consider the state of information at the moment of the decision, something that might be very difficult to achieve in practice. To build on a perfect forecast, he can only supply a meaningful variance analysis if he possesses all of the information before making the subsequent decisions.

► Example

It is assumed that the production process automatically runs according to parameters decided upon at the beginning of the production period. There are no stochastical mistakes in production or in the subsequent evaluation. The person responsible for production enters the budget parameter values to begin the process. Then the total variance is $\Delta C = C^a - C^b = 0$, provided that the budget parameters are also actually used. However, *the ex post* budgeted costs C^s may be lower than C^b because the machine scheduling could have been carried out better on the basis of changes to the original planned production schedule. The budgeting control shows an identical positive budgeting variance and positive implementation variance.

Case 1: The person responsible for the production has no additional information. He is not responsible for the positive, i.e. unfavourable implementation variance. The budgeting department can only be held responsible for the economic viability considerations underlying the budgets for the unfavourable budgeting variance.

Case 2: The responsible person knows exactly the situation relating to the machines. If he now uses the budgeting parameters, he is to be held responsible for the implementation variance. Nothing has changed in regard to the budgeting department's judgement against Case 1. ◄

To avoid this dilemma, use budgeting control *only* for the evaluation of the person responsible for budgets or *only* for the person responsible for the implementation. Alternatively, it could be possible to determine two different *ex post budget measures* and to calculate different budgeting and implementation variances.

The fact that the implementation can directly affect the environmental development must be viewed as another problem. If this influence cannot be adjusted *ex post*, the *ex post* budget measure is based on the execution and also indirectly on the *ex ante* budgets. If so, then it does not correctly and fully reflect the optimal results attainable *before* the implementation.

An extended budgeting horizon increases the likelihood of budgeting variances due to increased uncertainty.

6.6 Summary

Control aims to investigate and analyse variances between budgeted and corresponding actual values. Causes for variances can be controllable or uncontrollable. Controllable variances may be due to, for example, budgeting mistakes, execution errors, implementing mistakes or evaluation mistakes. The control has a decision support function, which aims to improve one's own decisions along with a behaviour-guiding function, which aims to influence the decisions of other decision-makers in the company.

The approach contains the determination of the control field (control object, control measure, control frequency), the determination of the budgeted and the actual measures, the comparison of both, the disaggregation of the total variance into single variances and, finally, the evaluation of the results.

With the disaggregation of the total variance, there is a problem that the influencing factors of the control object (costs, revenues) often do not additively contribute to the total variance, thereby causing variances of higher order to occur, which are partly dependent on each other. Then, a disaggregation based on causation is impossible. All methods can only be judged by their appropriateness. In relation to the most essential methods (method of differentiation, alternative method, cumulative method and symmetric method), the method of differentiation best fulfils the appropriateness criteria. However, in practice the cumulative method is applied most frequently.

Typical cost control variances are capacity, price and efficiency variances. Moreover, in an absorption costing system, (so-called) capacity utilisation variances appear, which correct the unitisation of the fixed costs. The efficiency variances are a result of uneconomical behaviour and of changes within production (special variances). Induced variances are variances that appear based on variances in another control object.

Revenue control is regularly connected with the problem that influencing factors are dependent on each other. Distinguishing between internal and external uncontrollable influencing factors can be carried out by determination of a marketing and a price efficiency variance, on the one hand, and an industry price and market size variance on the other hand. Contribution margin variances can be difficult to interpret due to algebraic sign changes of the contribution margins.

Budgeting control tries to separate budgeting errors from implementation errors (as well as distinguishing from evaluation errors). An *ex post* budget is constructed under utilisation of the information known later. This causes a number of problems, and it seems only partially suitable for the judgement of employees based upon the budgeting variance in addition to the remaining variance.

6.7 Assessment Material

Review Questions

1. Describe causes of variances and how they can be categorised.
2. What is the relationship between the function of control and the determination of the budgeted measures?
3. How does a third-order variance originate, and how can it be interpreted?
4. Are variances determined by the use of the symmetric method or the cumulative method always higher than the variances according to the method of differentiation?
5. Which measures can enclose implicit overlap problems in first-order variances?
6. Can a single positive variance by the inclusion and allocation of partly responsible variances of higher order change the algebraic sign and become negative?
7. What are induced variances?
8. What are external and internal variances within revenue control?
9. Under which assumptions can a budgeting department be held responsible for budgeting variances?

Exercises

1. **Cost variances under several methods:** The purchase price of an input material was budgeted at 12.5 per unit. It was assumed that, in producing 2,000 units of an intermediate product, it would use 3 units of the input material for each unit of the intermediate product. At the end of the period, it turns out that the purchase price had dropped to 4 and that the company was only able to produce 1,875 units of the intermediate product, for each of which, 10 units of the input material were required.

Perform a variance analysis using a reference system linked (a) to budgeted costs, and (b) to actual costs, disaggregating the total variance with the different methods of variance analysis, excluding the min method. In doing so, take into account all possible sequences of influencing factors.

2. **Production costs variances:** In the cost centre 'puncher' of the circuit board factory IBN, the circuit boards are transformed and then supplied to the following cost centres that process them further. By contract 20,000 circuit boards were delivered in the period as budgeted. Adverse technical circumstances led to a deterioration of the rate of yield. The production programme recognised this and tried to balance it by a short-term increase in production intensity. During intracompany transportation, 250 units were damaged. They could not be used for further processing and are now to be recycled.

Budgeted and actual data are:

	Budget	Actual
Production amount	20,000 units	20,000 units
Batch size (units per batch)	40	50
Duration of set-up processes (hours)	0.5	0.5
Rate of yield	50%	40%
Intensity (in units per hour)	100	125
Set-up costs per hour (variable costs)	300	
Production costs per hour (variable costs)	650	

Determine cost variances according to the method of differentiation and to the cumulative method.

3. **Revenue variances:** A single-product company assumes a price-demand curve of $p(x) = 1{,}240 - 2 \cdot x$ and a cost function of $C(x) = 10{,}000 + 40 \cdot x$. At the end of the period, it turns out that the company was able to achieve a price of $p^a = 580$, at which it realised a sales volume of $x^a = 310$ units.
   (a) What is the total revenue variance? How would this variance be divided into partial variances according to the method of differentiation? (Always use an actual/budget comparison with the reference system linked to budgeted figures). What conclusions can be drawn from such an analysis for assessing the realised pricing policies and other sales policies?
   (b) What partial variances arise for the various influencing factors that you additionally observe in the relationships described by the price-demand curve? How do the conclusions of the variance analysis change?
   (c) Now also take into account the industry price p_m and the market volume x_m. The related budgeted and actual figures are:

$$p_m^b = 680; p_m^a = 590; x_m^b = 3{,}000; x_m^a = 3{,}300$$

Ascertain the variances of the industry price, the market volume, the marketing efficiency and the price efficiency.

4. **Budgeting variance and implementation variance:** The cost centre RB 045 of a large cabinetmaker produces round teak wood tabletops, which are then supplied to the cost centre RB 046 for final assembly. During the oral discussion of the variances with the cost centre manager, the following information arises: according to the cost budgets a tabletop requires 11m^2 teak woods. However, the con-

struction plan only mentions $10m^2$. The error is caused by an incorrect conversion of the scale of the plan by an apprentice in the budgeting department. The price of the wood was budgeted at 300 per m^2. Due to the expected future import restrictions for tropical wood, a larger amount was available in the market at a price of 280 per m^2. Altogether 100 tabletops were produced in the period with actual, total material costs of 315,000.

Determine the budgeting variance and implementation variance.

Coordination, Budgeting and Incentives

Contents

P. Schuster et al., *Management Accounting*,
Springer Texts in Business and Economics,
https://doi.org/10.1007/978-3-030-62022-6_7

Learning Objectives

After studying this chapter, you should be able to:
- Present the reasons required for coordination.
- Analyse the different functions of budgeting.
- Demonstrate the interaction of budgeting and the appraisal of managers with the solution to coordination problems.
- Analyse incentives and the role of participation in the budgeting process.

7.1 Introduction

7.1.1 Coordination

Coordination is **the synchronisation of single activities** so as to **achieve superior goals**. Coordination is necessary for **non-personnel** or for **personnel reasons**. While the former is caused by various factual interdependences and relationships, the latter results from the fact that *different people* are involved in the preparation and implementation of company decisions and may *have divergent interests* and/or *different states of information*. Therefore, the reasons required for coordination are outlined in Fig. 7.1.

7.1.2 Non-Personnel Coordination

Four typical forms can be differentiated as follows:
- Joint resources.
- Profit linkage.
- Risk linkage.
- Assessment linkage.

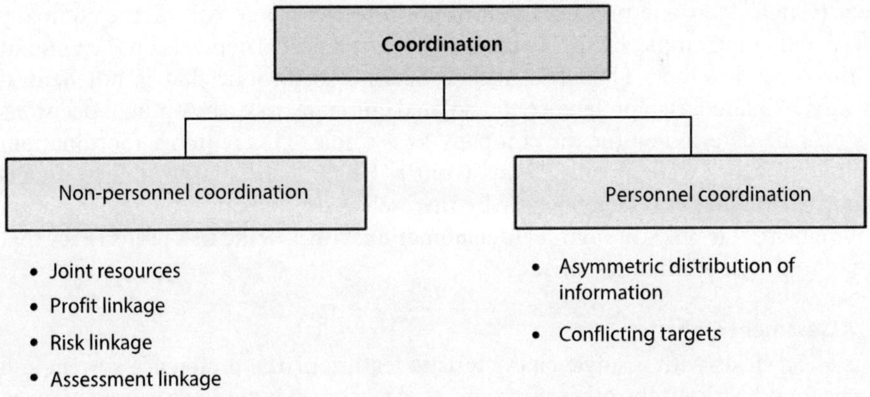

Fig. 7.1 Reasons required for coordination

■ **Joint Resources**

Resources are not unlimited. For example, the amount of sellable products depends upon the available capacities in the procurement and production divisions. If the company produces several product types, the sellable amount of each one also depends on the range of production capacities already used for their other product types. While, of course, an increase in capacity can be contemplated, this implies consideration of other factors like financial options and alternate investment opportunities. Therefore, divisional activities regularly reduce the extent of the activities that other divisions can undertake. From the perspective of the company as a whole; for an optimal solution to be determined, coordination amongst the activities of all divisions' is required.

■ **Profit Linkage**

Profit linkage exists when a certain activity's **contribution to profit** depends on the other activities executed simultaneously, earlier and/or planned in the future. If, for example, the quantity of units of another product affects the sales price achievable for a certain product, the considered product's contribution to profit cannot be determined in isolation. Similar relations arise in the procurement division if, for example, the price of a raw material used in several divisions depends on the discounts received in relation to the total amount procured of that raw material. This **interdependence** of the **profit function** requires consideration by the company as a whole. Such relations were previously discussed, for example, in an intertemporal form in ▶ Chap. 3. Due to the existence of learning and/or wear effects, the net present value contribution of a single unit cannot be found without consideration of both the expected future production programmes and previous production programmes.

■ **Risk Linkage**

Provided that **uncertain expectations** are considered for decision-making, risk interdependence can be present if the activities of different divisions are **stochastically dependent**. If the contribution margins of two products are uncertain and uncorrelated, then one product's contribution to the whole risk of the company (measured, for example, by the variance of the total profit) depends on the amount of the other product. Therefore, with a decision behaviour that is not neutral towards risk and a risk preference for isolated company risk, the optimal decisions can only be determined for the company as a whole. This requires coordination. Such approaches were already discussed in ▶ Chap. 4. It is important to understand that stochastical dependences by themselves do not cause the coordination requirement; it is only through their **combination** with specific **risk preferences** that a real need for coordination arises.

■ **Assessment Linkage**

This effect deals with a single characteristic feature of the **preference system** and can be found without the other three effects. An assessment linkage is present when the **subjective appreciation of a result** of a certain activity depends on the previous success level, and implicitly on the characteristics of the other activities. For example, in ▶ Chap. 4, the potential relevance of (certain) fixed costs was described; it was based on aspects of the assessment linkage because (certain) fixed costs assign the relevant part of the utility function for the specific decision problem. Provided that the utility function shows no constant attitude to risk in all parts of the function, an assessment linkage exists. With an existence of the assessment linkage only coordination of all activities can guarantee the optimal policy.

- **Solution of Such Coordination Problems**

From a *conceptual perspective*, the solution to these coordination problems is not difficult. As pointed out above, the necessity to consider the company as a whole is important for the determination of the optimal policy for the company. Therefore, **simultaneous planning models** that register company divisions with all interdependences should be applied as far as possible. The simultaneous decision-making models for investment and financing or production decisions, developed by the introduction of operations research methods, can be seen as examples of such approaches (e.g. Götze et al. 2015).

However, only from a conceptual perspective is this solution without any problems. The necessity for a simplification ('optimal degree of complexity') was pointed out in this text, due to the substantial problems in the procurement of information along with the computational solution of the models in their practical application. **Separation theorems** can help determine a solution, but an isolated treatment of *all* single aspects may not be possible. Therefore, **heuristical solution procedures** are needed that may not provide the optimal, but rather a solid and 'good' solution. Yet, the heuristical procedure does not conceptually change the principle of the above solution. Interdependence and economy of scope, provided they are regarded as important and economically useable, are to be considered as far as possible, especially if **separation theorems** do not allow isolated solutions for partial problems.

7.1.3 Personnel Coordination

The coordination problems are not yet fully described by the above description, as the presented solution implicitly assumes that the company acts like a monolith. At a senior management level, an integrative planning model is established and its solutions are simply to be implemented afterwards.

- **Asymmetric Distribution of Information**

In companies that consist of more than one employee, **responsibilities** and **decision-making power** are usually **divided** and **delegated** to several people, and the company's decision field is broken into several parts for specific managers (e.g. divisions, plants or market segments). Then, the procurement and processing of information for the respective partial decision fields becomes the responsibility of the divisional managers, who typically have better information about their divisions in comparison to head office. In other words, information is unequally distributed, i.e. there is an **asymmetric distribution of information**.

Reasons for this **asymmetric information include** information costs, the limited capacity of head office (e.g. in terms of the time needed to process information) or limited rationality. Decision problems are often very complex and connected to uncertainty. The game of chess exemplifies these ideas. Chess is a deterministic game (there is no uncertainty) and both players disclose all previous decisions (symmetric information) throughout the game. Nevertheless, the optimal decisions from the start up until the end of the game have not been found, and all strategies are based on heuristics.

The delegation of decisions does not change the problems of non-personnel **coordination** but implies modifications that are required for their solution. If head office is considering an integrative planning model to register the described effects and relations, the question must be asked as to where they (i.e. head office) would receive the specific information about the partial decision fields and their potential. One possibility would be to **duplicate** all **information procurement processes** of each divisional manager, but then delegation would be immediately and completely renounced. Alternatively, decisions could be made by head office based on their much lower state of information.

Another possibility is to encourage divisional managers to report their better state of information to head office. Provided this **reporting** is *truthful*, head office could finally utilise the divisional managers' better state of information, and the asymmetric distribution of information would no longer be a real problem. Rather, the *information procurement activities* would be divided amongst several people and existing information from different company areas only needs to be collected by head office and processed for the integrative planning model.

■ Conflicting Targets

Truthful reporting from divisional managers assumes that there are no **conflicts of interest** (and targets) between head office and the divisional managers. This is unrealistic. Conflicting targets amongst decision-makers have the following **main causes**:

- Different subjective preferences ('given' conflicting targets).
- Organisation-dependent differences ('produced' conflicting targets).

Responsibility in Decentralised Organisations

- The division of responsibility and decision power usually corresponds with certain performance measures. Typical forms of delegation are as follows:
  - ***Cost Centres***

    The responsibility here relates to the efficiency of production measured by costs. A prerequisite is that performance and the required costs can be determined. No responsibility exists for the capacity of the division as it is given by other divisions' demands. *Cost centres* are typical for production divisions with variance analysis utilised on the basis of standard costs for the measurement of efficiency. ***Service centres*** are often organised as *cost centres* as they provide internal, non-market services, for example, legal advice or public relations.

- ***Expense Centres***
  If the output cannot be directly measured or the relation between output and input is difficult to determine, costs are unsuitable for management's judgment, and therefore responsibility relates only to the amount of expenses incurred, measured against budget. Typical *expense centres* include research and development and marketing.
- ***Revenue Centres***
  Responsibility exists only for revenues, not for costs (usually in the form of standard costs). *Revenue centres* can be found in marketing but rarely in pure form because marketing efforts cause costs to be incurred within the responsibility of the particular divisions.
- ***Profit Centres***
  Here the responsibility relates to profit, that is, both the costs and revenues of the division. The management of a *divisional profit centre* has wide operational rights; as only investment and financing decisions are left to head office.
- ***Investment Centres***
  This encompasses the delegation of decisions about investment or capacity decisions to the respective division. Head office is only responsible for financing decisions. Therefore, the performance measure chosen must consider the resources used and the surplus achieved. Often, it is the *return on investment (ROI)* or the *residual income* (profit after the deduction of a given payment of interest on the capital invested).
- Which approach is preferred depends on a number of factors, such as the difference in the state of information between head office and the division, existing conflicts of interest along with the abilities and attitudes to risk of the respective divisional managers. Consideration of these factors usually requires a trade-off between the different economic effects.

Different subjective preferences appear due to different decision-makers' individual value attitudes. For examples, engineers have a reputation for preferring technically perfect, very creative product developments, regardless of the effect on customers' utility. Customers often do not recognise such technical tricks and would not be willing to pay a higher price for them. For divisional managers, extensive allocated resources can be connected with **non-financial advantages** (so-called private benefits of control, such as consumption on the job, power, prestige or influence). These resources are given, intrinsic and therefore rarely changeable. Divisional managers often neglect profitability and only focus on the fact that such resources reflect the 'importance' of the respective manager; he can demonstrate not only his importance but also exhibit more influence on subsequent collective decisions. Additionally, the resources can allow him to **substitute** his own efforts for other resource applications so that the disutility of work decreases.

Organisation-dependent differences are 'produced' by the company. A decision-maker has certain decision competences, and his performance is measured on the basis of certain criteria. These are frequently not in full agreement with the company or owners' targets. For examples, marketing managers are often judged on the basis of sales; the more sales the better. Costs and similar effects of marketing decisions are not in their field of vision. A *profit centre* manager is responsible for the profit of his *profit centre*; effects of his decisions on other *profit centres* might not be of interest to him. By no means do companies randomly choose such performance measures. For example, *profit* is chosen for a *profit centre* manager as it is in harmony with his decision competence. He should actually feel the success of his activities, assuming that 'his' division generates an acceptable level of profit. The possible disadvantages of effects on other divisions are consciously accepted because there is no 'optimal' performance measure suitable for all divisions simultaneously.

If a divisional manager is encouraged to report his (better) state of information, he will be conscious of the fact that this information provided to head office will be used for subsequent **planning** and **resource allocations**. This will affect his own self-interests, and it cannot be assumed that he would be indifferent to the level of resources provided for his disposal by head office due to, for example, low (reported) potential for success.

When **conflicts of interests** and **asymmetric distribution of information** appear **simultaneously,** a **personnel coordination problem** must be solved additionally. It is a **strategic interdependence** that can appear within a company as well as between companies. As with the delegation of decision-making power, not all decisions are made by head office. These aspects of personnel coordination surpass the problem of truthful reporting to head office. **Problems** appearing in this connection are represented, for example, by the following questions:

- Do managers report correctly?
- Is the available status of information being fully utilised by managers and in the interests of the company (and their owners)?
- Are there sufficient incentives for divisional managers to procure information and to act in accordance with company targets?

Even though the different coordination problems are treated as overlapping, they can exist independently of each other. For example, due to a lack of time and/or missing knowledge, a company owner hires a manager to take care of a certain project. The project may show no effects of joint resources and profit linkages with other projects of this owner, and the owner is risk neutral so that no risk and assessment linkages can exist. Nevertheless, there is a personnel coordination problem because the activities of the manager should be aligned with the owner's interest.

▪ Incentive Systems for the Solution of Personnel Coordination Problems

An incentive system would be a potential solution for personnel coordination problems. The following three components are determined by such incentive systems:

1. **Remuneration type**: The incentives can be of material or immaterial nature, that is, can consist of money or non-cash benefits. Examples of the latter are job promotions, awards or incentive trips. In the following, compensation in the form of cash is assumed, as all other remuneration types must also be uniformly

valued from the company's perspective so as to weigh the costs and benefits against each other.

2. **Performance measures**: They form the basis of the assessment of manager's performances. They can be quantitative or qualitative measures and can consist of a single measure or a combination of several measures. Several examples were given in the above section examining responsibility in decentralised organisations.
3. **Remuneration function**: Finally, remuneration consistent with the compensation function must be provided by defining the connection between the performance measure and the remuneration. For example, it can be an (optional) bonus payment for fulfilling a certain standard, in linear or non-linear form.

Figure 7.2 shows these components and some of their additional forms. From this, it becomes evident that incentive systems have many individual forms and looks.

Approaches to the solution of coordination problems have already been described in several parts of this text. Therefore, in the centre of the following figure is the additional problem of the need for **personnel coordination**.

This general approach, from the perspective of finding a **solution to coordination problems,** certainly appears both very plausible and needed, but in reality, it is too demanding. In addition to budgeting, psychological and sociological aspects also play a large role.

However, an analysis of the **features of specific types of solution**, which are propagated as coordination instruments either in literature or in company practice, can prove to be helpful. These solutions are judged by how they cope with the problems of conflicts of interest and asymmetric distribution of information. In

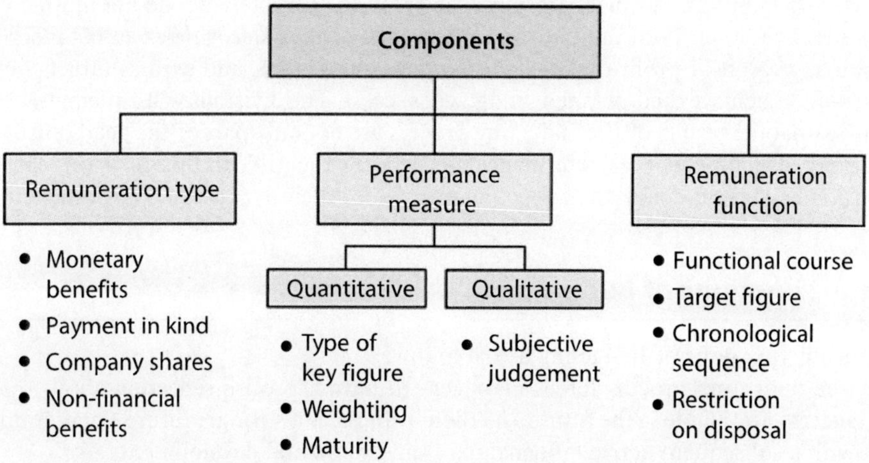

Fig. 7.2 Components of incentive systems

this respect, the fundamental perspective of the coordination problems remains unchanged and only the claim to the model-endogenous determination of the optimal solution is discarded.

Some of the following models allow for the determination of *first best* and *second best solutions,* yet in most cases, only within the given **organisational** or **delegation form**. For example, it can be possible to determine an optimal incentive system for a company divided into several divisions with a *profit centre-organisation*, but this does not answer the question of whether or not the *profit centre-organisation* could be improved upon by another form of responsibility delegation. The qualities of alternative forms of responsibility have been discussed in the informational economic literature.

This chapters deals with **budgeting**; whereas Chap. 8 is about **transfer prices and cost allocations**. The material outlined in both was chosen not only for its practical relevance but also due to the fact that within the recent *management accounting literature*, systems of budgeting and transfer prices are regarded as **extensive, general coordination instruments** and therefore **instruments central to management accounting**.

7.2 Budgeting and Management Assessment

7.2.1 Introduction

The terms *budget* and *budgeting* are not uniformly applied in the literature. In particular, their ranges vary widely. Anglo-Saxon literature often refers to *'budgeting'* as equivalent to *'profit planning and control'*. A **budget** is as a result of **planning,** and the budget always plays an important part in American *Management Accounting* textbooks.

A further-reaching view as to the definition of a budget stresses the **target aspect** for decision units and its **mandatory character**. Both characteristics do not mutually exclude each other. For example, the components of a *master budget* can be understood as a result of profit-oriented planning considerations, and used as targets for divisions to achieve their planned 'budgeted' success. The divisions will anticipate, of course, that the results of the budgeting process are not only part of the head office's plan but also applied as a **performance measure** for them. With this, however, each division will try 'to adapt' the budgeting process for their own use and advantage.

7.2.2 Functions of Budgeting

Typically functions of budgeting are as follows:

- The budgeting process forces managers to have a precise **reflection** about the **success attainable** in the future and thereby induces a stronger future orientation with a subsequent active influencing of environmental developments.
- Budgeting leads to the **coordination of all activities**. Budgets represent the outcome of the company's planning activities. For these plans to be meaningful, they must mutually coordinate all of the divisions within the company.

- **Communication** and the identification of **bottlenecks** or **problematic divisions** in the company are closely related to this. Due to delegation, successful budgeting requires intense exchanges of information between the divisions of a company and head office. Bottlenecks and problematic divisions therefore also become known to head office, which can then subsequently be used to provide support for future investments or disinvestments.
- Finally, budgets can be used to **assess the performance of managers**. Precise budgets clearly outline, for example, what profit contributions are expected from them. As long as the targets are accepted by divisional management as being fair and reasonable, the greater the likelihood of their **participation in its determination, which also improves planning** via the constant **exchange of information**. Analogously to variance analysis, budget variances require explanations, and the achievement or non-achievement of targeted budgets can influence rewards.

These four typical functions relate to the **material and personnel coordination problems** described above. The example of a *master budget* presented in the next section emphasises those four functions and demonstrates that budgeting is viewed as an extensive coordination instrument in the more recent management accounting literature.

However, the four functions only indicate **characteristics** one should expect from a coordination instrument from the point of view of decision delegation with **asymmetrically distributed information** and **conflicting goals**, and therefore based on intuitive considerations, one should realistically be able to achieve them from the use of budgeting.

If behavioural guidance is at the centre of attention, the **assessment of managers by budgets** plays a central role, whereas coordination effects depend on the **integration of budgets into the incentive systems**. If the budget and/or budget variances have no consequences for managers, it remains completely unknown as to what behavioural effects will arise, and also, why they are needed at all for any of the assumed effects.

This discussion can be seen as an example of the appropriateness of coordination for the management view of **management accounting**. A working solution for **coordination problems** requires the coordination of several subsystems and an *isolated* consideration of measures from the accounting system – for example, cost or profit budgets present a view too short, as they do not have consequences for the behaviour of managers. Instead, behavioural effects can only be analysed by a **certain organisational structure** and in connection with specific provisions of the **performance measurement** and the **incentive system**.

Approaches from information economics – analogously to the basic model of agency theory – are used in this chapter with only two participants (manager and head office). Initially, an example of a *master budget* is used to provide fundamental coverage of budgeting systems, followed by a simple situation of **cost budgeting** with **incentive effects** and problems of the manager's **participation**, which will be considered further.

- ***Expense Centres***
  If the output cannot be directly measured or the relation between output and input is difficult to determine, costs are unsuitable for management's judgment, and therefore responsibility relates only to the amount of expenses incurred, measured against budget. Typical *expense centres* include research and development and marketing.
- ***Revenue Centres***
  Responsibility exists only for revenues, not for costs (usually in the form of standard costs). *Revenue centres* can be found in marketing but rarely in pure form because marketing efforts cause costs to be incurred within the responsibility of the particular divisions.
- ***Profit Centres***
  Here the responsibility relates to profit, that is, both the costs and revenues of the division. The management of a *divisional profit centre* has wide operational rights; as only investment and financing decisions are left to head office.
- ***Investment Centres***
  This encompasses the delegation of decisions about investment or capacity decisions to the respective division. Head office is only responsible for financing decisions. Therefore, the performance measure chosen must consider the resources used and the surplus achieved. Often, it is the *return on investment (ROI)* or the *residual income* (profit after the deduction of a given payment of interest on the capital invested).
- Which approach is preferred depends on a number of factors, such as the difference in the state of information between head office and the division, existing conflicts of interest along with the abilities and attitudes to risk of the respective divisional managers. Consideration of these factors usually requires a trade-off between the different economic effects.

Different subjective preferences appear due to different decision-makers' individual value attitudes. For examples, engineers have a reputation for preferring technically perfect, very creative product developments, regardless of the effect on customers' utility. Customers often do not recognise such technical tricks and would not be willing to pay a higher price for them. For divisional managers, extensive allocated resources can be connected with **non-financial advantages** (so-called private benefits of control, such as consumption on the job, power, prestige or influence). These resources are given, intrinsic and therefore rarely changeable. Divisional managers often neglect profitability and only focus on the fact that such resources reflect the 'importance' of the respective manager; he can demonstrate not only his importance but also exhibit more influence on subsequent collective decisions. Additionally, the resources can allow him to **substitute** his own efforts for other resource applications so that the disutility of work decreases.

Organisation-dependent differences are 'produced' by the company. A decision-maker has certain decision competences, and his performance is measured on the

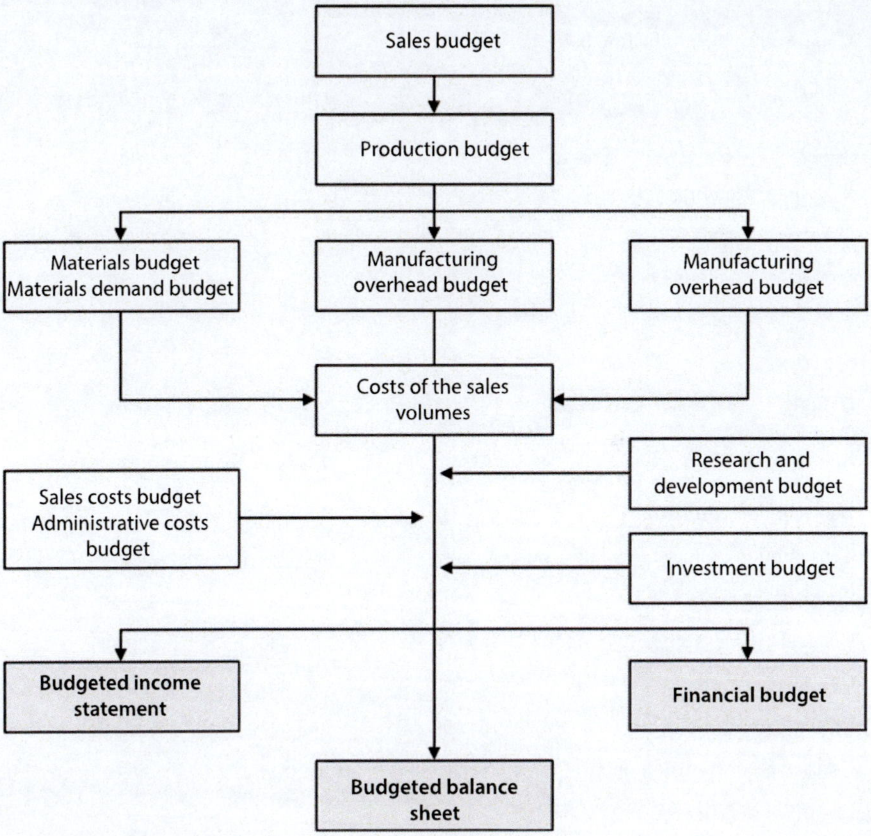

Fig. 7.3 Master budget

Table 7.1 The sales budget

Product	$j = 1$	$j = 2$
Sales volumes, x_j	20,000	30,000
Sales prices, p_j	100	120
Revenues, R_j	2,000,000	3,600,000

supplies are decided upon based on the company's expectations about sales and production on entering the period's budget. Given certain relevant values, the production budget is presented in Table 7.2.

Derived from production and sales budgets, the **materials budget** can be determined by multiplication of the product-specific consumption coefficients v_{ij} and the procurement prices r_i per factor unit. In the present case, three materials are used for the two products. Table 7.3 summarises them (rounding to 500).

Table 7.2 The production budget

Product	$j = 1$	$j = 2$
Sales volumes, x_j	20,000	30,000
Beginning inventory	1,000	5,000
Desired ending inventory	3,000	2,000
Production amounts	22,000	27,000

Table 7.3 The materials cost budget

Raw material	$i = 1$	$i = 2$	$i = 3$
Consumption coefficients, v_{i1}	5	1	2
Consumption coefficients, v_{i2}	2	3	3
Procurement prices, r_i	1	2.5	2
Demand by sales volume	160,000	110,000	130,000
Cost of sales	160,000	275,000	260,000
Required production volume	164,000	103,000	125,000
Costs of production amounts	164,000	257,500	250,000

The factor-specific cost of materials for production (sales) arises by the consumption coefficients of a factor type multiplied by the respective production amounts (sales volumes), then summed for both product types before being multiplied by the procurement price of the respective factor.

In the example, the respective **consumption** for sales volumes and production amounts is always **valued** with constant prices. It is implicitly assumed for the later profit calculation that inventories of finished products and products finished during the current period are of identical value. If this were not the case, inventory reductions of finished products would have to be dealt with based upon certain assumptions (e.g. LIFO, FIFO). This is not used here so as to not complicate matters.

The amount of materials consumed is not identical to the amounts procured. Analogously, for the derivation of the production budget from the sales budget, potential inventory changes also need to be considered here. Assuming certain values, the **materials demand budget** is summarised in Table 7.4.

The materials demand budget is relevant for **financial budgeting**, as the total demand related to the value of the budgeted production programme indicates the resulting cash outflow amount. The temporal distribution of these cash outflows within the budgeting period is open so that the materials budget represents only a **starting point** for other considerations.

Table 7.4 The materials demand budget

Raw material	$i = 1$	$i = 2$	$i = 3$
Required production amounts	164,000	103,000	125,000
Beginning inventory	10,000	15,000	6,000
Desired ending inventory	10,000	10,000	10,000
Total demand (amount)	164,000	98,000	129,000
Total demand (value)	164,000	245,000	258,000

Table 7.5 The direct manufacturing labour budget

Kind of work	$i = 4$	$i = 5$
Consumption coefficients, v_{i1}	1	1
Consumption coefficients, v_{i2}	0.75	1.5
Procurement prices, r_i	15	17
Cost of sales	637,500	1,105,000
Cost of production amounts	633,750	1,062,500

Table 7.6 The manufacturing overhead budget

Machine depreciation (fixed)	500,000
Factory building depreciation (fixed)	600,000
Maintenance and repairs (fixed)	150,000

The costs of product-related **work** (direct manufacturing labour costs) are usually registered based on product-specific consumption coefficients. These indicate the time required per unit produced. Here, it is assumed that two types of product-related work exist. They equal two other production factors symbolised by $i = 4$ and $i = 5$. Then, the **direct manufacturing labour budget** may have the form shown in Table 7.5.

For manufacturing overhead costs, three positions need to be considered, all of which are assumed to be fixed costs. The **manufacturing overhead budget** is given as in Table 7.6.

From these data, the total **costs of the sales volumes** can be determined. A marginal costing system is assumed, that is, that only variable costs are allocated to products. Since all of the manufacturing overhead costs are fixed, only the direct material costs and the direct labour costs remain. The company allocated fixed manufacturing overhead costs *en bloc* against the gross surpluses resulting from the sales volumes. The costs of the sales volumes then arise from the direct costs of the sales volume in addition to the separate components of the (fixed) manufacturing overhead costs. Through this, the values as in ◘ Table 7.7 are derived.

The **remaining budgets** (sales costs, administrative costs, research and development) are assumed as shown in ◘ Table 7.8.

Finally, all budgets flow into the **budgeted income statement** as shown in ◘ Table 7.9.

The **financial budget** follows next. Collectively, the forecasts and measures of all (sub)divisions of the company have an input into the budgeting process.

◘ **Table 7.7** Costs of the sales volumes

Direct material costs of the sales volumes	695,000
Direct labour costs of the sales volumes	1,742,500
Machine depreciation (fixed)	500,000
Factory building depreciation (fixed)	600,000
Maintenance and repairs (fixed)	150,000
Sum	3,687,500

◘ **Table 7.8** Other budgets

Sales costs budget	200,000
Administrative costs budget	100,000
Research and development	300,000

◘ **Table 7.9** The budgeted income statement

Revenues from sales volumes	5,600,000
Costs from sales volumes	−3,687,500
Sales costs	−200,000
Administrative costs	−100,000
Research expenses and development costs	−300,000
Budgeted profit	1,312,500

7.4 Participation and Budgeting

7.4.1 Degrees of Participation

If divisional managers pass on pieces of information to head office during the budgeting process, they typically have an influence on the final budgets, that is, they **participate**. However, the actual **degree of participation** can vary. Typically, three variations exist:

1. ***Top-down budgeting***. Head office determines the main data derived from strategic planning. The subordinated levels then specify and provide data in more detailed form. A major problem with this approach is the high demand for information required by head office along with the fact that the superior status of information from the subordinated levels is not utilised. **No participation** by divisional management takes place.
2. ***Bottom-up budgeting***. The budget is determined by the subordinated levels and then summarised by the different hierarchal levels that it is passed to. With this approach, better information from the subordinated levels can be used in the budgeting process. *Bottom-up budgeting*, therefore, is characterised by the divisional manager's **maximum degree of participation**. However, its problem is that these levels typically have no incentive to allow their information to enter the budgeting process unchanged. Another difficulty is related to the increased coordination demands that the use of this approach necessitates.
3. **Mixed top-down/bottom-up budgeting**. This is an iterative procedure, and the process typically begins with an approximate target set by head office (*top-down phase*) with *a subsequent bottom-up phase* to modify, and finally adapt, if necessary, modifications suggested by top level management. This variation uses **divisional** manager **participation** but with a smaller degree of influence than *bottom-up budgeting*. It aims to combine the advantages of *top-down* and *bottom-up* budgeting.

To be able to derive precise statements, a simple agency model will now be considered for the budgeting of costs and different forms of budgeting and participation will then be presented.

7.4.2 Model Assumptions

The model encompasses two participants: the head office (as principal) and a divisional manager (as agent) (the following model structure is a simplified version of the approach adopted by Kanodia 1993). Head office instructs the divisional manager on the management of the division in which a certain amount of production is produced (here exogenously provided). The manager should produce the required amount at the lowest cost. However, he possesses better information about the cost situation of his division compared to head office. The budgeting horizon is a specific time period. The temporal succession of the events is represented in ◘ Fig. 7.4.

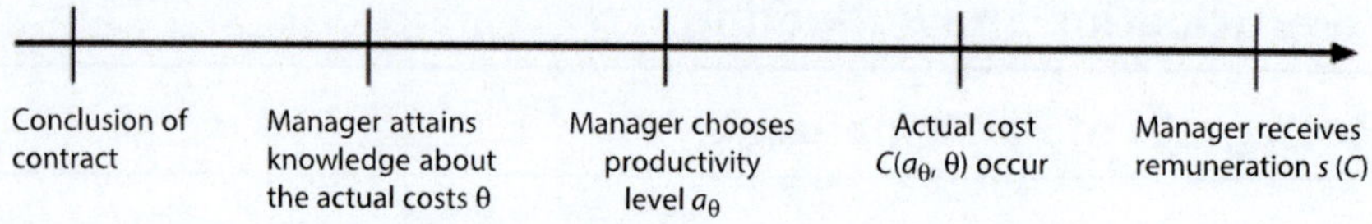

Fig. 7.4 Sequence of the model

With:
- *a* Productivity of the agent
- *s* Remuneration function
- *C* Actual costs
- θ (Uncertain) basic costs level

At the beginning of the period, the contract, including the incentive system, is agreed upon between the parties. It is assumed that only the **actual costs** *C* can be observed by the two contracting parties, and with it the **remuneration function** $s(\cdot)$ also depends only on *C*.

At the time the contract is completed **symmetric information** exists. However, directly afterwards, the divisional manager attains 'on the spot' superior knowledge about the actual costs of his division. This information, described by θ, is simplistically assumed as there are only two developments, *ex ante* with the probability ϕ_θ, $\theta = L$, low costs **and** $\theta = H$ high costs, that is, $L < H$. The cost function $C(a, \theta)$ is as follows:

$$C(a,\theta) = \theta - a \text{ for } \theta = L, H \tag{7.1}$$

with $0 \leq a < \theta$ assumed. θ is considered to be the **basic level of costs** that exist on the basis of a certain configuration of production conditions and procurement prices. However, costs can be affected by the **productivity** *a* of the manager. The cost reduction is assumed to be linear in *a*.

According to Fig. 7.4, the manager gets the information θ in time to be able to adapt his productivity. It is $a = a(\theta)$. Head office knows only *that* the manager receives the piece of information, but neither the information θ nor the productivity level $a(\theta)$ can be observed. In reference to the unobservability of the productivity level in the present example, it is important that the actual costs according to (7.1) are certain *for a given* condition θ.

Had head office knowledge of θ, it could *indirectly* control productivity using **cost budgets**. There is an unambiguous relation between *C* and *a* with θ assumed on the basis of (7.1). In the present example, the problem instead lies with the fact that such control of productivity is impossible because head office does not possess the same status of information as the divisional manager. The difficulties resulting from it are discussed in detail in the following section.

An additional specification of the preference system is firstly required. For the manager (agent), **an additively separable utility function** of the following type is assumed:

$$U^A = U(s) - V(a) = s - \frac{a^2}{2} \tag{7.2}$$

Therefore, the manager is risk-neutral with regard to financial measures. With regard to the **disutility** or degree of **'suffering at work'** $V(a)$ a square function is simplistically assumed so that the degree of suffering at work as well as the marginal degree of suffering at work constantly increases with more work. The assumption of a convex increasing disutility essentially serves to find explicit solutions in a simple form.

Head office (the principal) looks exclusively at financial measures and is risk-neutral. It aims to minimise the expected total costs TC which arise from the expected remuneration of the manager and the expected production costs. If one defines

$$C_\theta \equiv C\left(a_\theta,\theta\right)\ \theta = L,H \tag{7.3}$$

$$s_\theta \equiv s\left(C_\theta\right)\ \theta = L,H, \tag{7.4}$$

then head office's objective follows with

$$\min_{s}\ \mathrm{E}\left[\widetilde{TC}\right] = \sum_{\theta=L,H}\left(C_\theta + s_\theta\right)\cdot\phi_\theta \tag{7.5}$$

If the manager is to be engaged by the company, the offer to him must be at least as good as what he could otherwise achieve on the open market. Analogously to the basic model of **agency theory,** a **condition of participation** by the manager is to be considered, and the **reservation utility** of the manager is called $\underline{U}^A$. For *every* condition θ, head office must offer the manager the reservation utility, which is standardised without limitation to $\underline{U}^A = 0$, explained, for example, by the possibility of contract cancellation by the manager. If the manager recognises the real situation θ, and that he would face a disadvantage compared with his other options, he could dissolve the contract. Therefore, the contract must guarantee that the manager *always* receives at least the reservation utility, no matter what cost situation exists:

$$s_\theta - V\left(a_\theta\right) \geq 0\ \theta = L,H \tag{7.6}$$

The assumption of the **condition of participation** by the manager can also be interpreted in a slightly different manner. If the manager in *every* condition θ received the reservation utility offer, and the manager chooses his productivity level only after the observation of θ, it is equivalent to a situation in which the manager already possesses the information θ at the time of the contract completion. Head office does not know the status of the information of the manager but only the probabilities that the state of information at the time of the completion of the contract of the manager is θ. The manager will only accept the contract if he gets at least the reservation utility. The role of this condition of participation will now be shown for a *first best solution.*

7.4.3 The First Best Solution

For a better assessment of the effects of cost budgeting, it is appropriate to firstly acknowledge the characteristics of the *first best solution*. Initially, it is assumed that head office also possesses complete knowledge of the condition θ. Due to the state-conditional cost structure, **optimal costs**, and therefore indirectly also optimal working intensity – can be decided on directly by **head office**. Head office will grant the manager remuneration as a balance for the suffering at work and guarantee the reservation utility $\underline{U}^A = 0$. These payments are only made if the cost level required by head office for the entity/division is reached; otherwise, the manager receives nothing.

Assume that head office determines costs C_θ for the condition θ. According to (7.1), a working intensity follows from it in the amount of

$$a_\theta = \theta - C_\theta \tag{7.7}$$

For the desired level of costs only, the resulting degree of suffering at work must be balanced by the manager because of $\underline{U}^A = 0$, for which the following remuneration is necessary:

7

$$s_\theta = V(a_\theta) = V(\theta - C_\theta) \tag{7.8}$$

Now head office minimises the **total costs** for every condition

$$TC_\theta = C_\theta + s_\theta = C_\theta + V(\theta - C_\theta)$$

The state-conditional optimal **costs level** arises from the derivation

$$\frac{\partial TC_\theta}{\partial C_\theta} = 1 + \frac{\partial s_\theta}{\partial C_\theta} = 1 - V'(\theta - C_\theta^*) = 0 \tag{7.9}$$

With it, the intuitively understood condition is described based upon which reduction of costs is worthwhile as long as the additional payment required to the manager does not exceed the cost reduction. On the basis of the linear cost structure subordinated in this model (7.1), a state-independent *first best* productivity arises for which in (7.2) a disutility function always defines the value of 1. With it, the ***first best-costs level*** is:

$$C_\theta^{FB} = \theta - 1 \Rightarrow C_L^{FB} = L - 1 < C_H^{FB} = H - 1 \tag{7.10}$$

Therefore, the manager in every circumstance gets the remuneration:

$$s_\theta^{FB} = V(\theta - C_\theta^{FB}) = V(1) = \frac{1}{2} \cdot 1^2 = 0.5 \tag{7.11}$$

Therefore, the manager reaches his **reservation utility** after deduction of the degree of suffering at work in every circumstance, and head office reaching their target which amounts to:

$$\mathrm{E}\left[\widetilde{TC}^{FB}\right] = \mathrm{E}\left[\tilde{\theta}\right] - 1 + 0.5 \tag{7.12}$$

7.4.4 The Second Best Solution

If head office does not know the basic cost level θ, a direct state-specific solution can no longer be reached for the different levels of cost. Fundamentally, head office has two choices that can be interpreted as **budgeting variations**:

1. It simply determines a **remuneration system** for the manager dependent upon production costs.
2. It asks for a **report** on the production condition θ from the manager to determine the resulting remuneration.

It is obvious that the second alternative must be (weakly) dominantly better than the first one without considering the possible reporting costs. After receiving the report, head office is free to determine the remuneration that it would have found optimal based upon the first alternative. If it proceeded in the same manner with every report, it would actually find the solution of the first alternative. However, if it selected a different remuneration for at least one report, then the target reached by head office must evidently be higher.

Therefore, in seeking the *second best solution,* the **reporting** of the manager must be included. From the proposed solution, it can be determined whether this communication is actually valuable in the sense that the solution could not have been implemented without the reporting. By including the reporting, the reporting principle described above can be used again, that is, only remuneration structures are considered which leads to **truthful reporting** by the manager.

The following **procedure** arises from it:

1. The manager submits a report on the state of production.
2. Head office transforms this report into a cost budget, and a certain amount of remuneration connected with it will only be paid if the agreed costs would not be exceeded.
3. The manager performs his work intensely, and by the end of the period, the payment - as previously agreed by the contract - is made based on actual costs.

The requirement arising from the **reporting principle** for appropriate reporting in Step 1 implies that besides the state-specific conditions of participation (7.6), two **self-selection conditions** with regard to the reports now also have to be considered, which cater for the fact that the manager has no incentive to report untrue basic costs. Assume that the manager has knowledge about the existence of the favourable Condition L. Furthermore, in the case of a report of $L(H)$ head office offers the compensation $s_L(s_H)$ based upon the achievement of cost levels $C_L(C_H)$. The manager knows that for achieving these cost levels he must perform appropriate work according to the cost function (7.1). A manager in the condition L will, therefore, report only truthfully, if

$$s_L - V(L - C_L) \geq s_H - V(L - C_H) \tag{7.13}$$

The left side of (7.13) shows the **utility of the manager** with a report of L if head office offers the remuneration s_L and in return requires cost level C_L. The right side of (7.13) indicates the achievement of the manager's target if he wrongly reports H for which head office intends a remuneration s_H and a cost level C_H. The degree of suffering at work for the attainment of cost level C_H is determined according to the condition that L actually exists. For Condition H, the following analogously arises:

$$s_H - V(H - C_H) \geq s_L - V(H - C_L) \tag{7.14}$$

An important **quality** of the *second best solution* follows from these conditions. Because of $L < H$, the required effort to attain a certain level of costs in the condition L is lower than in the Condition H. This implies for the cost level C_H.

$$V(L - C_H) < V(H - C_H)$$

7

Due to the self-selection condition (7.13), it follows from it

$$s_L - V(L - C_L) \geq s_H - V(L - C_H) > s_H - V(H - C_H) \geq 0 \tag{7.15}$$

and the last inequality of the condition of participation corresponds with the Condition H. With it, the *second best solution* is characterised by the fact that the manager gets **more than his reservation utility** in the Condition L; as he achieves a so-called **information surplus**.

Background Information

The logic behind it is recognised when the *first best remuneration* and cost levels are examined for compatibility with the reporting principle. With this *first best* according to (7.10) and (7.11), the manager achieves no information surplus if he reports truthfully because it is:

$$s_L^{FB} - V(L - C_L^{FB}) = s_H^{FB} - V(H - C_H^{FB}) = 0$$

Now a manager in the Condition L would have an incentive to deliver the report H. His effort for reaching the *first best* cost level would be *lower* than that in the Condition H, but the *first best* remuneration aims for H. Therefore, it is

$$s_H^{FB} - V(L - C_H^{FB}) > 0$$

For analogous reasons, a manager in the Condition H has *no* interest in incorrect reporting because for him the effort would be so high for reaching the lower *first best* cost level of the Condition L that with the *first best* remuneration for L a negative utility would arise. Therefore, with the *first best contract*, head office would always get the report H and the cost level connected with it under asymmetry of information. Truthful reporting assumes that it grants the same utility to the manager in the Condition L as for untruthful reporting, and this is the basis for the existence of the information surplus in the Condition L.

The **quality** of the *second best solution* expressed by (7.15) allows for a reduction of the conditions, which are to be considered for the solution:

- Because the manager, in accordance with (7.15) in the state L, receives an information surplus, his **condition of participation** in this state is not **binding**.

- The **condition of participation** in the Condition *H* **is binding** because head office will determine the remuneration s_H just to balance the degree of suffering at work $V(H - C_H)$.
- Head office will set the remuneration s_L no higher than necessary. Therefore, ceteris paribus, a lowering of s_L until the **self-selection condition** (7.13) that **binds** (by lowering s_L the second self-selection condition (7.14) ceteris paribus remains fulfilled) makes sense.
- From this follows that the second **self-selection condition** (7.14) **does not bind**. If that were the case, then from (7.13) and (7.14), the following equation would result

$$s_L - s_H = V(L - C_L) - V(L - C_H) = V(H - C_L) - V(H - C_H),$$

which is impossible because of the convexity of *V*.

Solution

Therefore, as a result head office minimises the **expected total costs** taking into account the (binding) condition of participation in the state *H* and the (binding) self-selection condition (7.13) for the state *L*:

$$\min_{C_L, C_H} \phi_L \cdot (C_L + s) + \phi_L \cdot (C_H + s_H)$$

under the constraints of:

$$s_H - V(H - C_H) = 0$$

$$s_L - V(L - C_L) = s_H - V(L - C_H)$$

Set into the target function it leads to:

$$\min_{C_L, C_H} \phi_L \cdot C_L + \phi_H \cdot C_H + \phi_L \cdot \left[V(L - C_L) + V(H - C_H) - V(L - C_H)\right] + \phi_H \cdot V(H - C_H)$$

or

$$\min_{C_L, C_H} \phi_L \cdot C_L + \phi_H \cdot C_H + V(H - C_H) + \phi_L \cdot \left[V(L - C_L) - V(L - C_H)\right] \tag{7.16}$$

The condition of the first order for C_L leads to

$$\phi_L \cdot \left(1 - V'\left(L - C_L^*\right)\right) = 0 \Rightarrow C_L^* = C_L^{FB} = L - 1 \tag{7.17}$$

Therefore, the ***first best solution*** (and with it also the *first best productivity*) is realised in the positive Condition *L* with regard to the **cost level**. On the contrary, the condition of the first order arises *for* C_H

$$\phi_H - V'\left(H - C_H^*\right) + \phi_L \cdot V'\left(L - C_H^*\right) = 0$$

Because of $\phi_L + \phi_H = 1$ this corresponds to

$$\phi_H - (\phi_L + \phi_H) \cdot V'(H - C_H^*) + \phi_L \cdot V'(L - C_H^*) = 0 \quad \text{or}$$

$$1 - V'(H - C_H^*) = \frac{\phi_L}{\phi_H} \cdot \underbrace{\left[V'(H - C_H^*) - V'(L - C_H^*)\right]}_{>0} > 0 \tag{7.18}$$

In the state H, it is evidently no longer optimal to reach the *first best costs level.* Rather it follows:

$$1 - V'(H - C_H^*) > 0 \Rightarrow C_H^* > H - 1 = C_H^{FB} \tag{7.19}$$

The reason lies in the **trade-off between** the **information surplus and efficiency**. A decrease of the costs in the state H on the *first best level* would first induce additional payments to balance the degree of suffering at work in H itself. Furthermore, Condition (7.13) on the truthful reporting in state L must also be considered. As the degree of suffering at work for a given cost level in state L is lower than in state H, an additionally offered payment to the balance of the degree of suffering at work in the Condition H implies – from sight of the Condition L – a more than sufficient payment and, therefore, a utility rise by untruthful reporting. This raises the surplus in the state L again, and this affects the setting of a cost level in the amount of the *first best* optimum.

7

Value of Reporting

The above solution was determined with explicit inclusion of the manager's reports and with attention paid to the **reporting principle**. As shown at the beginning of this section, it does not compellingly imply that this solution does require reporting. Provided that the available cost levels can be **implemented** with the same level of remuneration as **without reports**, the communication has no real value.

This is actually the case. Assuming that a report is renounced and remuneration dependent on actual costs $s(C)$ is offered to the managers, it follows:

$$s(C) = \begin{cases} s_H^* & \text{if } C = C_H^* \\ s_L^* & \text{if } C = C_L^* \\ 0 & \text{otherwise} \end{cases} \tag{7.20}$$

If the manager is in the state L, he will realise from his own self-interest the cost level intended for this state, and he will achieve an information surplus, if he chooses instead the higher costs level of the Condition H. He also achieves a utility increase exactly in the amount of the information surplus on the basis of the remuneration offered for it so that the better solution for the principal can be assumed as before. Every other policy would confront a manager in the state L with lower target achievements and, therefore, would not be considered. If the manager, on the contrary, is in the state H, he would get just his reservation utility (to the amount of zero) by realisation of the higher cost level of this state. This is also considered if he exerts no effort. At the existence of state H, it would not be meaningful to aim towards the lower cost level because the productivity required for it would lead to a disutility exceeding the additional remuneration.

The contract expressed in (7.20) is purely dependent upon costs and induces the same allocations and target reaching for both head office and the manager. The ***second best solution*** can be implemented **without reporting**. However, the contract analogously considers the self-selection conditions (13) and (14), that is, the contract induces the manager to choose the allocation which would have been chosen by head office after receiving the report.

7.4.5 Variations of Participation

The above *second best* solution of the coordination problem contains specific remunerations, which are either dependent on the reporting and costs or exclusively dependent on the latter. At first glance, this would appear to have nothing to do with **budget targets**, and so the question emerges as to how budgets could find their way into this scenario. For the analysis, the contract given in (7.20) is reconsidered and can be interpreted as follows:

- Head office decides about **cost budget** $\hat{C} = C_H^*$ and offers a base remuneration amount of $\hat{s} = s_H^*$ for it.
- **Excesses** of the budget imply a remuneration of zero.
- **Staying below the budget** by at least $\Delta = C_H^* - C_L^*$ induces a bonus $B = s_L^* - s_H^*$.

Evidently, this rewording of the contract induces the same decisions and target achievements for both head office and manager, and the solution derived can now be presented in the form of **budgets, budget variances** and **bonuses**.

Participation Variations in the Agency Model

Before the analysis of the second best solution of the different variations, an interpretation of them within the context of the agency model has to be made:

- ***Top-down budgeting***. The budget is determined by head office and **without the participation of the manager**, that is, the manager has no influence on the determination of the budget.
- ***Bottom-up budgeting***. Head office expects a report from the manager about the actual costs. These reports remain unexamined by head office, so this system transfers the dominant influence on the specific budget to the manager.
- **Mixed top-down/bottom-up budgeting**. The manager also submits a report on the cost situation. This report remains not unquestioned but rather is transformed by head office in accordance with its own state of information and objectives.

Optimality of the Budget Variations

As seen in the previous section, the *second best* solution can be achieved within the presented scenario by both **top-down budgeting** and **mixed top-down/bottom-up budgeting**.

Mixed top-down/bottom-up budgeting actually corresponds to the approach for the development of the *second best* solution. Head office transforms the reports in accordance with their own objectives and state of information about the conditions and preferences of the manager into cost levels and remuneration (or budgets, budget variances and bonuses). The **self-selection conditions** are sufficient for the requirements of the reporting principle. This budgeting approach results in **truthful reports**, but only because there is a credible commitment to use these reports in a certain way, that is, to achieve specific remuneration at the different cost levels. The manager's interest in potentially untruthful reporting actually dominates the whole solution structure and leads to variances from the *first best* allocation. Therefore, the fact that no cheating takes place at the equilibrium does not imply that cheating is unimportant for the solution.

For an asymmetric distribution of information, it is intuitively obvious that mixed top-down/bottom-up budgeting is meaningful, but even more surprising is the fact that it is not really necessary. An **identical solution** can also be found with ***top-down budgeting*** by virtue of the **'dictation' by head office**. The key to understanding this result lies in the contract (7.20) shown at the top, which is completely free of the manager's reporting. This can be related to the **state-conditional cost structure** (7.1). For the *second best* solution, every report on the actually existing condition θ would relate to a certain cost level and the remuneration connected with it. Due to the state-conditional cost structure, cost-related variances of the cost level (and with it, the required working intensity) can be easily detected and sanctioned. The *second* best solution indicates cost levels for every state, and this solution can be easily found using a simple contract based on costs. This contract can also be formulated in a budgetary form. Therefore, ***top-down*** **budgeting is just as good as mixed top-down/bottom-up budgeting**.

Asymmetric information alone does not imply the superiority of mixed top-down/bottom-up budgeting. If internal reporting induces additional costs, the *top-down* solution would be strictly better in the present case. The abolition of the fundamental equivalence of *mixed top-down/bottom-up* budgeting and *top-down budgeting* requires an extension of the scenario by including additional uncertainties, as shown in the following section.

Pure ***bottom-up budgeting*** can hardly be optimal. An unexamined use of the manager's reports would mean that head office trusts these reports and tries to implement the *first best* solution. As shown above, this implies **untruthful reporting** by the manager, **high surpluses** and **low efforts**. It seems inconceivable that head office does not apply their fundamental knowledge of the manager's incentives in exchange for the agreement of a contract. This knowledge is connected to an explicit change of the applied mechanism, and finally, it leads to mixed top-down/bottom-up budgeting.

7.4.6 Participation Variants with Uncertain Costs Structures

The assumption of state-conditional cost structures allows for a simple analysis of the trade-offs relevant for the *second best* solution. An implication arising from these virtually certain cost relations is the uselessness of reporting and, therefore, the equivalence of *top-down budgeting* and mixed top-down/bottom-up budgeting. An extended scenario with additional **risks at cost** can demonstrate that the *second best* solution can only be reached by reporting, and thus, the mixed top-down/bottom-up budgeting is optimal.

It is assumed that the costs, like those in (7.1), depend on managerial effort a and the condition θ but are subject to risk, specifically to a **probability distribution**, dependent upon a and θ with the costs in a certain fixed interval:

$$\widetilde{C}(a,\theta) \in \left[\underline{C},\overline{C}\right] \text{ and } \mathrm{E}\left[\widetilde{C}(a,\theta)\right] = \theta - a \tag{7.21}$$

The condition and effort variable affect the cost distribution, and the previous relation (7.1) only describes the **expected value of the costs**. A certain cost relation cannot be used for conclusions about the productivity level.

In the present case, all participants are risk-neutral and therefore focus on expected values. These are not affected by assumption (7.21) as compared to the previous situation, so that the question emerges as to what really causes the change now. It is a severe one: based on (7.21) the previous scenario is characterised in such a way that the **expected value** of the costs can be observed beyond any doubt and can therefore be contracted. The costs are used in the basis model as an *ex ante* measure and for an *ex post* assessment basis of the remuneration. Therefore, variances from the *ex ante* measure can only be sanctioned *ex post*, enabling the *second best* solution described above. If only **costs** are observable, this possibility does not exist. A contract based purely on costs, as in (7.20), cannot implement the *second best* solution due to implicitly assuming that remuneration depends on expected values.

Yet, there is a possibility to achieve the identified *second best* solution with regard to allocation and distribution: to do so, a so-called **menu of linear contracts** is offered. Unlike previously, the manager delivers a **report**, and head office replies to this report, not with a definitive cost level or proposed amount of remuneration, but instead with a **linear remuneration structure**. This is analogous to the ***Osband/ Reichelstein* scheme** that depends upon the variances between a reference measure and the actual costs. Furthermore, the parameters of this linear remuneration also depend upon the report. Specifically, it is

$$s\left(\widetilde{C},\theta\right) = \alpha_\theta + \beta_\theta \cdot \left(\mu_\theta - \widetilde{C}\right) \tag{7.22}$$

Assuming the use of suitable parameters, the reason this remuneration function achieves the previous *second best* solution is shown in several steps.

▪ Determination of the Variables for the Remuneration Parameter

Head office determines the variable remuneration parameter as follows:

$$\beta_\theta = V'\left(\theta - C_\theta^*\right) = V'\left(a_\theta^*\right) \text{ for } \theta = L, H \tag{7.23}$$

With it arises the variable remuneration with positive **variances** from the reference value, and this dependence is stronger for the favourable state L than for the state

H. β describes the manager's incentive to reduce costs with a given report. Efforts in the state H exceed those in the state L in the *second best* solution. Thus, stronger incentives must be set for a report of L.

For example, the manager's incentives are now considered after reporting of L. Presumably, the manager is actually in the state θ. Now, by choice of the productivity level, he maximises the expected value of his remuneration according to (7.21), (7.22) and (7.23) reduced by the disutility,

$$\mathrm{E}\left[s\left(\tilde{C}(a,\theta),L\right)\right]-V(a)=\alpha_L+V'\left(a_L^*\right)\cdot\left(\mu_L-(\theta-a)\right)-V(a)$$

The condition of the first order with regard to a is

$$\frac{\partial\left(\mathrm{E}\left[s\left(\tilde{C}(a,\theta),L\right)\right]-V(a)\right)}{\partial a}=V'\left(a_L^*\right)-V'\left(a_\theta\right)=0$$

7

The optimal productivity $a_\theta = a_L^*$ follows from it.

Therefore, the manager chooses the productivity that he actually intended with a report of L. Analogous considerations apply for a report of H. Provided that these reports are **truthful**, in every state θ **an expected cost level** is achieved to the value of the previous ***second best*** **cost levels**, that is,

$$\mathrm{E}\left[\tilde{C}\left(a_\theta,\theta\right)\right]=\mathrm{E}\left[\tilde{C}\left(a_\theta^*,\theta\right)\right]=C_\theta^*$$

▪ Determination of the Reference Value and the Fixed Remuneration

The reference value and the fixed remuneration that still needs to be determined guarantee identical expected values for head office and the manager as in the basis model, with appropriate reporting provided. The **reference value** is determined by the amount of the state-specific intended cost levels of the previous *second* best solution:

$$\mu_\theta = C_\theta^* = \theta - a_\theta^* \qquad (7.24)$$

The fixed remuneration arises by adapting to the amount of the **remuneration optimal up to now** as

$$a_\theta = s_\theta^* \qquad (7.25)$$

If the manager is in the state L, assuming appropriate reporting and considering optimal working intensity he receives the following **expected utility**:

$$\mathrm{E}\left[s\left(\tilde{C}\left(a_L^*,L\right),L\right)\right]-V\left(a_L^*\right)=s_L^*+V'\left(a_L^*\right)\cdot\left(C_L^*-C_L^*\right)-V\left(a_L^*\right)=s_L^*-V\left(a_L^*\right)$$

Accordingly, it arises for the state H

$$\mathrm{E}\left[s\left(\tilde{C}\left(a_H^*,H\right),H\right)\right]-V\left(a_H^*\right)=s_H^*+V'\left(a_H^*\right)\cdot\left(C_H^*-C_H^*\right)-V\left(a_H^*\right)=s_H^*-V\left(a_H^*\right)$$

Appropriate reporting has allowed the managers and head office to achieve **identical** (expected) **target achievements** in comparison to the basis model.

- **Truthful Reporting**

The proof remains open that with the chosen parameters truthful reporting takes place. Literature describes models of the type regularly considered here for the continuous state variable θ, and for these cases, the quality of **truthful reporting** with the parameters of the underlying virtually certain basis model can be shown *precisely*.

In the discreet case with only two conditions, truthful reporting is valid for Condition H but not for Condition L, predominantly due to technical aspects. To induce truthful reporting, the fixed remuneration a_L would have to be raised slightly above s_L^* in Condition L. Further details are not presented here. The idea that the new underlying contract guarantees the allocation (and also the distribution) of the *second best* solution of the basis model by a suitable choice of parameters is important.

- **Value of Reporting**

With the additional cost risks included, the role of **reporting** now consists of selecting the specific **parameters of linear contracts**. The increase in the variable remuneration through the productivity incentives finally achieves identical (expected values of) cost levels than without cost uncertainty, while the choice of fixed remuneration and reference value adapts to the **expected target achievements**. In the basis model, the resulting *second* best mechanism (allocation of cost levels and remuneration as a function of reporting) was understood as a special case of a contract, independent of reporting, simply connecting certain remunerations with certain cost levels so that communication could also be renounced. Now this is impossible because the **contract itself is selected by the report** to guarantee the appropriate incentives for cost reductions.

Reporting now is strictly preferred, and the resulting contract type is similar to the ***Osband/Reichelstein scheme*** directly formulated in a budget form with which favourable variances from the reference value (costs below reference) are rewarded and unfavourable (cost excesses) are punished. In this extended situation, **mixed top-down/bottom-up budgeting** shows a fundamental **superiority** against the *top-down* approach. Internal *reporting systems* can be interpreted as the **participation** of **cost targets** and **bonuses** for unfavourable variances.

7.5 Summary

The coordination requirement of a company depends upon non-personnel and on personnel reasons. **Non-personnel coordination** is influenced by various interdependences between different **actions** and **divisions**, which regularly require a **consideration** of all activities together. Important forms are joint resources, profit linkage, risk linkage and assessment linkage.

Joint resources relate to competitive relationships, which appear from the common use of limited capacities by several company divisions. **Profit linkage** refers to interdependences in the profit function when the profit contribution of an activity depends upon the other activities executed at the same moment in time, earlier and/or in the future. **Risk linkage** aims at stochastical dependences between different activities, which can be important for decision-behaviour when a neutral attitude towards risk is not assumed. **Assessment linkage** relates to an appreciation of the profit and risk contributions of a measure depending upon which basic situation of the activity is realised.

The personnel coordination need finally results from the delegation of decision power and from the **simultaneous** appearance of **asymmetric distribution of information** and **conflicts of interest**. The managers typically possess a better state of information 'on the spot' in regard to the profit situation of his departments and divisions than head office themselves. For example, conflicts of interest appear because the manager is indifferent neither towards the *extent* of the resources assigned nor towards the factors of the degree of suffering at work, while exclusively financial aspects are relevant to head office in their capacity as the shareholders' representative. In addition, there can also be conflicts of interest for the financial aspects if **risk attitudes** of the managers and head office are different.

The personnel coordination can exist independent of non-personnel coordination; however, generally these factors can overlay it. From the perspective of head office, coordination problems can only be appropriately solved when the personnel coordination problems are solved. For this, **incentive systems which consist** of **performance measures** and **remuneration functions are implemented**.

From both a theoretical and a practical view, the solution of coordination problems in **budgeting** plays an important role. The **advantages** attributed to budgeting consist of the fact that managers are forced to have a precise reflection of future success potentials. Furthermore, coordination of activities takes place via the budgeting process, and bottlenecks and problematic divisions of the company are identified. Finally, the budgets should also serve as a basis for a **manager's assessment** and particularly the **participation** shows relevant meanings for the motivation and the quality of planning.

However, these expected advantages of budgeting depend on the information processed during the budgeting process. As this information is mainly at the disposal of the divisional managers, the problem of truthful reporting is of fundamental relevance.

A detailed examination of the incentive effects of budgeting systems was conducted in a scenario of **cost budgeting** with **asymmetric information**. The basis model contains no other cost risks, and with it the manager's efforts can be influenced by **specific cost budgets**. The *second best* solution of this model shows a **trade-off between surpluses** and **cost reduction efforts**. The manager's **reporting** turned out **not** to be **compellingly required** to implement this solution. The optimal contract dependent upon the report can be understood as a special case of a contract purely dependent upon costs without explicit reporting requirements. Therefore, in this scenario, the ***top-down*** **budgeting** as well as the **mixed top-down/bottom-up budgeting** leads to **identical results**, while *the bottom-up budgeting* is inferior.

An extended scenario registers the asymmetric information about the production situation and **stochastical costs**. Now it appears that **communication** can no longer be ignored to implement the *second best* solution. A contract type similar to the ***OSBAND/REICHELSTEIN scheme*** turns out to be optimal and is selected through parameters of the contract concerning the manager's report. In these cases, **mixed top-down/bottom-up budgeting** is superior to top-down budgeting.

7.6 Assessment Material

Review Questions

1. How do joint resources and profit linkage differ?
2. When do stochastical dependences of surpluses of several company divisions not lead to risk linkage?
3. Can there be an assessment linkage (risk linkage) without a simultaneously existing risk linkage (assessment linkage)?
4. Why must conflicts of interest and asymmetric distributions of information be present together to cause a personnel coordination requirement?
5. In what way does personnel coordination overlay the non-personnel coordination?
6. What are the general components of incentive systems?
7. What are the advantages of budgeting?
8. What is a *master budget*?
9. What is the meaning of the reporting principle, and which idea underlies it? Which relation exists between self-selection of head office and the possibility of getting appropriate information?
10. How can the relations between productivity level and cost budgets be explained? Which role do incentive systems play?
11. What considerations must head office make for *top-down* budgeting? What is the influence of the uncertainty level on the optimality of budgets?
12. Which effects can appear with *bottom-up* budgeting?

Exercises

1. **Profit linkage**. There is a company split into two divisions. The price demand curves of the two divisions are:

$$p_1(x_1) = 58 - 0.1 \cdot x_1; \quad p_2(x_2) = 120 - 0.05 \cdot x_2.$$

The sales volume for division 2 is limited to $x_2 \leq 200$. To manufacture their products, both divisions need *one* unit of a particular raw material of which the purchase price $r(q)$ per unit of volume depends on the following schedule of discounts for the *total* volume purchased q ($q = q_1 + q_2$).

$$r(q) = \begin{cases} 50 & \text{for } 0 \leq q \leq 100 \\ 45 & \text{for } 100 < q \leq 200 \\ 40 & \text{for } 200 < q \end{cases}$$

This schedule of discounts characterises a *triggered* discount, that is, the prices in each case are only valid for the interval of the quantities quoted.

The variable unit costs *excluding* the raw material are:

$$\bar{c}_1 = 14; \bar{c}_2 = 56$$

Why can this be regarded to be a case of profit linkage? What is the optimum solution bearing the effect of this profit linkage? What difficulties arise if both divisions are run as *profit centres* and if they accordingly determine their optimum by maximising the profit for their own division?

2. **Assessment linkage**. A company is able to carry out a project with a forecasted profit of 20 and an (isolated) standard profit variance of 35. The net profits of the new project are totally uncorrelated with those of the previous programmes. This new programme is viewed from two alternative starting points. In Situation 1, the previous programme has an expected profit of 180 and a standard deviation from the profit of 50. In Situation 2, on the other hand, the expected profit is 200 with the same standard deviation of 50.
   (a) Assume that the company maximises the following utility function:

$$U\left(\mathrm{E}\left[\tilde{\Pi}\right];\sigma\left(\tilde{\Pi}\right)\right) = \mathrm{E}\left[\tilde{\Pi}\right] - 0.05 \cdot \sigma\left(\tilde{\Pi}\right)$$

Does the degree of advantage offered by the new project depend on the starting point with this utility function?

   (b) Assume that the company maximises the expected *benefit*, whereby the following quadratic utility function applies.

$$U(\Pi) = 5 \cdot \Pi - 0.01 \cdot \Pi^2$$

How does the degree of advantage offered by the new project depend on the starting point of this utility function? (*Recommendation*: Start by formulating the expected *benefit* as a function of the expected profit and the standard variance.)

3. **Budgeting and incentive systems**. A budgeting system of the type described in the text with two equally probable conditions for the basic costs of $L = 10$ and $H = 10.5$. The actual costs are $C = \theta - a$. The manager directly attains precise knowledge of the actual condition before the choice of his productivity. His reservation utility amounts to $\underline{U}^A = 0$, and his utility function is $U = s - a^2/2$. A minimum payment must be offered in the amount of the manager's reservation utility for every condition. Head office maximises the expected remaining surpluses.
   (a) Determine the *first best* solution.
   (b) Determine the *second best* solution.

Transfer Prices and Cost Allocations

Contents

P. Schuster et al., *Management Accounting*,
Springer Texts in Business and Economics,
https://doi.org/10.1007/978-3-030-62022-6_8

Learning Objectives

After studying this chapter, you should be able to:

- Understand the functions of transfer prices and cost allocations along with the underlying conflict between coordination and profit allocation
- Analyse cost-based, market-based and negotiated transfer prices (in different forms) and their suitability (in general)
- Discuss market-based transfer prices in perfect and imperfect markets and the influence of synergies
- Understand marginal cost-based transfer prices for optimum coordination while being aware of the need to consider the problem of incentives and dysfunctional behaviour in the proposed solution
- See the distortion of cost structures as a major argument against the use of full costs; apply an agency model based on full costs to show that the optimum transfer price is above marginal costs and that market prices would interfere with the solution
- Understand the applicability of multi-tier transfer prices for solutions possibly leading to optimum coordination
- See dual transfer prices as an optional choice for solutions possibly leading to optimum coordination and understand any difficulties and problems arising
- Discuss negotiated transfer prices as one type of transfer price
- Learn how to share risk under uncertainty and witness the resulting behavioural effects
- Take and compare an ex post and ex ante view on transfer prices
- Show how to solve the capacity adjustment problem by using transfer prices and how to correct (i.e. punish) untruthful reporting by a specific transfer pricing mechanism
- Determine optimum transfer prices in a *Nash* equilibrium
- Discuss (in general) incorrect decisions caused by transfer prices, incorporating behavioural effects into the analysis of the decision problems and understand the effects resulting from asymmetric information

8.1 Functions and Types of Transfer Prices

8.1.1 Introduction

Transfer prices are values determined for inter-company products (intermediate products and services) that are purchased from (independent) company divisions, that is, the **transfer price** is the internal price of products created within the company. One of the main functions of transfer prices is to coordinate the management of both the selling and the buying divisions. **Cost allocations** are a special form of transfer prices. They are transfer prices based on the cost of the producing company division and the sum of the allocated costs equals the costs incurred. Thus, if a higher amount is allocated to one division, another division will inevitably have a lower amount allocated to them.

The major presupposition for the need for transfer prices and cost allocations is a **decentralised organisation** with divisional managers **responsible** for performance measures of their respective divisions, typically divisional profits or costs. Along with **budgeting systems** and **profit measures**, transfer prices are the most important instruments for **management control** available to divisional managers.

Responsibility in Decentralised Organisations
Typically, the divisions are organised as profit or investment centres within a company or legally independent subsidiaries. However, they can also be, for example, cost centres (see also ► Chap. 7). In a profit centre, the divisional manager can decide upon all operational business decisions and, therefore, is fully responsible for the profit of his division and is judged by it. Furthermore, it is assumed that divisional managers make their decisions in an attempt to maximise their divisions' profit. In the case of a cost centre, revenues are assumed to be constant.

It seems that production divisions are frequently organised as cost centres and not as profit centres. A **profit centre organisation**, however, can be meaningful when certain output characteristics are not directly measurable; an example would be product quality (which often becomes obvious after sales). The profit centre organisation can induce important incentives (e.g. by using the contribution margin of the sales division as the transfer price).

The idea of transfer price determinations is derived from the following considerations: transfer prices are based on the fiction of a '**market**' within the company. The divisions are supposed to act like independent companies, and this has the advantage that the decisions delegated to subordinated employees and managers should lead to entrepreneurial conduct. The ability to coordinate is expected by the internal (fictitious) market; the external market is excluded due to the internal organisation of the company. Therefore, the integration of all divisions within one single company must lead to advantages compared to independent companies, because the integration also causes costs to be incurred. Apart from missing the adjusting effect of the external market, coordination costs (including those caused by the use of transfer prices) appear. Without coordination, the advantages of integration would hardly work, and then independent companies would be better. Empirical studies confirm this (e.g. the so-called conglomerate discount, Porter 1985, p. 319). It is to be noted, of course, that integration for tax reasons can certainly count (an example is the enabling of an immediate loss of compensation if this was not possible with legal independence). **Advantages of integration** include, for example, improved capacity utilisation, a decrease in quality tests, lower marketing costs by utilisation of the company reputation or by improved access to identical market segments, better coordination of product developments as well as the use and concealment of knowledge and expertise. Such advantages generally arise from a reduction of the transaction costs. The described effects appear when, and because, markets are not perfect. Now, decentralisation and transfer prices again bring the market into the company. The problem is finding a transfer price that combines as many advantages as possible in comparison to its disadvantages. It is obvious that transfer prices must always be seen in **connection** with the **company's structure**.

8.1.2 Functions of Transfer Prices

The most essential functions of transfer prices (for internal use) are the following:

1. **Profit allocation** in order to assess divisional profits and for performance measurement purposes.
2. **Coordination, influence and guidance** for the divisions.
3. **Calculation and cost accounting** for decisions and for the justification of [transfer] prices.
4. **External regulatory purposes**, especially for balance sheet and profit and loss statements.
5. **Simplification** (the transfer price is applied as a normalised budget measure).

■ Profit Allocation

In decentralised companies, transfer prices are necessary for the determination of the divisions' profits, when the divisions trade amongst themselves. On the one hand, the transfer price is the (internal) revenue of the supplying division; on the other hand, it indicates the (internal) purchase cost of the buying division. **Divisional profit** is the basis for decisions for both divisional management and the company's upper management, who use it for strategic activities or budget allocations. It also contributes to the assessment of divisional management's performance. The profit contribution of every division thereby becomes visible, responsibilities are clearly presented, and cost transparency and awareness are both promoted.

The determination of divisional success requires an accurate demarcation of the success components, which can be assigned to the different divisions. When performance is to be measured, divisional profits have to be allocated, thus profit allocation is an important function of transfer prices.

Yet, the demarcation is difficult, for example, when two or more divisions are interwoven with each other. Such **interweaving** can appear in the following cases:

- Products of one division are bought in by another division (**sequential interweaving**). *Example*: a division produces an intermediate product, which is processed further by another division, made into a final product before being sold at market.
- Divisions compete for limited resources (**resource interdependencies**) or in a common (limited) sales market (**market interdependencies**); it is a joint resources group. *Examples*: two divisions produce substitute products, or two divisions need a quality test for certain components used during their production processes, which is executed by a special department that is at its capacity limit.

The success that appears as a result of common products is also named the **synergetic effect**. It cannot be split or divided on the basis of the individual divisions' contributions. From a theoretical view, it is impossible to execute such a split-up correctly, as the success results from common products only. Should one division be eliminated, the synergetic effect would be appropriately shortened, or perhaps, terminated completely. Due to a decision to, for example, close/eliminate a particular division, it might be possible to determine limits and ranges of such losses, or it might be possible to apply an average principle or to split up the effects equally. However, all of these possibilities are arbitrary.

» 'Trying to defend an [...] allocation is like clapping one's hands, then trying to defend how much of the sound is attributable to each hand'. (Ijiri 1967, p. 13).

SHAPLEY Value

The *SHAPLEY* value tries to create a 'fair' split-up of synergetic effects based on a concept of the cooperative game theory. For this, all possible coalitions of the contributing divisions are considered, and it is asked which advantage appeared, if the considered division is now included. Then the *SHAPLEY* value is determined as a weighted average value of the marginal advantages with every given coalition. Although this can be seen as a 'fair' result, the *SHAPLEY* value also remains arbitrary, just like any other split-up.

8

▶ Examples

Division B1 of a company constructed a brand name by intensive marketing activities at a cost of 1000. The brand name has received a very positive image amongst consumers. B1 achieves a contribution margin of 10,000. Now, another division, B2, would like to use this brand name for one of its products. B2's contribution margin rises with the brand name's use by 1,000 to 5,000. How high are the divisional profits of B1 and B2? The use of a brand name constructed within the company is a synergetic effect. If Division B2 had to construct its own brand name, this would be relatively expensive and probably less effective than the use of the already established name. ◀

■ Coordination Function

Divisional managers should work hard and give their best efforts for their division. Incentives are given to maximise their divisional profit. This can guide them to make decisions that are favourable and profitable from the perspective of their own division, but unfavourable from the view of the company as a whole. The effects of a division's decisions on other divisions are **externalities** that are not considered by the divisional manager.

▶ Examples

1. The marketing department promised a customer an extremely short delivery time, and to achieve this, the production department must deviate from their optimised production programme or must delay maintenance works.
2. The optimal market treatment from the perspective of Division 1 is to start a price war with a competitor, but it contradicts the company's strategy of following a high price strategy for all products.
3. A production division could achieve cost savings (producing a positive net present value) through an investment in the automation of the production process. However, it is forced to pass on part of the cost savings to the buying divisions ensuring that the net present value of the cash flows from the perspective of the production division will become negative. Therefore, it refrains from the investment. ◀

Transfer prices can be used to **influence** decentralised decisions. Assume that the divisional manager is responsible for short-term decisions. Head office announces a transfer price (or a transfer price scheme) to the manager for the inter-company transfer of intermediate products. The decision behaviour of the manager can be steered by influencing the divisional profit via the transfer price. A higher transfer price reduces the quantity bought-in by the purchasing division from another production division, or to accept a one-off special order less easily. A higher transfer price can change the producing division's production programme or the production amounts. Examples of such behavioural control effects will be given later in this chapter.

Coordination Function Versus Goal Congruency

Coordination function is a term used throughout this book. A similar concept is sometimes described as 'goal congruence' with suboptimal decisions as 'incongruent decisions'. We prefer the abstract term of 'coordination (function)' as the goals of different divisions usually will not be 100% identical and the perspective on goals seems very limited. Coordination, in contrast, indicates the primary function and stresses the linkage to behaviour guidance and **management control**, for example, in the case of head office's view of decisions made by divisional management.

- **Other Functions**

Transfer prices fulfil a number of other functions besides profit allocation and coordination, for example, **calculation** (of costs) for the determination of factors used in central decision-making when several divisions are involved or in affiliated group companies. The cost accounting system of such companies traces the relevant costs between different, legally independent divisions, which are then used for price calculations. The determination of **costs of goods produced** for external regulatory purposes or rectifications of prices against third parties are other functions of transfer prices.

From a company perspective, a primary issue is the optimisation of **taxes** and related payments. Transfer prices of multi-national corporations are often influenced by such considerations. These effects are ignored in this chapter, as profit allocation in that sense equals the manipulation and the allocation of profits to regions and countries that minimise tax payments for the company. The focus of the book is documented by its title, 'Management Accounting', it suggests that this book takes the approach of management accounting, that is, the **managerial use of accounting information for decision-making** respectively with a particular emphasis on the **decision-influencing** aspect. The OECD publishes guidelines for transfer prices in order to limit manipulation and applies the so-called arm's length principle. We ignore this perspective and relate our line of argument to the **management accounting view** and its **direct relationship to decisions**, in the described way, that is, we focus on **coordination** and **profit allocation** in the described sense.

Empirical Results

The *'Transfer Pricing 2003 Global Survey'* by Ernst and Young (2003) questioned 641 financial managers of internationally active parent companies and 200 managers of subsidiaries from 22 countries about their transfer pricing policies, with tax versus management targets playing an important role.

Eighty percent of the group companies preferred uniform transfer prices for both tax related and management related decisions; 40% of the parent companies responded that management aspects were more important than fiscal issues, and for 25% of the mother companies, the support of the company strategy was the exclusive driver of the transfer price policy.

In a similar study by Deloitte (2006), there were 240 companies with consolidated annual sales in excess of €500 million located in Germany. The four most important objectives of a transfer price system were shown as internal profit allocation, the support of the group strategy, the optimisation of company taxation and the control system for resource allocation. The companies confessed that not all objectives could be pursued simultaneously, and the top performer focused on internal control (and, therefore, less on fiscal) aspects more than the other companies.

In a questionnaire of Swiss companies, Pfaff and Stefani (2006) found that the majority of companies used uniform transfer prices for both external and internal functions. Market and full cost-based systems were predominant, and the companies seemed to classify the importance of synergetic effects for internal control as less important.

Transfer prices between legally independent company divisions are of special importance. In **commercial law,** transfer prices are important when the participation ratios of mother company and daughter company are not identical (e.g. if the daughter company has minority shareholders); then the **profit allocation function** is the focus of attention: the achieved profit should be divided 'fairly' and 'righteously' between the divisions to avoid discriminating against the minority partner. Effects caused by **tax law** can be similarly seen, as the total amount of taxes due can largely depend on the profit allocation, most apparent with transnational sales. The OECD has legislated directives for internationally uniform transfer price methods that are recommended to be adopted. As a 'correct' allocation of the profit earned in connection with several divisions, cannot succeed unambiguously, companies therefore have a certain leeway.

Finally, another function of transfer prices is the **simplification** of the cost accounting system by the use of **normalised measures**, frequently only to keep exogenous fluctuations of the input prices out of the subsequent analysis.

- **Asymmetrically Distributed Information**

Typically, models for the determination of transfer prices implicitly assume *symmetrically* distributed information, that is, head office has all the necessary information about the divisions, and with it could solve the coordination problem itself.

Simultaneously, a need for the profit allocation function would also not exist, as head office possesses all information anyway. Exaggerated, it could be argued that transfer prices solve a problem that does not exist at all.

More realistically, information will be **distributed asymmetrically** as the respective divisional manager is better informed about his division than head office. Several examples are shown throughout this chapter about **misleading control** effects that can be caused by certain transfer prices due to superior information held by the divisions.

Asymmetrically distributed information not only has the effect that head office can make less precise decisions, but also leads to the fact that divisional managers cannot be **assessed** by their real performance, but rather based on surrogates only. Such a surrogate is **divisional profit**, which was already mentioned in the previous discussion. With it, the objective of the divisional manager differs from the objectives of the company as a whole (i.e. conflicts of interest arise).

▪ **Conflicting Objectives**

The different functions of transfer prices frequently **compete** with each other. A transfer price that fulfils one function very well can be unsuitable or even counterproductive for another function. Particularly, the possibility for conflict between the **profit allocation** and **coordination functions** is vast. *Example*: the company likes to provide considerable leeway for price setting to the division that sells to the external market. For this, it is seen as necessary that marginal costs are applied to intermediate products sold within the company, because in the short term they correspond to the only relevant cost. With linear cost functions, the selling divisions producing these intermediate products, end up with a loss equal to their total fixed costs potentially resulting in a high divisional loss, while the purchasing division gains the total contribution margin. For the profit allocation function, such divisional profits are worthless and meaningless. It applies similarly to other functions, such as the tax-optimal determination of transfer prices. Such transfer prices are often very unfavourable for management control issues.

Conflicts of objectives are frequently found within the same function. Assume that head office would like to limit the demand for an internally produced product. One possibility is setting a high transfer price for it, as the purchasing division would then lower their demand for it if feasible to do so. At the same time, head office needs undistorted measures for their own decisions, for example, in deciding upon the allocation of resources to the divisions, and a transfer price set too 'high' is unsuitable for this.

Such conflicts of objectives can be solved in a relatively simple way, by the use of **different transfer prices**, one for every function. Every division determines two or more divisional profits, for example, one used for the manager's assessment and another indicating the 'real' profit. However, this solution frequently meets with difficulties in practice. How could it be explained that a divisional manager must pay marginal costs for the internal product (for coordination purposes), while his divisional profit is determined based on higher costs, with the subsequent profit used for measuring and assessing his performance? The coordination takes place by virtue of the fact that the performance measure (divisional profit) is *manipulated* in the way that divisional managers autonomously make decisions in the best interests of the company as a whole. In other words: '*In some cases, the impression is given to the divisional manager that he is playing a bookkeeping game*' (*Dearden* 1962, quoted by Thomas 1980, p. 209). However, if the assessment is disconnected from this manipulated profit, the coordination function of the transfer price could not be attained at all.

Another problem arises: typically, the **divisional profit** is dependent upon **strategic decisions** made by head office. The divisional manager can raise his profit if he receives higher resources. With this mechanism, the 'real profit', following the profit allocation function, will create reactions in the co-ordination and control system. For example, the manager will align his decisions not only with the transfer price installed as part of the management control system, but also with maximising the 'other' profit that will raise his profit through resource allocation. As a result, head office cannot receive an undistorted divisional profit and must also consider these incentives. With it, the profit allocation function is absorbed to a certain extent by the management control function.

For these reasons, companies usually use only one transfer price, and it arises from balancing the effects of different transfer prices on the respective functions.

Other optional solutions for the conflict amongst objectives are interventions in the decision autonomy of the divisions, for example, obligations of delivery and purchase commitments or restrictions, or changes to the organisational structure or the incentive system. Other performance measures, such as productivity ratios, could potentially replace divisional profit. Profit as a criterion has enough disadvantages by itself: profit is typically short-term based and highly aggregated. At first glance, a renunciation of the determination of separate divisional profits and the divisional managers' assessment based on the joint profit (*profit sharing*) appears to be a way out of the dilemma; however, there are also a number of negative side effects. Since every divisional manager is only connected to a small part of the positive and negative success, he can decide to reduce his individual efforts and to use them instead in other ways. How could motivation of decentralised decision-makers be achieved if they depend on profit figures that can only be found centrally, more or less in one account for all divisions?

8.1.3 Types of Transfer Prices

In theory and in practice, a range of different transfer price types are used. They can be summarised and categorised into three major **types**:
- **Market-based** transfer prices
- **Cost-based** transfer prices
- **Negotiated** transfer prices

All three types are regularly used in practice and the most frequently used are the cost-based transfer prices, followed by the market-based transfer prices.

The significance and informative value of such facts suffers from the realisation that the three types of transfer prices are **not entirely free of overlap**. *Example*: A construction and engineering company applies costs as a basis (i.e. proxy) for its market prices (i.e. offers) and negotiates these prices in that manner. For internally produced intermediate products that show the same characteristics, it is unclear as to whether the transfer price is market-based, cost-based or negotiated. Often, companies use several types of transfer prices simultaneously.

The operations research literature also explores transfer prices from different perspectives.

8.1.4 Organisational Settings

For the **practical application** of transfer prices, criteria like **simplicity** and **acceptability** play an important role. What use does a very ingeniously devised transfer pricing system have if no user is able to understand and administer it? For acceptability, it is essential to know whether the transfer prices lead to divisional results that are considered fair.

Therefore, apart from the choice of the type of transfer price, the following **questions** also need to be answered:

- Who determines the transfer price?
- What duration does the transfer price have, and what are the circumstances when it must be decided upon anew?
- Is the transfer price chosen permanently or dependent upon production volume?

Often transfer prices are only set for key products, while all other products transferred in insignificant amounts are based on simple rules such as the application of market prices.

Transfer prices cannot be assessed without consideration of the **company's structure**. Of particular importance for the function of transfer prices is the decision scope that the divisional manager possesses. In companies, certain organisational conditions, so-called **rules**, are defined for this purpose. Amongst other things, they are the following:

- Does one or every division have the choice to partially or fully buy in from the external market, or is there a strict rule to buy/sell internally?
- Are there priority rules for internal sales?
- Can a division freely make an external agreement according to its own conditions (*last call*)?
- To what extent must central services be bought internally?
- May a division produce a product themselves even if another division produces the same product?
- Up to what level of volume can a divisional manager make investment decisions?
- Can a divisional manager select staff?
- What are the informational obligations between divisions?

This chapter first discusses **sequential production** in vertically integrated companies. In their most simple form, there are only two divisions, a producing division and a purchasing division. It becomes more difficult in cases where the producing division also manufactures other products (e.g. how are the indirect costs allocated?), and in cases in which several divisions buy the internal products. **Resources and market interdependencies** are discussed afterwards; the chapter mainly focuses on **competition** amongst the 'purchasing' divisions for the limited resources of the producing division. The resource consumption is to be controlled, often by head office or a *service centre*.

8.2 Market-Based Transfer Prices

8.2.1 Applicability of the Market Price as the Transfer Price

The choice of the market price of a product that is equivalent and comparable to the intermediate product is one option for the determination of a transfer price. Ideally, the following **conditions** must apply:

1. A market for the intermediate product or a full substitute exists. In reality, this condition is often not fulfilled, as several products with different prices are offered for sale, which can serve more or less as a substitute for the internal product.
2. Transactions of the company divisions may have no influence on the market price, as otherwise, the divisions could affect the price. Nevertheless, this condition is fulfilled when perfect competition exists.
3. There is a uniform market price. If the market price is affected by the order amount, or if a certain order sum changes within a period (e.g. by discounts), which price should then be taken?
4. The market price should fit with the decision. It should not be affected by short-term price considerations (e.g. cut-price offers). For that reason, 'finding' a suitable price by an external offer might be problematic because the offer may be very low, simply set to clinch a business relationship with the expectation of later being able to raise the price when in a constant business relationship.

The better these conditions are fulfilled, and the more efficient the market for an intermediate product, the more appropriate is the market price as the transfer price. Then, such a transfer price is suitable to be used for the divisions' **profit allocation** as every division can simply be compared with the market situation. It is also suitable for **coordination**. A coordination requirement mainly appears as a result of synergetic effects, but these synergies do not exist in perfect markets, and thus, coordination is virtually guaranteed by the market. However, in practice, such markets or market prices are more the exception than the rule. Markets are typically imperfect – this is a reason why companies exist and are economically meaningful, as already shown. Therefore, in this case approximate solutions must be used.

> **Remark**
>
> A typical textbook recommendation for the transfer price is: 'If the market price exists (or can best be approximated [...]), use it'. (as one of many examples: Anthony et al. 1992, p. 233 f.)

Another advantage of a market price that fulfils the above conditions relates to **low manipulability**, as the market price does not depend on the (better) state of information of divisional managers and to a certain extent, is rather an 'objective' measure. With legal repercussions and effects, for example, if the divisions are legally independent, the market-based transfer price is recognised as being probably the best solution for the distribution of profits between the divisions.

From a taxation point of view, the **price comparison method** corresponds to this type of transfer price, and is based on the so-called **dealing at arm's length** rule requiring an external reference price, with a price offered to a third party (inner price comparison), and a price determined between negotiations of exclusively third external parties (external price comparison). Comparable conditions are required, such as in relation to product quality, additional components, risk taking, and the economic situation. Another approach would be to use the resale price, applied especially between mother companies supplying to daughter distribution companies; here, the transfer price arises on the basis of the retail price reduced by the usual market profit margin.

From a long-term view, **market prices** have an indicative function about the profitability of company divisions. If a division in the long-term view and at future market prices cannot earn profit (not: contribution margins), the company would probably be better off without this division, and selling it should be seriously considered (investment appraisal methods would need to be applied for the decision-making).

In summary, market-based transfer prices will tend towards being more appropriate and suitable:

- The more efficient the market,
- The smaller the **synergetic effects** and
- The smaller the volume of the internal sales.

In the cases described, the potential disadvantages hardly impair the advantages of market prices. However, it is obvious that under these conditions, little needs to be coordinated.

If the divisions can access the **external market unrestrictedly**, the transfer price (in the following called *TP*) *must* equal the **market price** for the intermediate product or the internal service p_1, as otherwise no internal transfer would occur. The reason: first, $TP \geq p_1$ must apply; as otherwise, the producing division would only sell to external buyers. At the same time $TP \leq p_1$ applies as otherwise the purchasing division would not buy anything internally and would instead use the external market. Therefore, $TP = p_1$ arises.

The use of market prices is not limited to situations whereby the divisions may actually use the market for intermediate products. Upper management can impose the policy that existing internal demand or supply has to be acknowledged. Vice versa, company policy may leave the decision about the extent of the inter-company business at the discretion of the divisions themselves. This should bring 'competition' into the company. With a view on price decisions, however, this can be problematic. Dependent upon the price calculation as well as the economic situation of competitors, incorrect decisions from the perspective of the company as a whole can arise.

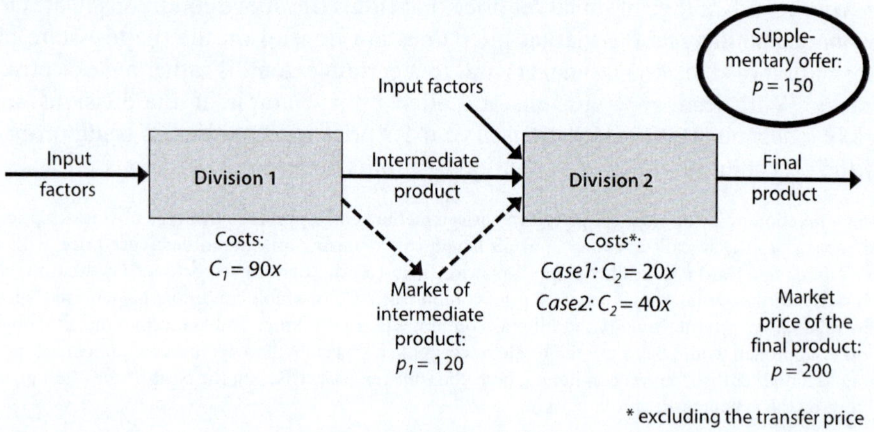

Fig. 8.1 Perfect market for the intermediate product

8

- **Example**

Division 1 produces an intermediate product, which is processed further into a final product by Division 2 and then offered for sale at the market price. This example relies on the simplifying assumption that the final product requires exactly one unit of the intermediate product (i.e. the consumption coefficient equals one). This is not restrictive, as with other consumption coefficients the amounts of the intermediate product or that of the final product only need to be adapted. The market price for the final product amounts to $p = 200$. The intermediate product is sold at a market price of $p_1 = 120$ without limits. In Division 1, the variable production costs are $c_1 = 90$, the costs of processing and sales in Division 2 amount to $c_2 = 20$ (Case 1) or alternatively $c_2 = 40$ (Case 2). Division 2 now receives an inquiry for a supplementary order at a price of $p = 150$ per unit. The acceptance of this additional order has no effect on their regular sales volume. In order to show the problems, it is assumed that both divisions have sufficient free capacities. Figure 8.1 shows this situation. Should Division 2 accept the order, and should Division 1 supply the intermediate product?

The perspective of the divisions and the company as a whole are summarised in Table 8.1.

The use of the market price as the transfer price for the intermediate product causes both divisions to be **indifferent** as to whether they supply internally, sell or buy in externally. Division 2, for example, might as well buy the intermediate product at the market price.

In Case 1, both divisions determine a positive contribution margin if the supplementary order is accepted. Therefore, both choose this option. The total contribution margin achieved equals the sum of the two divisions' contribution margins (30 + 10 = 40).

In Case 2, Division 2 determines a negative contribution margin and, therefore, rejects the supplementary order. At first glance, this hardly appears profitable from the company's perspective. Yet, it is the optimal decision, as Division 1 now can sell the intermediate product required for the rejected supplementary order at the mar-

Table 8.1 Contribution margins in a perfect market

Division 1		
Transfer price	120	
Variable cost	−90	
Contribution margin of the supplementary order	+30	
Division 2	Case 1	Case 2
Sales price	150	150
Variable cost	−20	−40
Transfer price	−120	−120
Contribution margin of the supplementary order	+10	−10
Company	Case 1	Case 2
Sales price	150	150
Variable cost of Division 1	−90	−90
Variable cost of Division 2	−20	−40
Contribution margin of the supplementary order	+40	+20

ket price of $p_1 = 120$ and achieve a contribution margin of 30. This equals the maximum contribution margin attainable, as Division 2 can gain no additional contribution margin. It is *higher* than the total contribution margin of 20 when the supplementary order was to be fulfilled. Thus, the acceptance of the supplementary order is also not optimal from the company perspective. Again, the market price totally fulfils the coordination function. The market for the intermediate product is perfect.

This example requires the existence of sufficient **free capacities** for the supplementary order. The other assumption in the example, namely, the constant market price without sales limits and constant variable cost leads to the fact that the full capacity utilisation is optimal from both divisions' perspective. Therefore, the assumption of free capacities implicitly requires further assumptions; for example, the existence of long-term relationships.

When the **capacities** were fully **exhausted**, the following solution would arise: for an acceptance of the supplementary order, Division 1 would have to redirect the required units of the intermediate product from market sales to Division 2. Then, the additional contribution margin of the supplementary order would equal zero, and Division 2 would always reject this order because it prefers the market price $p = 200$ as opposed to the price of the supplementary order $p = 150$.

Supply and sales limitations cannot lead to improvements but can instead act to reduce profits. Limitations have an effect only if the transfer price is determined at a price not identical to the market price. *Example*: assume $TP = 100$. Then Division 2 would accept the supplementary order and determine a divisional contribution margin of 150 – 40 – 100 = 10, and Division 1 would supply (although reluctantly) because its divisional contribution margin amounts to 100 – 90 = 10. However, this decision is not optimal from the perspective of the company as a whole because it prevents Division 1 earning a divisional contribution margin of 30 at the external market price.

Assume that Division 1 cannot sell any additional amounts of this intermediate product at the market. Then, the favourable choice (also from the company view) is lost, and the acceptance of the supplementary order becomes the optimal solution. However, Division 2 will still not be willing if the transfer price remains at the market price. The transfer price might not exceed 110 (= 150 – 40), and it could even be lowered down to 90 (= c_1), at which price Division 1 is still ready to supply the intermediate product.

8

▪ Extension of the Example

Division 1 has variable production costs of only 90 in the case of internal delivery; for external sales, additional variable costs of 16 appear as a result of additional sales activities, leading to increased variable costs of 90 + 16 = 106. The variable costs of processing and sales are 40 in Division 2 if the intermediate product is purchased internally and are 50 if bought in from the external market due to additional quality tests and freight charges. ◘ Figure 8.2 shows the modified situation.

Again, the perspective of the divisions and the company as a whole are summarised in ◘ Table 8.2:

Applying a transfer price equal to the market price, Division 2 again determines a contribution margin of the supplementary order in the amount of –10 and,

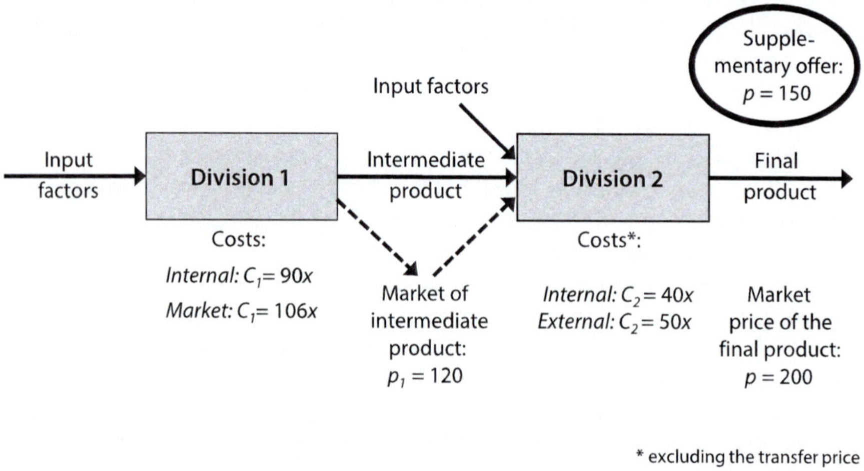

◘ **Fig. 8.2** Imperfect market for the intermediate product

Table 8.2 Contribution margins in an imperfect market

Division 1		
Sales	Internal	External
Transfer price	120	120
Variable cost	–90	–106
Contribution margin of the supplementary order	+30	+14
Division 2		
Purchase	Internal	External
Sales price	150	150
Variable cost	–40	–50
Transfer price	–120	–120
Contribution margin of the supplementary order	+10	–20
Company		
Division 1's sales	Internal	External
Sales price	150	120
Division 1's variable cost	–90	–106
Division 2's variable cost	–40	–
Contribution margin of the supplementary order	+20	+14

therefore, rejects the order. If Division 2 buys in externally, the negative contribution margin gets even worse due to additional costs of 10 and becomes –20. Division 1 can sell the respective amounts of the intermediate product not required by Division 2 at the market and achieves a positive contribution margin of 120 – 106 = +14 per unit. Based on a transfer price equal to the market price, this is also the total contribution margin in decentralised decision-making.

However, it is *lower* by 6 than the contribution margin of 20 that would arise for the company as a whole, with the acceptance of the supplementary order. Consequently, with the existence of synergies, the market price no longer leads to optimal coordination, as Division 2 makes a decision that is suboptimal, that is, incorrect, from the perspective of the company as a whole.

Does a transfer price exist in this situation leading to the optimal decision? Such a transfer price must guarantee a positive (additional) contribution margin for both divisions against the best alternative in each case (opportunity costs). Division 1 supplies to Division 2 at every price higher than its variable cost (including opportunity costs), so the internal sales are 90 + 14 = +104. Division 2 accepts the supplementary order at every transfer price lower than 110. Every transfer price within the following interval: $104 \leq TP \leq 110$ leads to the optimal decision from the company's perspective, that is, it fulfils the coordination function. At what exact price within the given range the transfer price should be set, firstly depends on whether it is given by head office or negotiated. A fair possibility would be the equal subdivision of the additional contribution margin of 6, resulting in a transfer price $TP = 107$. The results of these examples show a **general understanding as follows**:

A transfer price leading to decentralised decisions that are optimal from the perspective of the company as a whole often does not correspond to the market price of the intermediate product. Market-based transfer prices do not fulfil the **coordination function**.

The market price is only relevant through the amount of the opportunity costs (in the example: external sales with a contribution margin of 120 – 16 – 90 = 14) and thus far plays a role in the decision. It determines the lower limit of the possible transfer price.

8.2.2 Modified Market Price

It is by no means compulsory to use *the* market price as the exact transfer price. In practice different forms of modifications to the market price are used. One frequently used is the following **modification**:

Market price of intermediate product sold internally	
– Sales costs	
– Shipping costs	
– Omitted marketing costs	
– Imputed (fictitious) interest on accounts receivable	
+ Intra-company transportation costs	
= **Transfer price**	

The extent of the omitted cost for internal sales is subject to further specification and expansion (into greater detail).

This transfer price corresponds to the **marginal price of the supplying division**. With a given market price, the division is indifferent between internal and external sales at this transfer price, and the whole advantage of internal business rests with the buying division.

Alternatively, the market price could be raised by omitted procurement costs. This corresponds to the **marginal cost of the buying division**. Then the division is indifferent between internal and external purchases, and the whole advantage from internal business rests with the supplying division.

Interim solutions to these cases would be an equal division of the joint advantages of internal business or a combination of both methods.

- **Example**

The market price amounts to 100. The omitted cost of the supplying division is 5 and for the buying division is 3. The total advantage from internal business (synergetic effect) amounts to 5 + 3 = 8. They equal the 'cost' of the market utilisation.

- Marginal price of the supplying division: 100 – 5 = 95.
- Marginal price of the buying division: 100 + 3 = 103.
- Symmetric split-up (division) of the advantage: 100 – 5 + (5 + 3)/2 = 99.
- Combination of the methods: 100 – 5 + 3 = 98.

Fundamentally, every transfer price TP within the range of $95 \leq TP \leq 103$ leads to an incentive for *internal* transfer for both divisions. The splitting-up of the synergetic effect of 8 is completely arbitrary. In this respect, every modification is equally good or bad, provided that the incentive for *internal* transfer remains intact. However, the modifications differ concerning the question of whether it comes to a transfer *at all*. The previous example of the last section with an imperfect market of the intermediate product would produce a transfer price in the amount of $TP = 120 - 16 + 10 = 114$ for a combination of both methods. However, this price lies beyond the identified transfer price interval $104 \leq TP \leq 110$, meaning that Division 2 would reject the supplementary order which would not be the optimal decision for the company as a whole. This outcome would not be found in a decentralised organisation.

An advantage of the marginal price of the supplying division approach can be seen by the fact that it leads to a relatively low transfer price with which the buying division gains a rather large leeway for price setting, which typically is favourable from the perspective of the company as a whole. Another reason for such a modification could lie in the (relatively) lower risk that the supplying division would face.

Setting the transfer price below the market price can impose control effects if the supplying division can act monopolistically against the buying division, for example, to protect intellectual property. This leads to distortions of supply and internal demand for the intermediate product. With the help of a price drop induced by head office, the distortion, when limited capacity of the supplying division exists, can be reduced. With it, the internal sales volume of the intermediate product is increased with the reverse effect on the quantity of external sales. This is favourable from the company's view.

8.3 Cost-Based Transfer Prices

Transfer prices linked to cost figures in different ways are most frequently applied in practice. They encompass a relatively diverse group of different transfer price types, namely, based on the following:

- Actual costs or standard (budgeted) costs
- Marginal costs or full costs
- Costs or cost 'plus' surcharge

Empirical surveys show that transfer prices based on marginal costs are rather rare whereas those based on full costs are most frequently used. At first glance, this is surprising, but as will be shown in the following analysis: there are situations in which marginal costs optimally fulfil the **coordination function**, while it is difficult to find situations in which full cost-based transfer prices are optimal. Nevertheless, the following descriptions will also show the limitations of the coordination qualities of marginal cost-based transfer prices. In doing so, this might better explain the aversion towards such transfer prices in practice.

8.3.1 Actual Costs Versus Standard Costs

Transfer prices determined on the basis of **actual costs** lead to a precise coverage of the supplying division's (reported) costs in each case. However, the purchasing division only knows the transfer price afterwards, that is, once the goods/services have been produced/provided.

Therefore, this approach carries the entire risk of cost variations and must base its operational decisions on *expected* actual costs. The actual costs often also depend on the other divisions' demands. The transfer price is not 'isolating'.

▶ Examples

With increasing units per month, the cost per unit often declines. If a division can adjust (e.g. delay) its orders within a certain period, it will prefer to buy in the months, during which the other divisions buy in higher numbers. ◀

For transfer prices based on **standard costs** (or budgeted costs), the exact budgeted costs are covered. The difference between standard and actual costs (**cost variances**) affects the result only of the selling division, which therefore bears the entire risk. This has the advantage that divisional management has an **incentive** to act economically. In contrast, if all costs are covered anyway by the transfer price (determined ex post), any such incentive largely disappears. Frequently the cost variance consists of a **capacity variance**. Its allocation must be treated in a differentiated way according to its causation, that is, the reason why it arose. If the purchasing division decides on the quantity and if the supplying division must fulfil an internal demand, the capacity variance has to be allocated to the purchasing division, that is, the transfer price should instead be based on actual costs. To be able to allocate inefficiencies to the selling division, the transfer price would have to be set according to a flexible budget based upon the standard costs. If the supplying division has decision power in regard to the quantity and can determine its capacity itself, the capacity variance has to be allocated to them, that is, the transfer price should equal the standard costs.

A potential disadvantage of standard costs lies in the fact that **adaptation decisions** of the purchasing division cannot take place due to the actual cost change, because the information is not available in time. *Example*: the purchasing division has a substitutive production function. If an input factor purchased internally becomes more expensive, another minimal cost combination arises. If it is settled at standard costs, the division remains with its planned factor combination, although this is not optimal in the ex post view.

Alternatively, the **determination of standard costs** requires an additional step: if the divisions agree on standard costs, possibly on the basis of an offer with fixed prices, the supplying division can utilise its better state of knowledge about the real (expected) costs. If head office determines the standard costs, it will be suddenly involved again in the details of the operational business from which it wanted to free itself by decentralisation; furthermore, it requires the same level of information as that of the division. Depending on the situation of head office (i.e. whether the advantages or the disadvantages dominate), it could be meaningful on a cost-benefit basis, to allow head office to set the standard costs for the divisions. A partial allocation of the cost variances could also be considered.

8.3.2 Marginal Cost-Based Transfer Price

As can be formally shown, optimum, that is, profit maximising decisions, from the perspective of the company as a whole, can only be found using marginal costs, which are understood as relevant costs for short-term decisions. Thus, they solve the coordination problem. However, this is achieved based upon very specific conditions regarding the level and state of information of both head office and the divisions, and therefore only appears to be solved. The rare use of marginal cost-based transfer prices in practice also emphasises this.

- **The *Hirshleifer* Model**

Published in 1956 and 1957, papers by *Hirshleifer* forms the basis of the argument and the following example shows the relationships and their effects.

Example: Division 1 produces an intermediate product, which is further processed by Division 2 into a marketable final product. There is no market for the intermediate product, nor are there supply and purchase limits, which do not allow the divisions to use a market for this intermediate product. The processing costs of both divisions amount to the following:

$$C_1 = 20 + \frac{x^2}{2} \text{ and } C_2 = 2 + x \tag{8.1}$$

The market for the final product is monopolistic with a price demand function of $p(x) = 16 - x$. ◘ Figure 8.3 shows this situation. Both decentralised divisions should determine their output volumes. How high must the transfer price be, so that both divisions decide on identical amounts, which are also optimal from the company's perspective?

The **central solution** as a reference solution is determined by the maximisation of total profit Π:

$$\max_x \Pi = p(x) \cdot x - C_1(x) - C_2(x) \tag{8.2}$$

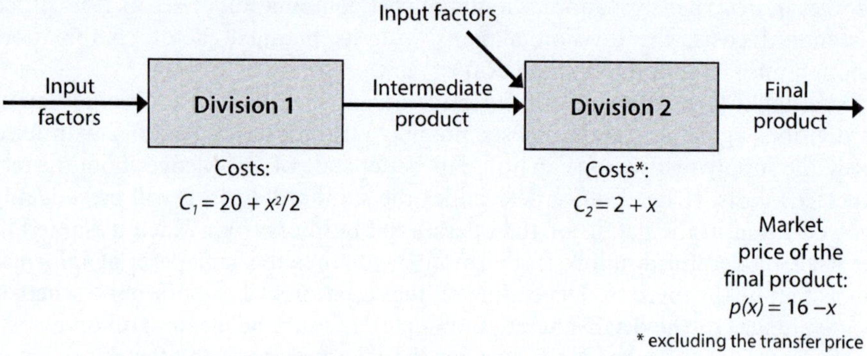

Fig. 8.3 The situation of the *Hirshleifer* model

A necessary condition is that the first derivation of the profit according to x equals zero, that is,

8

$$p(x^*) + p'(x^*) \cdot x^* - C_1'(x^*) - C_2'(x^*) = 0 \tag{8.3}$$

where x^* is the optimal (*Cournot*) amount that arises for the example as follows:

$$\Pi = (16 - x) \cdot x - 20 - \frac{x^2}{2} - 2 - x = -\frac{3x^2}{2} + 15x - 22$$

$$\Pi' = -3x + 15 \text{ and } x^* = 5$$

The second derivation is negative. Therefore, this is a maximum (here at the same time the global maximum). The maximum profit amounts to $\Pi(x^* = 5) = 15.5$.

Under **decentralised decision-making**, divisional managers independently determine their respective output volumes. Both maximise their divisional profits, taking the transfer price *TP* into account for the transferred intermediate product:

$$\max_x \Pi_1 = TP \cdot x - C_1(x) \tag{8.4}$$

$$\max_x \Pi_2 = p(x) \cdot x - TP \cdot x - C_2(x) \tag{8.5}$$

The optimal amount in each case depends on the transfer price *TP*. Table 8.3 gives three examples of transfer prices. It is obvious that the transfer price has no influence on the total profit $\Pi = \Pi_1 + \Pi_2$.

There is only one transfer price at which both divisions want to transfer the same amounts. This amount is also optimal from the company's perspective simultaneously. This transfer price equals the **marginal cost of the supplying division in the optimum**, namely, $TP = C_1'(x^*) = x^* = 5$. The optimal *divisional amounts* x_i, $i = 1, 2$ assuming the maximisation of the decentralised target functions according to the amount x:

$$\Pi_1' = TP - C_1'(x) = 5 - x \text{ and } x_1 = 5 = x^*$$

$$\Pi_2' = p(x) + p'(x) \cdot x - TP - C_2'(x) = 16 - 2x - 5 - 1 \text{ and } x_2 = 5 = x^*$$

Table 8.3 Optimal amounts for different transfer prices

Amount x	2	3	4	5	6	7
Transfer price = 3						
$Profit_1$	−16	**−15.5**	−16	−17.5	−20	−23.5
$Profit_2$	18	25	30	33	**34**	33
Total profit	2	9.5	14	**15.5**	14	9.5
Transfer price = 5						
$Profit_1$	−12	−9.5	−8	**−7.5**	−8	−9.5
$Profit_2$	14	19	22	**23**	22	19
Total profit	2	9.5	14	**15.5**	14	9.5
Transfer price = 7						
$Profit_1$	−8	−3.5	0	2.5	4	**4.5**
$Profit_2$	10	13	**14**	13	10	5
Total profit	2	9.5	14	**15.5**	14	9.5

Both divisions independently choose $x^* = 5$. There is *no other* transfer price that leads to the same result.

However, the use of marginal costs as the transfer price solves the coordination problem only *apparently*. Head office must determine the transfer price $TP = 5$, and the question arises of how it could know this transfer price. To be able to determine $TP = 5$, it must solve the decision problem. If that problem is solved, head office might as well stipulate the output volumes to the divisions. Therefore, decentralised decision-making, with an imposed transfer price solves, a false problem.

Additionally, the **profit allocation** of the divisions using a marginal cost-based transfer price is hardly sufficient, that is, suitable. The **split-up (division)** of total profits is entirely **arbitrary** and typically favours the buying division. Depending on its cost function, the supplying division 'gains' only its marginal cost and faces a loss, with a linear cost function in the amount of its fixed costs. If marginal costs are increasing, the loss becomes lower, or else higher.

Incentive Effects

Assume that head office only determines *how* the transfer price should be set, that is, based on the marginal costs of the supplying division. Then, new **problems** appear: Division 1 and Division 2 have an incentive to behave in a manner not desired by head office. As a consequence, in each case, the coordination function is not fulfilled.

Division 2 will recognise that the transfer price is actually a **function of the amount purchased**, that is, $TP = TP(x) = C_1'$, and not merely a constantly given value. It virtually becomes the monopolistic customer. Compared to (8.5), its decision problem changes into

$$\max_x \Pi_2 = p(x)\cdot x - TP(x)\cdot x - C_2(x) \tag{8.6}$$

$$\Pi_2' = p(x) + p'(x)\cdot x - TP(x) - TP'(x)\cdot x - C_2'(x) = 16 - 2x - x - x - 1 = 15 - 4x$$

The profit-maximising amount is now *lower* than x^*, namely $x_2 = 3.75$. The divisional profit of Division 2 rises from $\Pi_2(x^*) = 23$ to $\Pi_2(x_2) = 26.125$. However, from the perspective of the company as a whole, this amount leads to a less favourable situation with a lower total company profit.

Division 1 has to struggle with other problems. First, the delivery of the optimal *amount* x^* leads to a loss in the amount of $\Pi_1(x^*) = -7.5$. This is a **fundamental disadvantage** of the use of marginal cost-based transfer prices: as with the exception of the case of strongly increasing marginal costs, Division 1 will always incur **a loss**. Therefore, other measures (for instance, the imposed obligation to deliver the intermediate product) must guarantee that Division 1 actually produces the intermediate product for the subsequent company divisions.

8

However, Division 1 often has another choice of action in this situation. If its cost function C_1, is only known to itself (**private information**), head office or Division 2 (depending on who sets the transfer price) must ask Division 1 for this information. Divisional costs can hardly be seen and examined by 'strangers'. Assume that the division also produces other products than the intermediate product in question. As every allocation of fixed costs to products is arbitrary to a certain extent, enough leeway remains to distort these costs in one direction or another.

Division 1 can affect the selection of the transfer price by **untruthful information,** and with it, the amount purchased and its own divisional profit. Assume Division 1 reports its cost function as follows:

$$\widehat{C}_1 = 20 + \frac{3x^2}{2}$$

It indicates higher variable costs than actually arise. Head office (or the non-monopolistic customer Division 2) then determines:

$$\max_x \Pi\left(\widehat{C}_1\right) = p(x)\cdot x - \widehat{C}_1(x) - C_2(x) = 15x - \frac{5x^2}{2} - 22$$

The optimal amount is $\hat{x} = 3$ with the transfer price TP

$$\widehat{C}_1'(\ )x = 3x = 9$$

and the profit of Division 1 (Π_1) rises to +2.5. This is to the detriment of the company's profit and the profit of Division 2.

If the structure of the cost function is known by C1 = 20 + δ·x2 and the distortion is limited to the parameter δ, then the above distorted cost information is optimal from the perspective of Division 1.

False incentives in regard to decisions about production technology are to be expected, in so far as such decisions are made within *profit centre* responsibilities. The supplying division might oppose such a product technology investment considered favourable by itself, as it leads to higher divisional fixed costs but to lower variable costs. Similar effects appear with regard to investments in human resources, for example, improvements in staff qualifications.

■ Linear Costs and Revenues

The model shown up to now assumes that divisional profits are strictly concavely dependent upon the amount being transferred internally between the divisions. This was achieved in the example of Division 1 by a convex cost function and for Division 2 by a concave revenue function. In the following example, linear costs and revenues are assumed, and misguidance by the marginal costs is therefore less likely.

Example: Division 1 produces an intermediate product, which is processed in Division 2 into a final product before being sold in the external market. The sales price p is constant, and the cost functions are linear:

$$C_i(x) = C_1^F + c \cdot x \text{ for } i = 1, 2$$

In order to limit the solution, there must be a limited resource or bottleneck in at least one division. For each of the two divisions, (potentially effective) restrictions are assumed in the following way:

$$v_i \cdot x = \overline{V}_i \text{ for } i = 1, 2 \tag{8.8}$$

The consumption of one unit of output, v_i, uses the limited resource and $\overline{V}_i$ equals the available units of that resource (e.g. time, machine hours) in division i.

Division 1 decides as follows:

$$\max_x \Pi_1 = TP \cdot x - C_1^F - c_1 \cdot x \tag{8.9}$$

The solution is

$$x_1 = \begin{cases} 0 & \text{for } TP < c_1 \\ \dfrac{\overline{V}_1}{v_1} & \text{for } TP \geq c_1 \end{cases} \tag{8.10}$$

Analogously, the condition applies for Division 2 (the condition $x_2 = \overline{V}_2 / v_2$ is: $TP \leq p - c_2$). Assuming that both divisions must choose an equal amount it finally arises from $x^* = \min\{x_1, x_2\}$.

The **optimal solution** from the company perspective is identical to the **decentralised solution** when

1. $p - c_1 - c_2 \geq 0$ (production is profitable).
2. $c_1 \leq TP \leq p - c_2$ (the transfer price guarantees that both divisions will produce their respective output).

Head office does *not* necessarily need to know the restrictions, just as it is typically sufficient to possess only an *approximate* knowledge of the variable cost amounts, to fulfil the coordination function. The reason lies in the fact that the optimal solution reacts relatively insensitively concerning the underlying measures; this was not the case in the previous example. If the transfer price is set exactly at the marginal cost of the supplying division ($c_1 \leq TP$), this insensitivity is partly lost again.

- **Marginal Costs at the Limit of Capacity**

Marginal costs have to be modified at the **capacity limits**. Assume that Division 1 not only produces the intermediate product needed by Division 2 but also sells other products to other divisions or to the market, and it has now reached its capacity limit. Then, the transfer price must include the direct variable costs as well as the **opportunity costs** of the bottleneck, that is, the contribution margin crowded out by production of the intermediate product. If Division 1 only reaches its capacity limit based upon the internal demand of the intermediate product, the transfer price jumps from the original marginal costs to the new marginal costs (including the opportunity costs).

Then, taking the borderline case of the marginal costs equalling the **market price**: if a market exists for the intermediate product and if Division 1 has the possibility of selling the product at the market price, then this market price equals the relevant revenue measure for the determination of the opportunity costs in a bottleneck situation.

If the producing division decides its capacity, **false incentives** can arise: as the producing division is interested in a high transfer price and knows that the transfer price will rise in line with a shortage of capacity. Therefore, it might have the incentive to choose a capacity which is too small.

Vice versa, the buying divisions, during the budgeting phase, are inclined to overestimate their demand. Consequently, the producing division is pushed towards a high(er) capacity, and the probability of underutilisation increases.

8.3.3 Full Cost-Based Transfer Price

The basic idea of full cost-based transfer prices is that the producing division (on average) should be reimbursed to the amount of their **total** (or **full**) **costs**. The producing division is then not threatened by a loss, in contrast to the situation when marginal costs are the basis of transfer prices. Yet, the producing division does not generate a profit, in addition to the fact that the company profit is achieved by the purchasing division. With it, *an arbitrary* **division of the total company profit** is again visible.

Sometimes **combined transfer price systems** of the type where full costs are covered are found in practice, limited to the market price, if it is lower. The consequence for the profit allocation function is the fact that not only can the producing division not reach a profit but they often face a loss calculated as the difference between full costs and market price. This increases the pressure on the division to produce less expensively; however, it still does not lead to a divisional profit.

Transfer prices on a full cost basis are very **popular** in **practice**. Strictly speaking, this means that every company has practically one transfer price system applied in a simple way, that is, without further considerations, as it can be based on their cost accounting system, with little further adjustments.

In practice, the allocation of overhead costs is often excused and explained by the argument of creating cost awareness amongst divisional managers. As a rule, total costs are far higher than variable costs; and if only the latter were charged, divisional managers might get the impression that production costs are (too) small. The transfer price based on full costs should create an incentive to behave in a 'cost-aware' manner.

A major argument for the extensive rejection of marginal cost-based transfer prices in practice, and for favouring full cost-based transfer prices, is that an internal production of intermediate products is rarely completed with only a short-term perspective. Therefore, the usual argument, that *only* marginal costs fulfil the coordination function cannot be valid, as this is only applied to short-term decisions based on the definition of marginal costs. For **long-term decisions**, the use of marginal costs is unsuitable as a decision criterion; rather, relevant measures encompass all changes caused by the decision. However, *full costs* are similarly unsuitable for it because of the following:

1. Full costs encompass *all* costs, but it depends on the decision problem as to which cost components are relevant.
2. Full costs are often subject to variances according to the **capacity utilisation** of the producing division. This can be avoided by the use of budgeted capacity instead of actual capacity utilisation for the determination of full costs. Yet, this can lead to false incentives in the budgeting process.
3. If several products are produced by the producing division and only part of them are supplied internally, the well-known problem of **overhead costs' allocation** to products arises. This is generally solved **arbitrarily**, and with it, the full costs of the internal products are also arbitrary.

If decisions are to be made on the basis of costs rather than on cash outflows (as in investment appraisal), full costs can form a simplified **approximation** of the costs that are changeable by the decision in the **long term**.

The allocation of fixed costs, however, becomes necessary when the fixed costs can be influenced.

▶ Example

Head office considers investments in continuing education. The investment causes one time fixed costs, and as a result, a certain percentage reduction in the direct costs of each of the divisions arises. Head office does not precisely know the savings potential of the divisions. Unless the costs of the investment were not charged, every division would have an incentive to exaggerate this savings potential, as it would only gain advantages but not the costs of this investment. Therefore, from an *ex ante perspective*, the (later) fixed costs must be contained in the transfer price. ◀

The inclusion of fixed costs in the transfer price also serves to control the **demand for limited resources**.

▶ **Example**

A company acquires the authorisation to use a literature database. The monthly fee is 1,000 and includes 100 min of database searches each month. A 'normal' inquiry of this database is charged at 30 per min. How can the costs per minute be allocated to the internal divisions using the database?

At the beginning of the month, the number of minutes used for searches is not rateable. The marginal costs of the first 100 min amount to 0, the marginal costs of every exceeding minute amount to 30. If the *transfer price* is set at the marginal costs, the divisions will carelessly handle it, and only once 100 min are used, do they incur costs and this has to be compared to the benefit of further searches. The control effects are diminished if the principle of 'Who comes first, gets it free first' is applied. It might occur that the benefit of a search equals 5 per min and is only used because the search is (still) free. A search is considered as a virtually free resource. A search after the 100 min are used, and which perhaps leads to benefits of 25 per min would not be done, due to the fact that it happens later in the month.

It is not necessarily optimal to immediately charge the divisions 30 per min, because it might be that the 100 min are not exhausted and, therefore, the marginal costs actually amount to 0. ◀

Raising the price for the use of a resource **reduces the demand**. In the ideal case, the capacity is exactly utilised; its respective costs are the **opportunity costs** that can hardly be accurately estimated within practice. Opportunity costs can consist of the following:

- Costs of delays: costs as a result of the delayed fulfilment. *Example*: maintenance costs.
- Costs of quality deterioration: *Example*: because of work overload in the legal department, the quality drops or the duration of work increases.
- Costs of procurement from other sources or own production. *Example*: installation of its own legal department instead of hiring an external lawyer.

The allocation of full costs in such situations can represent a simple and economically justifiable attempt to **approximate** the undeterminable opportunity costs of centrally provided services. The quality of this approximation depends on the cost function and the (budgeted and actual) demand for the products. For certain assumptions, the quality of the approximation can be analysed.

▶ **Example**

Miller and Buckman (1987) showed a queuing model for a service department with random demands (with a Poisson distribution) and also random service work duration (with an exponential distribution). The capacity costs of the service department depend on the quantity of service work places X, $C_0 = c \cdot X^k$ with $k > 0$ and $0 < k < 1$. If k is close to 1 (i.e. there are almost no *economies of scale*), the fixed costs approximate the opportunity costs very closely. However, for a very small c the approximation is very bad; in this case it would be preferable not to charge the capacity costs. However, this result is of little help, as cost allocations have an effect, as a good approximation exactly in the cases in which the use of a centrally supplied service leads to limited advantages. ◀

■ Coordination Function

The transfer price on the basis of full costs contains components of both variable costs and fixed costs and possibly even part of the profits of the producing division. All of these are viewed by the buying division as variable costs. In reality, they actually are variable costs: as if one unit less is purchased, the costs decrease exactly by the amount of the transfer price. This can lead to **incorrect**, i.e. **suboptimal decisions** in scenarios that require the use of variable costs. An example is a one-off special order as shown in the following insertion.

▶ Example

A product is processed in two independent production divisions.

Variable costs (per copy) of Division 1	10	
Proportionate fixed costs	15	
Transfer price (supply from Divisions 1–2)		25
Costs for Division 2	25	
Variable costs (per copy) Division 2	6	
Proportionate fixed costs of Division 2	9	
Total costs per copy		40

Cost structure per copy (with given capacity in both divisions):

	Actual		Division 2' perspective	
Variable costs	16	40.0%	31	77.5%
Proportionate fixed costs	24	60.0%	9	22.5%
Total costs per copy	40	100.0%	40	100.0%

A supplementary order at a price of 30 would be rejected by Division 2 although it produces a positive contribution margin of 14 (ca. 47%). ◀

In addition, effects on the suitability of certain **cost accounting systems** can arise, depending on the cost structure, namely, the relation of the variable and fixed costs. If the real cost structure is distorted by transfer prices, a company can apply an unsuitable cost accounting system without recognising it. For example, due to the data, the company might believe that a high proportion of the product costs are direct costs and that a change towards another cost accounting system, which would trace the indirect costs more precisely, is not economical. Distortions and incorrect decisions increase due to the unsuitable suitable cost accounting system in use.

8.3.4 Multi-Tier Transfer Prices

Two-tier transfer prices split the transfer price into two parts:
- The current products are charged at **marginal costs**.
- Additionally, a **single amount** is charged in each period.

With this suggestion, the **characteristics** of marginal cost-based transfer prices remain intact for (short-term) decision-making. However, the disadvantage due to the marginal costs imposing losses on the producing division is reduced or avoided by the single period payment. This payment can be interpreted as a charge for the supply or reservation of the producing division's capacity.

It results in the reporting of fixed costs, yet remains **decision neutral** in the short-term, which is in contrast to the full cost approach. In view of the single payment, two-tier transfer prices are only meaningful for long-term transfer relationships.

In practice, two-tier transfer prices are rarely applied. However, certain market services (e.g. electricity and telephone services) are charged in this way. In principle, this equates to a flexible budget approach.

Concerning the fixed amount, considerable **flexibility** exists; it can be derived to cover budgeted or actual fixed costs. To induce an incentive for the producing division to produce at their optimal capacity, it is possible to only charge the costs of utilisation (i.e. capacity costs of the budgeted capacity utilisation). The amount due might also contain a profit surcharge.

If the fixed amount is interpreted as covering the reserved capacity, the question arises as to how to treat short-term **variances** from the budgeted capacity utilisation.

▶ Example

Two purchasing divisions, Division 1 and Division 2, reserve full capacity with 30% and 70%, respectively; they pay accordingly 30,000 and 70,000 to the producing division. By the end of the planning period, Division 1 still has 10% of its capacity available and will not need them. Presumably, Division 2 has fully exhausted its reserved capacities. Now Division 2 gets a supplementary order that needs 5% of its capacity. Division 2 has no available capacity while there is still free capacity available (and will not otherwise be used). How should they now proceed?

Because the capacity will probably not be useable otherwise from an ex post perspective, Division 2 should receive it free of charge. The capacity costs are *sunk costs* and should not affect the decision about the supplementary order. If Division 2 had to buy the required capacity from Division 1 at a price of, for example, 5,000, this amount would suddenly become relevant for the decision. This could lead to the supplementary order being rejected, despite being profitable from the perspective of the company as a whole. ◀

Yet, if a division can receive capacity free of charge *afterwards*, it will have an **incentive** to initially reserve a capacity that is too small (in tendency). Once the division exceeds the original reserved capacity, it receives additional capacity free of charge as long as there is additional capacity available. This can be examined further in the capacity decision of the producing division: if there is too small a demand predicted in the budgeting phase, the producing division will install a capacity that is too small, and the total capacity of the company as a whole could then be too low.

Whether the advantages of two-tier transfer prices in comparison to marginal cost and full cost-based transfer prices outweigh their disadvantages, must be judged individually.

8.3.5 Full Cost Plus Profit Surcharge as a Transfer Price

The transfer price must not always cover just the costs of the producing division; it can also contain a profit share, particularly in industries where orders are priced based upon cost plus a profit surcharge (*cost plus*). From the perspective of the producing division, this procedure provides equal treatment to both internal buyers and regular external customers.

The primary motivation to include a profit surcharge in the transfer price results from the **profit allocation function**. In the suggested way, the producing division can also achieve a profit. However, as already shown, every kind of profit division is arbitrary when synergies exist. The main problem with a cost plus profit surcharge as a transfer price is determining the 'appropriate' profit surcharge. The following **possibilities** can be used in this regard:

- A percentage of the full costs
- An appropriate interest charge on capital invested (return on capital)
- By negotiation between the divisions

A lower profit surcharge is frequently assumed for the internal buyers in comparison to the external customers, but again, in this regard every profit surcharge is arbitrary.

From the perspective of the **coordination function**, full costs plus profit surcharge may not necessarily be suitable. All arguments against the use of full costs also apply here, such as the risk of incorrect decisions or the distortion of the cost structure.

False incentives arise from the division of a jointly earned profit, if a division can improve their profit situation by individual activities. Because costs are recorded in each division while profit is shared amongst the divisions, activities might not be executed that are profitable from the perspective of the company as a whole. For example, every cost reduction activity with a proportional profit surcharge ceteris paribus leads to a decrease of the absolute profit amount.

▪ An Agency Model

The following section shows a situation in which full cost plus transfer prices provide the optimum solution and solve the underlying **coordination problem**. An agency model shows two sequential intertwined divisions (◘ Fig. 8.4).

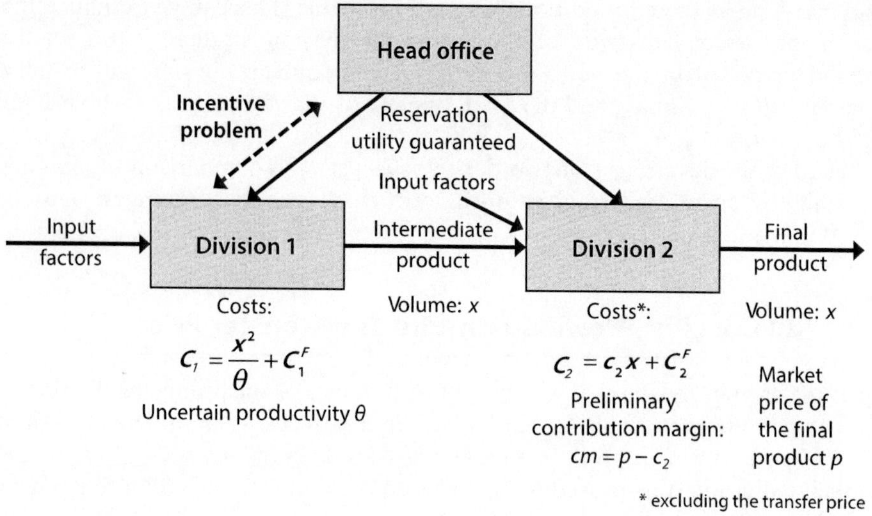

Fig. 8.4 The organisational structure in an agency model

The following scenario is given (for details see Wagenhofer 1992; the underlying model type was first examined by Sappington 1983): Division 1 produces an intermediate product which is processed further by Division 2. It is sold at the market where a perfect competition situation exists for a market price of p. The variable production costs in Division 1 are severely convex to the production volume x. Furthermore, the costs depend on the parameter θ – the 'type' of manager, that is, $C_1 = C_1(x, \theta)$. The type describes the expertise of the manager; and it can also represent the special production conditions in Division 1. The manager of Division 1 knows precisely his type. On the contrary, head office only has a priori expectations about it. A higher θ leads to a decrease of the production costs for any amount of x. The cost function is

$$C_1(x,\theta) = \frac{x}{\theta} + C_1^F \tag{8.11}$$

Only two types may be realistic, $\theta = 1$ (low productivity) or $\theta = 2$ (high productivity). The probability of both types is 50% in each case.

The subsequent processing and sales costs in Division 2 are linearly related to the amount x with $C_2 = c_2 \cdot x + C_2^F$. To simplify matters, the preliminary contribution margin (without the costs of the input factor bought from Division 1) $cm = p - c_2$ is assumed to equal 1. In regard to Division 2 where no asymmetric information exists, head office needs no indirect coordination instruments, such as a transfer price to control the division. Therefore, Division 2 can be omitted from the following analysis, and head office indirectly takes over their business relations with Division 1.

The manager of Division 1 is risk neutral. To motivate him to collaborate, head office must offer him at least as much remuneration as he would receive elsewhere (**reservation utility**). It is assumed that the divisional manager receives the full divisional profit (or alternatively, non-monetary utilities, such as praise, trust, power).

The reservation utility is assumed to equal $-C_1^F$ (thus, the transfer price must only cover the variable production costs). This must be guaranteed for every type.

A potential **false control** effect can result from the fact that the manager can report to be type $\theta = 1$, although actually being type $\theta = 2$. If head office can observe the costs afterwards, he only needs to use the difference between the actual variable production costs ($x^2/2$) of x and the required variable costs being type $\theta = 1$ ($x^2/2$) for other unnecessary things (such as business trips, customer visits, company cars). Head office wants to prevent this, through the use of the transfer price.

For a better comparison, the solution is firstly determined with symmetry of information, that is, head office knows the type θ (***first best solution***). Head office maximises:

$$\max_{x} \Pi = cm \cdot x - \frac{x^2}{\theta} = x - \frac{x^2}{\theta} \tag{8.12}$$

for $\theta = 1, 2$; $cm = 1$. The fixed costs are not relevant and, therefore, are not considered. The necessary condition of the first order is $1 - 2x/\theta = 0$, and the optimal amount x^* depends on θ:

$x^*(\theta = 1) = 1/2$ and $x^*(\theta = 2) = 1$.

Now, head office could impose the amount appropriate for every type θ, and with it, the imposition of a transfer price itself is not necessary. If head office determines a transfer price, it could be made dependent upon x and θ, that is, $TP = TP(x, \theta)$. The amount of the transfer prices would need to acknowledge the **reservation utility** of the manager:

$$\Pi_1 = TP(x,\theta) \cdot x - \frac{x^2}{\theta} - C_1^F \geq -C_1^F \text{ or } TP(x,\theta) \cdot x - \frac{x^2}{\theta} \geq 0 \tag{8.13}$$

for every θ. The lowest transfer price just fulfils this in the equation, that is, $TP(x, \theta) = x/\theta$. From it arises $TP(0.5; 1) = 0.5$, $TP(1; 2) = 0.5$ and $TP(x, \theta) \leq 0$ (sanctions) for other (x, θ) combinations ($TP = 0$ is a sufficient sanction because for each $TP \leq 0$ every type θ the amount $x = 0$ is chosen). It is assumed that the manager, in the case of indifference, produces the amount desired by head office. By *coincidence* the transfer prices are identical in the example for both types; normally it depends on θ.

In the case of **asymmetric information**, the transfer price can only depend on the amount x but not on the type θ, as it is unknown to head office. To determine the transfer price $TP(x)$ head office maximises the expected profit (before fixed costs and with $cm = 1$),

$$\max_{TP} E[\Pi] = \sum_{\theta=1}^{2} \frac{1}{2} \cdot \left[x_\theta - TP(x_\theta) \cdot x_\theta \right] \tag{8.14}$$

The amount x_θ equals the amount chosen by the manager on account of his respective type θ with the following equation:

$$\max_{x} \Pi_1 = TP(x) \cdot x - \frac{x^2}{\theta} - C_1^F \text{ for } \theta = 1,2 \tag{8.15}$$

Furthermore, head office must guarantee that the divisional manager will at least receive his reservation utility independent of his respective type θ:

$$\Pi_1(x_\theta,\theta) = TP(x_\theta)\cdot x_\theta - \frac{x^2}{\theta} - C_1^F \geq -C_1^F \text{ for } \theta = 1, 2 \text{ or}$$

$$TP(x_1)\cdot x_1 - x_1^2 \geq 0$$

$$TP(x_2)\cdot x_2 - \frac{x_2^2}{2} \geq 0 \tag{8.16}$$

This problem can be solved by a *Lagrange* approach. A deeper analysis of the **solution structure** is achieved by Condition (8.16): a type $\theta = 1$ manager will certainly have no incentive to imitate a type $\theta = 2$ manager, that is, to produce x_2 instead of x_1. Therefore, only the reverse case must be considered, namely,

$$TP(x_2)\cdot x_2 - \frac{x_2^2}{2} \geq TP(x_1)\cdot x_1 - \frac{x_1^2}{2} = TP(x_1)\cdot x_1 - x_1^2 + \frac{x_1^2}{2} > TP(x_1)\cdot x_1 - x_1^2 \geq 0 \tag{8.17}$$

8

In this case a type $\theta = 2$ manager receives more than his reservation utility, that is, achieves a **productivity gain** that is actually caused by the asymmetric information.

Certainly, head office could insist on the fact that *every* type produces just the *first best* amount. However, this would mean a relatively high payment to a type $\theta = 2$ manager. Therefore, it is preferable to impose a **lower amount** on a type $\theta = 1$ manager, which would result in lower costs to prevent a type $\theta = 2$ manager from imitating a type $\theta = 1$, and still producing the optimal, higher amount.

The solution of this model (***second best* solution**) is as follows: a manager with high productivity ($\theta = 2$) is motivated to produce the optimal amount $x_2 = x^*(\theta = 2) = 1$; a manager with low productivity $\theta = 1$ produces a lower amount, namely $x_1 = 1/3 < 1/2 = x^*(\theta = 1)$. Production is lower than in a case of symmetric information, head office must also pay less to the manager. Actually, the **transfer price** must be determined for both amounts x_1 and x_2, and amounts to the following:

$$TP(x_1) = \frac{1}{3} \text{ and } TP(x_2) = \frac{5}{9}$$

Head office can prevent other amounts from being chosen by sufficient sanctions (e.g. $TP(x) = 0$ for $x \neq x_1, x_2$). A manager of the type $\theta = 2$ is indifferent between the two amounts:

$$\Pi_1(x_2,2) = \frac{5}{9}\cdot 1 - \frac{1}{2} - C_1^F = \frac{1}{3}\cdot\frac{1}{3} - \frac{1}{18} - C_1^F = \Pi_1(x_1,2)$$

and it can be assumed that he in this case chooses x_2. On the contrary, a type $\theta = 1$ strictly prefers x_1:

$$\Pi_1(x_1,1) = \frac{1}{3}\cdot\frac{1}{3} - \frac{1}{9} - C_1^F = -C_1^F > \frac{5}{9}\cdot 1 - 1 - C_1^F = \Pi_1(x_2,1)$$

As a result, the divisional managers reveal their **real type** (in a consideration of multiple periods, this may not necessarily be the most favourable choice). The type $\theta = 1$ manager receives his alternative utility $\left(-C_1^F\right)$, and a type $\theta = 2$ manager the same plus an additional 1/18. Therefore, both will have an interest in cooperation. The solution can provide interesting insights into cost-based transfer pricing arguments and reveals the following **characteristics**:

- The optimal transfer price covers the **average costs**, that is, not the marginal costs, of production. In addition, the reservation utility of the divisional manager must be guaranteed. Therefore, it can contain a profit share, which is required to lead the manager to collaborate (due to the simplistic assumptions contained in the model, this is not explicitly expressed and shown).
- For a more productive division, the transfer price also contains a **profit share** (as a reward). This is required for the motivation of a more productive manager.
- A **market price** for the intermediate product, if it existed, would interfere in fulfilling the coordination function, if it cannot be used by Division 1. If Division 1 could supply externally, the market price would become the lowest possible limit for the transfer price. However, this was not explicitly included in the described model.

In the above simple model, all decision-makers are assumed to be risk neutral. Even if this is not the case, the transfer price can also fulfil a risk-sharing function.

The same solution structure arises even if **asymmetric information** is assumed in the other divisions. The **optimal transfer price** strongly depends on the individual division's as well the manager's circumstances, and coordination can be induced by head office in a similar manner to the procedure used in dual transfer prices (see below). However, implementation difficulties can arise when two divisions make arrangements that improve their situation to the detriment of head office.

Naturally, such a simple model does not solve the problems connected with a full cost approach in practice. It has a more **conceptual character** and serves for gaining an understanding of the relationship between the coordination and assessment functions, as well as on transfer prices which cover the costs *and* contain a profit surcharge.

However, coordination by means of transfer prices in this situation is not the only possibility. Head office could ask the manager of Division 1 for a **report on his *type*** θ and then impose the production amounts on the basis of the report, whose accuracy cannot be directly examined by head office. However, head office can induce incentives for truthful reporting by the manager.

8.3.6 Dual Transfer Prices

Dual transfer prices (sometimes called 'dual-rate transfer prices') make use of an optional variation in internal 'prices' unconsidered in the previous discussion: why must the *same* transfer price be applied to the supplying division and the purchasing division? Dual transfer prices set **different transfer prices** for the divisions. Head office fulfils a balancing function for the subsequent profits.

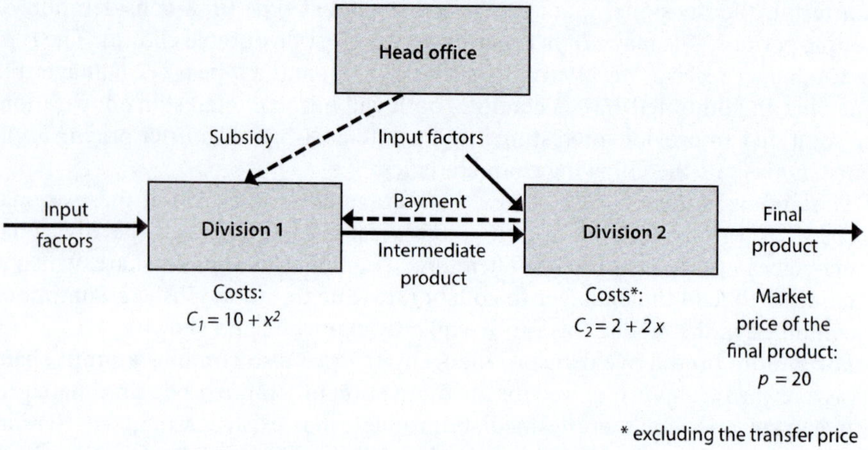

Fig. 8.5 Dual transfer prices

8

Example: Division 1 produces an intermediate product at costs of $C_1 = 10 + x^2$. Division 2 processes it further and sells it as a final product at the market for a constant price of $p = 20$. Its costs are $C_2 = 2 + 2x$. Figure 8.5 shows the situation. As a reference, the central solution arises by maximisation of the total profit:

$$\max_x \Pi = 20x - \left(10 + x^2\right) - \left(2 + 2x\right) = -x^2 + 18x - 12 \tag{8.18}$$

Setting the first derivation $\Pi' = -2x + 18$ to zero leads to the optimal amount $x^* = 9$. The total profit from the transaction amounts to $\Pi = 69$.

The **procedure** for the determination of dual transfer prices is the following (this is a simplified suggestion based upon Ronen and McKinney 1970):

1. Head office requires information about the (full) costs for different level of demands for Division 1. In the example, these are

$$c_1 = \frac{C_1(x)}{x} = x + \frac{10}{x}$$

This equals the transfer price TP_2, at which Division 2 procures the intermediate product.

2. Head office requires Division 2's preliminary contribution margins cm_2 (excluding the costs of the intermediate product) for different volumes of the intermediate product. In the example, these are

$$cm_2 = \frac{CM_2}{x} = 20 - 2 - \frac{2}{x} = 18 - \frac{2}{x}.$$

This becomes the transfer price TP_1, for which Division 1 sells the intermediate product internally.

The decentralised decisions with these transfer prices amount to:
Division 1:

$$\max_x \Pi_1 = TP_1 \cdot x - C_1(x) = \left(18 - \frac{2}{x}\right) \cdot x - 10 - x^2 = -x^2 + 18x - 12 \tag{8.19}$$

Division 2:

$$\max_x \Pi_2 = 20x - TP_2 \cdot x - C_2(x) = 20x - \left(x + \frac{10}{x}\right) \cdot x - 2 - 2x = -x^2 + 18x - 12 \tag{8.20}$$

The divisional profit functions are **identical** to the total profit function (8.18). Therefore, independently of each other, both divisions decide the (centrally) optimal amount $x^* = 9$. As an advantage of dual transfer prices, it can be seen that Division 1 gets closer to the market (of the final product) to a certain extent, because achievable contribution margins are imposed as the transfer price. Alternatively, Division 2 has to use a transfer price that corresponds to the intermediate product's production costs. Although the transfer price contains unitised fixed costs, they cease because of the multiplication of the amount and, therefore, are again not relevant for the decision (◘ Fig. 8.6).

Head office must balance the **difference** between the two transfer prices TP_1 and TP_2. Division 1 receives $TP_1 \cdot x = 18x - 2 = 160$, while Division 2 only pays $TP_2 \cdot x = x^2 + 10 = 91$. The difference of 69 is covered by head office and *virtually* forms a **loss balance**. With it, the total profit of the company cannot be determined as the sum of the divisional profits ($\Pi_1 + \Pi_2$). Head office *always* suffers a loss exactly equal to the total company profit as a result of the transaction. This is obvious because both divisions maximise the same profit function, and that is why every division achieves a profit of 69, despite the fact that this profit only occurs once. With transfer price types using identical transfer prices for both divisions, divisional profits *always* equals the sum of the total profit. Now the total profit corresponds to the sum of the divisional profits including the loss balance from head office.

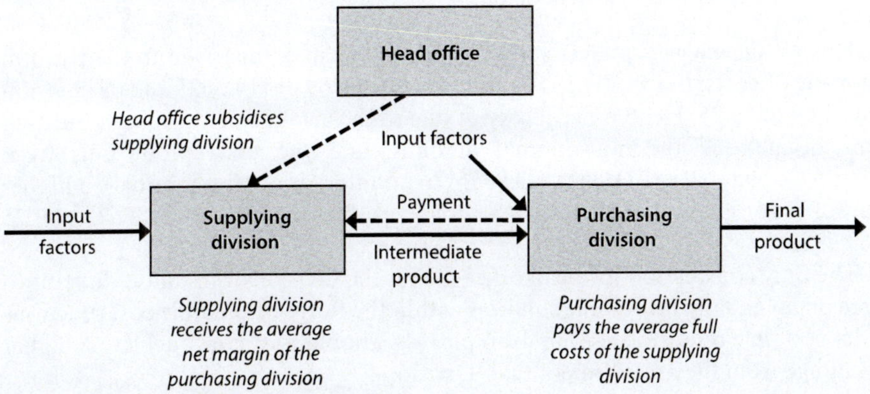

◘ **Fig. 8.6** Suggestion for dual transfer prices

A significant problem is the fact that both divisions achieve the same profit as the total company profit, independent of how well they have worked. Ranking the divisions, for example, according to their profitability, is impossible now, that is, the **profit allocation function** obviously cannot be fulfilled by using dual transfer prices. This consequence is one of the principal reasons why dual transfer prices are rarely used in practice and have a **low rate of acceptability**. It also suffers from the fact that two transfer prices for an identical product exist and the question emerges again, which one is the '*correct*' price? Every answer to this question remains unsatisfactory to a certain extent.

- **Incentive Effects**

Dual transfer prices can provide incentives for **distorted information** during the determination of the transfer prices. If one division deviates from its actual cost function, different amounts arise, so that it becomes obvious that one of the two divisions has supplied incorrect cost information. Therefore, it is not in the interest of the divisions to *individually* report incorrectly. However, this is different when the divisions make collusive **arrangements** between them, as by doing so, they can coordinate the amount.

Continuation of the example: Divisions 1 and 2 arrange for Division 1 to report a distorted cost function to head office. Instead of $c_1 = x + 10/x$, the following cost information is reported:

$$\hat{c}_1 = 0.8x + \frac{10}{x}$$

With it, Division 2 maximises its divisional profits $\Pi_2 = 18x - 2 - (0.8x^2 + 10)$ with an optimal amount of 11.25. Therefore, it must 'adapt' its cost report in a way that Division 1 also achieves the same amount. This is achieved by the following contribution margin per unit function:

$$c\widehat{m}_2 = 22.5 - \frac{2}{x}$$

Division 1 maximises $\Pi_1 = 22.5x - 2 - (10 + x^2)$ and an optimal amount of 11.25 arises from it.

This **arrangement** is **preferred** by both divisions in comparison to the truthful reporting of costs: the profit of Division 1 rises from 69 to 114.5625 and of Division 2 from 69 to 89.25. Head office loses out due to the arrangement between the divisions because of the non-optimal amount, and the total profit falls from $\Pi(x = 9) = 69$ to $\Pi(x = 11.25) = 63.9375$. In addition, both divisions have a higher share of the profits so that the *loss balance* of head office increases to 114.5625 + 89.25 − 63.9375 = 139.875.

The only consolation for head office is that the divisions will find it difficult to agree on an equally favourable solution within the range of credible cost functions under certain circumstances. For example, why should Division 1 achieve a higher advantage from the arrangement than Division 2?

As the internal transfers duplicate the profit from the perspective of both divisions, reduced incentives for efforts searching for more favourable **external options** arise and arrangements between the divisions may prevent the use of such superior external offers.

Other suggestions for dual transfer prices exist. A model by Zverovich and Schuster (2019) suggests a combination of a single cost-plus transfer price and the pragmatic process of negotiation and assumes non-linear net average revenue curves. In particular, typical quadratic functions are considered and corresponding transfer price schedules are determined. It is shown that a similar technique can be used for the transfer pricing problem with any net average revenue curve. A similar approach for a simpler revenue function was considered by Tomkins (1990).

8.4 Negotiated Transfer Prices

8.4.1 Effects From Negotiated Transfer Prices

Head office can refrain from determining transfer prices and leave it to the divisions themselves to agree on transfer prices that they find acceptable. Then, transfer prices are the result of negotiations between the divisions involved in the internal transfer of goods and/or services. However, as a prerequisite, the divisions must have the right to refuse internal business. If the internal transfer was imposed by head office, it would be difficult to see the logic of any subsequent negotiations, as neither division could really threaten retreat, that is, refuse internal transfers; and an arbitrary split-up of the joint profit would ensue.

In practice, it must be distinguished whether the negotiation is made on an **ad-hoc basis** with no advance planning for each transaction as it arises, or whether the divisions agree **generally** based on certain principles of how the transfer price can be determined in each individual case. The decision about that largely depends on the extent of the internal transactions. The more often it occurs, the more suitable is the application of a general rule. Cost-based transfer prices and particularly market-based transfer prices are often applied in this context. The negotiation of general rules to be applied is based on average, expected circumstances, while the case-wise negotiation strongly considers each **specific situation**.

Negotiated transfer prices provide **maximum autonomy** to the divisions, which has both advantages and disadvantages. They can act more independently and as a result should be better motivated. Another advantage is that divisions often possess a **much better state of information** about the mutual costs or revenue situation than head office, so they can make better decisions than if they were confronted with a transfer price set by 'misinformed' head office.

On the other hand, it enables the divisions to make decisions that are optimal for them, but not necessarily for the whole company. If the result of the negotiations is a transfer price other than the one that fulfils the **coordination function** as well as possible, it leads to incorrect decisions from the perspective of the company as a whole. The outcome of the negotiations will almost always lie somewhere between the costs of the producing division and the contribution margin of the buying division. Therefore, head office will only find it meaningful to leave the determination of the transfer price at the disposal of the divisions if the advantages outweigh the disadvantages.

■ **Influence Factors on the Negotiation's Results**

An agreement between the divisions on the transfer price only occurs if the internal transaction brings *both divisions* an advantage compared to the **best alternative to a negotiated agreement (BATNA)**. Therefore, the said alternatives determine the **zone of potential agreement (ZOPA)**. The better the alternative options, the smaller the range of outcomes within which the negotiations can lie.

Example: Division 1 and Division 2 negotiate the transfer price for a copy of a product that Division 2 would like to buy from Division 1. The marginal costs of Division 1 amounts to 120, the sales price of the final product produced by Division 2 is 200 and the marginal costs of completion amounts to 30. Therefore, the preliminary contribution margin equals 200 – 30 = 170. Assume that the divisions have no alternatives so that the ZOPA lies between [120, 170]. If Division 1 could sell its product to another customer for only 145, the delivery to Division 2 would cause opportunity costs of 145 – 120 = 25. The ZOPA then shrinks to [145, 170].

Assume now that Division 2 also has the option to purchase the product from another supplier at 160, then the ZOPA further decreases to [145, 160]. If Division 2 could externally buy the product even at 140, there would no longer be a ZOPA, and both divisions would follow their alternatives. However, this would be favoured from the perspective of head office because the sum of the divisional profits then amounts to (145 – 120) + (170 – 140) = 55 compared to 170 – 120 = 50 in the case of an internal transaction. ◘ Figure 8.7 presents the changes to the ZOPA for the described example.

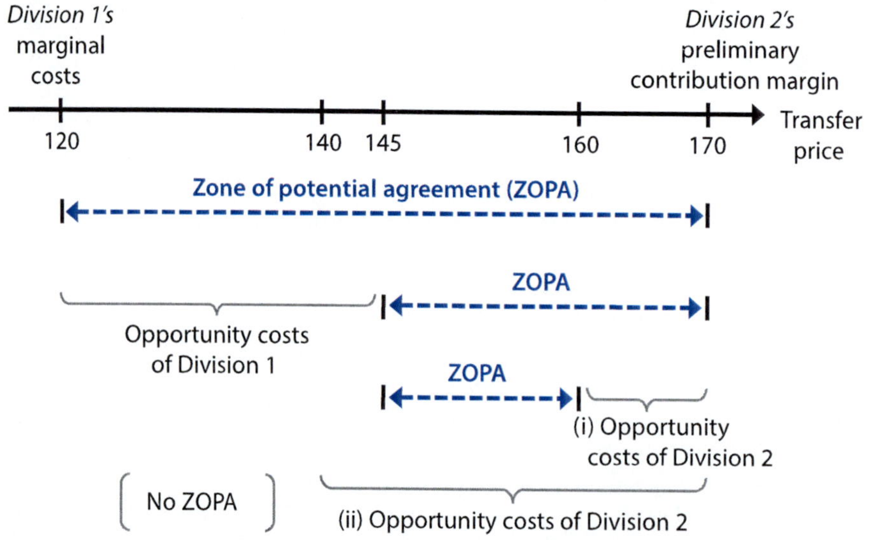

◘ **Fig. 8.7** Zone of potential agreement

A division is a priori favoured by the existence of **strong alternatives** because it shifts the limits of the transfer price in a direction favourable for the division. Therefore, both divisional managers will try to find suitable alternatives, for example, by obtaining external offers. However, in practice, it is often difficult to find externals willing to partake in such a game, especially if a new order only materialises occasionally. In practice, for standard products a part of the amount to be procured will often be kept internally with the other part for that reason kept externally.

However, **within the zone of potential agreement** the outcome of the negotiations' is hardly predictable as it depends on the specific situation and individual circumstances. Negotiating power (based on better alternatives) plays an essential role. Other effects such as time pressure and stress, along with the different individual negotiating skills of the divisional managers, can also influence the transfer price. The more 'skilful' manager can significantly influence the transfer price. Negotiating skill is certainly an important managerial quality; however, divisional profit should instead measure the economic viability of production, and this is sometimes overlooked.

Remark

'There is possibly no single accounting topic that consumes more management time and energy in multi-profit centre companies than the business of establishing acceptable transfer prices. The expenditure of energy in this division far exceeds that expended on pricing products sold to outside customers' (*Seed* quoted in Thomas 1980, p. 117).

Negotiated transfer prices have the **disadvantage** that negotiations can raise a multiplicity of **conflicts** between the managers of a company. This can negatively influence the 'climate' in a company and endanger the required co-operation of divisional managers. In addition, negotiations are often very **time-consuming**.

Conflicts Between Divisions

An empirical questionnaire survey of 84 large U.S. companies (Lambert 1979) brought the following results:

1. Negotiated transfer prices lead to significantly larger conflicts than cost-based or market-based transfer prices.
2. The conflicts are stronger if the divisions cannot use an external market.

It is better to agree on a **conciliation procedure** in advance. The divisions can probably more easily agree on such a procedure at a time during which the actual circumstances are not yet obvious, than later on with a particular *outcome of the negotiations*. Alternatively, head office can suggest such a conciliation procedure to intervene in the negotiation process. It could be based on fundamental principles of advanced consensus, such as fairness. In general, a solution regarded as being '*fair*' lies in an equal division of the joint profit, that is, the centre of the ZOPA. One problem of this equal division of the joint profit is that the ZOPA is often only known to the respective divisions. The divisions will not reveal their alternatives during negotiations, as it would be to their disadvantage to do so during this time.

NASH Negotiation Solution

The *NASH* negotiation solution determines a transfer price that maximises the combination of the profit increases (against the respective alternative) in both divisions within the corresponding limits. This solution is the only one that fulfils the following five axiomatic requirements of a negotiated solution:

- Individual rationality (both divisions expect a positive profit).
- Symmetry (if the situations of both divisions are symmetrical).
- Pareto optimality.
- Independence against linear transformations.
- Independence against irrelevant alternatives.

8

Example: TP is the transfer price to be determined, and g_1 and g_2 are the respective opportunity costs of Division 1 and Division 2 if the internal transfer is not made. c_1 equals the variable costs of Division 1, and $cm_2 = p - c_2$ the preliminary contribution margin of Division 2 related to the same amount as in Division 1, then the transfer price is derived as follows:

$$\max_{TP}\left[\left(TP-c_1\right)-g_1\right]\cdot\left[\left(cm_2-TP\right)-g_2\right]$$

In the case of a zero-sum game (i.e. c_1 and cm_2 are constant) and if opportunity costs are $g_1 = g_2 = 0$, TP lies right in the middle between c_1 and cm_2, i.e. $TP = (c_1 + cm_2)/2$.

If transfer prices are negotiated, a **conciliation board** (e.g. the management accountants) or a procedure to solve conflicts is often inevitable. This can range from common agreements to assisting the search for a solution up to the determination of the transfer price by the conciliation board itself. It is important that the conciliation board is not addressed too often, as this would require a change in the procedure for the determination of the transfer prices.

8.4.2 A Hold Up Model

At least in one way, negotiated transfer prices resemble transfer prices that contain a profit surcharge: this has the **disadvantage** of possibly delaying favourable investments by a division as the investing division carries the entire cost but only partially participates from its success. This so-called ***hold up* problem** is presented in the following simple example.

Assume that Division 1 produces an intermediate product, which is further processed by Division 2 and sold at the market. The **revenues** (sales) as a function of the production amount x equals:

$$R(x) = \alpha - \beta \cdot x$$

The processing costs in Division 2 are $C_2(x) = c_2 \cdot x$. Division 1 can achieve a reduction in its variable cost, by for example, innovation procedures, investments in cost cutting activities or employees' training. The production costs are $C_1(x, a)$, with a as **work productivity** or as an **investment**. The private costs of Division 1 amount to $v(a)$. Furthermore, the costs depend on an uncertain environmental condition θ. Simplifying, the following linear relationship is assumed:

$$C_1(x,a,\theta) = (c - a - \theta) \cdot x$$

In the first step, Division 1 must determine the level of its **work productivity**. This is done before the environmental condition θ is known. Once revealed, both divisions negotiate the transfer price and the quantity to be transferred.

A determination of the transfer price after disclosure of θ enables **risk-sharing** between the two divisions. With risk-averse divisional managers, this may lead to the acceptance of a risky order, due to the fact that part of the risk is transmitted to the supplying division via the *transfer price* depending on θ.

The **outcome of the negotiations** depends on the negotiating power of both divisions. Assume that the divisions agree on the idea that the actual contribution margin from the sales of the products would be shared 'fairly' (but to not consider the advanced costs of the productivity level a). The contribution margin with productivity a and environmental condition θ follows as:

$$\begin{aligned} CM(x,\theta) &= \underbrace{R(x) - C_2(x)}_{CM_2(x)} - C_1(x,a,\theta) \\ &= \left(\underbrace{a_2 - c_2}_{\equiv \alpha} - \beta x \right) \cdot x - (c - a - \theta) \cdot x \\ &= (\alpha - c + a + \theta - \beta x) \cdot x \end{aligned}$$

It needs to be considered that the amount x is a function of a and θ as it is chosen after these measures are observed. To simplify, it is assumed that only direct functional dependences exist, for example, $CM = CM(x, \theta)$. Through the dependence of the amount x on a, CM also becomes dependent on a. The **(division) split-up rule** should be that Division 1 receives a proportion γ of CM and Division 2 the remaining part ($1 - \gamma$ with $\gamma \in [0, 1]$. A $\gamma = 0.5$ equals the *NASH* negotiation solution. The transfer price TP^V arises from Division 1's proportion of the contribution margin and the production costs:

$$TP^V(x,\theta) \cdot x = C_1(x,a,\theta) + \gamma \cdot CM(x,\theta)$$

Division 1 determines its amount by maximising its **profit**.

$$TP^V(x,\theta)\cdot x - C_1(x,a,\theta) = \gamma\cdot CM(x,\theta)$$

Division 2 maximises its profit.

$$R(x) - C_2(x) - TP^V(x,\theta)\cdot x = (1-\gamma)\cdot CM(x,\theta)$$

Both are interested in an ex post **efficient decision** about the amount $x(a, \theta)$, given a and θ. This arises from the maximisation of $CM(x, \theta)$ according to x,

$$\max_x CM(x,\theta) = (\alpha - c + a + \theta - \beta x)\cdot x$$

to

$$x^*(a,\theta) = \frac{\alpha - c + a + \theta}{2\beta}$$

8

Division 1 anticipates this decision and chooses its **productivity** a^V before observing θ by the maximisation of its expected profit

$$\mathrm{E}\left[\gamma\cdot CM(x^*,\theta) - \frac{a^2}{2}\right] = \mathrm{E}\left[\gamma\cdot\left(\frac{(\alpha - c + a + \theta)^2}{4\beta}\right) - \frac{a^2}{2}\right].$$

From this it is obvious that the chosen productivity level is not **optimal** from head office's perspective, as long as $\gamma < 1$. Division 1 only receives a part γ of the gained advantage of its productivity, while it carries all of the costs, resulting in an **under investment** in productivity a compared to the situation in which head office could decide the productivity level. Finally, the maximisation of Division 1's objective function proves an optimal productivity a^V of

$$a^V = \frac{\alpha - c + \mathrm{E}[\theta]}{\frac{2\beta}{\gamma} - 1}$$

The productivity a^V rises in γ and reaches its maximum at $\gamma = 1$.

- **Monopoly Price-Based Transfer Price**

Another variation to solve the **coordination problem** lies in the assignment of all of the **negotiating power** for the transfer price to Division 1. Then, Division 1 determines the price after knowledge of θ (as a function of the demand), and Division 2 determines its resulting optimal amount. There is no further negotiation, and head office simply devolves the negotiating authority to the divisions.

This approach equals a **monopolisation** of the supplying division. This is not identical to complete negotiating power ($\gamma = 1$), as Division 2 reacts to a given transfer price, while in the situation described above the amount and price were determined simultaneously. Division 1 utilises its knowledge of the **reaction function** of Division 2 to maximise its profit (the so-called ***Stackelberg*** **solution**). Division 2 decides on the maximisation of its profit with a given transfer price $TP(\theta)$:

$$\max_{x} CM_2(x,\theta) = R(x) - C_2(x) - TP(\theta)x = (\alpha - TP(\theta) - \beta x)\cdot x$$

An optimal *amount* x^M arises from it:

$$x^M = \frac{\alpha - TP(\theta)}{2\beta}$$

Now Division 1 determines the **transfer price** TP^M by maximisation of its profit, with a given a and θ:

$$\max_{TP} (TP - c + a + \theta)\cdot\frac{\alpha - TP}{2\beta}$$

From it arises as a transfer price

$$TP^M = \frac{\alpha + c - a - \theta}{2}$$

TP^M applied to the optimal amount x^M leads to x^M as half of the efficient amount x^*. This **reduction** in the amount of **production** is an essential disadvantage of such a transfer pricing system. It results from the monopoly price determination.

The **inefficient decision** also induces ex ante an inefficient level of **productivity**. Before observation of θ, Division 1 maximises its expected profit, taking into account the following decisions with regard to the transfer price and the induced amount. **The expected profit** amounts to

$$\mathrm{E}\left[(TP - c + a + \theta)\cdot\frac{\alpha - TP}{2\beta} - \frac{a^2}{2}\right] = \mathrm{E}\left[\frac{(\alpha - c + a + \theta)^2}{8\beta} - \frac{a^2}{2}\right]$$

By derivation towards a, the optimal productivity a^M arises as

$$a^M = \frac{\alpha - c + \mathrm{E}[\theta]}{4\beta - 1}$$

A **comparison** of the productivity a^M with the level of activity arising due to a negotiated transfer price a^V shows that

$$a^V = \frac{\alpha - c + \mathrm{E}[\theta]}{\frac{2\beta}{\gamma} - 1} > a^M = \frac{\alpha - c + \mathrm{E}[\theta]}{4\beta - 1} \Leftrightarrow \gamma > \frac{1}{2}$$

If the **ex post negotiating power** of Division 1 is higher than that of Division 2 ($\gamma > 0.5$), then Division 1 has the incentive to increase its productivity with this negotiated transfer price, compared to a monopoly price-based transfer price. Since the ex post amounts are simultaneously **efficient**, this implies that negotiated transfer prices with $\gamma \geq 0.5$ are superior, from the short-term view of head office, as compared to the monopoly price-based variation. However, for $\gamma < 0.5$ this result can be reversed: the ex post inefficient **amount decisions** can be counterbalanced by higher incentives to increase **productivity**.

8.5 Transfer Prices and Behavioural Control

The focus of the analysis thus far has been on the coordination of internally transferred amounts between the production and purchasing divisions incorporating sequential production. However, coordination can encompass another level: in the following, examples of cost management and strategy penetration are discussed to examine the issue of transfer prices from a slightly different perspective.

8.5.1 Introduction

Transfer prices and cost allocations can serve as instruments of (personnel) coordination if a decentralised decision-maker (e.g. manager, employee) pursues other objectives than those pursued by head office and when head office has no sufficient means to directly affect the decisions taken. With the help of a cost allocation chosen in a meaningful way, the decision problem is distorted in such a way that the decision-maker himself chooses a decision that meets the objective of the company as a whole.

8

Behavioural control is basically achieved by **influencing** the **price structure of the input factors**. Prerequisites for efficiency are as follows:

- The manager applies the price of the internal product for his decision-making.
- The decision is **sensitive** to the price of the internal product.
- The decision influences the **objective measure** used for assessing the decision-maker's performance.
- The transfer price is regarded as acceptable by the decision-maker.

In many cases, deliberately **distorted** costs appear, that is, they are allocated either too high or too low. The divisional manager is supposed to optimise the distorted divisional profit, and at the same time the performance measurement and managerial assessment must be made based on this distorted divisional profit, even if is known that this is not the 'correct' profit. This typically contradicts the **profit allocation function** of transfer prices.

8.5.2 Cost Management and Strategy Penetration

Transfer prices generate an internal market. Depending on the extent by which the divisions may use an external market, different forms of internal market arise. If supply and purchase limits exist, a bilateral **monopoly** results. Both divisions typically act sensitively to price changes, and a higher price will reduce the demand for the internal product and with it, the amount transferred internally, even if the producing division wanted to offer higher quantities. A lower price will reduce the supply and with it the transferred amount. Similar relations apply for other 'market' configurations. Head office can use this 'market' to induce certain **behaviours** amongst divisional managers. Some examples are discussed in the following paragraph.

Products or production procedures can be presented as less expensive to guide the product manager's behaviour. Short-term profit maximisation can be affected by a 'subsidy' of long-term decisions. On account of his short **planning horizon**, assume that a divisional manager invests too little in research and development. From the perspective of head office, they can influence this by offering results from a central research department for a transfer price below its costs.

Another *example*: head office has the impression that the management accounting department produces too many reports beyond the informational needs of the users. The demand can be limited by determination of specific (transfer) prices, and a division will then only 'buy' a report, when its utility exceeds these costs.

Another *example*: a company produces video recorders in several divisions. Head office is convinced that competitive advantages can only be gained by speeding up **automation**. The central overhead costs are allocated on the basis of *direct labour* to each division. This leads to an indirect **rise** in overheads allocated on the basis of direct labour and to a relative preference for automated production processes from the perspective of the divisions. It is interesting to note that cost allocation is obviously against the causation of the costs, but this is irrelevant, as only the induced effect is important.

Additionally, it is interesting that the pressure for automation will be larger for a division when other divisions have already heavily automated. This exemplifies possible advantages of cost allocations as compared to transfer prices. **Cost allocations** are transfer prices that fulfil an additional condition: that is, that the sum of the allocated costs equals the costs incurred. Thus, if a higher amount is allocated to one division, another division will be allocated a lower amount.

Behavioural Control in Product Development

A product developer or technical designer often values the technical elegance of a product solution essentially higher than the market and company management. However, due to the lack of expert knowledge, he cannot decide about the sufficient development time that is actually necessary. Therefore, upper management cannot prescribe this development time, but does possess some indirect possibilities to guide the product developer to greater efficiency from the company's perspective.

For example, the 'imputed' overhead costs can be charged on a basis exceeding the true costs, with the effect that the cost of development hours increases. To avoid endangering the introduction of a new product on account of high costs, the product developer will be careful to spend less time on inefficient designs or to engage in excessive trialling of different designs. Similar effects can be seen by charging distorted costs for required parts: standard parts can be charged too low, and special parts relatively too high, to motivate the product developer to prefer the use of standard parts.

8.5.3 Coordination of Price Decisions

The following case study analyses the coordination of divisions with existing market interdependencies. **Competitive situations** between divisions can happen in decentralised organisations, as they can also occur between external competitors.

Case Study Assumptions

Division 1 produces the electronic control unit, S_1, that is used for the final products. Division 2 specialises in analogous technology, and Division 3 in digital technology. Amongst other products, both divisions (2 and 3) produce the measuring instruments, M2 and M3, both of which require the electronic control unit produced by Division 1. The organisational form for this example has been chosen as the technology applied is one of the essential aspects of specialisation that requires a division of activities.

The variable costs of S1 amount to 10, the subsequent processing costs for the production of M2 an additional 10 and of M3 an additional 15. There are no effective capacity limits. To a certain extent, both instruments, M2 and M3, are substitutes in the market. The following price demand functions describe the market (x_i equals the amount of the instrument M_i and p_i its price for $i = 2, 3$):

Instrument M2 : $x_2 = 100 - 2p_2 + p_3$

Instrument M3 : $x_3 = 200 - 2p_3 + p_2$

Both managers determine their optimal price from their respective perspectives based on a *Nash* **equilibrium**. The optimal price of M2 arises from the maximisation of the contribution margin CM_2:

8

$$\max_{p_2} CM_2 = (p_2 - c_2) \cdot x_2 = (p_2 - c_2) \cdot (100 - 2p_2 + p_3) \tag{8.21}$$

and $c_2 = 10 + TP$. The first derivation is

$$\frac{\partial CM_2}{\partial p_2} = 100 - 2p_2 + p_3 - 2p_2 + 2c_2 \tag{8.22}$$

Setting (8.22) to zero leads to the **optimal price** as a function of the price of M3,

$$p_2^* = \frac{1}{4} \cdot (100 + 2c_2 + p_3)$$

Analogously, the optimal price of M3 arises by maximisation of CM_3 to the following:

$$p_3^* = \frac{1}{4} \cdot (200 + 2c_3 + p_2)$$

The mutually rational expectations about the price determination result in optimal prices at the *Nash* equilibrium. If these optimal prices are applied in the reaction function of the respective division, the following **optimal prices and amounts** arise:

$$p_2^* = \frac{1}{15} \cdot (600 + 8c_2 + 2c_3), p_3^* = \frac{1}{15} \cdot (900 + 8c_3 + 2c_2)$$

$$x_2^* = \frac{2}{15} \cdot (600 - 7c_2 + 2c_3), x_3^* = \frac{2}{15} \cdot (900 - 7c_3 + 2c_2)$$

None of the divisions can improve their profit by a unilateral change of their price, given the optimal price of the other division. The **transfer price** *TP* for the control unit S1 is determined as the variable costs of both divisions, that is, $c_2 = 10 + TP$ and $c_3 = 15 + TP$. In the following section, the effects of several transfer price types on the contribution margins achieved are analysed.

Table 8.4 Initial solution

	Division 1	Division 2	Division 3
Unit cost	10	20	25
Transfer price or optimal price	10	54	76
Sales volume	170	68	102
Divisional contribution margin	0	2,312	5,202
Total contribution margin			7,514

Transfer Price Equalling the Variable Costs

The results are summarised in Table 8.4. Based upon their internal sales, Division 1 achieves a contribution margin of zero. Division 3 can use the favourable market conditions and despite higher costs for M3, they achieve a contribution margin of more than double the contribution margin of Division 2.

Transfer Price Equalling the Market Price

Assume that the market price for S1 is 25. In this case, unit costs for both purchasing divisions are 15 higher, and both divisions analogously determine their new optimal prices, which now lie appropriately higher. The consequence is that Division 1 achieves a positive contribution margin and the contribution margins of the two other divisions are reduced. Table 8.5 states the results of this situation.

The essential result of this situation is the fact that the total contribution margin has risen by almost 9%. Clearly, two effects of the transfer price can be recognised:

1. **Distributive effect**: the transfer price redistributes the total contribution margin between the supplying and purchasing divisions.
2. **Productive effect**: the total contribution margin is changed. This is as a consequence of the behavioural control.

The transfer price changes the **relevant unit costs** for managers of Divisions 2 and 3, and with it, their price behaviour. They set higher prices for their instruments. This decreases the expected sales, and as can be expected, has negative consequences for both divisional contribution margins. However, the loss is lower than the gain achieved by the supplying Division 1. The reason for this is the substitutive relationship of the two instruments M2 and M3. A coordination of the prices typically leads to higher prices, in comparison to cases where the divisions act like independent companies in competition with each other. However, the decentralised profit centre organisation does not enable such coordination, because both divisions only consider their own profits. Finally, they are assessed by them.

Table 8.5 Solution with market price

	Division 1	Division 2	Division 3
Unit cost	10	35	40
Transfer price or optimal price	25	64	86
Sales volume	150	58	92
Divisional contribution margin	2,250	1,682	4,232
Total contribution margin			8,164

- **Optimal Transfer Price**

The optimal transfer price from the perspective of head office (i.e. the company as a whole) maximises the **sum of the contribution margins** from all three divisions based upon the autonomous decentralised pricing policy for both Divisions 2 and 3, that is,

$$\max_{TP} \underbrace{(TP-10)\cdot\left(x_2^*+x_3^*\right)}_{CM_1}+\underbrace{\left(p_2^*-10-TP\right)\cdot x_2^*}_{CM_2}+\underbrace{\left(p_3^*-15-TP\right)\cdot x_3^*}_{CM_3}$$

Finally, if the appropriate equations for the prices and amounts that depend on TP are used, an optimal transfer price of $TP = 41.875$ arises. Table 8.6 presents the results. Using this transfer price, Division 1 achieves the highest contribution margin of all of the divisions. Attention should be paid to the fact that the purchasing Divisions 2 and 3 are forced to buy internally from Division 1, as the market price of 25 (plus procurement side costs if required) is less than this transfer price. Therefore, head office must limit the Divisions' autonomy.

Fundamentally, the use of the **market price** as a transfer price does not solve the coordination problem. This is completely independent from the well acknowledged problems associated with the determination of 'the' market price. The **optimal transfer price** also has no connection to the relevant costs of the intermediate product. Furthermore, it does not depend on whether a division achieves a profit or not. Until now, capacity costs (fixed costs) were not considered, as they are not required for the result. The optimal transfer price is not only dependent on the market situation but also on the cost situation in the purchasing division.

If the final products were complementary instead of substitutive, the prices would have to be set lower for M2 and M3 than in the initial solution (Table 8.4). The transfer price would then be less than variable costs, and Division 1 would always achieve a negative contribution margin.

This example clearly shows the **conflict** between the **coordination function** and the **profit allocation function** of the transfer price as the divisional contribution margin does *not* adequately measure the performance of the respective divisions. Without doubt, Division 1 is not the only division contributing to the company's

Table 8.6 Solution with the optimal transfer price

	Division 1	Division 2	Division 3
Unit cost	10	51.875	56.875
Transfer price or optimal price	41.875	75.25	97.25
Sales volume	127.50	46.75	80.75
Divisional contribution margin	4,064.06	1,092.78	3,260.28
Total contribution margin			8,417.13

success. However, due to the profit linkage based upon the market interdependence, the individual division's success and performance cannot be precisely separated.

Centralised Organisation

For a comparison of decentralised organisations versus centralised organisations, it is now assumed that head office possesses full information about the situations in both divisions and determines the sales prices of both instruments (M2 and M3) itself. Then head office maximises:

$$\max_{p_2,p_3}(CM_1+CM_2+CM_3)=0+(p_2-c_2)\cdot x_2+(p_3-c_3)\cdot x_3=$$
$$(p_2-20)\cdot(100-2p_2+p_3)+(p_3-25)\cdot(200-2p_3+p_2) \tag{8.23}$$

This leads to optimal prices $p_2^* = 76.67$ and $p_3^* = 95.83$ and a **total profit** of 8,429.17. This solution would only be attainable using a transfer price system, if the transfer prices of both divisions could be set at different amounts (here, for Division 2 a little bit higher and for Division 3 a little bit lower than 41.875).

8.5.4 Strategic Transfer Prices

Another important function of transfer prices is their **relational effect** on external competition. If a market equilibrium with simultaneous decision-making about prices (price competition in a *Bertrand* equilibrium) or production/sales volumes (*Cournot* equilibrium) is assumed, a company can gain a **competitive advantage** over its **competitors**, when it is able to commit itself to certain decisions in advance. Thereupon, the (rational) competitor must make its own decisions as to the best response to the strategy of the company. Typically, this situation evolves into a disadvantage for the competitor company.

The basic idea is illustrated by a **specific situation** (adapted from Göx 1999). Assume that two companies are in price competition and their (inverse) price demand functions are symmetrical and given as

$$x_i = \alpha - p_i + \beta \cdot p_j \tag{8.24}$$

for $i, j = 1, 2$ and $i \neq j$. The variable production costs per unit are identical for both companies' $c > 0$, and no fixed costs occur. It further applies that $\alpha > c$ and $0 < \beta < 1$. The price demand function describes (partial) substitute products.

If no company can itself engage in a specific price strategy, market equilibrium is achieved by the following situation. Every company determines its reaction function, that is, a strategic response to the competitor, by the maximisation of its profit function:

$$\Pi_i = (p_i - c) \cdot x_i = (p_i - c) \cdot (\alpha - p_i + \beta \cdot p_j)$$

$$\frac{\partial \Pi_i}{\partial p_i} = \alpha - 2p_i + \beta \cdot p_j + c = 0 \tag{8.25}$$

As both companies face the same situation, this condition is also considered for p_j. By applying p_j into p_i, it finally results in the **equilibrium prices**

8

$$p_i^* = \frac{\alpha + c}{2 - \beta} \text{ for } i = 1, 2 \tag{8.26}$$

Finally, **the profit** of each company amounts to the following:

$$\Pi_i^* = \frac{(\alpha - (1 - \beta) \cdot c)^2}{(2 - \beta)^2} \tag{8.27}$$

Now, it is assumed that each company **decentralises** its **pricing decision** by hiring a **manager** and asking him to maximise the divisional profit of his respective profit centre. Similar effects arise if only one enterprise decentralises its decision-making. Simultaneously, the respective head office sets the transfer price TP for the input factors. This is generally known. The **divisional profit** is

$$\Pi_i^B = (p_i - TP) \cdot (\alpha - p_i + \beta \cdot p_j)$$

With an analogous calculation to (8.26), both managers determine their **sales prices** as follows:

$$p_i^B = \frac{\alpha + TP}{2 - \beta} \text{ for } i = 1, 2. \tag{8.29}$$

However, the **profit of the companies** is determined on the basis of the real costs c and not the transfer price TP. With the given transfer price, it is

$$\Pi_i^{\text{strategic}} = (p_i^B - c) \cdot x_i = \left(\frac{\alpha + TP}{2 - \beta} - c \right) \cdot \frac{(\alpha - (1 - \beta) \cdot TP)}{2 - \beta} \tag{8.30}$$

According to the transfer price TP, the optimisation of (8.30) provides the following condition, and both companies again choose the same transfer price as a result of the symmetry of the situation:

$$\frac{\partial\left(\Pi_i^{\text{strategic}}\right)}{\partial TP}=\frac{1}{(2-\beta)^2}\cdot\left[\alpha-(1-\beta)\cdot TP-(1-\beta)\cdot(\alpha+TP-2c+\beta\cdot c)\right]=0$$

Finally, the **optimal transfer price** arises as

$$TP_i^*=\frac{\alpha\cdot\beta+c\cdot(2-\beta)\cdot(1-\beta)}{2\cdot(1-\beta)}=c+\frac{\beta\cdot(\alpha-(1-\beta)\cdot c)}{2\cdot(1-\beta)}>c \tag{8.31}$$

The optimal transfer price is higher than the variable costs per unit (because $\alpha > c$ the fraction is higher than zero). In other words: the transfer price has a strategic effect. If (8.31) is set into (8.30), the profit is

$$\Pi_i^{\text{strategic}}=\frac{(\alpha-(1-\beta)\cdot c)^2}{4-4\beta} \tag{8.32}$$

A comparison of (8.32) with (8.27) shows that $\Pi_i^{\text{strategic}}$ is higher for all $\beta > 0$ than Π_i^* and that the difference rises with β.

The **reason** for this transfer price induced effect is that the price, which the managers require in equilibrium, increases with the transfer price. A higher price for both companies reduces the strength of the competition in the market, and both companies benefit from it. The more intense the competition, that is, the higher β, the more distinctive is the advantage from the strategic transfer price. This is a comparable effect to the one shown in the last section, containing two divisions of the same company competing at market.

Why is this solution only possible with decentralised price decision-making and the introduction of a transfer price? Without decentralisation, the announcement by one of the companies of a price higher than the equilibrium price would not be credible or trustworthy. For example, if one company choose a higher price p_i instead of its equilibrium price p_i^*, the other company could improve its position based on its optimal reaction function (8.25) by choosing a new price $p_j(p_i)$. The definition of market equilibrium shows that there is only one pair of prices $\left(p_i^*,p_j^*\right)$, from which no company wants to individually deviate from. However, the contract with the manager, by which he is urged to maximise his divisional profit according to the given transfer price gives **credibility** to a higher price, as the manager sets this price in his own best interests. From the perspective of the company, the manager is only used to setting a price strategy divergent from the original equilibrium, in a convincing manner. However, a prerequisite is that the contracts and the transfer prices are observable and cannot be amended later.

8.6 Summary

The **main functions** of transfer prices are for the **coordination** of management and for the **profit allocation** of decentralised units. They are an instrument for the overall **company** and must be regarded and evaluated in conjunction with other instruments, for example, sales and purchase limits.

Transfer prices are required to be able to determine separate **divisional profits** despite **interdependencies** amongst the divisions, particularly mutual product transfers; and are also needed, to assess divisional profitability and the activities of divisional management. **Market-based transfer prices** are suitable when there is a (nearly) perfect market for the internal products, if only low synergetic effects exist or the transfer volume is relatively small. The divisions then act as if they were independent companies.

In practice, **cost-based transfer prices** are the most frequently used types. Transfer prices based on **marginal costs** fulfil the coordination function for short-term decisions under certain circumstances; however, for the assessment of divisions, they are not suitable, because they typically discriminate against the producing division. Transfer prices, based on **full costs**, can represent a good **approximation** for the relevant costs in the long-term. However, they typically lead to incorrect decisions in the short-term, particularly if they contain a profit surcharge. A special form of transfer prices on a full cost basis, is a **two-tier transfer price**. Each transaction is based on marginal costs, and for the capacity supplied, a certain fixed amount per period is determined. **Full costs plus a profit surcharge**, as a transfer price, can have negative effects on several decisions but can also be favourable if the productivity of a division is unknown.

Dual transfer prices consist of different transfer prices for the producing and buying divisions. They are rarely regarded as being acceptable in practice, as the sum of the divisional profits exceeds the total profit of the company.

With asymmetrically distributed information, all cost-based transfer prices potentially lead to **incentives** for distorted and untruthful cost reporting and can cause incorrect decisions from the perspective of the company as a whole.

Negotiated transfer prices exemplify and bestow the greatest possible autonomy to divisional managers with potentially positive motivational effects. If the divisions possess a high level of knowledge about the mutual situations, better decisions can arise, than when head office prescribes a transfer price. However, negotiations can lead to conflicts within the company. Transfer prices can be applied to **risk sharing**, by adapting them dependant on environmental situations.

The coordination function of transfer prices and cost allocations can be used for the **behavioural control** of divisional managers, if the transfer prices are strategically set.

Decentralised organisations, for example, a profit centre organisation, are created to improve the entrepreneurial conduct of managers. Yet, there is no such thing as an ideal solution for transfer prices and furthermore, there is not even a 'fair' transfer price.

The conflict between coordination and profit allocation, that is, decentralised decisions that are in the best interest of the company as a whole on the one hand, and transfer prices that allow the calculation of reliable and trustworthy divisional profits on the other hand, is evident in most of the examples provided in this book. The divisional contribution margins and profits, as illustrated in the case study, do not adequately measure the performance of the respective divisions. Decentralised decision-making, applying any of the transfer price types discussed, did not find the real optimum solution.

Transfer prices, as seen, are of major importance in the reality of company practice, and therefore deserve considerable focus and increased attention in the area of Management Accounting.

8.7 Assessment Material

Review Questions

1. To what extent does a conflict exist between the different functions of transfer prices?
2. Under which circumstances does coordination by the market not lead to the total company profit optimum?
3. What causes the difference between a market-based transfer price with or without sales and purchase limits for the intermediate product at the external market?
4. Can the use of the market price as a transfer price lead to arbitrary profit allocations of the affected divisions?
5. When do marginal cost-based transfer prices lead to optimal coordination?
6. Does the supplying division with a marginal cost-based transfer price always incur a loss, and if so, how could the transfer price be modified to exclude this?
7. What is the reason that causes a dual transfer price system to achieve optimal coordination? Can it be profitable for a division to distort its information, and if so, in which direction?
8. Transfer prices, which are negotiated by the divisions involved, potentially cause conflicts. A company determines the following conciliation procedure: if the divisions do not agree within an appropriate time, the transfer price is prescribed by the group controller as full costs plus a 3% profit surcharge. What effect does this have on the negotiation of the divisions?
9. Can head office force the divisions to always report truthfully? If so, is this more favourable or unfavourable for head office than a situation in which the divisions can supply distorted information – with head office considering this?
10. Many companies impose a so-called last call principle, according to which, the supplying division can receive the same conditions as an external customer of

the buying division. What advantages and disadvantages does such a principle, have?

11. What types of transfer prices can be derived in an agency model?
12. What advantages and disadvantages does a cost allocation based on the average principle, have?
13. How can the allocation of fixed costs be economically justified for divisions that do not make the decision that causes these fixed costs themselves?
14. What advantages could divisions identify for arranging a given cost division plan?
15. Under which conditions, and why, can it be profitable to employ a manager and to impose on him a transfer price above the costs for the internal transfers?

Exercises

1. ***Hirshleifer* model.** A company is divided into three divisions: Division 1 produces an intermediate product and supplies it to Division 2. Division 2 processes this and sells it as an intermediate product to Division 3, which converts it into a marketable final product. There is no market for the two intermediate products.

   (a) Determine the optimum transfer prices so that all divisions choose the same amounts that lead to maximising the company's profit. Corporate head office has insight into the following divisions' cost functions and the price demand curve:

$$\text{Division 1}: C_1(x) = 20 + \frac{x^3}{6}$$

$$\text{Division 2}: C_2(x) = 60 + \frac{x^2}{2}$$

$$\text{Division 2}: C_3(x) = 45 + x^2$$

$$\text{Price demand curve}: p(x) = 108 - \frac{x^2}{6}$$

   (b) Division 2 anticipates its loss situation and decides to inform head office of a modified cost function. Calculate the effects on the company's profit and for the reported profits of the individual divisions if Division 2 announces the function as $\hat{C}_2(x) = 60 + x^2$.

   (c) If Division 2 announces that the modified cost function is $\hat{C}_2(x) = 100 + \frac{x^2}{2}$, what effect does it have on the overall profits?

2. **Dual transfer prices.** Division 1 produces an intermediate product costing

$$C_1(x) = 40 + \frac{x^3}{6}$$

and supplies it to Division 2, where it is further processed into a marketable product at costs of

$$C_2(x) = 35 + x^2.$$

There is no market for the intermediate product. The price demand function is $p(x) = 82.295–0.05x$.

Determine the dual transfer prices at which head office can motivate the profit-optimising amount in the interest of the company as a whole. How high are divisional profits if you use dual transfer prices?

3. **Cost allocations.** The IT department is organised as a central service of a company. The costs of providing the central services amount to 1200. To simplify matters, let us assume that we are only dealing with fixed costs (such as labour costs and depreciation). Plans indicate that two divisions draw on different IT services as follows:

Planned requirement	D1	D2	Capacity
PC and software maintenance	15	9	30
Internet access	15	3	30
Central ordering	6	5	12

If each division were to install its own IT or buy in the service from outside, this would result in costs for Division 1 of about 1,000 and for Division 2 of about 500. The divisions' results before allocating the IT costs are 2,000 for Division 1 and 1,600 for Division 2. How high are the divisional results after the allocation of the IT costs?

4. **Cost allocations.** For the produced amount x, a production process causes costs of: $C(x) = \sqrt{x}$. The company consists of one division producing (indexed at 0) and three divisions, B_1, B_2 and B_3, purchasing. They buy in the amounts $x_1 = 3$, $x_2 = 5$ and $x_3 = 2$. The total costs (rounded) are:

$$C_0(x) = \sqrt{10} = 3.162$$

   (a) How high is the cost advantage from centralised production?
   (b) What is the minimum and maximum amount that should be allocated to each division?
   (c) How should the costs $C_0 = 3.162$ be divided between the three divisions?

5. **Full cost allocation** (adapted from Magee 1986, p. 338 f.). Borel manufactures all kinds of toys driven by a small electric motor. Division A produces the electric motors. Division B specialises in little railways manufactured using injection-

moulding technology, installs the motors and eventually sells them. Division B's variable costs are more or less constant for the railways at an average of 100. The fixed costs are 34,000 per month. The company currently produces around 4,000 railways per month which are sold at an average price of 200. Division A generally passes on the costs of the electric motors monthly to the divisions asking for them. Their (monthly) cost function is

$$C(x) = 100{,}000 + 50x$$

Besides Division B, Division C also needs electric motors. Its requirements, however, are extremely volatile with the most recent estimates indicating a need for 2,000 or 6,000 motors with an equal level of probability in each case.

Now Division B receives an additional order of 2,000 railways at a special price of 154.5 each.

(a) Assume that Division B wants to maximise its divisional profit. Should it accept the additional order or not?

(b) B's divisional manager receives a bonus for a monthly profit in excess of 100,000. Will this affect his decision regarding the additional order?

8

6. **Cost allocations and capacity adjustments** (adapted from Magee 1986, p. 341 f.). OX Ltd. has seen strong growth in recent years. Management has now suggested hiring a commercial lawyer who could do the advisory work in-house which had previously been given to two law practices. The management accountant, Thomas Prad, who is involved in this, has the following data. The law practices charge 200 per hour on average. The commercial lawyer with a secretary would probably cost 200,000 p.a. The problem is that the number of hours of advisory work needed each year is uncertain. Thomas Prad had the impression from discussions with *OX Ltd's* two divisions that they knew very well how many hours of advisory work they needed, but did not want to be pinned down by him. The two divisional managers are each interested in maximising their respective divisional profits. Based on his own research, Thomas derives the following probabilities of hours needed:

	400 h	**500 h**	**600 h**
Division 1	50%	50%	-
Division 2	-	50%	50%

The controller, Thomas Prad, now faces the task of determining the pros and cons of setting up a legal department.

(a) Based on Thomas's *ex ante* level of information, should the department be set up or not?

(b) Assume that Thomas would like to motivate the two divisions to declare their actual needs. To this end, he proposes to the two divisional managers that the in-house advisory work will be made available free of charge. What

will the divisional managers claim (in relation to hours required) and what will be the decision on the department?

(c) What would happen if Thomas proposes that the divisions be allocated the 200,000 in costs based on the figures given by them for their requirements?

(d) What would happen if the proposal looked like this: each division declares its requirements for hours of advisory work and the legal department will only be set up if the total is equal to or greater than 1,000, whereby 40% of the costs will be allocated to Division 1 and 60% to Division 2?

Supplementary Information

P. Schuster et al., *Management Accounting*,
Springer Texts in Business and Economics,
https://doi.org/10.1007/978-3-030-62022-6

References

Anthony, R. N., Dearden, J., & Govindarajan, V. (1992). *Management control systems* (7th ed.). Boston: Richard D. Irwin Inc.

Banker, R. D., & Hughes, J. S. (1994). Product costing and pricing. *The Accounting Review, 69*, 479–494.

Banker, R. D., & Johnston, H. H. (1993). An empirical study of cost drivers in the U.S. airline industry. *The Accounting Review, 68*, 576–601.

Banker, R. D., Potter, G., & Schroeder, R. G. (1995). An empirical analysis of manufacturing overhead cost drivers. *Journal of Accounting and Economics, 19*, 115–137.

Bol, G. (1980). *Lineare Programmierung – Theorie und Anwendungen*. Königstein/Ts: Athenäum.

Clark, J. M. (1923). *Studies in the economics of overhead costs*. Chicago: The University of Chicago Press.

Cooper, R., & Kaplan, R. S. (1991). Profit priorities from activity-based costing. *Harvard Business Review, May–June*, 130–135.

Deloitte. (2006). Teile eines Ganzen – Empirische Studie zur Steuerung von Konzernen mit transnationaler Wertschöpfung, www.deloitte.de

Dopuch, N. (1993). A perspective on cost drivers. *The Accounting Review, 68*, 615–620.

Ernst & Young. (2003). Transfer Pricing 2003 Global Survey. www.ey.com

Ewert, R. (1997). Target Costing und Verhaltenssteuerung. In C.-C. Freidank, U. Götze, B. Huch, & J. Weber (Eds.), *Kostenmanagement – Aktuelle Konzepte und Anwendungen* (pp, 299–321). Berlin et al.: Springer.

Ewert, R., & Wagenhofer, A. (2014). *Interne Unternehmensrechnung* (8th ed.). Berlin et al: Springer.

Foster, G., & Gupta, M. (1990). Manufacturing overhead cost driver analysis. *Journal of Accounting and Economics, 12*, 309–337.

Franzen, W. (1984). Entscheidungswirkungen von Voll- oder Teilkosteninformationen. *Zeitschrift für Betriebswirtschaftliche Forschung, 36*, 1084–1091.

Gordon, L. A., & Silvester, K. J. (1999). Stock market reactions to activity-based costing adoptions. *Journal of Accounting and Public Policy, 18*, 229–251.

Gosselin, M. (1997). The effect of strategy and organizational structure on the adoption and implementation of activity-based costing. *Accounting, Organizations and Society, 22*, 105–122.

Götze, U., Northcott, D., & Schuster, P. (2015). *Investment appraisal: Methods and models* (2nd ed.). Heidelberg et al.: Springer.

Göx, R. F. (1999). *Strategische Transferpreispolitik im Dyopol*. Wiesbaden: Gabler.

Göx, R. F., & Wagenhofer, A. (2007). Economic research on management accounting. In T. Hopper, D. Northcott, & R. S. Scapens (Eds.), *Issues in management accounting* (3rd ed., pp. 399–424). Harlow et al.: Prentice Hall

Hertz, D. (1964). Risk analysis in capital investment. *Harvard Business Review*, 95–106.

Hirshleifer, J. (1956). On the economics of transfer pricing. *Journal of Business, 29*, 172–184.

Hirshleifer, J. (1957). Economics of the decentralized firm. *Journal of Business, 30*, 96–108.

Ijiri, Y. (1967). *The foundations of accounting measurement: A mathematical, economic, and behavioral inquiry*. Englewood Cliffs: Prentice Hall.

Innes, J., Mitchell, F., & Sinclair, S. (2000). Activity-based costing in the U.K.'s largest companies: A comparison of 1994 and 1999 survey results. *Management Accounting Research*, 349–362.

Jensen, M. C. (2003). Paying people to lie: The truth about the budgeting process. *European Financial Management*, 379–406.

Johnson, G. L., & Simik, S. S. (1971). Multiproduct C-V-P analysis under uncertainty. *Journal of Accounting Research*, 278–286.

Kanodia, C. (1993). Participative budgets as coordination and motivational devices, pp. 172–189.

Kennedy, T., & Affleck-Graves, J. (2001). The impact of activity-based costing techniques on firm performance. *Journal of Management Accounting Research*, 19–45.

Kilger, W., Pampel, J., & Vikas, K. (2012). *Flexible Plankostenrechnung und Deckungsbeitragsrechnung* (13th ed.). Wiesbaden: Gabler.

Künzi, H. P., & Krelle, W. (1979). *Nichtlineare Programmierung* (2nd ed.). Berlin et al.: Springer.

Lambert, D. R. (1979). Transfer pricing and interdivisional conflict. *California Management Review, 21*, 70–75.

Luptácik, M. (1981). *Nichtlineare Programmierung mit ökonomischen Anwendungen*. Königstein/Ts: Athenäum.

Magee, R. P. (1986). *Advanced managerial accounting*. New York: Longman.

Miller, B. L., & Buckman, A. G. (1987). Cost allocation and opportunity costs. *Management Science*, 626–639.

Miller, R. E., & Morris, M. H. (1985). Multiproduct C-V-P analysis and uncertainty: A linear programming approach. *Journal of Business Finance and Accounting*, 495–505.

Miller, J. G., & Vollmann, T. E. (1985). The hidden factory. *Harvard Business Review, September–October*, 142–150.

Noreen, E., & Soderstrom, N. (1994). Are overhead costs strictly proportional to activity? Evidence from hospital service departments. *Journal of Accounting and Economics, 17*, 255–287.

Noreen, E., & Soderstrom, N. (1997). The accuracy of proportional cost models: Evidence from Hostpital service departments. *Review of Acccounting Studies*, 89–114.

Pfaff, D., & Stefani, U. (2006). Verrechnungspreise in der Unternehmenspraxis: Eine Bestandsaufnahme zu Zwecken und Methoden. *Controlling*, 517–524.

Porter, M. A. (1980). *Competitive strategy*. New York: Free Press.

Porter, M. A. (1985). *Competitive advantage*. New York: Free Press.

Ronen, J., & McKinney, G. (1970). Transfer pricing for divisional autonomy. *Journal of Accounting Research*, 99–112.

Sakurai, M. (1989). Target costing and how to use it. *Journal of Cost Management, Summer*, 39–50.

Sappington, D. (1983). Limited liability contracts between principal and agent. *Journal of Economic Theory, 29*, 1–21.

Schmalenbach, E. (1934). *Selbstkostenrechnung und Preispolitik* (6th ed.). Leipzig: Gloeckner.

Schuster, P. (2015). *Transfer prices and management accounting*. Heidelberg et al.: Springer.

Shank, J. K. (1989). Strategic cost management: New wine, or just new bottles? *Journal of Management Accounting Research, Fall*, 47–64.

Shank, J. K., & Govindarajan, V. (1992a). Strategic cost management: The value chain perspective. *Journal of Management Accounting Research, Fall*, 179–197.

Shank, J. K., & Govindarajan, V. (1992b). Strategic cost management and the value chain. *Journal of Cost Management, Winter*, 5–21.

Shank, J. K., & Govindarajan, V. (1993). *Strategic cost management*. New York et al.: Simon & Schuster.

Sharman, P. A. (2004). Kritische Betrachtungen zum Stand der Kostenrechnung in den USA, in: Der Controlling-Berater, pp. 273–284.

Thomas, A. L. (1980). *A Behavioural analysis of joint-cost allocation and transfer pricing*. Lancaster: Stipes.

Tomkins, C. (1990). Making sense of cost-plus transfer prices where there are imperfect intermediate good markets by a 'pragmatic-analytical' perspective. *Management Accounting Research, 1*, 199–216.

Troßmann, E. (1992). Gemeinkosten-Budgetierung als Controlling-Instrument in Bank und Versicherung. In K. Spremann & E. Zur (Eds.), *Controlling – Grundlagen, Informationssysteme, Anwendungen*, (pp. 511–539). Wiesbaden: Gabler.

Wagenhofer, A. (1992). Verrechnungspreise zur Koordination bei Informationsasymmetrie. In K. Spreman & E. Zur (Eds.), *Controlling – Grundlagen, Informationssysteme, Anwendungen*, (pp. 637–656). Wiesbaden: Gabler.

Wagenhofer, A. (1997). Kostenrechnung und Verhaltenssteuerung. In C.-C. Freidank, U. Götze, B. Huch, & J. Weber (Eds.), *Kostenmanagement – Neuere Konzepte und Anwendungen*, (pp, 57–78). Berlin et al.: Physica.

Zimmerman, J. L. (2006). *Accounting for decision making and control* (5th ed.). Boston et al.: McGraw-Hill.

Zverovich, S., & Schuster, P. (2019). Transfer pricing in non-linear revenue settings. In W. D. Nelson (Ed.), *Advances in business and management* (Vol. 16, pp. 151–175).

Index

N

O

P

R

S